'An immensely user-friendly introduction to International Relations, replete with diagrams, maps, illustrations and helpful summaries of the material covered. Such care for a student text has not been taken for a very long time.' – **Stephen Chan OBE, Professor of World Politics, SOAS University of London, UK**

'*Foundations of International Relations* delivers a comprehensive explanation of International Relations that includes a thorough introduction to critical theories and non-western viewpoints alongside established IR theories and narratives. The approachability of the text and relevant case studies will leave students with the tools needed to understand and analyse international events.' – **Jessica Neafie, Assistant Professor of International Relations, Nazarbayev University, Kazakhstan**

'The core strength of this textbook is the clarity it brings to explaining the many concepts and theories that make up International Relations – it introduces students to the nuance and complexity of the field in an exciting and accessible way. An excellent educational resource.' – **Zoë Jay, Lecturer in Politics and International Relations, University of Tasmania, Australia**

'This introduction to International Relations is one of the most original and interesting to come to the market in a long while. Moving away from a purely European perspective, students will gain an understanding of traditional ideas about international organisation, whilst also appreciating how issues such as COVID and food security are truly international in scope.' – **Anthony F Lang, Professor of International Political Theory, University of St Andrews, UK**

'Stephen McGlinchey has brought together a fantastic collection of authors who together present a wide-ranging, critical and accessible introduction to International Relations. Supported by helpful case studies, key insights and key term features, the book will enable its readers to navigate the complexities of global politics.' – **Peter Sutch, Professor of Political and International Theory, Cardiff University, UK**

'*Foundations of International Relations* is a wonderfully rich, yet highly accessible, introduction to International Relations, both as a subject and as a discipline. Students are brought on an engaging intellectual journey through a range of contending perspectives and issues, whilst being encouraged to think critically throughout. They will find it challenging and rewarding in equal measure.' – **Stephen Hill, Lecturer in Politics and International Relations, University of Edinburgh, UK**

'This innovative and well-written textbook takes students on an exciting historical, theoretical, geographical and thematic journey of International Relations. It is truly attentive to the multiplicity of (state and non-state) actors in global politics, as well as non-Western approaches. The book presents an impressive and well-thought pedagogical outline leaving students critically engaged and encouraged to apply their new knowledge of IR to specific, concrete cases. I highly recommend this unique book to both beginner and more advanced students.' – **Andréas Litsegård, Senior Lecturer in Peace and Development Research, University of Gothenburg, Sweden**

FOUNDATIONS OF INTERNATIONAL RELATIONS

Edited by
Stephen McGlinchey

BLOOMSBURY ACADEMIC
LONDON • NEW YORK • OXFORD • NEW DELHI • SYDNEY

BLOOMSBURY ACADEMIC

Bloomsbury Publishing Plc

50 Bedford Square, London, WC1B 3DP, UK

1385 Broadway, New York, NY 10018, USA

29 Earlsfort Terrace, Dublin 2, Ireland

BLOOMSBURY, BLOOMSBURY ACADEMIC and the Diana logo are trademarks of Bloomsbury Publishing Plc

First published in Great Britain 2022

Cover design: Louise Dugdale

Cover image © Mr.IIkin / Adobe Stock

A catalogue record for this book is available from the British Library.

Library of Congress Cataloging-in-Publication Data
Names: McGlinchey, Stephen, editor.
Title: Foundations of international relations / Edited by Stephen McGlinchey.
Description: New York: Bloomsbury Academic, 2022. | Includes bibliographical references and index.
Identifiers: LCCN 2021051690 (print) | LCCN 2021051691 (ebook) | ISBN 9781350932579 (hardback) | ISBN 9781350932586 (paperback) | ISBN 9781350932609 (pdf) | ISBN 9781350932593 (epub) | ISBN 9781350932616 (XML)
Subjects: LCSH: International relations. | International organizations. | Global politics.
Classification: LCC JZ1242 .S544 2021 (print) | LCC JZ1242 (ebook) | DDC 327–dc23/eng/20211202
LC record available at https://lccn.loc.gov/2021051690
LC ebook record available at https://lccn.loc.gov/2021051691

ISBN: HB: 978-1-3509-3257-9
           PB: 978-1-3509-3258-6
           ePDF: 978-1-3509-3260-9
           eBook: 978-1-3509-3259-3

Typeset by Integra Software Services Pvt. Ltd.

Printed and bound in Great Britain by Bell and Bain Ltd, Glasgow

To find out more about our authors and books visit www.bloomsbury.com and sign up for our newsletters.

BRIEF CONTENTS

LONG CONTENTS

LIST OF FIGURES, MAPS, TABLES AND PHOTOGRAPHS

Figures

Maps

Tables

Photographs

LIST OF BOXES

Key People

Case Studies

ABOUT THE AUTHORS

Editor

Stephen McGlinchey is a Senior Lecturer in International Relations at the University of the West of England, Bristol (UWE Bristol). He is Editor-in-Chief and Publisher of E-International Relations.

Authors

Shazelina Z. Abidin is the Director General of the Institute of Diplomacy and Foreign Relations of Malaysia. She received her PhD from the University of Sheffield.

Amitav Acharya is Distinguished Professor in the School of International Service, American University.

James Arvanitakis is the Executive Director of the Australian American Fulbright Commission and an Adjunct Professor at the Institute for Culture and Society at Western Sydney University.

Katherine E. Brown is a Senior Lecturer in Islamic Studies at the University of Birmingham.

Carmen Gebhard is a Senior Lecturer in Politics and International Relations at the University of Edinburgh.

Dana Gold works in regulatory strategy and research for the Ontario Public Service. She was a PhD candidate in Political Science at the Western University between 2012 and 2018.

Andreas Haggman is Head of Cyber Advocacy at the United Kingdom's Department for Digital, Culture, Media and Sport. He holds a PhD in Cyber Security from Royal Holloway, University of London.

David J. Hornsby is Associate Vice-President (Teaching and Learning) and Professor at the Norman Paterson School of International Affairs, Carleton University.

Natalie Jester is a Lecturer in Sociology and Criminology at the University of Gloucestershire.

Mukesh Kapila CBE is Professor Emeritus of Global Health and Humanitarian Affairs at the University of Manchester. He is a former Director at the World Health Organization and the United Nations.

Anitta Kynsilehto is a Senior Research Fellow at Tampere Peace Research Institute, Tampere University.

Raffaele Marchetti is a Professor of International Relations at LUISS.

Sahil Mathur is a PhD candidate in International Relations and an adjunct instructor at the School of International Service, American University.

Raul Pacheco-Vega is an Associate Professor at the Methods Lab of the Facultad Latinoamericana de Ciencias Sociales (FLACSO) Sede Mexico.

John A. Rees is a Professor of Politics and International Relations at the University of Notre Dame Australia.

Robbie Shilliam is a Professor of International Relations at Johns Hopkins University.

Clare Stevens is a Teaching Fellow in International Security with the Portsmouth Military Education team at the University of Portsmouth.

Knut Traisbach is Adjunct Professor of International Law and Human Rights at the University of Barcelona and at ESADE, University Ramon Llull.

Peter Vale is a Senior Fellow at the Centre for the Advancement of Scholarship, University of Pretoria, and Nelson Mandela Professor of Politics Emeritus at Rhodes University.

Rosie Walters is a Lecturer in International Relations at Cardiff University.

Günter Walzenbach is a Senior Lecturer in European Politics at the University of the West of England, Bristol (UWE Bristol).

ACKNOWLEDGEMENTS

This book owes a debt of gratitude to Bill Kakenmaster who offered extensive editorial assistance across the full manuscript and also to Andrew Malvern who was instrumental in getting the book off the ground. The following members of the E-International Relations editorial team gave valuable feedback and assistance: Jane Kirkpatrick, Tomek Najdyhor, Majer Ma, Christian Scheinpflug, Farah Saleem Düzakman, Clotilde Asanga, Anjasi Shah, Pedro Diniz Rocha, Marianna Karakoulaki, Akshaya Jose, Assad Asil Companioni, Kieran O'Meara, Marcelle Trote Martins, Mathias Gjesdal Hammer, Bárbara Campos Diniz, Alessandro Burrone, Benjamin Cherry-Smith, Bernhardt Fourie, Rodrigo Ventura De Marco, Taylor Knecht-Woytsek, Zachary Hadley, Natalie Alfred, Rainer Ricardo, Jakob R. Avgustin, Max Nurnus, Christy Davidson-Stearn and Jason Reynado. Lloyd Langman, Peter Atkinson, Milly Weaver, Becky Mutton and the anonymous reviewers were all generous with their time and expertise. Finally, and most importantly, I would like to thank the authors of each of the chapters for working so hard through the disruptions and hardships of the Covid-19 pandemic to help this book come together.

Stephen McGlinchey

John A. Rees thanks Ms Jasmine Robertson for research assistance in the writing of the Tamrazyan case study in Chapter twelve.

TOUR OF THE BOOK

The chapters are arranged in three parts, bookended by introduction and reflection chapters. Together they offer a broad sweep of history and theory (Part one), outline important global structures (Part two) and identify the key global issues that concern the discipline (Part three). All of the book's chapters, with the exception of the introduction, are structured in a unified format as follows:

Question: Within the vastness of the global system can one person's voice have an impact?

Opening and closing questions
Each chapter begins with a question that primes you to think critically about the subject before you read the chapter. This question will be recalled directly in the conclusion of each chapter, which will remind you of some of the ways the chapter addressed that question. Each chapter ends with a set of discussion questions that you can try to answer yourself and/or discuss with others, to think over and apply what you have learned.

1492 as a map of the present

The year 1648 remains an important date in provided for the principles of mutual recog that came to be represented as the Europea about 1492. Instead of sovereignty and nc conquest and discovery – the cardinal norr with a holy hierarchy of humanity (Jahn ; history of discovery and conquest with a sovereignty it would be more accurate to i sub-section of political actors (male, white, of humanity continued to suffer the legacie and bondage.

Still, it would be fair to ask whether the historical importance. Well, it is certainly n whole edifice of European empire over the the cartography associated with 1492 – its principles that animate their interaction, rei instance, the question of whose humanity is is made by reference to geographical origin/ Now think of the contemporary Black Liv

Main body
This is the longest section of each chapter where all the central information is given. It starts by introducing the subject matter at hand and is split into several headed sections to allow you to navigate the range of information on display. Each chapter assumes no prior knowledge (other than the content covered in the previous chapters). So, the main body of each chapter is built to take you from no knowledge to competency on each issue, and to gradually build momentum as you advance through the book.

Case studies
Each chapter, with the exception of the introduction chapter, has two case studies following the main body section. The case studies focus on something specific – such as a real-world event – to help unpack the more abstract and complex issues explored in each chapter. The case studies are followed by the chapter's conclusion.

 CASE STUDY 2.1: Regulating nuclear weapons

Photo 2.3 Atomic cloud formation from the Baker Day explosion over Bikini Lagoon, 1946

Credit: National Archives/Hulton Archive/Getty Images

The quest to regulate nuclear weapons offers a glimpse of interactions between states that were sworn enemies and had little in common due to incompatible economic and political systems. Yet, through diplomacy and the influence of the United Nations, they were

the United Kingdom (1952), France (1960) and China (1964). As the number of nations possessing nuclear weapons increased from one to five, there were fears that these weapons would proliferate (spread rapidly). This was not only a numbers issue. As the weapons developed, they became many orders of magnitude more destructive. By the early 1960s, nuclear weapons had been built that could cause devastation across over one hundred square kilometres. Recognising the danger, the United Nations attempted in vain to outlaw nuclear weapons in the late 1940s. Following that failure, a series of less absolute goals were advanced, most notably to regulate the testing of nuclear weapons. Weapons that were being developed required test detonations – each releasing large amounts of radiation into the atmosphere, endangering ecosystems and human health. By the late 1950s, diplomacy under a United Nations framework had

Pedagogical resources

Pedagogy is a term teaching professionals and authors use to describe tools used to help students learn. The pedagogical resources this book uses are found in the boxes and images that are set apart from the text throughout each chapter. These are arranged in four groupings:

Key people – a short profile of a figure of importance to International Relations.

5.3 – KEY PEOPLE: Osama bin Laden and Julian Assange

Photo 5.1 Osama bin Laden in Kabul, November 2001

Photo 5.2 Julian Assange in London, August 2014

Credit: Hamid Mir/Wikimedia Commons

Credit: David G. Silvers/Cancilleria del Ecuador/Flickr

Osama bin Laden led a global terrorist network, al-Qaeda, based on his own religious and political visions and masterminded the 9/11 attacks on the United States. Julian Assange spearheaded a whistleblowing campaign leaking government secrets via the website WikiLeaks – most notably

5.5 – KEY TERMS: Methods

Methods are specific ways of doing things. If the methods are both within the reach/means of the researcher, and used correctly so they are likely to provide the information or insight needed to answer a research question, then this would be what academics call a valid research **methodology**. Levels of analysis is a vital component of any good methodology. When used to help shape other valid research methods, such as interviews, fieldwork, surveys – and even the basic academic staple of textual analysis (reading different available sources such as journal articles, books and other documents) – it will help to produce answers that are both self-aware (of their limits) and persuasive. As a student, then, persuasion is the key. It is not your job to find *correct* answers as these rarely exist in the questions that International Relations generates. Rather, the key to a successful research strategy is to gather relevant information and use appropriate methods in order to reach a well-crafted analysis. In this sense, it is not just *what* you say or write that is important in academic work, but also *how* you express it.

Key terms – concise descriptions unpacking terms central to International Relations, each of which is essential to understanding the discipline.

Key insights – brief explorations of a real-world event and/or an intellectual development that offer targeted insights to the themes in the book.

1.3 – KEY INSIGHTS: Reading academically

By making notes you will form a reading strategy that will allow you to retain the most important information and compress it into a smaller set of notes integral to revision for examinations and preparation for discussions and assignments. You should also note down the citation information for each set of notes so that you can identify the source if you need to reference something later in any written work. You should adopt this approach with everything you read during your studies. It's best to use digital means (laptop/tablet) so you can create backups and not risk losing valuable paper notes. If you do prefer handwritten notes, use your phone to take pictures of them to back them up. There will be times in the year when panic sets in as deadlines approach or unexpected life events occur, but if you have already developed a good reading strategy you will find you have built up a good momentum and can better overcome obstacles and regain your footing.

Table 3.1 Comparing images of 1648 and 1492

1648	1492
* Nation-states face each other with no higher power to rule their conduct existing in a state of international anarchy. * The practice of diplomacy and the principle of non-intervention in the affairs of other Christian rulers, regardless of denomination, mitigate against war. * Although some are strong and some weak, all are the same kind of unit – a sovereign, territorially bound state.	* Imperial powers colonise indigenous peoples while claiming that they are doing God's work. * Humanity is divided by religious authorities into those whose Christian faith compels them to conquer and enslave and those non-Christians whose idolatry allows them to be conquered and enslaved. * The world is comprised of a *hierarchy* of these qualitatively *different* entities.

Figures, maps, tables and photographs – to help you learn visually.

DIGITAL RESOURCES

E-INTERNATIONAL RELATIONS

SUBMISSIONS   ADVERTISE   DONATE   JOIN OUR TEAM   ABOUT   Search...

HOME   ARTICLES   BOOKS   INTERVIEWS   REVIEWS   STUDENTS   RESOURCES

Foundations of International Relations Online Area

This is the online area for Foundations of International Relations. It features freely accessible articles, audio and video content, and learning aids to help you work with – and reach beyond – the content within each chapter of the book.

Getting Started

CHAPTER 1

Introduction to International Relations

Part One: History and Theory

CHAPTER 2

International Relations and the Global System

CHAPTER 3

Discovery, Conquest and Colonialism

CHAPTER 4

Towards a Global International Relations

CHAPTER 5

Levels of Analysis

CHAPTER 6

Traditional and Middle Ground Theories

CHAPTER 7

Critical Theories

This book has been developed in partnership with E-International Relations. Beyond signposting E-International Relations (www.E-IR.info) for the extensive resources it offers – from dozens of academic books to thousands of in-depth articles and shorter expert reflections on current events – it also hosts a dedicated online area to accompany this book. Everything on E-International Relations is free to view, ensuring you will never run out of accessible material to explore.

The online area features multimedia resources for each chapter that have been curated to accompany the book. This includes articles, audio and video content, and learning aids to help you work with – and reach beyond – the content within this book.

Link: https://www.e-ir.info/resources/foundations/

The online area is arranged visually around the book's chapters, allowing you to navigate it effectively. You will find, amongst other things:

- Multimedia resources on the case studies for each chapter.
- Extensive links to further reading to deepen and widen your subject knowledge.
- More information to accompany the pedagogical resources in each chapter (key people, key terms, key insights, etc.).
- Extended profiles of all the authors of each chapter, allowing you to find out more about their work and other publications.

Instructor resources

The freely accessible website bloomsbury.pub/foundations-of-international-relations contains a selection of resources to help instructors plan and deliver their courses. These include:

- A test bank containing 500 multiple-choice questions organised by chapter
- Essay style questions for each chapter
- Lecture slides to aid teaching

Foundations of International Relations
Edited by Stephen McGlinchey

Home
Lecturer Resources

An engaging introduction to the core concepts, theories, actors and issues in global politics. Featuring a combination of chapters authored by leading scholars, researchers and practitioners from around the world, this textbook takes into account the historical development of international relations and the web of dynamics that forms the subject, resulting in a clear analysis of the field from a variety of perspectives.

Password-protected resources for lecturers are available by clicking on the link in the sidebar, and student resources are available at https://www.e-ir.info/resources/foundations/

FOUNDATIONS OF
INTERNATIONAL RELATIONS

Edited by
Stephen McGlinchey

BUY THE BOOK

GETTING STARTED

As the title on the cover instructs, this is a book that seeks to give you a foundational understanding of International Relations, both in practice and in terms of how academics understand it. International Relations examines just about everything that concerns how we have organised our world. In addition, it reflects upon our fate by unpacking our shared challenges and opportunities and opening those up to competing viewpoints. Because of its breadth and depth, it is one of the most dynamic and important academic disciplines in the world today. The book will hopefully encourage you to see International Relations as something that is plugged into the real world, always adapting to events and is therefore a never-ending journey of discovery.

INTRODUCTION TO INTERNATIONAL RELATIONS

This introductory chapter of the book gets you started in two ways. Firstly, it introduces some of the basics of the discipline of International Relations to help give a flavour of what is ahead in the rest of the chapters. Secondly, it offers some primers on how to establish good academic practices so you get the most out of this book and build up the skills that will serve you well throughout your studies.

Introducing International Relations

Each academic discipline has its own unique language, usually referred to as 'jargon'. This comprises a range of specific terms that have been developed by scholars to describe certain things. Throughout this book, and throughout your studies, you will come across terms such as nation-state, sovereignty, global system, anarchy, development, globalisation, norms – and many more. As a result, a lot of the time you spend learning a discipline is spent learning its jargon so that you can access and understand the literature. In this book we have tried to ease you into the terminology that International Relations scholars use so that you build up the proficiency to understand the advanced literature that you will soon encounter – much of which is signposted throughout the chapters.

Understanding key terms even applies to something as basic as how to express the term 'International Relations'. The convention is to capitalise it (International Relations, often abbreviated as 'IR') when referring to the academic discipline – that is, the subject taught in university campuses all over the world. International Relations does not describe events; rather, it is a scholarly discipline that seeks to understand and analyse the events, issues and actors within the global system (Box 1.1). Although the chapters will progressively build up the picture of how the discipline sees the world, we will briefly touch on some of the terms listed above to help you get a sense of the road ahead.

1.1 – KEY TERMS: The global system

The phrase 'international relations' – not capitalised – is used to describe relations between nation-states, organisations and individuals at the global level. Lowercase 'international relations' is interchangeable with terms such as 'global politics', 'world politics' or 'international politics'. What all these commonly used terms refer to are activities within the **global system** that both overlay, and undergird, life on planet earth. Traditionally, International Relations has understood the system at its most basic level as a dynamic between three key actors: **(1) nation-states, (2) international organisations** and **(3) individuals**. These key actors react to, are subject to, and sometimes shape, the events and issues that drive international relations. In reality, the picture is more complex than this and things will be unpacked further as the book progresses. Yet, simplification devices such as this, illustrated in Figure 1.1, are helpful to orient yourself.

Figure 1.1 The global system

We can start with the idea of political power, which has found its ultimate form (so far) in the creation of the nation-state. Yet, 'nation-state', most commonly referred to in the shorter form of 'state', is a jargon term that you might not often hear. Instead you may hear people say 'country' or 'nation'. But these terms, although widely recognised, are technically incorrect at describing nation-states, which are one of the three key actors within our global system. We will cover the importance of sovereignty and the state in depth throughout the book – especially in Chapters two, three and four – but it is helpful to begin to unpack this important term now with some examples.

France is a nation-state. It also happens to be a country and a nation, but then so is Scotland. Yet, Scotland is *not* a nation-state. It is one of four different countries within the United Kingdom of Great Britain and Northern Ireland. Like France, the United Kingdom *is* a nation-state because it possesses 'sovereignty' – which is yet another key term central to International Relations (see Box 1.2). Scotland's well-publicised quest for independence is therefore a quest for sovereignty. For those familiar with federal systems the term 'state' is also used in that context, which can be confusing. For example, Texas is one of the 'states' within the nation-state of the United States of America. Another example, Penang is a state that forms part of the nation-state of Malaysia. But, as will hopefully be clear by now, although Penang and Texas are 'states' (perhaps unhelpfully for students of International Relations), they are *not* nation-states.

1.2 – KEY TERMS: The nation-state

'Nation-state' is a compound noun that joins two separate political entities together. A **'nation'** is a group of people who share many things in common, such as language, territory, ethnicity or culture. Typically, a nation is forged over a longer period of history and shared experiences. When that nation is ruled by one system of governance, a **'state'**, the two join and form a 'nation-state'. A state is a set of institutions, with a defined leadership, that has uncontested authority over the nation (the people). This authority is superior to any local, federal or regional government structures, which exist only through the consent of the state. A state's power is typically expressed in political, military and legal power – but it can also include other categories such as religion. Historically, states came to rule over nations of people for many reasons, and they have taken many forms through history – often through patterns of domination rather than consent. But, taken broadly, it is most useful at this early stage to see establishing a state as a compromise that allows a nation of people to live under defined shared rules and structures, and thereby achieve a basic sense of security that allows their shared culture to endure in an insecure world.

You may not be satisfied that International Relations is just reflections on politics between or among nation-states. Economics is also involved, and this has evolved to the extent that we are often said to be living in a 'globalised' world characterised by the relatively free movement of people, goods, services and finance. Similarly, ideas can rapidly spread and affect people in other places. This can be something that leads to positive change, such as raising awareness of political corruption or environmental issues – or negative, such as when criminals or terrorists use the internet and other elements of global interconnectivity to operate more effectively. Understandably, this requires International Relations to incorporate an understanding of international organisations (both governmental and non-governmental) and businesses that operate internationally (transnational corporations). Looking even wider, individual people – you and I – are also important. After all, our global system at its root is essentially one of interaction between human beings. International Relations is, then, appropriately described as 'a broad church' due to the extent of what it covers.

Most scholars consider such concepts as those explored above fundamental for understanding International Relations. But, they often approach them in different and interesting ways. So, simply learning the definition of a key term is just the first step and you will quickly find each term is interpreted in different ways. For example, some scholars think nation-states are a fixed element of the global system that we should not critique too much, whilst others would like to see nation-states dissolved entirely and replaced with a different way of organising the world's people. Similarly, some regard the idea of a globalised world (known as 'globalisation') as a tangible phenomenon to study. Yet, others think it is no more than a trendy buzzword with no real substance. Previewing complexity like this may make such a dense library of key terms appear as a dizzying prospect. But it should become clear how unavoidable such terms are and why students need to use them with due care and attention. Even making the simplest point about something within the sphere of International Relations draws on specific terms, and taps into sometimes intense debates, that need to be appreciated. As such issues arise, this book aims to get you oriented by starting with the basics and then giving you sufficient context to think for yourself and read more deeply and widely.

If you are feeling a little overwhelmed already, that's okay. Everything covered in this introductory chapter is carefully unpacked and explained again later in the book when it next appears – and thereafter developed further through later chapters. You may also be needing some tips about how to read academically, which is where we turn to next.

Establishing good academic practice

As this is designed to be the very first book you will read in your International Relations journey, it is also likely to coincide with the start of your university studies. So, before we move on to the subject matter of the book, it is worth setting out some general advice that will help you get the most out of the book and also help you establish a firm footing academically. If you are coming to this book later in your studies, these tips are also worth considering as a refresher.

Firstly, it is important to establish good basic study habits so you can read and think without distractions. Smartphones are a fantastic feature of our world, but they can also prove a source of distraction when considering their frequent alerts. For this reason, the first step in establishing good academic practice is to put your devices on silent, out of view (perhaps turned facing downwards) and find a good physical space in which to work. Some students find that listening to music helps them concentrate, others prefer to work in silence. It is also important not to overdo things. Arrange ten-minute mini breaks every hour to do other things and make sure to eat a decent meal before, and at the midpoint, of your study session. Finally, get a good night's sleep and find time for sport and leisure activities as your brain does not absorb or retain information very well when you are sleep deprived, overworked or hungry. The key is to balance your study time with a healthy routine.

Secondly, reading for scholarly purposes is not the same as reading for pleasure. You need to adopt a reading *strategy*. Everyone has their own way of doing this and there is no single magic formula, but the basic element to scaffold everything else around is this: *take notes as you read*. If you find that you don't have many notes or your mind goes a little blank, then you might be reading too quickly or not paying enough attention. If this happens, don't worry: just go back to the start of the paragraph, section or chapter (wherever you started having difficulty) and begin again. Often, reading something a second time is when it clicks. Best practice is to make rough notes as you read through each chapter. When you get to the end of a chapter, compile your rough notes into a list of 'key points' that you would like to remember. This will be useful when you come to revise or recap an issue because you won't necessarily have to read the entire chapter again. Your notes should trigger your memory and remind you of the key information.

1.3 – KEY INSIGHTS: Reading academically

By making notes you will form a reading strategy that will allow you to retain the most important information and compress it into a smaller set of notes integral to revision for examinations and preparation for discussions and assignments. You should also note down the citation information for each set of notes so that you can identify the source if you need to reference something later in any written work. You should adopt this approach with everything you read during your studies. It's best to use digital means (laptop/tablet) so you can create backups and not risk losing valuable paper notes. If you do prefer handwritten notes, use your phone to take pictures of them to back them up. There will be times in the year when panic sets in as deadlines approach or unexpected life events occur, but if you have already developed a good reading strategy you will find you have built up a good momentum and can better overcome obstacles and regain your footing.

Thirdly, referencing sources is very important. It is the way we attribute the work of others, whether we use their exact words or not. For that reason, you will see numerous such references in this book, pointing you to specific sources of information or ideas. It is an important element of scholarly writing, and one that you must master during your own studies. When we need to point you to more specialist literature, for example to invite you to read a little deeper, we do so by inserting in-text citations that look like this: (Ringmar 2017). These point you to a corresponding entry in the references section towards the back of the book where you can find the full reference and follow it up if you want to. Typically, these are books, academic journal articles or websites. In-text citations always include the author's surname and the year of publication. As the reference list is organised alphabetically by surname, you can quickly locate the full reference. Sometimes you will also find page numbers inside the parentheses (brackets). Page numbers are added when referring to specific arguments, or a quotation, from a source. This referencing system is known as the 'Author-Date' or 'Harvard' system. It is the most common, but not the only, referencing system used in International Relations. Your own institution will likely have detailed guidance on referencing which you should seek out.

When the time comes for you to prepare your own assignments, think of using sources as if you were a lawyer preparing a court case. Your task there would be to convince a jury that your argument is defensible, beyond reasonable doubt. You would have to present clear, well-organised evidence based on *facts* and *expertise*. If you presented evidence that was just someone's uninformed opinion, the jury would not find it convincing and you would lose the case. Similarly, in academic writing you have to make sure that the sources you use are *reputable*. You can usually find this out by looking up the author and the publisher. If the author is not an expert (academic, practitioner, etc.) and/or the publisher is unknown/obscure, then the source is likely to be unreliable. It may have interesting information, but it is not reputable by scholarly standards.

It should be safe to assume that you know what a book is (since you are reading one) and that you understand what the internet is. However, one type of source that you will find cited in this book and may not have encountered before is the journal article. Journal articles are typically only accessible from your university library as they are expensive and require a subscription. They are papers prepared by academics, for academics. As such, they represent the latest thinking and may contain cutting-edge insights. But they are often complex and dense due to their audience being experts and this makes them hard for a beginner to read. In addition, journal articles are peer reviewed. This means they have gone through a process of assessment by other experts and editors before being published. During that process many changes and improvements may be made – and articles often fail to make it through peer review and are rejected. So, journal articles are something of a gold standard in scholarly writing.

In addition to being available through your university library search functions, most journal articles are now available on the internet. This leads to confusion as students can find it difficult to distinguish a journal article from other sources such as an online magazine, a policy report, or an online newspaper article. Works such as these are not peer reviewed and conform to different standards. In this case, while the internet is the source of the confusion, it is also the source of the solution as it allows you to carry out a search for the publisher and the author and do a little detective work to find out who/what they are, and if they are credible academic sources. By using this simple and accessible method, you should quickly discern whether you are looking at a genuine journal article. Another helpful tip is length. A journal article will typically be 10–25 pages long (7,000–12,000 words); articles of online journalism or commentary will usually be shorter.

A final note on the subject of sources: the internet is something of a Wild West. There is great information there, but also a lot of rubbish. It can often be hard to tell them apart.

But, again, if you follow the golden rule of looking up the author and looking up the publisher (using the internet), you can usually find your way. However, even some of the world's most well known websites can be unreliable. Wikipedia, for example, is a great resource, but it often has incorrect information because it is authored, and usually edited, by ordinary people who are typically enthusiasts rather than experts. In addition, its pages are always changing (because of user edits), making it hard to rely on as a source. So the rule of thumb with the internet is to try to corroborate anything you find on at least two good websites/from at least two reputable authors. Then you can use the internet with confidence and enjoy its benefits while avoiding its pitfalls. When preparing assignments, however, you should only use the internet to supplement the more robust information you will find in academic journals and books.

 ## END OF CHAPTER QUESTIONS

1. What are the key components of a nation-state?

2. Why, and when, do we capitalise 'International Relations'?

3. The global system's three key actors react to, are subject to and sometimes shape the events and issues that drive international relations. Are there any specific events and issues from your own experience that you consider most important as you begin your journey with International Relations? Write them down and come back to your notes later as you advance through the book to see how your thoughts may have developed.

4. Have you ever considered how 'globalised' the world is today? If so (or if not), write down some of your first impressions about what this might mean.

5. What are the most important points to remember about reading academically and using sources?

HISTORY AND THEORY

The first part of the book starts with three chapters that deal with different interpretations of how historical events have laid important foundations, ideas and critiques that allow us to understand today's global system. Starting with an appreciation of history is essential as it paints a picture of 'how we got here'. Assuming that you could analyse today's world without historical grounding would be like setting out on a journey without knowledge of the terrain. Following that, Part one continues with three chapters looking at how we can interpret the world, primarily through theories, which comprise the main analytical toolkit for how students and scholars analyse events and generate ideas. Theory deepens and widens our knowledge about how the world works and reveals what insights are available to solve problems and open up new opportunities. History and theory are therefore essential starting points for any student of International Relations.

INTERNATIONAL RELATIONS AND THE GLOBAL SYSTEM

Stephen McGlinchey

Question: There were two world wars in quick succession in the twentieth century. Why has there not been a third?

The world today may seem to be in disarray. However, by historical standards, it is actually relatively orderly and fixed into place. Those that were born in the early part of the last century lived (if they were fortunate enough to survive) through a global pandemic, a global recession and two world wars. Life in prior centuries was even more perilous. Hence, there is no better place to start with International Relations than by explaining how the modern global system came into being, primarily out of the ashes of such events. This chapter deals with what can be described as the conventional origin story of International Relations. It sets out that International Relations as a discipline, and the global system it seeks to understand, was (and still is) dominated by warring nation-states that over time became somewhat moderated by international organisations and the characteristics that they embody – such as diplomacy and trade. Late in the story, individual human beings began to have limited agency. As the two chapters that follow this one will later detail, this origin story is under significant critique due to its limitations. Yet, it remains important as a starting point in any journey through International Relations to understand the history of the academic discipline by overlaying it on significant global events – as this chapter does.

The foundations of International Relations

You may have been drawn to studying International Relations for many reasons. But it is likely that part of what shaped your thinking began with a memorable event – perhaps one that occurred in your own lived experience or made it to the headlines. Such events are diverse and fall into many categories. As the book progresses, we will focus on those more. However, historically, significant events have typically involved violence between peoples through warfare and to a lesser extent large-scale regional or global economic events (Box 2.1). Indeed, it was the issue of warfare, and the seemingly endless occurrences of it, that birthed the discipline of International Relations in 1919 in the United Kingdom at Aberystwyth, University of Wales. Later that same year, Georgetown University in the United States followed suit and a trend had thus been established that universities should study and teach International Relations. Before long, there were groups of scholars spread across different continents working on one principal issue: how to build a discipline that could explain, and potentially solve, the problem of warfare.

2.1 – KEY INSIGHTS: Landmark eras for International Relations

The First World War (1914–18). Before 1914, a system of agreements and actions known as the 'concert of Europe' was orchestrated between the larger powers in Europe aimed at preserving the status quo (keeping things as they are) in the continent. The collapse of this system led to war and the European powers, divided in two broad groupings, drew their overseas colonies and other great powers such as Japan and the United States into the conflict. At the time, it was known as the 'Great War' as its global scale was unprecedented.

The Interwar Years (1919–38). An initially optimistic period in which the first attempts at global governance were built, watermarked by the creation of the League of Nations, based in Geneva, which provided a forum to manage disputes through negotiation rather than war. During this period a stock market crash occurred in the United States in 1929, causing the 'Great Depression' that spread worldwide during the early 1930s and brought significant economic decline. This event marked out the importance of economics to the global system, especially in terms of how quickly it can cause negative effects spreading from one place to another.

The Second World War (1939–45). Certain states were unhappy with the status quo in the interwar years, most notably Germany and Japan, which sought to grow their power and acquire more territory by invading neighbouring states. This led to the collapse of the League of Nations and another world war as a group of states (the United States, China, the United Kingdom, France and the Soviet Union) formed an alliance to oppose the expansionist powers, eventually triumphing following the occupation of Germany and the surrender of Japan in 1945.

The Cold War (1947–91). The Cold War was known as such because the presence of nuclear weapons made a traditional war between the rival parties (in this case the United States and the Soviet Union) unlikely as they each had the power to destroy each other and in doing so jeopardise human civilisation as a whole. This was known as 'Mutually Assured Destruction (MAD)'. For that reason, smaller-scale conflict and competition existed but a major 'hot' war, such as those in prior decades, was avoided. This period also underlined the importance of ideology in shaping global conflict, principally between *capitalism* and *communism*, which produced two incompatible international systems.

The New World Order (1991–2000). A short period following the end of the Cold War in which it was assumed that the international organisations built post-1945 (such as the United Nations) would finally come of age and provide a more secure and peaceful order based on globally shared ideas and practices. Francis Fukuyama's idea of the 'end of history' (1989, 1992), in which he posited that liberal democracy was the only viable long-term political system to complement a capitalist world, watermarked the era. Yet, critics of such ideas highlighted their shortcomings as an overly Western image of world order.

The post-9/11 era (2001–19). On 11 September 2001, al-Qaeda – a terrorist group opposed to Western (chiefly American) dominance in the global system – attacked the United States by hijacking four commercial airliners and crashing two of them into the Twin Towers of the World Trade Center in New York and a third into the Pentagon (the headquarters of the US Military in Arlington, Virginia). The fourth plane crashed before hitting its target, which was presumed to be a political building in Washington, DC. The event led to the United States starting its 'War on Terror', seeking to rid the world of terrorists and governments that supported or enabled them. United States actions – together with further operations by al-Qaeda and similar terrorist groups – shaped the first two decades of the twenty-first century and led to material changes in the nature of both domestic, and international, politics.

The post-Covid-19 era (2020–). People have always travelled from place to place and exchanged goods and cultural artefacts. What has changed, due to advances in technology and transportation, is the *speed* and *intensity* of this process. Embodying this shrinkage of time and space, the term 'globalisation' is a major part of how we perceive today's world. When the novel coronavirus that causes Covid-19 became a pandemic in 2020 it brought two points into focus. Firstly, transnational terrorism was no longer the central issue that it once was. Secondly, the pandemic questioned images of an interlinked, interdependent world as borders closed and most states initially turned inwards to tackle the problem for themselves rather than look outwards to pursue a global solution for all. Consequently, it is likely that the era that emerges from this crisis will be one where the global system's resilience, and the very nature of globalisation, are stress tested for an extended period.

The year 1919 was a landmark for many reasons. Not only was it the birth-year of International Relations as a discipline, but it also followed the end of the First World War (1914–18) which involved over thirty states and resulted in over 20 million deaths. Building on this, a common feeling at the time was that a war of such scale would not, or could not, happen again due to the financial costs and the toll it took on human life. Despite this, it was surpassed only twenty years later by an even more deadly conflict, the Second World War (1939–45), which took the lives of approximately 75 million people, 2.5–3 per cent of the world's population at the time. The Second World War is the most significant war in history due to its scale and impact. It reinforced to scholars that warfare seemed to be endemic to humankind's past and was therefore likely to be a central problem in our future. This reflected the so-called first 'great debate'. Firstly, there were those who sought to develop the discipline with scholarship that sought to manage warfare. This would be done by developing and promoting strategies to help states manage their participation and survival in the inevitable wars of the future. Secondly, there were scholars who sought to focus on how war could be gradually replaced, or downscaled, by emphasising the benefits of established patterns of peaceful interaction (mainly trade) and building new structures that would restrict war and formalise diplomacy (international organisations) such as the United Nations.

This early period left us with a discipline that focused on two key actors within the global system: (1) nation-states, the formal name for the political communities in which each of us lives and (2) international organisations, which provided a forum for states to discuss their differences whilst also helping to facilitate international trade. Gradually over time, a third element would emerge within the system: individual human beings. This was due to the rising issue of human rights, inspired by the atrocities of the Second World War and a desire to prevent that kind of mass suffering and death from happening again. Yet, it would take many more decades for individuals and the non-state groups they sometimes form to more fully rise to prominence. These three key actors of International Relations – nation-states, international organisations and individuals – were all in place by the mid-twentieth century and they still encompass the basic shape of how we make sense of the world today.

In attempting to make sense of history in all its complexity, scholars often use a simplification device to break the last 100+ years into different 'eras' (defined periods of time) as seen in Box 2.1. For example, the post-9/11 era consumed much of the debate in International Relations for the first two decades of the twenty-first century. In a darker sense than with human rights, it reinforced the growing importance over time of the actions of individuals – this time manifested through non-state terrorist groups. It is hard to say what the characteristics of our 'present' era are, that will only emerge in hindsight. However, we can say it is likely to be defined by responses to shared threats and shared opportunities beyond terrorism, which is no longer a top order global issue when taken against pandemic disease, climate change and new patterns of state rivalries.

The making of the modern world

Of all International Relations' key actors historically, the emergence of the nation-state is the most important in terms of how the global system is shaped. Today, there are 193 defined and internationally recognised territories, which we formally call nation-states (or more commonly just 'states'). To fully understand their importance, we need to look further back in history.

2.2 – KEY TERMS: Sovereignty

Map 2.1 Illustrating sovereignty

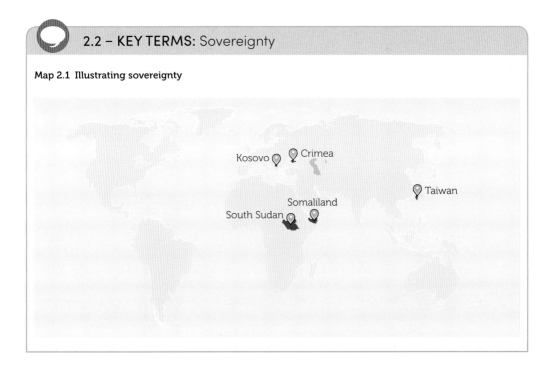

When you look at a map of the world today all the earth's landmasses are divided by lines (borders). Each of these borders are made (and remade) through historical events reflecting the key ordering principle of our global system – 'sovereignty' – which must be in place for a people to be recognised as a nation-state. Sovereignty has two benchmarks, both of which must exist simultaneously. First, there must be no major internal competition over who or what rules the territory. In practice this could be a parliament (or a similar set of institutions) in which power is regularly transferred to different elected officials. Or, it could be a monarch or dictator who rules until they are succeeded in some way by an equivalent figure. Second, there must be no significant external competition for that people's territory. In practice this means that no overseas power claims ownership.

In practice, sovereignty is fluid. For example, should a state be attacked by another (an external competitor) it may result in that state being absorbed into the aggressor's territory should they lose. In the modern day this is uncommon, but not unheard of. For example, Russia 'annexed' Crimea – part of Ukraine – in 2014. Additionally, if a group of people within a state start a movement (an internal competitor) and succeed this may sometimes create a differently composed state (carrying a new name and/or a new flag) occupying the same territory. We can see this in the case of China in 1949, which became the People's Republic of China, and later in Iran in 1979, which became the Islamic Republic of Iran – both after successful revolutions. In these cases, other states gradually recognised the sovereignty of the new leadership as the internal competition had been settled. Finally, sometimes groups of people within states seek to break away and form an entirely new state. This occurred most recently when South Sudan seceded (legally broke away) from Sudan. As the existing state of Sudan did not contest this (removing the factor of internal competition) and no external competitor existed, South Sudan became the world's newest nation-state in 2011.

There are territories often represented on maps which are described by terms such as 'self-declared' or 'partially recognised' because the two benchmarks of sovereignty are not yet fulfilled due to ongoing internal or external challenges. Among others, these include Taiwan, Kosovo and the Republic of Somaliland.

In Westphalia in 1648, part of today's Germany, a peace treaty was agreed between a set of warring parties that had won the Thirty Years War (1618–48). With over 8 million dead, the so-called 'Peace of Westphalia' was notable not just for ending what had been a brutal war, but also for providing the origins of our modern global system. Prior to Westphalia, Europe had been comprised of a fluid set of city states and smaller territories, many of which were overseen in some way by the church (under the guise of the 'Holy Roman Empire'), which provided a guiding set of principles to each ruler (see Ringmar 2017). Under this arrangement, borders and the distribution of power were unclear and often undefined. The Peace of Westphalia set out a system whereby authority going forward would be based on the political idea of sovereignty, rather than religious structures. Formalising this, each participant in the Treaty agreed on a set of defined borders marking their territory, which the others recognised in turn. This led to the redrawing of the European map and the gradual emergence of the idea of today's nation-states as territorially bound units, recognised by other such units as mutually sovereign. Sovereignty came hand in hand with the principle of non-intervention of a foreign power in another state. Nevertheless, non-intervention has always been a point of tension – especially when relations between states break down.

Of course, peace did not come to Europe for long. In fact, Europe saw an ever-escalating series of wars for several hundred years thereafter, ultimately culminating in the two world wars. As power was (post-Westphalia) seen in the accumulation of territory, and the resources and peoples therein, many leaders sought to expand their territory by taking over the territory of others. This led to frequent conflicts that regularly redrew the European map as existing states grew (or shrank) in size, new states were created, and others vanished entirely. It escalated further as European powers exported their continental rivalry to Africa, Asia and the Americas, which they raced to colonise (control a foreign territory and its people). As a result, by 1945, one third of the world's population were living under colonial rulers.

Following the Second World War, the global system began shifting to incorporate ideas of human rights and to recognise the illegitimacy of empire. This change was broadly inspired by the growing power of the United States, which had emerged from the Second World War in a stronger economic and political position relative to the other powers. It sought to use that leverage to influence a different world order beyond empire. Considering that the United States had freed itself from the colonialism of the British in the late 1700s during its own struggle for independence, its ideas when matched with its growing influence had sufficient gravity to reorder the system. Scholars have called this the beginning of a period of 'pax Americana' denoting the United States' key role internationally from this point forwards.

The process of decolonialisation did not happen overnight, but gradually through the second half of the twentieth century empires were almost entirely dissolved. A system of establishing self-determination for formerly colonised peoples was overseen by the newly formed United Nations. In that system, those colonised peoples had only one path to independence – becoming nation-states along the very lines Europeans had established in 1648. This process gradually gave us the world map we recognise today as new borders were drawn worldwide. As had been the case in Europe, this was not always a peaceful process and a range of challenges to sovereignty, both internal and external, continue to this day across all continents. In that sense, our world map undergoes occasional updates as this process evolves with time.

The ubiquity of sovereignty in today's global system, embodied in the nation-state and the quest for peoples who do not have a state to form one, is best represented numerically. In 1945 there were fewer than seventy nation-states. Today, there are almost 200. In that sense, today's global system – represented by the division of the earth into territorially sovereign units – is a system made first in Europe and then exported to the rest of the world. It overrode pre-modern and alternative forms of arranging peoples and distributing power. It endures to this day as the so-called global 'Westphalian' system, as key elements of the logic and structure trace back to 1648.

Beyond the understanding of the Westphalian system and the ever-increasing patterns of historical conflict it led to, the Cold War, which emerged in parallel to the decolonisation process, is of central importance in reminding us that large-scale war was not over in 1945. Pax Americana translates from Latin as 'American peace', suggesting that the new values of the global system would lead to a more peaceful world than the one overseen by the frequently warring European colonial powers. However, while there has been no third world war, large-scale state conflict would evolve to take on different forms – primarily due to the arrival of a new technology, nuclear weapons. After the first uses of an atomic bomb by the United States on Japan in August 1945, reports and pictures of the devastation caused by the two bombs that the United States dropped on Nagasaki and Hiroshima confirmed that the nature of warfare had changed forever. As one reporter described the scene: 'There is no way of comparing the Atom Bomb damage with anything we've ever seen before. Whereas bombs leave gutted buildings and framework standing, the Atom bomb leaves nothing' (Hoffman 1945).

Nuclear weapons were soon developed by other states, resulting in an entirely new set of conditions in the global system. It may seem strange but, despite their offensive power, nuclear weapons are primarily held as defensive tools – unlikely to be ever used. This is due to a concept central to IR known as 'deterrence'. By holding a weapon that can (if used) endanger the very existence of an opponent by potentially wiping them out, such an opponent is unlikely to attack you as the risk is too high. Especially if your nuclear weapons can (at least partially) survive that attack and allow you to retaliate. This is why states frequently move their nuclear weapons around, place them in submarines or aircraft, and even sometimes install them beyond their borders by agreement with an allied host state. In an environment as insecure as the Cold War, gaining a nuclear arsenal was a way to achieve deterrence from being attacked and thereby a measure of security that was not otherwise attainable. And tens of thousands of nuclear weapons were built and stockpiled by states during the Cold War. Underlining the logic of deterrence, nuclear weapons were never again used in anger after their initial use by the United States in 1945. Yet, in recognising the danger of the unmoderated spread of these weapons, a norm of non-proliferation of nuclear weapons became one of the central ideas of our global system, which is explored later in the chapter in the first case study.

The Cold War was responsible for the historical image of a world divided into three zones. The 'First World' was the 'Western' nations (this is where the term 'the West' comes from). These states were allied with the United States, broadly followed an economic system of capitalism, and (at least aspirationally) a political system of liberal democracy. The 'Second World' was the Soviet Union and a range of 'Eastern' states that were governed predominantly by communist (or socialist) parties who rejected capitalism as an economic model. This conflict between the first and second world went beyond economics and created two irreconcilable international systems – leaving other states a stark choice to operate within one system or the other. That led to some states opting out and declaring themselves 'non-aligned' – creating a 'Third World'. As most of those states were newly formed and/or developing it became a term often used to describe economically poorer states and is still sometimes used as such.

Despite the added ideological element of communism versus capitalism, the Cold War resembled other wars before it in that it became a battle for control over territory. Instead of meeting directly on the battlefield, both sides took part in 'proxy wars' as they fought to either support or oppose elements within states who sought to (or appeared to) move between the First and Second Worlds. The most well-known instances of this occurred in Asia, in Korea (1950–3) and Vietnam (1955–75), each of which resulted in several million deaths. As this took place in a time of decolonisation, the goal in this period was not to be seen to directly conquer other states, but to influence their political and economic development and in doing so increase the power of one 'World' and diminish the other.

The Cold War ended when the Soviet Union collapsed internally between 1989 and 1991 due to endemic corruption, popular resistance and economic decline. The 'Second World' was therefore no more, having lost its anchor. Virtually all of the world's states then transitioned to capitalism, if they had not already done so. At this point, the term 'globalisation' became widely used by scholars and policymakers more generally to describe the process of the First World's image gradually becoming representative of the entire world. For the first time in history a truly 'global' system had been born. States then became categorised more loosely within that global system by their economic levels of development post-1991, with 'Global North' sometimes used to represent the most historically developed economies, and 'Global South' essentially replacing the term 'Third World'.

The Cold War is therefore an interesting culmination in our journey of understanding the global system as being one comprised of historically warring nation-states. In this period, and continuing into the present, nuclear weapons helped prohibit the type of large-scale war seen pre-1945. In that sense, although the Cold War is over, it demonstrated a point in history where the global system changed materially in terms of how states can

Photo 2.1 The BRICS leaders in 2019. Left to right: Xi, Putin, Bolsonaro, Modi and Ramaphosa

Credit: Alan Santos /PR/Flickr

Global North/South distinctions are not as categorical, or as mutually exclusive, as the three worlds image they replaced. For example, when searching for an image that embodies the Global South we might reach for an image of the annual meeting of the BRICS – a loose association of five states (Brazil, Russia, India, China and South Africa) that are classified as amongst the most significant emerging economies. However, Russia was once a superpower and would likely not consider itself 'Southern'. Furthermore, China is the world's second largest economy and therefore hard to usefully categorise as 'developing'. Finally, geographically, only Brazil and South Africa are in Earth's Southern hemisphere, providing further fuzziness in the use of 'South'.

act internationally, especially when in conflict. This materially shaped the development of the discipline of IR and also gave way to the modern image of a world embodied by one global system. Not only has this changed the nature of warfare, it has also emphasised the importance of non-violent forms of engagement by states, allowing us to explore other elements in the system.

Beyond a world of warfare?

When military theorist Carl von Clausewitz remarked in the early 1800s that war was the continuation of policy by other means, he sought to normalise the idea of war in politics. Indeed, his words were reflective of the world at that time, as has been explored earlier in the chapter. But his words also indicated that actions short of war are available to help states achieve their objectives. These are typically the actions of diplomats. Their work is often far less expensive, far more effective and much more predictable a strategy than war. In fact, unlike in centuries gone by when war was common, diplomacy is what we understand today as the normal state of affairs governing international relations. When understood in tandem with the growing importance of international trade and the associated links between individuals in today's global system it allows us to expand our journey through history while also adding more analysis to account for why we have not had a third world war after witnessing two in short succession in the twentieth century.

2.3 – KEY TERMS: Diplomacy

Photo 2.2 Carter, Sadat and Begin after the Camp David Accords, 18 September 1978

Credit: David Hume Kennerly/Hulton Archive/Getty Images

Diplomacy is a process between actors (diplomats, usually representing a state) who exist within a system (international relations) and engage in private and public dialogue (diplomacy) to pursue their objectives in a peaceful manner. Diplomacy is part of the broader category of foreign policy. When a nation-state makes foreign policy, it does so for its own national interests. And these interests are shaped by a wide range of factors. In basic terms, a state's foreign policy has two key ingredients: its actions and its strategies for achieving its goals. The interaction one state has with another is considered the act of its foreign policy. This act typically takes place via interactions between government personnel, sometimes the leaders of states themselves – as pictured in the image celebrating the Camp David Accords. Historically, to interact without diplomacy would limit a state's foreign policy actions to conflict (usually war, but also economic sanctions) or espionage. In that sense, diplomacy is an essential tool required to operate successfully in today's global system and a major explanatory factor that accounts for what Gaddis (1989) called the 'long peace' due to the absence of major war since 1945.

While you will now be familiar with the concept of war in its varying forms, diplomacy, due to its nature, may present itself as something alien or distant. Diplomacy is most often an act carried out by representatives of a state, usually behind closed doors. In these instances, diplomacy is a silent process working along in its routine (and often highly complex) form, carried out by rank-and-file diplomats and representatives. More rarely, diplomatic engagements can drift into the public consciousness when they involve critical international issues and draw in high-ranking officials – and in tandem the media. An example of this would be a high-profile event marking a major peace agreement such as the Camp David Accords between Israel and Egypt in 1978, in which the respective leaders appeared together and shook hands – an unexpected gesture considering the deep tensions between both nations which had led to several wars over prior decades.

Records of regular contact via envoys travelling between neighbouring civilisations date back at least 2500 years. They lacked many of the characteristics and commonalities of modern diplomacy such as embassies, international law and professional diplomatic services. Yet, communities of people, however they may have been organised, have usually found ways to communicate during peacetime and have established a wide range of practices for doing so. The benefits are clear when you consider that diplomacy can promote exchanges that enhance trade, culture, wealth and knowledge. The applicable international law that governs diplomacy – the Vienna Convention on Diplomatic Relations (1961) – references only states as diplomatic actors. Yet, the global system also involves powerful actors that are *not* nation-states. These include international organisations, which regularly partake in areas of diplomacy and often materially shape outcomes. For example, the United Nations materially shaped diplomacy in the regulation of nuclear weapons – which will be covered in the first case study later in this chapter.

Building on diplomacy, trade is another means to mitigate war. When the Cold War ended in 1991 the idea of global trade came of age. There were no more images of different worlds but instead an image of one world open for business. Still a world of nation-states, but one where the barriers between them were at a historical low and a system of shared practices (such as resolving disputes diplomatically) was enshrined in international organisations. The complex nature of global trade, where each nation-state's economy is dependent on imports and exports to other states, is another development that makes war less likely. This is especially evident amongst the bigger powers in the global system who would likely be near-bankrupt and devoid of important commodities without the trade they generate between their peoples and businesses. The Covid-19 pandemic underlined this as, despite the unprecedented shutdowns of borders and restrictions on the movement of people, global trade – seen via the movements of goods and services – continued due to its necessity. Even the vaccines that were developed by pharmaceutical companies in certain states could not be manufactured at any scale without the materials and services found elsewhere.

What also makes war less likely is the fact that due to the instant communications we now enjoy via smartphones and global media, we can more easily see 'the other' as fellow human beings and as a result, it is much harder to justify acts of state aggression and to rally citizens to support a war. It is also easier to see (and therefore empathise with) individual human suffering, whether from war or from other manmade or natural factors, in other parts of the world. In this sense, the arrival of the globalised world in the 1990s also coincided with the gradual mainstreaming of ideas such as human security that took place both in the world of policymaking and in International Relations scholarship. It was as the twentieth century ended, the bloodiest century in recorded history, that individuals (and the groups they sometimes comprise) rose to prominence in the global system. In that sense you might view history as a dark place for people, but the foundations laid in the 1940s to emphasise the importance of human beings within the global system are gradually becoming more visible, as is explored further in the second case study later in the chapter.

Globalisation, especially when taken to be an unstoppable process within today's global system, raises a number of questions. When we try to answer these questions, we quickly find new ones emerging. For example, if we settle on an idea of globalisation as the emergence of a shared global culture where we all recognise the same symbols, brands and ideals, what does that mean for local products and customs that may be squashed out of existence? Examples like this build around the question of whether globalisation is more negative than positive. In this sense, it can be seen to represent the imposition of Western political ideas and neoliberal capitalist economics – which can be viewed as unrepresentative and/or exploitative. Critiques such as this have inspired an anti-globalist (or 'alter-globalism') movement which is active in society and academia (see Chang 2002). The wide-ranging debate that just one term evokes is characteristic of the discipline of International Relations itself and the complexity it attempts to navigate. As noted earlier, globalisation also comes with a darker side via the opportunities it provides for criminals and terrorists to operate more effectively. Yet, beyond these issues, it is a useful way to visualise the importance of global trade and interconnectedness in a tangible sense. When taken alongside diplomacy it offers a more holistic picture of the ways states have options beyond war in today's global system.

Adding trade and diplomacy, and the international organisations that facilitate them, allows us to see the world as one that is not static. New elements can sometimes appear and when they do, they can alter the nature of the system. Indeed, when recalling the presence of nuclear weapons, another factor within our system that disincentivises major war, it is clear to see that there are many reasons why today's world is more peaceful in absolute terms than it has been historically. This does not take away from the reality that war still occurs, both between states (interstate war) and within states (civil war or intrastate war). Indeed, there are hundreds of instances of these post-1945. Yet, unlike in historical situations, these have not escalated to become systemic events (large-scale regional or world wars). All of this does not mean that major war is impossible. It just indicates that due to the shape of today's global system, such a large-scale conflict is less likely to occur than in the different systems of the past.

2.4 – KEY TERMS: Polarity

The Cold War represented a global system of **bipolarity**. A bipolar system is one where two powers dominate. In that case, it was the United States on one side, and the Soviet Union on the other – with each side assembling their allies into their sphere of influence.

When the Cold War ended, a debate raged over how to describe the system. Some maintained that it was a system of **unipolarity** – as there was only one superpower remaining, the United States. This idea was captured by Krauthammer (1991) when he described it as a 'unipolar moment' in which the United States stood in an unprecedented historical situation where one state was significantly more economically, militarily and politically powerful to the extent that it would take a generation or more for a competitor of equal stature (a peer) to emerge.

Others have argued that the world has entered a period of **multipolarity**. Multipolarity is the historical norm as it describes a system with multiple competing powers. The last defined multipolar system ended shortly after the Second World War, which had left the European powers depleted – giving way to the Cold War bipolar system. Multipolarity today can be represented not just by rivalling states as it was in the past, but by the emergence of ideas of global governance through international organisations which compete with, and often constrain, the power of states.

Some suggest that bipolarity may return with the growing rivalry between the United States and a rising China shaping the twenty-first century. Others have suggested that a system of **tripolarity** may emerge, adding a resurgent Russia (or perhaps a different rising power) into the United States-China picture. While these perspectives draw on historical patterns for their inspiration, Acharya (2017) describes today's system as one of **multiplexity** – a new type of order in which several systems exist independently at the same time, but not necessarily in conflict, much like the idea of different movies screening under one roof in a multiplex cinema.

It would be deceptive to end the origin story of International Relations without re-emphasising the role of the nation-state. Despite the other key actors that have emerged within the system, it is still only the state that holds sovereignty. This remains the true bottom line in terms of power, and this is also reflected in International Relations scholarship which has traditionally been very state centric. When Covid-19 was officially declared a pandemic by the World Health Organization (denoting an epidemic occurring in multiple places) the decentralised and individualistic behaviour of states in response was more reminiscent of historical patterns than that of a supposed interconnected, globalised world. Rather than work together, states acted individually – often at odds, or in competition, with each other. This served as a reminder of their unmatched power to shape events within the global system. Later in the crisis when the race to deploy vaccines became the dominant objective, most states continued this path by competing to secure doses for their own populations first rather than prioritising international schemes (such as COVAX) to ensure everyone had equal access to vaccination.

Yet, a note of optimism. Major historical events, especially those that involve global crises (as noted throughout this chapter), do tend on average to result in shifts over the longer arc of history that come to improve how international relations operates. This typically only becomes clear in hindsight once the instinctual behaviour of states for short-term actions and reactions to crises gives way to opportunities for collective measures and working together.

CASE STUDY 2.1: Regulating nuclear weapons

Photo 2.3 Atomic cloud formation from the Baker Day explosion over Bikini Lagoon, 1946

Credit: National Archives/Hulton Archive/Getty Images

The quest to regulate nuclear weapons offers a glimpse of interactions between states that were sworn enemies and had little in common due to incompatible economic and political systems. Yet, through diplomacy and the influence of the United Nations, they were able to avoid war and find ways to achieve progress in the most critical of areas. It also gives us one possible answer to the question posed at the start of this chapter as to why there has not been a third world war.

Although the United States was the first state to successfully detonate a nuclear weapon, others soon followed – the Soviet Union (1949),

the United Kingdom (1952), France (1960) and China (1964). As the number of nations possessing nuclear weapons increased from one to five, there were fears that these weapons would proliferate (spread rapidly). This was not only a numbers issue. As the weapons developed, they became many orders of magnitude more destructive. By the early 1960s, nuclear weapons had been built that could cause devastation across over one hundred square kilometres. Recognising the danger, the United Nations attempted in vain to outlaw nuclear weapons in the late 1940s. Following that failure, a series of less absolute goals were advanced, most notably to regulate the testing of nuclear weapons. Weapons that were being developed required test detonations – each releasing large amounts of radiation into the atmosphere, endangering ecosystems and human health. By the late 1950s, diplomacy under a United Nations framework had managed to establish a moratorium (suspension) on nuclear testing by the United States and the Soviet Union. However, by 1961 a climate of mistrust and heightened Cold War tensions between the two nations caused testing to resume.

One year later, in 1962, the world came to the brink of nuclear war during the Cuban

Missile Crisis when the Soviet Union placed nuclear warheads in Cuba, a communist island nation-state approximately 150 kilometres off the southern coast of the United States. Cuban leader Fidel Castro had requested the weapons to deter the United States from meddling in Cuban politics following a failed US-sponsored invasion by anti-Castro forces in 1961. As Soviet premier Nikita Khrushchev (1962) put it, 'the two most powerful nations had been squared off against each other, each with its finger on the button'. After pushing each other to the brink of a nuclear war, US President John F. Kennedy and Khrushchev found that via diplomacy, they could agree to a compromise that satisfied the basic security needs of the other. Over a series of negotiations, Soviet missiles were removed from Cuba in return for the United States agreeing to remove missiles they had deployed in Turkey and Italy. As the two sides could not fully trust each other due to their rivalry, the diplomacy was based (and succeeded) on the principle of verification by the United Nations, which independently checked for compliance. Building further on the momentum, in July 1963 the Partial Test Ban Treaty was agreed, confining nuclear testing to underground sites only. It was not a perfect solution, but it was progress. And, in this case it was driven by the leaders of two superpowers who wanted to de-escalate a tense state of affairs.

Although early moves to regulate nuclear weapons were a mixed affair, the faith that Kennedy and Khrushchev put in building diplomacy facilitated further progress in finding areas of agreement. In the years that followed the Cuban Missile Crisis, Cold War diplomacy entered a high-water-mark phase in what became known as a period of 'détente' between the superpowers as they sought to engage diplomatically with each other on a variety of issues, including a major arms limitation treaty. In that climate, progress was made on restricting nuclear proliferation.

The Treaty on the Non-Proliferation of Nuclear Weapons (1970) – often known as the Non-Proliferation Treaty – sought to channel nuclear technology into civilian uses and to recognise the destabilising effect of further nuclear proliferation. It was a triumph of diplomacy. The genius of the treaty was that it was aware of the realities of the international politics of the time. It was not a disarmament treaty as great powers would simply not give up their nuclear weapons, fearful their security would be diminished. So, instead of pursuing an impossible goal of eliminating nuclear weapons, the Treaty sought to freeze the number of nations that had nuclear weapons at the five states that already possessed them. Simultaneously, those five nations were encouraged to share non-military nuclear technology with other states – such as nuclear energy and nuclear medicine – so that others would not feel tempted to pursue nuclear weapons. In short, those who had nuclear weapons could keep them. Those who did not have them would be allowed to benefit from the non-military research and innovation of the existing nuclear powers.

Due to the well-considered design of the treaty and its enforcement, it has been highly successful. Following the end of the Cold War, the Non-Proliferation Treaty was permanently extended in 1995. Granted, it has not kept the number of nuclear nations to five, but there are still fewer than ten – which is far from the twenty or more projected before the treaty entered into force. States with nascent nuclear weapons programmes, such as Brazil and South Africa, gave them up due to international pressure. Today, only a small number of states are outside its bounds. India, Pakistan and Israel never joined as they (controversially in each case) had nuclear ambitions that they were not prepared to give up due to national security priorities. Underlining the weight of the Non-Proliferation Treaty, in 2003, when North Korea decided to rekindle earlier plans to develop nuclear weapons, they withdrew from the treaty rather than violate it. To date, North Korea remains the only state to withdraw from the Non-Proliferation Treaty.

The non-proliferation regime is not perfect, of course – a situation best underlined today by North Korea. It is also a system with an inherent bias, since a number of states are allowed to have nuclear weapons simply because they were among the first to develop them, and this continues to be the case regardless of their behaviour. Yet, while humankind has developed the ultimate weapon in the nuclear bomb, diplomacy has managed to prevail in moderating its spread. When a state is rumoured to be developing a nuclear bomb, as in the case of North Korea, the reaction of the international community is always one of common alarm. We call ideas that have become commonplace 'norms' and non-proliferation has become one of the central norms within our global system.

Photo 2.4 Kennedy and Khrushchev in Vienna, April 1961

Credit: The U.S. National Archives/Flickr

 CASE STUDY 2.2: Human rights and sovereignty

Photo 2.5 Eleanor Roosevelt holding a poster of the Universal Declaration of Human Rights, New York, November 1949

Credit: FDR Presidential Library & Museum/Flickr

During the Second World War, Adolf Hitler's Nazi regime that had ruled Germany since 1933 had been discovered to have undertaken a programme of exterminating Jews and other unwanted peoples such as homosexuals, political opponents and the disabled. In what is now known as the Holocaust, an estimated 17 million people were killed by the Nazis through overwork in labour camps, undernourishment and various forms of execution – which included gas chambers and firing squads. Of those, approximately six million were Jewish – two-thirds of the European Jewish population. Especially with

reference to the fate of Jewish people, the phrase 'never again' became synonymous with these events. Not only was there a desire to prevent mass slaughter of human beings in a third world war – which would likely be nuclear – there was also a pressing desire to establish an international standard of human rights that would protect people from atrocities like the Holocaust and from unnecessary large-scale warfare.

Set up to represent all the earth's recognised nation-states, the United Nations became ground zero for discussion of human rights. Just three years after the organisation was created, the 'Universal Declaration of Human Rights' (1948, pictured being held by Eleanor Roosevelt in Photo 2.5) had been agreed by virtually all of the United Nations' member states outlining thirty articles that – in principle – extended to all the earth's people. As a snapshot, the first three articles are as follows:

» Article 1. All human beings are born free and equal in dignity and rights. They are endowed with reason and conscience and should act towards one another in a spirit of brotherhood.

» Article 2. Everyone is entitled to all the rights and freedoms set forth in this Declaration, without distinction of any kind, such as race, colour, sex, language, religion, political or other opinion, national or social origin, property, birth or other status. Furthermore, no distinction shall be made on the basis of the political, jurisdictional or international status of the country or territory to which a person belongs, whether it be independent, trust, non-self-governing or under any other limitation of sovereignty.

» Article 3. Everyone has the right to life, liberty and security of person.

Upon reading this, three thoughts may cross your mind. The first is that it represents a step change in history. For the first time, an international document existed that sets all nation-states a set of benchmarks upon which their behaviour towards individuals will be judged. Secondly, the aforementioned comes from an international organisation that is now part of the global system, in addition to states. Here, it is important to understand the limits of the United Nations and the principles and declarations it may proffer. The United Nations is not sovereign. It does not have a territory, or a people. Instead it is an organisation run by, and through, the voluntary participation of its members. In that sense, it *appends* rather than *replaces* nation-state power. This leads us to the third thing that may have crossed your mind upon reading the articles above – that even with the most basic understanding they do not reflect today's global system, which remains one scarred by warfare and well-publicised failures to protect human rights. In that sense, it is easy to regard human rights as a failure because, much like international organisations, individuals have not become sovereign the way nation-states are.

Such a conclusion, while factually true and the product of our global system's enduring foregrounding of the nation-state, risks betraying the momentum that has gathered around human rights. Firstly, if we reverse to the pre-1945 period, states often acted with impunity by waging ever-escalating wars for selfish reasons – and also by colonising or enslaving human beings. There may be no international sovereign to impose legal punishment on states in the way a person would be prosecuted by the legal system within a state for a crime. But, the normative power of human rights is a growing element within our global system that has made such historical violations a rarity today. We can account for this further by looking at a range of international crimes that have been named and developed – with the bulk highlighting cases where states directly cause (or indirectly allow) unacceptable harm to people, including in times of war. Of these, perhaps the most well known is genocide, which denotes the deliberate killing of a defined group of people (usually defined by nationality, religion or ethnicity) – precisely what the Nazis did to Jewish people.

Building on the momentum of establishing a range of legal norms, the Responsibility to Protect (2001), sometimes referred to as 'R2P', was endorsed by all member states of the United Nations in 2005. It sought to build further on the Universal Declaration of Human Rights and subsequent documents by establishing higher levels of punishment for the worst violations by states. In principle, this involves a reinterpretation of sovereignty (at times) to the level of the individual. To illustrate this, under the Responsibility to Protect, sovereignty can be imagined as similar to a mortgage given by a bank (the United Nations) to a homeowner (a nation-state). Should states keep up their repayments (by treating their people well) then the bank will never trouble the homeowner. However, if the state does not keep up its repayments (by acting in ways that cause its people undue harm and suffering) then that state may be repossessed by the

Photo 2.6 Protesters hold signs relating to 'R2P' as they take part in a demonstration against the military coup in Yangon, Myanmar on 12 April 2021

Credit: STR/AFP/Getty Images

international community, under the authority of the United Nations. In practice, this could mean that a state comes under an increasing level of actions, up to and including a regime being forcibly removed from power through invasion. The caveat is, as with any major issue involving international security, it has to be agreed by the world's major powers – again reinforcing where the real bottom line of sovereignty lies.

The Responsibility to Protect has been invoked in well over a hundred resolutions at various levels within the United Nations, signifying that it is not just something that exists on paper, but that human rights in the decades since the Universal Declaration have come a long way. During the 2021 coup in Myanmar pro-democracy protesters even held up 'R2P' signs (Photo 2.6) showing how deeply and widely understandings and expectations of this norm have proliferated. Of course, some states still mistreat their people and international action is often insufficient to prevent it or stop it, or agreement on an action cannot be reached – as prolonged civil wars in Yemen and Syria demonstrate. Yet, understanding how the global system incorporates human rights in ways that go beyond the merely aspirational, and the related place of international organisations, is to understand that both the aforementioned exist in a position that is gradually challenging the once absolute monopoly on sovereignty held by states. It also adds further weight to the layer cake of reasons why there has not been a third world war – in this case adding a legal and normative architecture that restrains states from endangering human security on the scale that has been evident in history.

Conclusion

Our global system, in reality and as understood intellectually by International Relations scholars, is built on historical events. These events have resulted in a world dominated by nation-states which are influenced by international organisations in a dynamic system that has also opened a growing space for the voices and concerns of individuals. Future events will most likely continue to alter the system, just as past ones – such as the Treaty of Westphalia, the invention of nuclear weapons and the emergence of a global economic system of capitalism – have left indelible marks. Critiquing this origin story is our next step in the chapters ahead, which look deeper into our history and also ask questions of our present. We hope this will encourage you to not see this book, or the discipline it introduces to you, as something you can memorise as a series of events or static concepts. Instead, you should see International Relations as a living, challenging and sometimes confrontational journey of different perspectives. There are no correct answers for how we should understand the world. Indeed, there is no correct answer for the question posed at the start of the chapter of why we have not had a third world war. It may be because of nuclear weapons, it may be because the United Nations exists, perhaps it is born from a commercial desire to protect the global economy from a major disruption, or it may be because we just don't want to solve disputes in that way any more due a rising norm of human rights. Each of these are relevant starting points and each may lead to different, yet legitimate, answers.

END OF CHAPTER QUESTIONS

1. In what ways has warfare been central to International Relations from its inception as a discipline?

2. What is the 'Westphalian system' and why is it so important?

3. With diplomacy, and the international organisations underpinning it, do we now have the tools we need to mitigate major war?

4. What type of 'polarity' do you think best represents today's global system?

5. The post-Covid-19 era is hard to describe as it has only just begun, and we do not (yet) have the benefit of hindsight. Since you are living through it, what are your own impressions of it so far and how would you describe it?

DISCOVERY, CONQUEST AND COLONIALISM

Robbie Shilliam

Question: If the age of colonialism is over why do we still need to discuss it?

As the previous chapter argued, 1648 was the origin point for our global system. However, another year is worthy of mention. In 1492, Christopher Columbus sailed from the Canary Islands off the north-west African coast, crossed the Atlantic, landed in the Bahamas and thus inaugurated the age of European empire and the rise of what we nowadays call 'the West'. From the introduction of potatoes into culinary diets worldwide, to the genocides of indigenous peoples, to slavery and abolition, and to the creation of the most powerful military force the world has ever seen (the United States), the 'discovery' of the Americas has come to fundamentally shape our present. This chapter situates the idea of discovery within the European mapping of the world prevalent in Columbus's era. This map sketched out a hierarchy of human beings, with those belonging to European Christendom occupying the apex position, thus justifying the conquest of non-European, non-Christian peoples. The chapter also asks whether the 'conquest' and 'discovery' associated with 1492 might contain deeper-determining norms and practices than those of 'non-intervention' and 'sovereignty' associated with 1648. Comparing the perspectives in this chapter with the prior chapter should allow you to understand the contested nature of history and the ways in which this impacts our view of the present. This chapter therefore builds on our understanding of history by suggesting that ideas such as sovereignty and diplomacy have always been entangled with conquest and colonialism.

The 1492 map of the world

Different points of departure can give rise to different narratives that open up important nuances for anyone beginning their journey with International Relations. Consider, for instance, the Treaty of Tordesillas between Portugal and Castile (part of today's Spain), which in 1494 granted jurisdiction over the Americas to the two European powers. Instead of illustrating the rise of a modern state system (as we saw following the Peace of Westphalia in 1648), this departure point highlights the pre-existing logic of European imperial expansion and the consolidation of colonialism. In that sense, while the state system has outlasted imperialism, it can also be argued that five hundred years of colonial rule have nonetheless fundamentally shaped the political, economic, social and cultural dimensions of our 'post'-colonial global system. Strangely, 1492 does not feature prominently in the years of departure with which we normally sketch out our understandings of the contemporary world. To answer why, we need to once more reconsider the image garnered from Westphalia in 1648 where you will most probably imagine armies fighting across central Europe. Here, events happen on land. But think 1492, and you will imagine discovery and conquest across the ocean (see Table 3.1).

Table 3.1 Comparing images of 1648 and 1492

1648	1492
* Nation-states face each other with no higher power to rule their conduct existing in a state of international anarchy. * The practice of diplomacy and the principle of non-intervention in the affairs of other Christian rulers, regardless of denomination, mitigate against war. * Although some are strong and some weak, all are the same kind of unit – a sovereign, territorially bound state.	* Imperial powers colonise indigenous peoples while claiming that they are doing God's work. * Humanity is divided by religious authorities into those whose Christian faith compels them to conquer and enslave and those non-Christians whose idolatry allows them to be conquered and enslaved. * The world is comprised of a *hierarchy* of these qualitatively *different* entities.

Cartography is the art of map making. It involves arrangement (how the parts are defined and laid out) and animation (what each part does and how are they connected to each other). By using 1492 as our departure point, we must grapple with different cartographic challenges to that of 1648. Instead of mainland Europe, we can look to the oceans and non-European islands and landmasses. Instead of sovereign territories in Europe we can sketch out an expanding imperium (the area under imperial rule spread more globally). Instead of non-intervention, we must consider conquest to be an organising principle of how actors carve out their space. And, rather than diplomacy and war being the practice that animates these actors, we must look towards the act of discovery and the pursuit of colonisation.

Considering these factors leaves us with a range of issues to ponder, each of which allows us to build on or perhaps challenge the traditional image of history that was outlined in the previous chapter. Firstly, 1492 might be a far more portentous date for humanity than 1648, as the act of discovery might be more important for scholars than the recognition of sovereignty. Secondly, we might need to refresh our cartographic skills – our physical, but also mental, map-making abilities – to not only attend to peace-making in Europe but also the imperial expansion across the world that followed Columbus's journey. Towards this aim, we can think of different ways of defining and laying out the constituent parts of International Relations. We can also think more deeply about what principles animated these parts to action. Above all, we can think about what discovery meant for Columbus, and how its meaning and practice were embedded within broader policies of imperial expansion amongst the polities of European Christendom, especially the Spanish and Portuguese.

It is also important to fully understand what we mean by 'discovery'. In Columbus's era, 'discovery' did not necessarily refer to *unknown* land. Rather, to discover meant to *uncover* land that was known to exist yet had remained hidden (Washburn 1962). This might seem like a pedantic distinction to make. It is, though, a crucial one. The expansion of European Christendom across the world was not conceived of as a haphazard process but as one that was divinely ordained. In order to understand why in 1492 Columbus took upon himself and his crew the risk of sailing across the Atlantic Ocean into the unknown we first need to examine how the scholarly community of European Christians of that age mapped out the world.

Medieval Christendom had many different maps of the world. All of them were based upon geographical knowledge inherited from ancient Greek, Roman and Islamic scholars. Perhaps the most influential model was the 'five zone' model provided by fifth century BCE philosopher Parmenides (see Photo 3.1). Known as the 'five zone' model, maps based on Parmenides' writings split the world into a sphere comprising two frigid zones (the poles), two temperate zones (between the tropics and the poles) and one torrid zone (the tropics). The frigid and torrid zones were considered to be uninhabitable, while the northern temperate zone comprised the lands of Europe, Asia and Africa known to the Greeks. These lands were divided from each other by the Mediterranean (which ran east to west globally) and the Nile River (which ran north to south globally). Finally, the world was encircled by a huge 'ocean river' (Sanderson 1999). Greek scholars also argued that celestial bodies affected the human body and influenced behaviour. Building on observations such as this, many scholars of the time claimed that where people were geographically located beneath the stars and planets had an effect on their conduct. Put this arrangement and principle of animation together, and you have the classical Greek map of the world. The cold regions – that part of the northern temperate zone that verged on the frigid zone – produced fierce yet unwise people. The hot regions of the temperate zone, which verged on the torrid zone, produced wise yet tame people. It was only the middle of the temperate zone – that is, the parts of Europe that lay next to the Mediterranean – that produced a well-balanced people who were both wise and spirited. In other words, the European Mediterranean people, Greeks specifically, accorded to themselves the exclusive ability to govern and thus rule over peoples from the 'hot' and 'cold' nations.

Hundreds of years later, medieval scholars took the Greek map and translated its arrangements and principles of animation into biblical lore. The celestial region became God's incorruptible heavens, which regulated the terrestrial world of 'fallen' humans. Furthermore, the division between temperate, cold and hot nations was mapped onto the sons of the biblical figure, Noah (Shem, Japheth and Ham). In this way, every human being occupied a geographical place according to their divinely ordained and biblically narrated nature. Of special importance is the prevailing association at this time of the word Ham with 'hot'. Add to this the infamous 'curse of Ham', which in Genesis 9: 20–7 placed Ham's descendants in servitude to the descendants of Shem and Japheth.

Photo 3.1 Diagrammatic zonal world map, eleventh century

Building from all these associations, Christian scholars typically cast the people who lived on the African continent as natural slaves to those who lived in the temperate European zone.

This cartographic reasoning justified the first reported abduction and enslavement of Africans at the Bay De Rio de Ora in North-western Africa under the Portuguese flag in 1441. It was widely assumed that the habitable world ended just north of where the abduction occurred, specifically where Cape Bojador on the African mainland flanks the Canary Islands (see Map 3.1). Portuguese sailors were usually loath to venture beyond this point into the torrid zone. Some scholars of the ancient world had claimed that any humans living in this zone had to be unnatural, accidents deformed by nature's excessive heat. Many Christian scholars repeated this belief and attached it to the curse of Ham. Africans, then, appeared on the world map not only as natural slaves but even, possibly, as sub-human monsters. This biblically sourced belief maintained traction, even when evidence was presented to the contrary.

By 1482, the Portuguese had established their first fort south of the Sahara Desert at Elmina on the coast of current-day Ghana; and in 1488 Bartolomeu Dias rounded the Cape of Good Hope in the south-west of the African continent. Portuguese outposts relied

Map 3.1 Cape Bojador's location

on trade with local Africans. Yet the myth of monstrous people and natural slaves remained attached to the West African coastline and was still widespread when Columbus was planning his journey.

Conquest and conversion

Theologically, the Christian map of the world justified the connection between discovery and conquest. In practice, the justification of expansionary warfare in defence of Christianity was established with the 'Reconquista' – a centuries-long struggle by Christian forces to take back the Iberian Peninsula (today's Spain and Portugal) from the Islamic dynasties of the Moors. While the reconquest began in the early 700s, its framing through religious ideology began with the idea of a Christian 'holy war', or crusade, against Islam. The reconquest featured a particular system of economic extraction that underwrote military campaigning on the Iberian Peninsula. At the centre of this system lay the *encomienda*, a grant to conquerors of land taken from Muslim owners or rulers. Backed up by the Spanish Crown, the *encomienda* system permitted the extraction of labour and tribute from the defeated population. From the Crusades onwards, then, it was deemed entirely right for Christians to conquer non-Christian lands and hold their people in effective bondage.

3.1 – KEY TERMS: The Crusades

In 1095, and in response to a request from Byzantine (the eastern Roman Empire), Pope Urban II proclaimed a Crusade to clear the 'holy lands' around Jerusalem of Muslim rule. To facilitate the recruitment of an armed force, which the Catholic Church alone could not raise, Urban II offered to Christian men absolution (forgiveness) of their sins in exchange for fighting the 'Saracens' – principally, people of Islam – although Jewish peoples were also on occasion set upon and massacred. Theologically, 'holy war' justified, albeit in particular circumstances, the forceful taking of lands belonging to non-Christians and the placing of non-Christians into bondage. Ebbing and flowing, often due to the shifting geopolitical interests of European Christendom's numerous rulers, the Crusades ran for several centuries. After the late thirteenth century the locus of conflict moved from the eastern Mediterranean to the Iberian Peninsula. The Crusades finished there, in 1492, with the surrender of Muhammad XII of Granada.

Crucially, even before 1492, the Reconquista was an intrinsically extra-European affair. While the Portuguese were busy making judgements about people living on the north-west African coastline, the attention of the Spanish fell upon the Canary Islands. The War of Castilian Succession (1474–9) was fought in part due to an attempt by the king and queen of Castile and Aragon, what was to become the Kingdom of Spain, to encroach upon the trade that the Portuguese king, Afonso V, enjoyed on the Atlantic African mainland coastline. A good part of the war featured naval battles around the Canary Islands. The Treaty of Alcáçovas (1479) ended the war by preserving Portuguese influence over the African mainland and giving Spain dominion over the Canary Islands. This was perhaps the very first treaty between European leaders to divide up lands outside their Christian homelands into spheres of influence – a term that would later become central to International Relations.

The Treaty, however, was legally predicated upon two prior Papal decrees, issued by Pope Nicholas V in 1452 and 1455, and acknowledging the right of the Portuguese King Afonso V to trade on the Atlantic African coast. The 1452 Papal decree also justified African slavery by granting to the Portuguese:

> Full and free permission to invade, search out, capture, and subjugate the Saracens and pagans and any other unbelievers and enemies of Christ wherever they may be, as well as their kingdoms, duchies, counties, principalities, and other property ... and to reduce their persons into perpetual servitude.

What is notable in this decree is the way in which the crusade against Islam (Saracens) was made to justify the enslavement of Ham's descendants (Africans), many of whom were not Muslim. The discovery of torrid zones and the enslavement of the people who lived there became justified under the religious ideology of a holy war. The Spanish reconquest of Iberia and the Portuguese conquest of the African coastline were both justified by Papal decrees as holy wars. Practically, this justification allowed for the removal of lands belonging to non-Christians as well as the enslavement or bondage of non-Christians – Jews, Muslims and especially Africans. Thus, by 1492 Christian scholars presumed that conquest and discovery were the same animating principle by which to map out the world into which the Spanish and Portuguese kingdoms were expanding as imperial powers.

Crucially, though, the Papal decrees that concerned the Spanish rule over the Canary Islands had said something quite different about the treatment of non-Christians there – the indigenous inhabitants who lay in the way of Christian expansion. Back in 1435, Pope Eugene IV decreed that natives of the Canary Islands who were converting, or had converted, to Christianity must not be enslaved. In 1476, and as part of the war against Portugal, Ferdinand and Isabella turned their attention to establishing direct monarchical rule over all the Canary Islands. At this point, Pope Sixtus IV – who would a few years later confirm the right of the Portuguese to enslave Africans – reaffirmed his predecessor's decree of 1435 *against* the enslavement of Canary natives who were in the process of being converted.

The presence of indigenous peoples in the Canary Islands complicated the principles of holy war primarily because they did not fit neatly into Christian cartography. The islands existed on the very border of the torrid zones, just above Cape Bojador. But curiously, these peoples did not appear in the biblical genealogy of the descendants of Adam and Eve. They could not then be regarded as the descendants of Ham, who had a prominent place in the genealogy of the Old Testament, supposedly as the rightful slaves of Japheth (Europeans). Nor could they be conflated with Muslims. These indigenous peoples had not rejected the gospel of Christ as they had not yet been exposed to it. Hence, while Canary Islanders might be said to naturally come under the domination of European Christendom, as innocents they could only be dominated through the process of peaceful conversion to the faith. Indeed, as 'hot' nations, the inhabitants could be considered wise and tameable – that is, capable of peaceful conversion to Christianity.

That was the reasoning of the Papacy. But the Spanish Crown had to contend with the practicalities of colonising the Canary Islands, which in part undermined the Papacy's lofty position. As they pushed forward their conquest of the Canary Islands, Ferdinand and Isabella also began the final push to reconquer the Iberian mainland, warring with the last Islamic polity, the Emirate of Granada, between 1482 and 1492. During this time, Pope Sixtus IV granted tithing revenue (essentially taxes that Christians gave to the church) to the Spanish monarchs so that they could finance the war. And the Pope gave the same right to the monarchs when it came to the Canary Islands. Peaceful conversion was therefore key to a successful conquest for the Spanish monarchs, both religiously and economically: once converted, these peoples would become taxpayers to the Crown. But the monarchs were not the ones doing the actual conquering; they entrusted this dirty work to mercenaries – hired hands. Paradoxically, mercenaries would be locked out of any revenue streams if the indigenous peoples peacefully submitted to Spain. This is why, despite Papal decrees and the like, conquistadors pursued the final conquest of the Canary Islands with the same method as those who conquered Granada. It did not matter if the peoples were (guilty) infidels or (innocent) heathens. In both cases, lands were expropriated through brute force and oppression and their peoples oftentimes placed into bondage.

So, by the time that Columbus was planning to set sail, the conquest of the Canary Islands had already presented a set of deep cartographic challenges to the mapping of the world. Above all, if conquest and discovery, combined, animated the world map, this combination became troublesome in the already-inhabited Atlantic islands. Significant questions arose, such as: what did the location of the natives say about their characteristics? How did these natives fit into a holy war of conquest when they were not even mentioned in the Bible? And how could religious, political and economic interests be reconciled so as to peacefully incorporate these natives into the church and empires of European Christendom? Such conundrums and questions were ultimately resolved by brute force in southern Spain and in the Canary Islands. These questions – and their violent resolutions – would soon travel with Columbus to a set of islands on the other side of the Atlantic (Fernández-Armesto 1994).

Discovery and the apocalypse

In April 1492, Columbus met with Ferdinand and Isabella to petition support for his voyage. Technically, the question as to whether land could conceivably exist across the Atlantic revolved around the prospective proportion of land to water in the circle of the earth. On this question, Columbus favoured a higher proportion of land to water, which logically allowed for the argument to be made that land across the Atlantic (what was believed to be the east coast of India, as the continent of America was not known to exist) was much closer to Europe than otherwise thought. His opponents favoured the opposite – and of course they were correct as it would later be discovered that the earth is approximately two-thirds covered by water. Columbus made four different voyages to the Americas (see Map 3.2). Famously, when he first arrived, he thought he had reached the Indies, not knowing that the American continent existed and stood between Europe and Asia.

Map 3.2 The voyages of Columbus

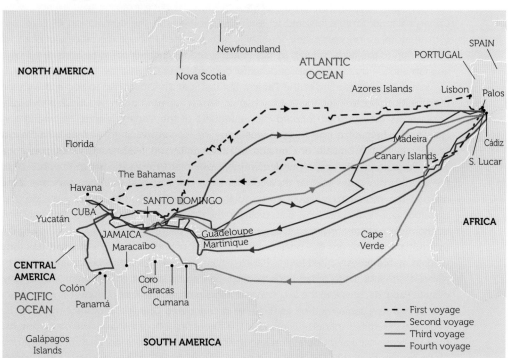

Far more important than the science argument was a religious one: Columbus's opponents charged him with heresy. Primarily, they drew upon the authority of Saint Augustine of Hippo (354–430 CE) who had believed that the geographical dispersal of humanity after the biblical flood was delimited to the known world, that is, the known landmasses of Europe, Asia and Africa. Columbus responded by mapping discovery onto the apocalyptic calendar of Christianity. In theological terms, 'apocalypse' does not mean the cataclysmic end of the world but rather the final revelation of divine mystery. The biblical Book of Revelations sets out a cryptic narrative, detailing the rise of an anti-Christ before the final return of the Messiah. Literature in Columbus's era strongly associated the

Photo 3.2 Portrait, said to be of Christopher Columbus

Credit: The Metropolitan Museum of Art/Wikimedia Commons

timing and events leading to the apocalypse with the crusading wars against unbelievers, especially Muslims.

Columbus himself considered the liberation of Granada and the end of the crusades, also in 1492, to be a sign that he was living in apocalyptic times and that the Spanish monarchs were God's powers on earth. This religious justification of political power was quite different to that which underlaid the Peace of Westphalia: Columbus conceived of the monarchy as a divinely mandated imperial force, whereas the Westphalia principle of *cuius regio eius religio*, 'whose realm, their religion', curtailed a monarch's religious authority to his realm. Columbus thus considered himself to be an emissary of God's temporal power (the Spanish monarchy) and he conceived of his venture as bringing into the fold the whole of humanity for the final revelation. This was what animated Columbus's mapping of the Americas. And that is why he believed that he had uncovered the Caribbean islands from their 'hiding' place. Their discovery inaugurated a new spiritual dispensation: a 'new heaven and earth', or what we colloquially call today 'the new world' (Watts 1985).

That, though, was the source of his heresy. Columbus disputed the assertion that the tropics were uninhabitable because they were torrid. He had himself experienced the opposite in a 1482 visit to the Portuguese fort at Elmina in present-day Ghana. Not only did Columbus note the rich trade in enslaved humans, gold, ivory and pepper, he also reported that the area was densely populated and, to a good extent, temperate. Crucially, his journey west was also a journey south – into the tropics. Influenced by Marco Polo's travelogue, and especially his mention of the most easterly islands (Japan), Columbus believed that the 'Indies' stretched from the temperate zone into the tropics and that they could be approached, as such, by crossing the Atlantic (see Gómez 2008). His journey was therefore doubly heretical: he did not only wish to find new temperate lands that were not in the Bible, he also wished to find tropical peoples who, he argued, against the convention of existing Christian maps, could be converted to Christianity.

This is why Columbus began his voyage at the end of the so-called inhabitable world – in the newly conquered Canary Islands, just north of Cape Bojador. And existing questions over the nature of those island's native inhabitants travelled with Columbus as he imagined what kinds of human being he might uncover across the Atlantic and bring into the Christian fold. Columbus was certain of one thing, at least. The peoples he would find in what would become known as the Western Indies were heathens; their existence was not even recorded in the Bible. And that meant that Columbus had full licence to bring them into Christianity, which at this apocalyptic time was protected by the Spanish monarchy. Just like the indigenous peoples of the Canary Islands, those across the Atlantic were to be conquered.

But at the same time, and like the Canary Islands inhabitants, those across the Atlantic might be capable of conversion by peaceable means. They could not be treated as if they were Muslims: they had not refused the word of Christ; they had not even heard the word. What is more, just like Canary Islands natives, they could not be the children of Ham as

3.2 – KEY INSIGHTS: Black Lives Matter

Photo 3.3 George Floyd protest in Times Square, New York, 26 July 2020

Credit: Ira L. Black-Corbis/Getty Images

Photo 3.4 George Floyd mural in Minneapolis, Minnesota

Credit: Lorie Shaull/Flickr

Black Lives Matter, often abbreviated as 'BLM', refers to the legacies of slavery in the Americas wherein Black peoples were legally, culturally, economically and politically valued as less than fully human. The movement began in 2013 as a hashtag in response to the acquittal of George Zimmerman who had been on trial for the fatal shooting of an African American teenager, Trayvon Martin. It became a regular presence in the streets of the United States, protesting police violence and repression targeted at Black communities. Protests reached a high-water mark following the death of George Floyd in May 2020 after a Minneapolis police officer, Derek Chauvin, knelt on his neck for over nine minutes while a crowd of bystanders looked on pleading for him to let Mr Floyd breathe. Protests also erupted beyond the United States in places that, due to various histories of empire and colonialism, had a minority Black population. The wider movement, which is largely decentralised, takes issue at the debilitating effects of over-policing and disproportionate criminalisation of Black communities such that even with conferment of citizenship after abolition, Black peoples have yet to enjoy a full and equal humanity vis-à-vis white citizens. It is also a testimony to the long tradition of Black women's organising, worldwide, that seeks justice for all.

their geographical location lay outside the Bible's map. Hence, they could not be treated as natural slaves. Additionally, if the tropics could be temperate (if humans could live there without degenerating into unnatural monsters) then these natives across the Atlantic might have the same characteristics as 'hot' nations that lived in the temperate zone: wise, yet tameable – perfect converts. At this point it is helpful to turn to Columbus's own words on how he described the first peoples he met in the Americas, on the island of Guanahani, in the present-day Bahamas:

> They should be good and intelligent servants, for I see that they say very quickly everything that is said to them; and I believe that they would become Christians very easily, for it seemed to me that they had no religion.

But just as had been the case in the Canary Islands, so in the Caribbean did demands by the Spanish Crown for religious conversion clash with the demands by conquistadors for economic enrichment. After 1513, a legal instrument was presented as a resolution to this clash. The *Requerimiento*, a declaration by the Spanish Crown enunciated by conquistadors, demanded that native 'Indios' accept the conquistadors' dominion as well as their right to preach and convert. Crucially, the declaration also warned that rejection of Christian rule, and the consequences of it, would be the fault of the Indios themselves. Effectively, then, the Crown provided a legal pathway by which conquistadors could still treat native Indios as they had Canary Islands natives – as spoils of holy war, Muslims and/or children of Ham. Hence the path was cleared for the expansion of the brutal *encomienda* system to the Americas.

Discovery and conquest were animated by an apocalyptic vision. The mapping of the New World relied on old world cartographies, although their principles of arrangement and animation would transform numerous times in the proceeding centuries (Wynter 1991). Ultimately the violence enacted in the Canary Islands, despite religious callings for peaceful conversion, was enacted in the New World – and to an unimaginable extent. After just one hundred and fifty years only 10 per cent of the indigenous populations remained across the Americas. Most were killed through war, land dispossession, and the diseases that took hold in the turbulence of colonisation (see Cameron et al. 2016). Kidnapped Africans (slaves) began arriving in Hispaniola (the island that is divided into today's Haiti and Dominican Republic) in 1501 and by the mid-sixteenth century had begun to replace indigenous peoples as the prime source of bonded labour. This all gives a very different interpretation of the apocalypse: less a revelation and far more a genocide.

1492 as a map of the present

The year 1648 remains an important date in European history. Yet the Treaty of Westphalia provided for the principles of mutual recognition only within that portion of humanity that came to be represented as the European and Christian 'family of nations'. Now think about 1492. Instead of sovereignty and non-intervention, this date is associated with conquest and discovery – the cardinal norms of empire that sought to cover the globe with a holy hierarchy of humanity (Jahn 2000). Rather than 1648 replacing the prior history of discovery and conquest with a new dispensation of non-intervention and sovereignty it would be more accurate to imagine this as being put in place only for a sub-section of political actors (male, white, and of European Christian heritage). The rest of humanity continued to suffer the legacies of conquest through violent dispossession and bondage.

Still, it would be fair to ask whether the difference between 1492 and 1648 is only of historical importance. Well, it is certainly not the case that 1492 alone gave rise to the whole edifice of European empire over the next five hundred years. But that being said, the cartography associated with 1492 – its arrangement of peoples and places and the principles that animate their interaction, remains pertinent to our present. Consider, for instance, the question of whose humanity is sacred, and the way in which this evaluation is made by reference to geographical origin/location and biblical narrative.

Now think of the contemporary Black Lives Matter movement whose struggle against anti-black racism resonates across the globe. Think of the less-than-human treatment of refugees, especially arriving from the Global South, and the denial of even basic rights of protection to children who cross borders. And consider the way in which politicians demonise migrant groups arriving from particular geographical locales as the supposed vector of disease, crime and poverty – a demonisation that often utilises categories of race and religion. A 1492 departure point would help us to think through these globally expansive hierarchies of humanity that even today justify violence, oppression and inequality. A 1648 departure point would have little to say directly on the matter. For these reasons, the deep and sometimes peculiar history lesson within this chapter reveals itself to be a vital part of the history of International Relations – adding a new layer of insight into our past and present.

Additionally, 1492 helps us to think about the continuation of global networks of bonded labour as well as the phenomenon of 'land grabs' – the repurposing of agricultural lands that once provided for local staples into agri-businesses that instead grow crops for export. This has given rise to food insecurity on a global scale. Yet we should also not lose nuance as we seek to apply understandings of the past to the present. For example, it would be wrong to map what is called the 'new slavery' – various forms of bonded labour embedded in global networks of forced migration – directly onto the historical slavery of the Americas, least of all because slavery is now outlawed by various international instruments and new forms of human slavery are mostly part of an illicit economy. Similarly, contemporary land grabs do not map directly onto the imperial history of territory acquisition; in fact, some governments in the Global South such as Ethiopia have leased out (rather than sold) vast tracts of land to outside entities – a theme explored further across later chapters.

Nonetheless, we should not confuse the legal prohibition or formal abeyance of an action (slavery) with its practical absence. Recall that religious edicts designed to protect 'innocent' souls did not stop conquistadors from dispossessing land and putting peoples in bondage. These imperial practices and their norms, logics and techniques have outlived the particular edicts and laws that birthed them. Somewhere between legality and lived experience these practices continue. The minority of humanity in the 'Global North' or 'West' whose bodies are protected from oppression or abuse, and who enjoy inviolable rights to their property, might be living in a 1648 world. Yet, as highlighted by Black Lives Matter and related movements, the majority of humanity still lives in the aftermath – and afterlives – of 1492.

CASE STUDY 3.1: The Valladolid Debate

Photo 3.5 Monument dedicated to Bartolomé de las Casas, Seville

Credit: Hispalois/Wikimedia Commons

Bartolomé de las Casas (1484–1566) was a Dominican Friar, the first resident Bishop of Chiapas (in present-day Mexico), and first official 'Protector of the Indios'. Las Casas became an influential scribe. It is from Las Casas's copies of the original that Christopher Columbus's diaries are known to us today. Las Casas also provided a damning account of Spanish colonisation in the New World. But before any of this, Las Casas arrived with his father in Hispaniola (present-day Haiti and Dominican Republic) with the first wave of Spanish settlers. On the island, Las Casas benefited from the *encomienda* system, which enabled settlers to expropriate lands from the Taino peoples while at the same time placing them under a brutal labour regime. In 1510 Las Casas was ordained a priest, the first such ordination in the Americas. But this did not stop him from taking part in the violent conquering of the neighbouring island now known as Cuba.

In 1515 Las Casas had a spiritual awakening. From here on, he would wage war on two fronts: a) to save the indigenous peoples from extermination; and b) to save the souls of Spanish settlers from damnation due to their acts (Wynter 1984). Late in his life, back in Spain, Las Casas joined in an influential debate with

Juan Ginés de Sepúlveda organised by the church to evaluate the treatment of indigenous peoples in the Spanish empire. This debate happened in the city of Valladolid from 1550 to 1551, where Columbus was buried. The Valladolid debate provides a different perspective on the issue of rights than those found today. Rights in modern-day International Relations are primarily debated with regards to the legal and normative frameworks of global governance, which was introduced in the prior chapter and will be expanded upon in later chapters. Most influentially, some in International Relations have looked towards 'scaling up' domestic laws to the global level. In contrast, the Valladolid debate was not concerned with scaling up a domestic issue. The debate began with an issue that was already globally inscribed in the mapping out of Spain's imperial expansion. The key ethical question arose from discovery and conquest: who was sufficiently 'human' to afford the natural protections provided by God to his highest creations?

Sepúlveda argued that indigenous peoples across the Atlantic, the 'Indios', were by nature slaves who were 'deficient in reason' – a result of their geographical location to the West and South that made them weak. Sepúlveda drew upon the established hierarchies of humanity that had been mobilised to justify European Christendom's holy wars. Las Casas disagreed, and he did so by critically rereading the Christian sources and arguments that Sepúlveda drew upon.

We can unpack the logic of Las Casas's argument from his *Apologetic History of the Indies* (no date). When it came to the claim that inhabitants of the tropics (the 'torrid' zone) were less-than-human, Las Casas argued that God could not have been so 'careless' when he made such an immense number of 'rational souls'. In fact, Las Casas followed Columbus in arguing that the tropical climate of the Caribbean actually enjoyed a 'favorable influence of the heavens' leading to a 'healthfulness of the lands, towns and local winds'. Just as importantly, Las Casas drew on the ambiguities that surrounded the Canary Islands natives. Turning to Aristotle's influential description of what counted as a 'barbarian', Las Casas pointed out that not all barbarians lacked reason. They could simply be 'offspring of people who have not yet been saved by Christ'. Moreover, Las Casas argued, even if they did not know Christ, the Indios still exhibited collective virtues that were lacking in the conquistadors and were perhaps greater developed than in the cultures of ancient Greece and Rome. In other words, native Indios were eminently equipped with the character and disposition to receive Christ and thus become good Christians.

Overall, Las Casas departed from Sepúlveda by challenging one of the key tenets of Christian cartography at the time, namely, that climate produced a hierarchy of humans. Instead, he claimed that it was possible for humans to exhibit reason wherever they were 'found' under the heavens. What truly mattered was whether indigenous peoples demonstrated the dispositions that would enable a peaceful conversion to Christianity and thus inclusion into the only human family that really mattered.

There is one more element to Las Casas's criticism of conquest that deserves mention. While he was committed to opposing the hierarchy of humanity proposed by the model of different climatic zones, for much of his life, Las Casas found less urgency in contesting the way in which the so-called sins of Ham found their way into this model. In 1516, Las Casas suggested that, in order to alleviate the suffering of native Indios, the Spanish Crown could replace those bonded under the *encomienda* system with '20 negroes or other slaves for the mines'. As late as 1543, Las Casas was advocating for replacement of the slave population: Africans for native Indios. By the time of the Valladolid debate Las Casas had experienced a second awakening, albeit almost forty years after his first revelation in Cuba. He now judged African enslavement to be 'every bit as unjust as that of the Indios', and that it was not right that 'blacks be brought in so Indios could be freed' (Clayton 2009). One should not fault Las Casas's final position on discovery and conquest. Nevertheless, the subject of the Valladolid debate was the treatment of Indios and not Africans. In this respect, Las Casas's early defence of native Indios was never fully integrated with his later defence of African peoples. Not even Las Casas arrived at a fully inclusive conception of the 'human'.

Thus, the Valladolid debate was not primarily about rights – domestic or international – but more fundamentally a question of humanity. Specifically, who was sufficiently competent to exercise their humanity so as to be protected by natural rights. The debate turned on the extent to which and the means by which an already geographically diffused and diverse humanity could (or could not) be converted to the one true religion: peaceful and consensual, or violent and coercive (see Blaney and Inayatullah 2004).

Paradoxically, the Valladolid debate reflects the logic behind many recent justifications for humanitarian intervention to protect people from harm –the Responsibility to Protect being one example. When it comes to such humanitarian action, the political question is usually over *who* has the authority to determine that one principle – non-intervention – should be put aside for the preservation of another principle – protection. The Valladolid debate suggests that this humanitarian question has always been answered by those who wish to intervene ascribing to themselves a moral superiority over those whom they wish to protect. While such justifications do not reference religious affiliation, they are nonetheless predicated upon the age-old idea that there are 'saviours' who have the right (or the duty) to save 'victims' who must accept that help or be classified as unruly and disorderly (see Mutua 2001). In other words, debates over humanitarian intervention still operate with a similar logic to debates over discovery and conquest: humanity is hierarchically ordered rather than equally created.

CASE STUDY 3.2: The First Continental Conference on Five Hundred Years of Indigenous Resistance

Photo 3.6 Members of CONAIE march in Quito against the 2002 summit of the Free Trade Area of the Americas (FTAA/ALCA)

Credit: Donovan & Scott/Wikimedia Commons

In 1990, indigenous peoples in Ecuador blocked access to highways across the country as part of a non-violent demonstration designed to raise awareness of injustices and discriminations that indigenous people had suffered, especially with regards to land reform. The uprisings began just before the June solstice and were subsequently called the Inti Raymi – Festival of the Sun. During the uprising, the Confederación de Nacionalidades Indígenas del Ecuador (CONAIE), founded in 1986 as a representative body for all indigenous peoples in Ecuador, presented a set of demands concerning indigenous control over indigenous affairs across a range of economic, political and cultural issues. Most importantly, CONAIE demanded that the Constitution recognise the 'plurinational' character of Ecuador.

This was a significant challenge to the norm of state sovereignty. Recall that the Treaty of Westphalia was supposed to have established the principle of non-intervention. Many International Relations scholars build on this principle, often presenting state sovereignty as an indivisible quality: to be sovereign is to exercise sole political rule over a territory, including representing the polity on the world stage (via diplomacy). Any qualification to this rule and representation is an abrogation of sovereignty. Indigenous peoples do not necessarily challenge the integrity of state sovereignty if their presence is legislated in terms of a minority group.

But to legally present your group as a self-determining nation *within* a state, and even more so, living side by side with other indigenous nations across state borders, certainly does challenge state sovereignty to its core.

This is the depth of political transformation that CONAIE sought.

Just one month after the uprisings, CONAIE, along with the Organización Nacional Indígena de Colombia (ONIC) and the South American Indian Information Center (SAIIC), organised the First Continental Conference on Five Hundred Years of Indigenous Resistance. Representatives from 120 indigenous nationalities and organisations spanning the Americas attended, demanding meaningful self-government. The Conference also sought to pre-empt and critique celebrations that were to accompany the five-hundredth anniversary of Columbus's landfall in the Bahamas.

Attendees formed a set of commissions that discussed the anniversary, human rights, self-determination, land claims and the role of women. The result of the conference was the Declaration of Quito, Ecuador (July 1990), which claimed the following:

The Indios of America have never abandoned our constant struggle against the conditions of oppression, discrimination and exploitation which were imposed upon us as a result of the European invasion of our ancestral territories ... We must guarantee the necessary conditions that permit complete exercise of our self-determination; and this, in turn must be expressed as complete autonomy for our Peoples. Without Indian self-government and without control of our territories, there can be no autonomy ... The achievement of this objective is a principal task for Indian Peoples however, through our struggles we have learned that our problems are not different, in many respects, from those of other popular sectors. We are convinced that we must march alongside the peasants, the workers, the marginalized sectors, together with intellectuals committed to our cause, in order to destroy the dominant system of oppression and construct a new society, pluralistic, democratic and humane, in which peace is guaranteed.

In many ways the declaration can be considered an international rather than domestic document. Recall the idea of 'plurinationality'. The declaration presents an alliance of indigenous peoples and nations whose populations and lands are situated within and across sovereign state borders. Yet this alliance is also committed to finding solidarity with other classes and groups within and across state borders to confront a global system of oppression begun with the discoveries and conquests of 1492. This commitment is evident in the name 'Abya Yala', which has increasingly been used to reference all the lands uncovered by Columbus. Abya Yala is from the language of the Kuna people of San Blas, meaning land of vital blood, or full maturity. San Blas is in the state of Panama, comprised of a stretch of land that forms an umbilical cord connecting the Northern and Southern hemispheres.

Of course, indigenous organising on a continental scale is a practical and political undertaking, and as such it has not been without significant challenges. For instance, one major geopolitical difference pertains to the far greater percentage of indigenous peoples relative to state populations in the South of the Americas compared to those in the North. In Ecuador, indigenous peoples make up approximately 40 per cent of the population compared to less than 1 per cent in the United States. This means that there are different organising capacities and strategies between indigenous peoples that might not always align. Despite these challenges, hemisphere-wide indigenous networking and organising became somewhat more regularised after 1990.

Indigenous organising of this depth and magnitude challenges the norms and practices of state sovereignty. True, descendants of settlers in the Americas have claimed every territory as part of a sovereign state. The exception is Haiti, which was claimed by the enslaved in revolution who then named their newly independent state after the indigenous name for what the Spanish had called Hispaniola. But this exception proves the rule. When US President James Monroe promulgated his famous doctrine in 1823 that no European imperial powers should meddle in the affairs of the Americas, he excluded Haiti from this protection expressly on account of the fact that it was a Black polity. It might be descriptively correct to present states as 'like units' due to their formal equality under international law. Yet not all sovereign polities were or are conceived or treated as equals. Perhaps it is more accurate to conceive of international relations as comprising hierarchically ordered and differently valued political entities, all of which possess a stunning range of distinct yet overlapping structures. From perspectives such as these, a departure point of 1492 helps us to access a far richer panorama of contending sovereignties than 1648 would afford us.

Conclusion

In 1492 Columbus uncovered the New World with an unshakeable principle: no native group could be allowed to retain their own understandings of land, time and political organisation. So 1648 and 1492 provide very different maps of the same world and require us to pursue different cartographic investigations concerning the arrangement and animation of the actors of global politics. The conventions of non-intervention and sovereignty are certainly important for International Relations, but they might not be more important than the politics eventuating from conquest and discovery. Put provocatively, we still need to discuss colonialism in International Relations because conquest and discovery might be more foundational to the making of today's global system than non-intervention and sovereignty. That is the provocation that leads many scholars to seek to better understand our contemporary global predicaments, which are still laden with the after-effects of colonialism and all that came with it.

 END OF CHAPTER QUESTIONS

1. What does a 1492 departure point tell us about International Relations that a 1648 departure point might not?

2. How did religion factor into the politics of discovery and conquest?

3. How similarly, and how differently, were Indigenous and African peoples treated by the Spanish and Portuguese?

4. Why should we consider Columbus an influential figure in the making of International Relations?

5. In what ways do contemporary movements such as Black Lives Matter relate to events that took place in previous centuries?

CHAPTER 4

TOWARDS GLOBAL INTERNATIONAL RELATIONS

Sahil Mathur and Amitav Acharya

Question: What would a non-Western view add to how we think of, and locate, aspects of the global system?

The study of International Relations is growing rapidly in universities outside the West, especially in large states such as China, India, Turkey, Brazil and Indonesia. However, the subject is primarily taught by drawing on examples from the history of Western Europe and the United States. For instance, as the previous two chapters outlined, nation-states are considered the basic form of political organisation because that is how society came to be organised in Europe post-1648, before that system spread to the rest of the world. For reasons such as this, despite its increasing geographical spread, International Relations is not yet a truly global discipline that captures the full range of ideas, histories and experiences of both Western and non-Western societies. It often neglects experiences and relationships in the non-Western world, or as we now refer to it, the Global South. This chapter expands the range of historical sources for understanding state behaviour beyond Europe and the Americas to the whole world, adding a third and final perspective to our journey through history. It looks across all forms of political organisation, including the idea of different civilisations. Adopting this broader perspective allows us to highlight the role and contributions of non-Western peoples through history in shaping our global system, which in turn shapes how we think about International Relations.

Unpacking Western-dominated understandings of International Relations

Although International Relations was first established in the United Kingdom, the discipline took off in the United States after the Second World War, with multiple International Relations departments being founded. In this sense, the 'foundational' understandings of the discipline are of the West, by the West and for the West. There are many reasons for the Western dominance of International Relations. One is the privileged status and position in the discipline of Western scholars, publications and institutions and their perception that Western scholars have discovered the right answers to the puzzles and problems of the day. Compounding the problem is that in the Global South, International Relations is often a niche subject and competes for limited institutional resources. Add to this the challenges scholars from non-English-speaking countries face in getting published in major journals or to understand, let alone contribute to, the major debates and developments in the field, which are mainly carried out in the English language.

Further, there is a tendency among many scholars in the Global South towards an uncritical acceptance of concepts developed in Western International Relations – and a resulting lack of confidence to challenge these concepts. In this situation, scholars often apply these Western concepts and models to study the South, rather than utilising, at least in a complementary manner, indigenous ideas and insights from local practices (Acharya and Buzan 2010). For example, analyses of India–Pakistan relations regularly use concepts of animosity between neighbouring states and the quest for power, developed from the history of conflictual relations between European nation-states, to understand the two neighbours' behaviour towards each other. While no doubt relevant, this framework often fails to take into consideration the cultural commonalities of northern India and Pakistan, especially prior to their partition in 1947, and their impact on current relations. A common heritage could either lead to building bonds across borders on the basis of that commonality, thus favouring cooperation, or it could lead to competing claims over elements of that culture, potentially increasing tensions. But since dominant theoretical perspectives assume that the two states' national interests necessarily clash, scholars have not yet adequately explored whether and to what extent culture matters in this relationship.

4.1 – KEY INSIGHTS: Bretton Woods institutions

In 1944, the United States hosted an international conference at Bretton Woods, New Hampshire to discuss the post-war international economic order. The conference led to the creation of the International Monetary Fund (IMF) and the World Bank, together known as the Bretton Woods institutions. Although these institutions were meant to serve all countries, they were, and continue to be, skewed towards the interests of the United States and its allies, despite their worldwide membership. The initial drafts of the design of the IMF and the World Bank were negotiated between the American and British delegates. Their agreement favoured the promotion of free trade combined with exchange rates pegged to the US dollar, aimed at helping the war-ravaged Western economies recover and grow. These drafts were only shared with other countries late in the process, giving them little opportunity to make meaningful contributions (Steil 2013). The final design of the Bretton Woods institutions gave much higher vote shares to the Western industrialised countries, on the basis of their economic and financial strength, compared to the countries in what was then referred to as the 'Third World'. In recent decades, emerging states such as China and India have gained significant economic power. Yet, this emergence has not been adequately reflected in the Bretton Woods institutions as vote shares are still heavily skewed in favour of Western countries – more than their current economic power would warrant.

Shaped by the ideas and practices of the West, the field of International Relations paid little attention to the Global South, except as recipients of Western ideas and institutions. Forcing Western ideas and practices on Southern countries sometimes had detrimental effects. For example, while fulfilling its role as an international lender of last resort, the IMF regularly imposed mandatory changes in borrowing countries' economic and industrial policies (known as 'conditionality') that forced them to open up their economies to free trade before the loans could be disbursed. The IMF imposed conditionality because of a belief in the benefits of globalisation. In reality, however, these policies often caused more harm than good (Easterly 2006). They were particularly devastating in sub-Saharan Africa. In Ghana, for instance, IMF-imposed policies increased socioeconomic inequalities and crippled local private industry (Konadu-Agyemang 2018). Instilling a more global view, one that recognises and values Southern perspectives on and contributions to the international order, holds significant promise not only in advancing the discipline but also in potentially improving global governance through steps to achieve a better fit with different societies across the world – rather than taking a one-size-fits-all approach.

International Relations as a discipline might have been invented in the West, but relations between peoples did not begin in 1648. Rather, Westphalia, which has deeply influenced Western thinking about International Relations, merely marked the beginnings of the period of Western dominance. Yet, older civilisations – such as the Sumerian (fourth millennium BCE), Near Eastern (fourteenth century BCE), Chinese (dating back to the thirteenth century BCE), Indian (dating back to the third millennium BCE) and Islamic (eighth to fourteenth century CE) civilisations (Map 4.1) – pioneered international systems and world orders that bore several similarities to, as well as many differences from, the Westphalian system. International systems can be studied in terms of not only political-strategic interactions but also cultural and civilisational interactions. Many of the so-called modern concepts such as economic interdependence, balance of power and collective security – which are often traced to Europe – actually have multiple points of origin, both within and outside Europe. Tracing the history of these ideas and practices across non-European civilisations allows us to appreciate the global origins of the system we live in.

Map 4.1 The international relations of Southern civilisations

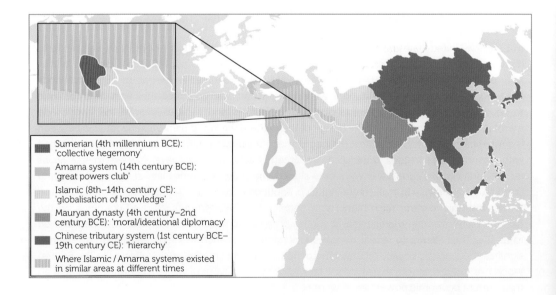

The international relations of Southern civilisations

Scholars often speak of the concept of 'anarchy' – the lack of an overarching world government – drawing from the historical examples of the system of Greek city-states in antiquity and the European system after 1648. But digging deeper into world history provides us with a more diverse set of examples from which to draw (Acharya 2020). The Sumerian civilisation of Mesopotamia, a region in modern-day Iraq, was a system of city-states. This system operated in the fourth millennium BCE, well before the Greek city-states. While the Sumerians did have a king, each city-state was politically independent. The king did not rule over the city-states; instead, his role was only to arbitrate conflicts that would arise between them. Significantly, when the king failed to adequately perform his duties, the city-states brought him down and selected another ruler (McNeill 1991, 69–83). This suggests a different form of hegemony compared to ancient Greece, which we can label 'collective hegemony' or 'shifting leadership': the ruler's legitimacy depended not on force, but on efficient performance of his assigned role. Another example of an anarchical system is the Warring States period of Chinese history, which lasted for approximately 250 years from 475 to 221 BCE. Throughout this period, seven different Chinese states were engaged in a constant quest for power and territory and frequently fought each other in military campaigns (Li 1985).

Upon moving to ancient Near Eastern history, we find evidence not only of anarchy, but of a 'great powers club'. In the fourteenth century BCE, there operated an 'Amarna system' of diplomacy between the five large states of Babylon, Hatti, Egypt, Mitanni and Assyria. Named after the archaeological site where the 'Amarna letters' (clay tablets) were found, this system was characterised by exchanges or 'dialogues' between the rulers covering communication, bargaining, signalling, persuasion and pressure tactics. Like modern diplomacy, the interactions were couched in polite terms, with the leaders addressing each other as brothers or fathers. But the symbolism of family served to mask the underlying political calculations and considerations behind the messages (Cohen and Westbrook 2002).

4.2 – KEY TERMS: Freedom of the seas

International trade is central to modern ideas of globalisation and the international economic order. Economic interdependence is often seen as incentivising interstate cooperation. These ideas are rooted in the concept of the 'freedom of the high seas' – that all states are free to navigate the ocean beyond territorial waters and should not fight wars in the high seas. This principle, embodied in international law under the United Nations Convention on the Law of the Sea (UNCLOS), traces its origin to the Indian Ocean trade in South and Southeast Asia. Starting in the fifteenth century CE, there emerged a thriving system of international trade between the various kingdoms of China, India and Southeast Asia, with the Indian Ocean serving as a connector. Dutch philosopher and jurist Hugo Grotius, who wrote about the idea of *mare liberum* (or 'freedom of the seas') and whose 1609 book by the same name became the basis for international law on the high seas, likely derived his concepts from his familiarity with the maritime rules and commercial practice in Asia, which he learnt about as a counsellor for the Dutch East India Company.

Elements of globalisation, particularly as it relates to the transfer of knowledge, can be found in the history of the Islamic civilisation, especially Muslim Spain (711–1492 CE). The Islamic civilisation helped spread ideas contained in Eastern texts to Europe and helped revive the historical and scientific texts of ancient Greece, which were preserved in Arabic. In this sense, it was a 'carrier' or 'messenger' civilisation. The city of Córdoba served as a centre of learning during this era, and these ideas eventually fuelled the European Renaissance (Attar 2007; Hobson 2004). The spread of ideas and morals is further captured in the efforts of Indian emperor Ashoka of the Mauryan dynasty, who ruled in the third century BCE. After witnessing the immense destruction and devastation caused by his conquest of the kingdom of Kalinga, Ashoka had a change of heart. He converted to Buddhism and undertook to spread its teachings far and wide. This was 'a conversion as historic as [Roman Emperor] Constantine's [conversion to Christianity] and would transform Asia forever' (Thant 2007, 48). Ashoka sent out missionaries propagating Buddhism and, over the next century, it would become the dominant religion in large swathes of Asia, including China, Japan, Korea, Myanmar, Sri Lanka and Thailand (Sen 2003).

Some periods of history lead us to conceptualise fundamentally different forms of international order than the Westphalian order. The history of the Chinese tributary system – which was in place for nearly two millennia – is one such example (see Map 4.1). This system was 'hierarchical', rather than 'anarchical'. Under this system, China engaged in political and economic ('diplomatic') relations with several neighbouring states, while viewing itself as culturally superior. Conducting trade with China was a privilege granted to the tributary states. The system was so named because the Emperor collected 'tribute' from several states in East and Southeast Asia, such as Korea, Thailand (Siam) and Vietnam (Annam). The 'hierarchical' nature of the system was further underscored by the requirement for emissaries to kowtow before the Emperor. Despite apparent unequal political and economic status, the system was often mutually beneficial. For instance, very often the Emperor's return gifts would exceed the value of the tribute received (Fairbank 1968).

Ancient civilisations, overlapping in time and space, form the world's foundational multiplex. With a wider historical and geographical scope, International Relations offers more space to the histories, cultures, economic systems, interactions and contributions of non-Western civilisations and states. In this broader sense, International Relations is best understood as the product of interactions and mutual learning between all civilisations and states, even as some have been more powerful than others at different stages in history.

Towards 'Global International Relations'

There are several ways of instilling a more 'Global' approach to how we think about and study International Relations. First among these is a new understanding of universalism, which is the idea that European-derived ideas are universally relevant and should be applied to all parts of the world. This sinister conception served as justification for European imperialism, which was discussed in the prior chapters. Instead, we can better recognise and respect diversity among nations and civilisations and simultaneously look for common ground. For example, norms such as human rights and free trade don't just spread from the West to 'the Rest'. They can also find support in the Global South and diffuse around the world.

4.3 – KEY TERMS: Non-intervention

Although we have previously explored how this issue goes back to 1648, if not earlier, the norm of non-intervention in the internal affairs of other states is now present in the UN Charter. Importantly, it can be superseded by the Security Council. This norm was affirmed in a more absolute form – without the possibility of supersession – in a 1954 treaty between China and India. Subsequently, it formed the centrepiece of the 1955 Bandung Conference of African and Asian nations. The trend continued and today the countries of the Association of Southeast Asian Nations (ASEAN) are staunch adherents to this norm. Although Westphalian in origin, this norm eroded in the West with increasing intervention from the United Nations and Western countries. Yet states of the Global South have become champions of the non-intervention norm.

Second, as we are establishing in this book, International Relations should be more authentically grounded in world history by including the ideas, institutions, intellectual perspectives and practices of both Western and non-Western societies. This entails applying lessons from one region's history to study another region. One example of a perspective based on Southern experiences is 'dependency theory', which originated in Latin America. Dependency theory dwells on the economic relationship between Latin American countries and Western industrialised states: the former served mainly as a supplier of raw materials to the latter and consumer of manufactured goods produced by the latter. Latin America was in this sense 'dependent' on the West. The dependency framework was applied to study economic relations in other Southern contexts such as Africa and the Arab world, both of which had somewhat similar 'dependent' relationships with the West (Amin 1977, 1982).

Third, a Global International Relations approach would subsume, rather than supplant, existing knowledge. This means that we should not reject Western perspectives; rather, we should seek to enrich them with perspectives from the Global South, in addition to deriving independent theoretical propositions from Southern history. Several concepts about nation-states and international diplomacy exist in political and philosophical treatises written by thinkers from Southern history. The ancient Sanskrit text *Arthashastra* – written sometime between the second century BCE and the third century CE by Kautilya, a scholar who served as advisor to Mauryan emperor Chandragupta Maurya – contains concepts such as the primacy of national interest, the importance of constantly seeking more power and hegemony, and preparing for the threat of war even while engaging in diplomacy (Shahi 2019). Similarly, Chinese statesman Han Feizi wrote during the Warring States period of the importance of military training and conquering the enemy, even if it meant placing strategy over ethics (Fu 1996). In the process of 'bringing in the Rest', the focus should be on finding points of commonality and difference between Western and Southern perspectives, not pitting them against each other as irreconcilable.

Fourth, regions should take centre stage in the study of International Relations. Regionalism is sometimes viewed as a stumbling block to global cooperation, but it can often serve as a stepping stone. Regional intergovernmental organisations such as the European Union, ASEAN and the African Union, in addition to carrying out their own activities, frequently work with the UN in peacekeeping, humanitarian operations and conflict management. African regional organisations have been pioneers on this front (Adebajo 2002). For example, the Economic Community of West African States (ECOWAS) played a crucial role in the end of the Second Liberian Civil War. It deployed a peacekeeping force – the ECOWAS Mission in Liberia (ECOMIL) – to oversee a ceasefire in September 2003 before the UN Mission in Liberia (UNMIL) took over.

4.4 – KEY TERMS: Exceptionalism

Exceptionalism is the tendency to present the characteristics of a social group as homogeneous, collectively unique and superior to those of others. Exceptionalism has historically served as justification for the dominance of great powers over the weak. Instead of touting exceptionalism, concepts derived from one part of the world – be it the Global South or the West – must travel and have broader resonance if they are to be legitimate in a truly global system.

Fifth, truly Global International Relations cannot be based on cultural exceptionalism. Today, the rise of China has raised the possibility of a regional system in Asia dominated by traditional Chinese values that seek to replicate hierarchical family structures in relations with other states. Although contemporary Chinese policymakers are hesitant to directly reference the tributary system since it conceives of China as superior to other states – hence going against Westphalian state equality – elements of contemporary Chinese foreign policy echo this system. For example, China's Belt and Road Initiative (BRI), aimed at infrastructure development in Asia, Africa, Europe and the Pacific with China holding the reins, can be compared to the historical tributary system. However, this does not necessarily entail regional domination. Just as, in history, the tributary states tended to benefit from China's lavish gifts, a powerful and prosperous China might fuel prosperity in East Asia (Kang 2010).

Sixth, a Global reading of International Relations takes a broad view of agency. Agency is the ability to foster change through action. This can be exercised by individuals, states or other groups. Agency can be material (based on physical resources) or ideational (based on the power of ideas). It need not be the prerogative of the strong, but can manifest as a weapon of the weak. There are numerous examples of Southern agency in international relations. For example, Latin American countries can be credited with foreshadowing the idea of universal human rights: they adopted a human rights declaration several months before the Universal Declaration of Human Rights was drafted at the United Nations in New York, which borrowed significantly from the Latin American declaration. Another example is South Asian economists Mahbub ul Haq from Pakistan and Amartya Sen from India, who challenged the Western model of development that focuses on economic growth, as measured through Gross Domestic Product (GDP), by putting forward an alternative, broader idea of 'human development' and the corresponding Human Development Index (HDI), which, in addition to GDP, focuses on enhancing individual capabilities through primary education and health. Taking this idea even further, Bhutan developed the idea of measuring happiness – the Gross National Happiness Index. After presenting this idea to the UN General Assembly in 2011, a *World Happiness Report* has been published annually since 2012. As is evident from these examples, Southern actions are not meant just for specific regions or for the South, but for global governance as a whole.

Seventh, and finally, we should reconceptualise globalisation. Rather than just an economic phenomenon of the world becoming more interconnected and 'progressing' unimpeded, globalisation includes political and social aspects of increasing interconnectedness as well as potential adverse consequences for the world. The drivers – and consequences – of globalisation have become planetary in scale. This has led to a set of shared fates, in which all of humankind is ensnared and for which responsibility is collective. For example, the Covid-19 pandemic spread rapidly because of global interconnectedness and has had far-reaching, global effects. Climate change is another example of a shared fate. Owing in part to geography and in part to lower infrastructure and development levels, the Global South is much more vulnerable to the ill effects of climate change. In the 2015 Paris Climate Agreement, Southern countries agreed to take more proactive measures on climate change than previous international climate treaties that had put the onus on developed countries.

A multiplex world order

To consider what a global, rather than Western-centric, world order would look like, we can consider the idea of a 'multiplex' world order. Multiplexity describes a world where there are many important actors and an array of ideas, institutions and approaches to peace, security and development. Building on the insights of a Global South appreciation of International Relations, it adds another possible structure for world order to the established ideas of unipolarity, bipolarity and multipolarity.

In a multiplex world, established powers would continue to dominate some aspects of global governance (such as the IMF), emerging and established powers would collaborate on some issues (as in the G20 – a forum for governments and central bank governors from developed and emerging countries, plus the EU) and emerging powers would compete with established powers on other issues (Chinese overseas investment and infrastructure loans – against projects led by the World Bank). Additionally, non-state actors are placed in lead roles rather than consigned to the sidelines. These include 'good' actors such as international nongovernmental organisations (Amnesty International, Human Rights Watch) and civil society activists (Greta Thunberg, Malala Yousafzai) as well as 'villains' such as terrorist groups, drug cartels and human traffickers. These aspects of the multiplex world order are to a great extent already in place – these are not futuristic

4.5 – KEY TERMS: Multiplexity

A multiplex world order is not anchored by a hegemon. Instead, it is culturally and politically diverse yet economically interconnected, where challenges to peace, security and welfare are increasingly transnational. It involves a dispersal of power and influence amongst both established and emerging powers, small states, global and regional bodies and non-state actors. For example, we can consider the role of the United States, which has exercised a form of hegemony through its spearheading of the 'liberal' international order post-1945, through the metaphor of a cinema showing only one movie at a time – one that was scripted, produced and directed by the United States, with itself as the lead actor. In the multiplex world, by contrast, the American movie is joined in a modern multiplex theatre by a variety of others, especially cinema from the Global South, with different plots, producers, directors and actors each playing simultaneously on other screens. Multiplexity therefore represents diversity and plurality, rather than homogeneity, whilst also recognising the interdependence at play as each 'movie' depends on the good functioning of the multiplex theatre itself (which can be seen as representing world order at large).

Multiplexity is different from multipolarity, which refers mainly to a distribution of material capabilities. The vision of a multipolar world order today might simply add several emerging countries, such as China and India, or regional powers like Nigeria and Turkey, as new 'poles' to the list of established Western powers. But it does not capture the broader complexity of interactions that define the contemporary global system. Multiplexity entails much more than the mere distribution of power. It is also about distribution of ideas, cultures and civilisations.

visions. The fragmentation or pluralisation of global governance, a key aspect of the multiplex world order, is visible with more regional and plurilateral governance arrangements such as the Asian Infrastructure Investment Bank (AIIB) – a major multilateral development bank spearheaded by China – and more complex, hybrid or multi-stakeholder arrangements in areas ranging from cyberspace to climate protection. But adopting a global approach to the study of International Relations is essential to be able to begin to see this phenomenon in practice.

The idea of multiplexity takes into account dispersed leadership, where no single state or institution leads in every issue area. Instead, states and non-state actors provide leadership in different issue areas, with multiple but overlapping conversations taking place around the world on various issues of importance to world order. For example, let's imagine one representative moment in the international relations of 2021: as discussions on conflicts in Syria and Yemen occur between state representatives at the UN Security Council in New York, a global climate summit involving states, civil society climate activists and transnational corporations takes place in Glasgow. Meanwhile, the summer Olympic games featuring elite athletes from all countries are held in Tokyo, and leaders from all around the world gather in Southeast Asia to discuss Asian regional issues at the ASEAN summits. Multiplexity recognises this dispersed, yet overlapping, set of events as the very essence of modern international relations. It is more inclusive and broader than the ideas of a unipolar American-led world or a multipolar world.

While a multiplex world order seems likely to emerge and grow, it is by no means guaranteed. Even as non-state actors gain in international prominence, states might continue to exercise overwhelming dominance. For example, in the case of new security technologies such as drones and artificial intelligence (AI), innovation by private technology developers has driven their rise in prominence (Cronin 2020). Yet, massive amounts of funding from states, especially great powers, and their militaries have since been channelled into these new technologies, suggesting that private innovators' salient international role was temporary. Around the world, civil society action and protests have increased in recent years. This could trigger a backlash from states and spur them to privilege traditional means of state-to-state diplomacy. Some scholars argue that while US hegemony may be declining, American soft power might carry on (Nye 2019). Hollywood, for instance, could cast a long shadow and influence several aspects of world cinema. Yet, it is hard to see the damage done by President Donald Trump (2017–21) to US prestige and credibility disappearing easily. Further, even as emerging powers and other Southern actors acquire more wealth and influence and exhibit higher rates of economic growth than Western nations, they are not immune to economic shocks of a local, regional or global nature.

One criticism of the idea of a multiplex world order is conceptual. To some analysts, the idea of a multiplex world may seem vague or too broad an umbrella. As a notion that goes beyond the distribution of power, the idea of a multiplex world presents analytical challenges to scholars. The liberal international order that is undergoing a rapid transformation today has been around since at least 1945. If conceived as an extension of the age of Western dominance, it has been around for a few centuries. Consequently, scholars are accustomed to the Eurocentric language of polarity (multipolar, bipolar, unipolar). Conceptualising the shift to a multiplex vision of world order, which requires a greater acceptance of the role of non-Western countries and Southern ideas and institutions that were heretofore marginal, will encounter hurdles. Doing so requires conceptualising an entirely novel global system and investigating its myriad implications. This is a challenging task, to say the least. Trends suggest that a multiplex world is already in formation. Inhibiting this process will require substantial reversals in the approaches and economic and cultural trajectories of the established powers, which appears difficult.

CASE STUDY 4.1: The United Nations Environment Programme in Nairobi, Kenya

Most of the global (i.e. not regional) international organisations that appear prominently in the news and feature in scholarly and policy analyses are headquartered in the West. The United Nations, the keystone organisation of the post-war international order, has its headquarters in New York. The World Bank and the IMF, cornerstones of the international economic and financial order, are headquartered in Washington, DC. The main office of the World Trade Organization, which was created in 1995 to replace and carry forward the General Agreement on Tariffs and Trade, is in Geneva. Geneva, in fact, is a hub for international organisations' headquarters. It is a 'second home' for the United Nations, with several of its agencies including the UN High Commissioner for Refugees and the UN Conference on Trade and Development headquartered there. Geneva also houses the International Committee of the Red Cross, the International Labour Organization, the International Organization for Migration and the World Health Organization, among others. Other major centres include Paris and Vienna.

These organisations all have global mandates: their activities are not restricted to the West. While they usually have 'field offices' in other, Southern states, their main offices remain in the West. Why is this so? The simple answer is that international organisations are largely Western creations and hence remain centred in the West. Another reason is that developed Western states have more resources to host these large headquarters. This overall narrative suggests that the states of the Global South are passive recipients when it comes to the operations of international organisations.

The UN Environment Programme (UNEP) was founded in 1972 as a result of the UN Conference on the Human Environment – the first large-scale international summit devoted to discussing environmental issues – held in 1972 in Stockholm. The programme's purpose is to coordinate activities related to the environment carried out by different UN agencies. A key – indeed necessary – point of discussion that followed UNEP's formation was on where to build its new headquarters. All the usual suspects – Geneva, London, New York, Vienna – were in the race and one of these centres seemed the obvious choice. However, to the surprise of most states, the Kenyan permanent representative to the UN Joseph Odero-Jowi not only threw Nairobi's hat into the ring, but launched a defiant bid, forcefully advocating for the new headquarters to be 'given to the Third World'. He argued that the West's monopoly over international organisation headquarters was 'unjust' as the Third World was being denied the opportunity and privilege. In Odero-Jowi's words, 'we are members of the UN, all of us, and all UN headquarters are in USA or Western Europe. None in Asia, none in South America, none in Africa, none in Eastern Europe… [and the reasons behind this] were not technical… but historical and political' (Johnson 2012, 29–31).

Anticipating that the thought of having a global international organisation headquartered in the developing world would be difficult for the West to entertain, Odero-Jowi, along with Kenyan Foreign Minister Njoroge Mungai, actively lobbied for support, first among African countries and then in the G-77 grouping of developing countries (which today has 134 members). After gaining a large number of signatures, the Kenyan delegation filed the draft proposal, which was centred less on Kenya and more on 'justice for the Third World'. Bravely taking on a Western 'whispering campaign' that maligned Nairobi for not having adequate hotels or a suitable airport and being 'too far' (from the West), Odero-Jowi defended his proposal with a document detailing Nairobi's world-class facilities, including the upcoming Kenyatta International Convention Centre that would host the headquarters. Realising the force of Kenya's push and the large support it had amassed, all Western cities withdrew their candidatures. Towards the end of the debate, Nairobi's only remaining contender was New

Delhi, India. Given its top-level participation at the Stockholm Conference – where Prime Minister Indira Gandhi had given a stirring speech on poverty and need as the biggest polluters – India had aspirations of hosting UNEP. But it eventually agreed to vote for Nairobi as a sign of goodwill and solidarity among the Third World. With that, Nairobi gained its place as the first Southern host to a UN headquarters.

The victory notwithstanding, there remained doubts. As one observer wrote, 'lacking the perspective of time, nobody could be sure yet whether the choice of Nairobi was a historic blunder or an act of statesmanship' (Irwin, cited in Johnson 2012, 35). Today, these doubts have abated. Following UNEP, Nairobi was awarded yet another headquarters in 1978 – this time of the UN Human Settlements Programme (UN-Habitat). In 1996, a brand-new building styled as the UN Office in Nairobi – the United Nations' only major office outside the West – was opened to host both UNEP and UN-Habitat. In addition, that office today has grown to host the regional offices of around thirty other UN agencies. It is, therefore, an understatement to say that Kenya has been a pillar of progress for the United Nations, representing a prominent and visible Southern contribution to global governance (Photo 4.1).

At the time UNEP was founded, 'global' international organisations formed the epicentre of global governance. Yet, various regional initiatives around the world were also beginning to form. What we see today, therefore, is that rather than Southern countries simply vying to host global international

Photo 4.1 The UN-Habitat offices in Nairobi

Credit: Kip254/Wikimedia Commons

organisations as Kenya did, we are also witnessing a strengthening, and growth, of 'Southern' international organisations. For example, the AIIB, headquartered in Beijing, is rapidly reaching lending levels similar to the World Bank. Reflecting a multiplex world order, the future of global governance will see multiple centres of power in the Global North and South, at times competing and at other times collaborating in their endeavours. In that sense, the example of Nairobi can be read as not just driving international organisations Southwards, but also as part of a larger direction of travel in international relations towards the Global South.

 CASE STUDY 4.2: Xi Jinping at Davos

The World Economic Forum, founded in 1971, has become prominent in international affairs owing to its yearly meeting at the Swiss mountain resort of Davos. For many years it restricted itself to inviting business leaders from Western Europe, before gradually opening up to the rest of Europe and the

United States. The annual meeting has grown to serve as an informal international summit of the world's top economic, business and political leaders. In recent years, the Forum has also offered heads of state from emerging powers of the Global South the opportunity to make the keynote address at the annual

Photo 4.2 Xi Jinping delivers his speech on the opening day of the World Economic Forum, Davos, 17 January 2017

Credit: FABRICE COFFRINI/AFP/Getty Images

meeting. In this respect, despite its location in the West, the World Economic Forum is giving space to Southern leaders to bring their contributions to and visions of international politics into the limelight.

In 2017, President Xi Jinping's presence at Davos represented the first time a Chinese head of state attended the event. The themes contained in Xi's keynote address suggested a different place for China in the international order: as the leader and shaper of, rather than most prominent challenger to, global governance and the international order. China has historically had a mixed relationship with the idea of globalisation. Beginning in the late 1970s under Deng Xiaoping, China had opened its economy to globalisation while remaining politically 'communist'. This has been described as 'communism with Chinese characteristics'. In his speech, Xi launched a staunch defence of economic globalisation, arguing that it has caused tremendous social, scientific and technological progress. Xi went on to highlight that the world needs to work together to drive and sustain growth in the global economy and overcome crises. To do so, it needs an effective global leader at the helm steering the global economy, and since developing countries account for the majority of global economic growth, that leader should come from the South. More specifically, that leader should be China, as it will be attuned to addressing the needs of the developing South and global inequalities while simultaneously instilling and spearheading a

dynamic and technologically driven global economy (Kennedy 2018).

Xi's speech exuded a lot of the rhetoric about the market economy that Western industrialised states normally use. It was also conveyed in a manner that suggested that the major problems lay elsewhere – not in China – and China could proffer sound global solutions. Again, this was a style of delivery and content ordinarily associated with the Western leaders of the so-called liberal international order. Xi's address marked an inflection point in international politics. It was made at a time when US President Donald Trump was pursuing policies and rhetoric that seemed to amount to the United States retreating from its position as global leader, as evidenced through Trump's withdrawal from the Paris Climate Agreement, the Trans-Pacific Partnership and the 2015 nuclear agreement with Iran. Xi therefore positioned himself as the new leader of the world (although not the 'free' world), which would additionally benefit the Global South given China's concern for the developing world via its own Southern heritage.

At the 2021 Davos Agenda virtual event, Xi reaffirmed China's support for globalisation despite the Covid-19 pandemic's de-globalising effects. However, it remains essential to parse the reality of Chinese intentions from the rhetoric. Since the 2017 speech, China's relations with several countries in the Asia-Pacific region – such as Australia, India, Malaysia and Sri Lanka – have deteriorated significantly. Issues of contention include territorial conflict, foreign political influence and unsustainable debt created by BRI lending. Indeed, Xi's speech at the 2021 Davos Agenda virtual event struck a far more assertive tone. China has also faced international pushback because of its mishandling of the initial outbreak of Covid-19. Yet, these tensions do not occur in isolation. Trade with China, while witnessing some decline, has remained high, with China continuing to serve as the largest trading partner for several countries.

An analysis of Xi's speech and subsequent events points to elements of a multiplex world order – characterised by multiple and overlapping realms of cooperation and contestation. While the United States is no longer a worldwide hegemon, China does not simply replace it. Global governance in the multiplex world order would be neither parochially Southern nor anti-West, but rather a mix of both South and West. The large, universally beneficial elements of the post-1945 liberal international order would remain, but would be strengthened by Chinese cognisance of and experience with the issues of developing countries. Traditional issues of national security remain significant, but alongside a range of other issues that constitute international relations.

This case study exemplifies the essence of a global perspective – drawing on and highlighting the experiences and ideas of the neglected parts of the world, namely the Global South, in order to enrich existing concepts through diversification, not replacement. Scholarship in the so-called 'Chinese school' of International Relations has been pioneering in this respect (see Zhang and Chang 2016). Zhao Tingyang (2019) has adapted the concept of 'tianxia', or 'all under heaven', which formed the basis of the historical Chinese Empire, to outline its relevance to the contemporary world order by highlighting the 'all-inclusiveness' principle that promotes global harmony. Yan Xuetong (2011), drawing on ancient Chinese history,

has asserted the importance of 'morality' in international affairs in conjunction with state power. Similarly blending Chinese political thought with Western social theory, Qin Yaqing (2018) has stressed the importance of analysing relations among international actors, rather than studying them separately.

The above case does, however, also highlight possible divisions within the Global South itself. China represents the 'power South', not the 'poor South' (Acharya 2018). Privileging China's position as Xi seeks may come at the expense of continuing to neglect poorer and less prominent states. However, as the world becomes more interconnected and globalised, one could imagine significant effects on the practice of international relations itself. As the concept of a multiplex world order envisions, other fora focusing more on Southern issues – and hosted in Southern locations – such as the BRICS have emerged, altering the landscape of global economic governance. If these initiatives sustain strength and momentum, global stewardship by Southern leaders, as displayed by President Xi at Davos, could become the norm rather than the exception.

Conclusion

A non-Western view of how we think of, and locate, aspects of the global system reveals that it features a multiplicity of actors drawn from all parts of the world. In turn, International Relations is gradually getting in tune with the practices of people and states across all parts of the world. The expansion takes place not just across space, but across time to a longer history that includes ancient civilisations. It has also opened the locations of international relations to begin a slow shift beyond their traditional homes in the West, as evidenced in the diffusion of global governance and the rise of non-Western groupings and initiatives. Gaining a global appreciation of the discipline that incorporates these developments and recognises a more diverse history will reap multiple dividends. First, it will carve a dent in the image that international relations is composed solely of elites engaging behind closed doors with little consideration of culture and society. By celebrating and sharing non-Western ideas, all the world's citizens contribute to global diversity, challenging the simplistic notion of a homogeneous world. Second, by appreciating how each of our own states' unique positions and historical experiences shapes its outlook, we can broaden our thinking on the motivations behind state actions. These observations all require more learning about the Global South's contributions and how these could shape a world order that is likely to be truly different from those of the past.

END OF CHAPTER QUESTIONS

1. How does studying the political systems of ancient civilisations enhance our understanding of international relations today?

2. Are concepts derived from practices in one region of the world useful in analysing international relations in other regions? Consider some examples to support your thoughts.

3. What does a Global approach to International Relations entail?

4. What is a multiplex world order and how is it different form a multipolar world order?

5. In what ways has the Global South contributed to the ideas, practices and locations of global governance?

CHAPTER 5

LEVELS OF ANALYSIS

Carmen Gebhard

Question: Within the vastness of the global system can one person's voice have an impact?

More than at any time historically, our global system involves not just states and international organisations, but also individual voices from the rich and powerful, right down to ordinary people. To help account for this ever more complex picture, this chapter details the analytical tools that scholars have developed in an attempt to make International Relations' task of interpreting the world more manageable. The previous chapters have set the foundations for understanding the making of our global system, through outlining and then critiquing history. With that context in mind, we will now turn to the next step in our journey, which involves three chapters unpacking how International Relations as an academic discipline analyses our world in deeper ways – chiefly through a theoretical toolkit which allows us to analyse our history and our present. Before fully engaging with International Relations theory, this chapter lays the building blocks that are faced by all students and academics when they seek to build an analysis – something that is best captured by identifying and using different 'levels of analysis'. We need such a device because the vast array of themes, actors and issues we face can quickly become overwhelming. Without separating these at times, such as with the levels of analysis detailed in this chapter, it would be a daunting task to make enough sense of things to build, or utilise, a theory that would allow us to pose viable answers to research questions.

Establishing the four levels of analysis

Academics spend quite a lot of time thinking about effective ways of structuring their thinking and of processing the complexity of the reality they endeavour to study, analyse and understand. A lot of this kind of analytical sense-making happens in the form of theories, which help explain and capture the meaning of real-life events in the form of abstract interpretations and generalised assumptions. Before scholars develop or adopt any specific theories, however, they take what is often an intuitive decision over the focus and scope of their analysis: the international system as a whole, parts of the system in interaction with each other, or some of its particular parts, down to the individual decision-maker. This is what one of the most common ways of structuring scholarly debates in International Relations is about: the distinction between different 'levels of analysis' and how they form an analytical framework that helps us think productively. On the one hand, they can be thought of as 'social structures' whose properties condition and even determine the behaviour of actors within them. On the other hand, we can also look at them as spheres of action and influence for these actors who then contribute to

5.1 – KEY TERMS: Levels of analysis

The four levels of analysis, summarised in Figure 5.1 are:

» The **system level** comprises the global system in its entirety and looks at issues like the distribution of political power, the economic system, global governance (international organisations, laws and norms) and the diffusion of technology. Importantly, it also considers how these factors create conditions that impose themselves structurally on the other levels.

» The **state level** looks at nation-states as actors in a set of particular external conditions, and actors with particular internal characteristics (such as whether they are democracies or whether they are large or small) and considers their strategic and economic positions.

» The **group level** looks at actors within their social, organisational, professional and bureaucratic context, and points to the way in which they interact with their surroundings. Examples are political decision-makers in the context of governmental structures like political parties, non-governmental organisations and interest groups acting at the intersection between governments and societies.

» The **individual level** looks at the behaviour and decisions of people both in governmental and non-governmental roles, examining their beliefs, fears and their personalities.

Figure 5.1 The four levels of analysis

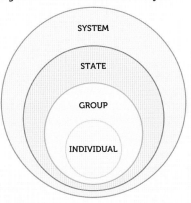

structures at this level and beyond (Temby 2015, 722). Different levels emphasise different actors, dynamics and processes and thus produce different kinds of arguments in pursuit of research questions.

One of the advantages of using this framework is that it helps us locate 'units of analysis', meaning the actors whose behaviour we are seeking to explain or analyse. Each level tends to emphasise different processes, structures and actors. Singer (1961) identified it as an analytical device that also allows us to capture the *scope* of our analysis: whether we focus on macro-level questions that involve wider issues in relation to one of the levels (e.g. how the system persists or fluctuates in different contexts, how different levels relate to each other) or whether we are looking at micro-level questions that are concerned with one of the units that operates at that level (e.g. the state). Levels of analysis can also be employed to indicate cause-and-effect relationships between our dependent variable (what we are trying to explain) and the independent variables (the explanations). Before we look at these more closely, it is important to look back at the way the discipline has evolved and how analytical ambitions have changed to accommodate concerns more specific to each level.

The emergence of today's four levels of analysis was not immediate. In the early days of International Relations – from 1919 until after the Second World War – a lot of what could be called traditional or conventional International Relations was not concerned with clear distinctions between different levels of analysis or theoretical perspectives. Waltz (1959) introduced an analytical framework for the study of International Relations that distinguished between what he referred to as different 'images' of an issue (in his case, the decision of a state to go to war). While acknowledging Waltz's attempt to distinguish between these different explanatory realms, Singer (1961, 78) lamented that scholars still had a tendency to

---

5.2 – KEY PEOPLE: Kenneth Waltz

Kenneth Waltz (1924–2013) is one of International Relations' most influential figures. Amongst his earliest works was *Man, the State, and War* (1959) where he identified three images that were central to International Relations as he saw it:

1 **The individual** – which was conditioned by human nature. Human nature arguments are often used to define the limits of human action, suggesting that our biology somewhat predestines us to certain negative patterns of behaviour (taken broadly) such as fear and selfishness.

2 **The state** – characterised by its internal properties (what kind of political/cultural/economic system) with its broader preferences pre-set to maximise power in order to compete with other states, and ultimately survive.

3 **The system** – characterised by absence of a world government to mitigate inter-state aggression.

Waltz's main analytical ambition with these 'images' was to try and break down and specify the location of possible explanations (independent variables) for his dependent variable – the decision to go to war. In doing so, he was attempting to answer such questions as: is humanity's innate aggression the main cause of war? Are some types of state more aggressive than others? Or is the nature of the international system the 'permissive' cause of war – the fact that there is 'no system of law enforceable' between states, which means that 'conflict, sometimes leading to war, is bound to occur' (Waltz 1959, 159)? Waltz's thinking became one of the forerunners of today's levels of analysis.

roam up and down the ladder of organizational complexity with remarkable abandon, focusing upon the total system, international organizations, regions, coalitions, extra-national associations, nations, domestic pressure groups, social classes, elites, and individuals as the needs of the moment required.

Singer sought to help overcome this by introducing an analytical model based on 'levels of analysis', notably, however, one that only consisted of the system level and the state level, with states operating as constituent parts of the whole (the system) and thus making up most of the causes of what happens at the system level.

However important these historical contributions were, both Waltz's and Singer's work featured what we recognise in hindsight as an expression of the traditional focus on the state as the dominant unit of analysis. For Waltz, states were the main vehicle of human action but one that was largely conditioned by an overwhelmingly powerful set of conditions that were imposed by the global system (principally the lack of global leadership and the insecurity that caused). Singer, too, maintained a view that studying International Relations was by definition a matter of dealing with states as units of analysis (see Temby 2015). This predominant focus on the state was strongly related to the assumption that the state was also the main location of power within the international sphere. This relative state-centrism was characteristic of the whole discipline while the main focus of analyses remained on how states related to each other at the system level, how power was distributed between them and how this produced different kinds of 'polarity' that determined international dynamics, as shown in Chapter two.

There was much debate about the definition of levels of analysis, their relative importance and how they relate to each other. For a major proportion of its history much of International Relations' focus, as is reflected in its original labelling as 'inter-national' (derived from Latin, 'between states'), lay on the system and the state levels. However, there were notable exceptions such as Kelman (1970), who pioneered analysis at the individual level. The system- and state-level fascination was mainly inspired by the context of the Cold War and the kinds of challenge the reality of a looming nuclear confrontation produced. There seemed little scope for a mainstream focus on sub-state levels, organisations, groups or individual decision-makers – let alone common individuals – to play an essential role in what appeared to be a monumental set of problems. Although the Cold War has long since passed, much of today's political life remains managed within the state framework and is based on issues like national security or internal stability. States form the primary kind of actor in major international organisations such as the United Nations, they feature prominently in the global discourse on most of the major challenges of our time, and states still hold what Max Weber called the 'monopoly on violence' – the exclusive right to the legitimate use of force.

The state as a unit of analysis and frame of reference will certainly not go away any time soon, nor will the interactions of states as a key level of analysis in International Relations. However, following the end of the Cold War we can also detect dynamics shifting as power became more dispersed across governmental, economic and global settings (Keohane 2016). This challenged the conventional conception of 'international relations' in the narrow sense as a matter of state interaction at the systemic level. Perspectives thus broadened to include the study of relationships between all sorts of political entity and types of actor. These include international organisations, non-state groups (such as charities and religious organisations) that operate across national boundaries, transnational corporations, and finally individuals and the groups they form in pursuit of their endeavours. The majority of global interactions, therefore, no longer occur via state channels the way they once did. Hence, there has been a gradual shift away from the near-exclusive focus on formal interactions of the state, its official representatives and its constituent parts to include informal relationships and non-official exchanges of information, communications, services and people. This has led to a broadening of the scope of what is considered a relevant event, actor, behaviour or characteristic – partly explaining both the rise of importance of the individual level and the group level of analysis.

5.3 – KEY PEOPLE: Osama bin Laden and Julian Assange

Photo 5.1 Osama bin Laden in Kabul, November 2001

Photo 5.2 Julian Assange in London, August 2014

Credit: Hamid Mir/Wikimedia Commons

Credit: David G. Silvers/Cancillería del Ecuador/Flickr

Osama bin Laden led a global terrorist network, al-Qaeda, based on his own religious and political visions and masterminded the 9/11 attacks on the United States. Julian Assange spearheaded a whistleblowing campaign leaking government secrets via the website WikiLeaks – most notably material that undermined the US-led War on Terror that was itself launched in response to bin Laden's attacks. Both Assange and bin Laden, although very different in nature despite their proximity to the modern debate on terrorism, have had a lasting impact on international relations from the position of a private person with no official political status or role.

While a heightened focus on the individual level reflects the modern shape of International Relations, attention on the group level is another sign of the times. The group level captures actors within their social, organisational, professional and bureaucratic context, and points to the way in which they interact with their surroundings. For instance, decision-makers in the context of governmental structures, non-governmental agents, such as scientific experts giving evidence in parliament, and interest groups acting at the intersection between governments and societies. Arguably, many of the groups addressed at this level are still contained within the state as a broader framework. What happens analytically, however, is that the state is no longer treated as a 'black box' and is instead broken down into further layers of action that are generally non-hierarchical in nature (see Jacobsen 1996).

Applying levels of analysis to the Covid-19 pandemic

To be able to use the levels of analysis as an analytical device, we need to be clear about what we are most interested in when discussing a particular theme or issue. The best way to introduce this is to apply the technique rather than talk about it in the abstract. If we were to study the global consequences of the Covid-19 pandemic, for example, there would be various ways of approaching, discussing and presenting the issue based on the level of analysis most suited to our interest (see Box 5.1).

As the pandemic swept the globe in the early months of 2020, *Foreign Policy* (2020) asked some leading International Relations scholars for their first impressions on how the world would look after the pandemic. While they all start out with the same question, they locate the causes of change at different levels of analysis. G. John Ikenberry foresaw an initial resurrection of nationalism but also pointed to new types of cooperation and internationalism that would develop in the long run (*system level*). Stephen M. Walt focused on the trend of states preparing for extended periods of economic self-isolation (*state level*) and concluded that this will undermine former incentives for states to collaborate globally. Third, Nicholas Burns emphasised the constructive power of key societal *groups* such as doctors, nurses, leaders and ordinary citizens who each demonstrated resilience and different forms of leadership. Collectively, he argued, their human spirit can counterbalance the failure of governments to develop an adequate response. Finally, Joseph S. Nye Jr. focused his analysis on US leadership, and in particular President Trump's general isolationist approach (*individual level*) to the pandemic and to other challenges the United States was facing. This example shows that how we start our investigation, or where we look, can determine what we see (or what we do not see) as we try to answer research questions. In that sense, any or all the above interpretations could be (somewhat) accurate, or (somewhat) inaccurate. Being aware of different perspectives thus guides us through the process of investigation and analysis and determines the kind of information we would need to gather in order to draw persuasive conclusions.

5.4 – KEY INSIGHTS: Jacinda Ardern and Covid-19

Jacinda Ardern, who was elected Prime Minister of New Zealand in 2017, was widely praised for her handling of the Covid-19 crisis. New Zealand took swift action, closing its borders and establishing various levels of quarantine and social distancing. As a result, New Zealand had only twenty-five deaths in the first year of the pandemic, and a similar number in 2021, from a population of approximately five million. When attempting to think about why this result occurred, levels of analysis allow us to target our search in our quest for answers. In the end, as with any example, we may find insights at one, or all, levels.

» **System level** – The perceived successes would allow an analysis of whether New Zealand's profile in the system changed in

Photo 5.3 Jacinda Ardern in Wellington, November 2020

Credit: New Zealand Government/ Wikimedia Commons

relation to more powerful states, perhaps giving it a better position in the system post-Covid. A system-level analysis would also allow for comparisons to be drawn among other smaller, or geographically peripheral, states to see if they too emerged differently in relation to larger states in terms of how Covid-19 impacted them. It may also highlight that, upon investigation, Covid-19 did not change the system much at all.

» **State level** – This could be analysed focusing on New Zealand's act as one of self-interest in rapidly taking actions to protect its own population, with little regard to the implications of these actions externally. Again, this could be compared to other states who took similar action to determine whether New Zealand is perceived, or acted, any differently as a result.

» **Group level** – A good place to start would be to examine the grouping of political parties in New Zealand. In that sense, we can ask whether the actions taken were not driven by Ardern, but instead driven by her party – Labour – to shore up its electoral power and influence as a group. Labour was governing as part of a coalition, having secured only a minority of the votes in New Zealand's prior election. By considering the group level of a political party seeking to show strength we can consider how certain actions may help their quest to gain a majority in an upcoming election, which would allow them to rule without needing a coalition partner (which is indeed what transpired).

» **Individual level** – All leaders survive based on their record. Politics is full of examples of parties in parliamentary systems (such as New Zealand's) turning on leaders who fail to keep the party's broad confidence. Taking a similar approach to the group level above, but focusing it directly on Ardern, her individual actions in decisive leadership, ensuring that she was highly visible through all these measures, can be seen as an attempt to shore up her own personal political power by leading her party along a certain path and extending her leadership ambitions further into the future. This can be taken in addition, or apart, from an analysis that may investigate to what extent Ardern's own moral or ethical views over protecting her population from the pandemic (rather than political aspirations) drove her decision-making.

This example illustrates that specific perspectives greatly influence our findings (our 'explanations') while, on the whole, the real-life events we are analysing remain the same, of course. They show how important it is to be aware of the potential limitations and gaps in our observation as well as any kind of bias or selective attention that could result from our analytical choices. In line with Heisenberg (1963, 58) it is worth considering 'that what we observe is not nature in itself, but nature exposed to our method of questioning'.

A system-level ('systemic') study would need to consider global linkages that go beyond single interactions between states. In more traditional International Relations, this mainly meant looking at the balance of power between states (Haas 1953), the degree and nature of their political and economic interdependence and how that determines what happens in global politics (Keohane and Nye 1973; Morse 1969). In contemporary International Relations, however, this could include developments that are outside the immediate control of any particular state or group of states, such as the global economy, transnational terrorism or the internet. This strand in the literature will naturally feature prominently in the scholarship about the consequences of the Covid-19 pandemic, considering how it has repercussions that span across the realm of state, group or individual levels. An account of this kind of perspective can be found in the work of Barua (2020) on what he terms 'Coronanomics', where he traces the likely long-term changes in world trade patterns, following an initial phase of de-globalisation between states. Biscop (2020) presents a more conventional system perspective by considering the balance of power among states after the crisis ends.

A state-level study would require careful consideration of what kinds of state we are looking at, their type of government, how societies within them are managed politically, their geographical position, their historical ties and experiences and their economic standing. The distinction here is not quite as rigid in practice because the state level is rarely looked at in isolation but more in its wider systemic context. On that basis it would look at the foreign policy of states, meaning their approach to and practice of interacting with other states, based on their internal characteristics, domestic limitations and national preferences (Allison 1971). Key manifestations of state foreign policy would be the policies proposed and decided by governments, statements of top-level politicians but also the role and behaviour of diplomats and their adjoining bureaucratic structures. This is where the analysis might intersect with group- and individual-level aspects (see Kaarbo 2015).

A group-level analysis would again need to try and break down the analysis into certain kinds of group, how they relate to the state level, how the state level constrains them both domestically and between countries, and where they position themselves with respect to the global dimension of the issues they are dealing with. All of these kinds of issues would escape a traditional state-level analysis. Jordana and Triviño-Salaza (2020) indicate what might be useful empirical starting points for developing a study at the group or organisational level of analysis in the context of the Covid-19 pandemic. They highlight the constraints under which public health agencies and pertaining public health experts in Europe and the United States had to operate as the pandemic evolved, indicating that transboundary cooperation was hindered by this.

If looking at individual-level dynamics in developing International Relations perspectives on an issue we would likely need to engage with the implications of human nature and the psychological context of decisions and actions. As much as psychological factors, there can also be relevant cognitive and perceptive issues, structural problems of equality and access to information as well as the divergent individual capacity to make a difference (not least between different national contexts) and therefore point to possible explanations for a research problem. At first, the Covid-19 pandemic appears to be much like a natural disaster that affects masses of people simultaneously and indiscriminately, and that therefore does not seem to lend itself very well to an individual-level argument about the International Relations-related long-term consequences. There is, however, a common approach that involves looking at the decision-making setting of individual leaders to then be able to compare and draw cross-state conclusions and explain international outcomes and prospects. In this spirit, Tourish (2020) presents a set of leadership analyses of the early phase of the pandemic, ranging from a progressive and collectivist Jacinda Ardern, a populist Donald Trump and a denialist Boris Johnson.

The added value of a levels of analysis framework

While we need to be clear about our particular focus, and refrain from overgeneralising our findings, it is also plausible within the levels of analysis framework to build an argument that spans across the different levels of analysis and use the perspectives provided by each 'level' in conjunction. Many of today's global challenges are so complex that they require our analyses to span across various levels. Indeed, this is one of the main strengths of the levels of analysis model.

5.5 – KEY TERMS: Methods

Methods are specific ways of doing things. If the methods are both within the reach/means of the researcher, and used correctly so they are likely to provide the information or insight needed to answer a research question, then this would be what academics call a valid research methodology. Levels of analysis is a vital component of any good methodology. When used to help shape other valid research methods, such as interviews, fieldwork, surveys – and even the basic academic staple of textual analysis (reading different available sources such as journal articles, books and other documents) – it will help to produce answers that are both self-aware (of their limits) and persuasive. As a student, then, persuasion is the key. It is not your job to find *correct* answers as these rarely exist in the questions that International Relations generates. Rather, the key to a successful research strategy is to gather relevant information and use appropriate methods in order to reach a well-crafted analysis. In this sense, it is not just *what* you say or write that is important in academic work, but also *how* you express it.

We can derive some useful examples from the literature that focuses on explaining foreign policy decisions. Any state's activities that cross their national borders will have implications for the way in which they deal and interact with other states. We can look at foreign policy at the state level by analysing government policies and diplomatic decisions in isolation. However, governments are also actors on the world stage and their foreign policies contribute to what we call international relations. As highlighted above, foreign policy can also be explained by looking at the individual level, for example, the psychological and political factors that guide leaders and their advisers in their foreign policy decisions. Those decisions in turn then feed into decisions that matter at the state level and in relation to other states.

It can be helpful to think of foreign policy behaviour as something that is influenced by a range of factors. Some of them can be found within a state, in its political traditions, its socioeconomic profile, its political party system or in the minds of leading politicians. Others come from outside, from the global system that builds the context within which states operate. This does not mean that every meaningful discussion of foreign policy needs to look at all these aspects. However, investigations at one particular level should be used very carefully to draw conclusions about a different level. Where the levels overlap, we need to be aware that each one will require us to look at different kinds of evidence.

There is no dearth of scholarly opinions on the weaknesses of a 'levels of analysis' approach. Some have even argued that it should not be pursued further at all, such as Patomaki (2002), who criticised that any definition of such levels was ultimately arbitrary and based on assumptions that were not normally clarified. What is more, some International Relations approaches have an (often implicit) preference for a conception of politics as a process rather than an arena with various distinctive levels. Leftwich (2004), for instance, has argued that thinking of international relations as something that takes place in a certain site or location is just *one* possible way of looking at things. He calls this the 'arena' approach given the way in which it focuses on the location, or 'locus' of interactions, on different platforms that provide the stage to particular events and instances of international relations. He distinguishes this 'arena' approach from what he calls the 'processual' approach, which assumes that international relations can instead be thought of as a complex web of processes taking place simultaneously between people.

So, an alternative way of studying International Relations is to focus on interactions as opposed to physical structures and locations, such as the state or particular institutions within states. An example of such a perspective can be found in environmentalism or so-called 'Green Politics', which traditionally refuses to think of the practice of international relations as something that can be studied at different 'levels' of analysis. This is mainly because analysts pertaining to this approach perceive any proposed division of political reality into arenas or any attempts at physically locating a problem in a particular context as arbitrary and misleading. They would also argue that thinking in those divisions conveys a false sense of structure or 'law-like regularities' (Joseph 2010, 51), when societal challenges are fundamentally interconnected and should thus be studied in a 'holistic' way, meaning, in conjunction with each other. We will not develop these kinds of perspective further at this point, but it is nevertheless useful to highlight them briefly to challenge the assumption of there being any kind of clear-cut structure or specific levels of analysis that we can rely on as students and analysts of International Relations. Much like examples of history being broken into 'eras' as detailed in Chapter two, the levels of analysis are merely a helpful simplification device that gives us a better chance of understanding a complex world than would be the case without them.

Regardless of the limitations, we can use the levels as a way of structuring our thinking in a more basic sense in order to be able to then turn to explanatory theories of International Relations with a clearer sense of direction – which we will do in the chapters that follow. Regardless of the theoretical perspective we decide to use to develop explanations, it is important to be aware of the multiplicity of actors and processes that make up the global system. Reminding ourselves of the complexity of the issues that we study also equips us with the ability to recognise any overgeneralisations as they are being presented to us by the media, by political leaders, activists, pressure groups and through our social networks. This makes us more informed, nuanced and rounded in our thinking.

CASE STUDY 5.1: Social media and the Arab Spring

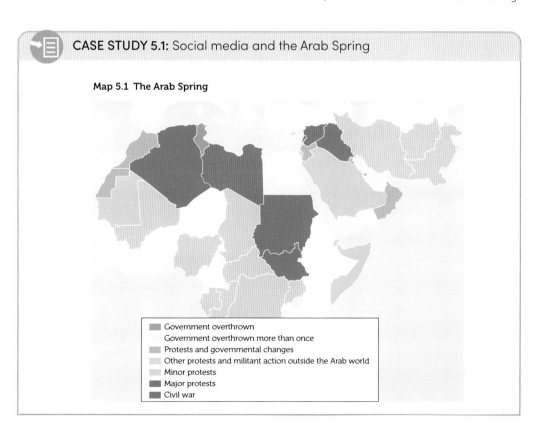

Map 5.1 The Arab Spring

Government overthrown
Government overthrown more than once
Protests and governmental changes
Other protests and militant action outside the Arab world
Minor protests
Major protests
Civil war

International commercial aviation and the rapid spread of information technologies has increased people's mobility and the rate at which interactions occur across and beyond state borders. The ability for common people to store, transfer and distribute large amounts of information, the possibility for data to travel across the world in virtually no time, and the increasing reach of the internet have not only changed lives at personal and community levels but also dramatically altered the dynamics in politics and global affairs. To a member of the general public, social media services appear to serve entertainment purposes with the added value of making information readily available. These social platforms become a relevant matter to International Relations where they enable common people to communicate, network, organise, influence, mobilise and even delegate over potentially any societal issue of our time including those with global repercussions. Taking us back to the question posed at the start of this chapter about whether one person's voice can have an impact, this phenomenon not only extends to those who own and operate such services, such as Mark Zuckerberg, whose company 'Meta' owns Facebook, Instagram and WhatsApp (see Abdelhaey 2019), but increasingly to the everyday people who use these accessible platforms to project and promote ideas across borders at virtually no financial cost to themselves (see Shirky 2011).

Political agendas – be they progressive, revolutionary or outright dangerous – can unfold and be reproduced in what seems to be a relatively uncontrolled way (particularly in democratic societies), often posing real challenges to governmental agencies and the political leaders that try to control and direct them. As a result, random individuals, or so it seems, can potentially start a revolution from their homes, bypassing conventional conceptions of power and transcending boundaries to the point where political activity and even confrontation become weightless and immaterial altogether (see Seib 2012). Many introductory textbooks will not go into great detail about the role of everyday individuals in the war and peace process. And yet, individuals have sometimes greatly shaped the course of events in conflict-ridden parts of the world. Even more so, they have influenced the way the sources of conflict and potential avenues of resolution are perceived externally.

The 'Arab Spring' offers a powerful example of the effect everyday people can have internationally. In December 2010, 26-year-old Tarek el-Tayeb Mohamed Bouazizi, a street vendor in Tunisia, set himself on fire in an expression of personal desperation over his living and working conditions and limited prospects for changing them. Not least because of its symbolic power (particularly also as it happened in a predominantly Muslim state where self-inflicted death is a religious taboo), this protest suicide of a single individual went viral on social media and brought global awareness to what would otherwise have been a local issue. Within days of his death, Bouazizi became an icon of a disenchanted generation of young people across the predominantly Arab world of the Middle East and North Africa. These individuals drawn from a range of different states felt similar anger over spending their lives in relative poverty, exacerbated by a culture of political corruption and repression that had become endemic across the region's governments. Demonstrations reached no fewer than eighteen states and resulted in four governments being overthrown and a number of civil wars breaking out.

Social media is where real-life events including instances of violent war-like conflict become uniquely interlinked with the crowds that follow, interpret, judge and react to what is happening. Apart from providing a platform for communication and the exchange of ideas between the spectators of crucial events and thus changing external perceptions, however, the amplifying effects of social media also matter a lot for the way in which information travels. Not least with the help of web-based communication, public unrest in Tunisia formed quickly and first set off in Bouazizi's home region. An entire society was soon mobilised through social media, thus placing unprecedented pressures on the well-established political practices within their host state and its sovereign representatives. Long-standing president Ben Ali resigned less than a month after Bouazizi's self-immolation over mounting pressures from the uprisings that followed. The decision of a single individual to protest in this way, amplified regionally and globally by social media, triggered what turned out to be a watershed in the entire region and beyond.

The image of the martyrs of a revolution was also powerfully reproduced in the case of Khaled Saeed, whose violent death at the hands of Egyptian police went viral in June 2010. Similar to the trigger event in Tunisia, this sparked widespread protests, carried substantially by a youth movement that organised itself predominantly through social media. Its founder, computer engineer Wael Ghonim, Head of Marketing of Google Middle East and North Africa at the time, collaborated with local protesters and used the Facebook group events function to support the movement from his base in Dubai. One could of course say that there was at the time a particular momentum in the region for a widespread societal revolution. However, the actions of individuals like the ones described here substantively shaped the course, speed and character of the uprisings, and social media played an essential role in each of the cases. By recognising this and focusing our analysis at the individual level, we can more effectively reveal the impact of their actions.

That said, we should also be careful not to indulge in 'techno-utopianism' and subscribe to the belief that social media can easily erode state power or oppression (see Christensen 2011). The political role of social media is contested, particularly where access to certain apps and websites, and denial thereof, is used as a form of political control and a means of social and cultural oppression. China is among the most commonly cited cases of a state where the internet is walled off and only approved sites are allowed by the government, and in China's case these do not include Twitter, Facebook or even Google and Wikipedia. Within those that are sanctioned, they are aggressively monitored and censored by operatives of the Chinese state. In other cases, rather than permanently blocking these services, states undergoing domestic protests or sensitive political incidents have temporarily shut down social media services, or even the entire internet for a period, to suppress dissent or prevent an Arab Spring-like event taking hold. In that sense, although tools such as social media empower individuals, they are not the only actors operating in that space and the state still wields significant power to (attempt to) control access if so desired.

 CASE STUDY 5.2: Greta Thunberg and climate activism

Photo 5.4 Greta Thunberg addresses climate strikers at Civic Center Park in Denver, 11 October 2019

Credit: Andy Bosselman/Streetsblog Denver/Flickr

If it was not already evident, by reading the account of the Arab Spring above it will be a liberating thought that as an individual you are not confined to being a passive subject directed by political elites and official state actors. Each of us has the means of being an actor in our own right, given the right conditions. This realisation can feel empowering, but it should also give a sense of responsibility and the need for self-moderation, particularly when it comes to the use of social media for political purposes, cultural communication and social activism.

The role of individuals in international relations is probably most often talked about in the global debate about climate and environmental issues. Within this area, there is one particular case that comes to mind: Greta Thunberg. The Swedish climate change activist, a 15-year-old high school student at the time, started her protest in the most low-tech kind of way: by sitting in front of the Swedish Parliament during school hours, holding up a handmade sign 'School strike for the climate'. She did, however, also upload a photo of herself in this very situation to her Instagram and Twitter accounts. Thunberg's protest rapidly gained attention as high-profile activists and stakeholders re-tweeted her photo and continued to repost her daily updates on Instagram. On day three of her protest, Thunberg was excited to see more than thirty people join her in front of the parliament. Two months later, her #FridaysForFuture hashtag had gone viral and student-led protests of the same kind had spread across the world.

After initially writing her posts in Swedish, she switched to English, presumably to facilitate the spread of her political message. She has since also engaged in some highly visible acts of protest including her crossing of the Atlantic on a sailing boat (rather than a plane, making a point about the harm caused by fossil fuels), and speeches at the United Nations Climate Action Summit and the World Economic Forum in Davos. Today, Thunberg is a celebrity activist with millions of followers on social media. Beyond (but importantly through her visibility on) social media, her cause was, among others, officially endorsed by the Club of Rome (a humanitarian and environmentalist NGO), the Scientists for Future (a collective of academic climate change experts), and by *Science* and *Nature*, two of the most prominent academic journals.

Thunberg's rise to global fame and visibility has come at a time when the general awareness of the consequences of climate change is higher than ever before, particularly amongst younger generations. Born out of dissatisfaction with the lack of progress in global environmental matters following the UN Conference of 1992 in Rio on the Environment and Development, the 2000s saw the establishment of a more mainstream environmentalist global narrative. In 2001 the 'Global Greens' were created, an international network of political parties, movements, partner networks and non-governmental organisations advocating the 'Global Greens Charter'. Thunberg has been able to reinvigorate this global debate and shown that more than ever before, by way of advanced and increasingly accessible information technology, there is the scope and potential for activism.

Localised 'grass-roots' activism – as with Thunberg's – can quickly morph into a wider political movement, sparked by individuals whose actions and the political messages they convey cannot only penetrate local and national societies but also transcend borders and even achieve global impact.

However, scholars have warned of the modernist and somewhat simplistic assumption that this technology has a democratising effect in its own right. Morozov (2009) cautioned against the misguided belief that all activity online was well intentioned, warning of a darker side of internet freedom and the way it can equally empower illiberal forces. Also, social media may bear the potential for individuals to get more involved but many forms of this kind of participation are more inspired by 'slacker activism/slacktivism' with little material impact on the cause (Dennis 2018). In these cases there is a perception that simply 'liking' something on social media or signing a petition is sufficient and/or allows an individual to appear to be part of a movement. Yet, in reality such actions (by themselves) are 'virtually' worthless. So, what we are looking at with this phenomenon is more of a relatively novel range of possibilities for self-expression, activism and mobilisation, but not without their caveats and limitations.

A related concept is the one of celebrity activism that finds itself enabled by internet-based communication technology (see Farrell 2019). On the one hand, this includes established celebrities that make use of digital media to advocate a cause, such as in the case of the #BringBackOurGirls campaign led by Western female celebrities such as Michelle Obama, Cara Delevingne, Julia Roberts and Keira Knightley to put pressure on the Nigerian government and push for Western intervention to free hundreds of girls who had been kidnapped by the terrorist group Boko Haram (see Hopkins and Louw 2019). On the other hand, we also see this kind of activism by self-promoted 'influencers', who make use of their digital platforms to support and mobilise support for transboundary issues (see Lewis 2020). In these cases the results are mixed, but can sometimes have a real world effect.

Not everyone who voices political opinions online will be a Greta Thunberg, but her example shows that it is possible that any individual could find their voice amplified if they were sufficiently inspirational, motivated and fortunate. If International Relations was still stuck in its state- and system-level fascinations, scholarship would miss – or dismiss – much of the impact of this important level of analysis. Together with the previous case of the Arab Spring, Greta Thunberg's example is a testament to the importance of the rise of the individual and the impact one person's voice can have in the vastness of the global system.

Conclusion

This chapter has introduced you to the idea of levels of analysis as an analytical device that makes the variety of issues in International Relations more comprehensible. More specifically, we have distinguished between the system, state, group and individual levels, highlighting differences as well as connections between them. When analysing something, you will always have material constraints such as time, availability of material, or a word count. In that sense, making a conscious decision about what level of analysis you will explore will allow you to develop a more focused piece of work and simultaneously trains you to approach complex issues with an academically satisfying method that will produce results. Levels of analysis also help us better comprehend the various theory families that we will explore over the next two chapters. We have also shown that the discipline has gradually moved away from its focus on the state and the system to deal more with the roles and perspectives of groups, and especially individuals. Although the global system is vast, changes in technology clearly demonstrate that one person's voice can reach farther than at any time in history. It will hopefully be refreshing to find that as you start to study International Relations, it has never been so representative in its quest to appreciate the active role that each individual can take on.

 ## END OF CHAPTER QUESTIONS

1. Think of, and evaluate, examples beyond those mentioned in this chapter where everyday individuals gained influence (positive or negative) in international relations.

2. The example of Greta Thunberg gives us insights into the role of an individual in the context of climate change. What additional insights might be found if looking at climate change through the other three levels of analysis?

3. What makes up the 'international community' if we no longer think of it as simply a community of states?

4. Analyse the ways your own state reacted to Covid-19 using the four levels of analysis. See what insights you can develop.

5. Which level of analysis resonates with you most at this point in your journey, and why?

CHAPTER 6

TRADITIONAL AND MIDDLE GROUND THEORIES

Stephen McGlinchey and Dana Gold

Question: Can International Relations theory be simplified to an argument between optimists and pessimists?

A good understanding of history, as the earlier chapters have detailed, will allow you to understand what happened, why it happened and to what extent it remains important today. However, you will need tools that allow you to dig deeper than this, and that's where International Relations theory comes in. Theory allows us to ask questions of our history, our present, and even gain insights into our future. It builds on the perspectives gained by appreciating the different levels of analysis and gives us a toolkit that forms an essential part of International Relations as an academic discipline. This chapter, and the one that follows it, are both designed with three objectives. First, we show when and why each successive theory emerged. Second, we outline the central features of each theory so that you can understand the basics of how they work and get an appreciation of the insights they offer. Finally, we unpack certain elements of the theories to reveal some of their complexity.

Making sense of theory

Due to its complexity and diversity, it is common for newcomers to have some difficulty in grasping International Relations theory. So, in order to consider the field as a whole for beginners it is necessary to simplify International Relations theory. This chapter works together with the one that follows it by splitting theory into three basic categories – 'traditional', 'middle ground' and 'critical'. This chapter deals with those theories we have put in the traditional and middle ground categories. In order to simplify further, the various named theories will be presented as theory families. We hope this is an analogy that will be easy to understand.

6.1 – KEY INSIGHTS: Theory families

Much like real families, International Relations theory families have members who disagree on many things – but they still share many commonalities. A proven way to find your footing with theory is to focus first on identifying and understanding those commonalities within each approach. In time, you will need to unpack the differences and factions within each theory family – and we will help you get started with this in the case studies later in the chapter. But, for now, understanding the core, shared, assumptions of each theoretical approach is the best way to build your confidence with what is perhaps the most complex area of International Relations. Should you get confused when grappling with a theory in all its complexity later in your studies, returning to its core familial elements (as presented in this chapter and the one following it) should help you reorient yourself.

Theories allow us to understand and try to make sense of the world around us through different perspectives – each of which are ways to simplify a complicated world. Theories are like maps. Each map is made for a certain purpose and what is included in the map is based on what is necessary to direct the map's user in a clear, and useful, manner. Some students love studying theories because they open up interesting questions about the world we live in, our understanding of human nature and even what it is possible to know. Other students, however, are eager to get straight to the real-life (often described as 'empirical') case studies of world events that made them want to study International Relations in the first place. For these students, studying theory might even seem like a distraction. Yet it is crucial to point out that embarking on the study of International Relations without an understanding of theory is like setting off on a journey without a map. You might arrive at your destination, or somewhere else very interesting, but you will have no idea where you are or how you got there. And you will have no response to someone who insists that their route would have been better or more direct. Theories give us clarity and direction; they help us to both defend our own arguments and better understand the arguments of others.

Take a look at part of Singapore's Mass Rapid Transit (MRT) network map (Photo 6.1). What you see there are lines, stations and some basic visual information to help commuters, such as the location of the most visited destinations, like the airport. You will not see roads, shops (and the like) charted as these are not essential to travelling on the system. Theories do a similar thing. Each different theory puts different things on its map, based on what its theorists believe to be important. Variables to plot on an International Relations map would be such things as states, organisations, individuals, economics,

Photo 6.1 Section of Singapore's MRT

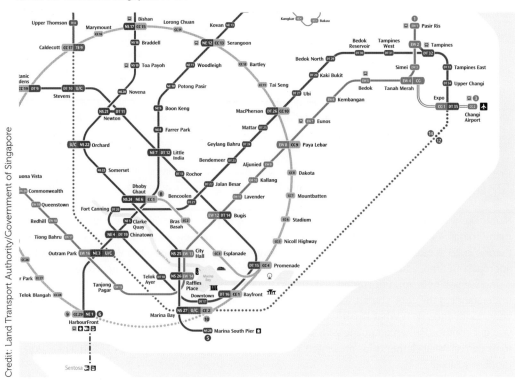

history, class, power, gender and so on. Theorists then use their chosen variables, and omit the others, to construct a simplified view of the world that can be used to analyse events – and in some cases to have a degree of predictive ability.

It is important to note that newer theories are constantly emerging and competing with existing ones. This can be disorientating at first, but it is a necessary reaction to the ever-changing nature of our world. Before we move ahead, one important point. You may notice that some of the theories you are introduced to here are referred to by names that also occur in other disciplines. Sometimes this can be confusing as, for example, 'realism' in International Relations is not the same as realism in art. Similarly, you may hear the word 'liberal' being used to describe someone's personal views, but in International Relations liberalism means something distinct. To avoid confusion, this note will serve as a caveat that in this book we only refer to the theories concerned as they have been developed within the discipline of International Relations.

Liberalism and realism

As International Relations itself was born out of the need to address the causes of war in the early twentieth century, the two traditional theories of the discipline – liberalism and realism – offered their own unique contrasting responses. Both theory families have been robustly challenged in the modern era, essentially because of their focus on issues at the system and state levels – like war and peace, for example – at the expense of other issues at the group and individual levels. Yet, despite these challenges, both liberalism and realism remain central to the discipline because of the distinctive insights that they offer.

Liberalism grew out of a set of principles based in idealism, which asserted that a better world was possible. Liberals view human beings as innately good and believe peace and harmony between nations is not only achievable, but desirable. Immanuel Kant developed the idea in the late eighteenth century that states that shared liberal values should have no reason for going to war against one another. In Kant's eyes, the more liberal states there were, the more peaceful the world would become, since liberal states are ruled by their citizens and citizens are rarely disposed to desire war. This is in contrast to the rule of kings and other non-elected rulers (who today we may call dictators or autocrats), who frequently have selfish desires out of step with citizens and are typically quicker of mind to make decisions that would send ordinary people into danger. Kant's ideas have resonated and continue to be developed by liberals, most notably in the democratic peace theory which posits that democracies do not go to war with each other – for the very reasons Kant outlined. To take this idea further, the theory argues that the more democracies there are, the more peace there will be in the international system. A common misunderstanding is often found here: democratic peace theory does not mean that war will end, but that its occurrences will shrink in number over time as more liberal democracies emerge. It also does not exclude the fact that liberal democracies will sometimes go to war with illiberal/non-democratic states for perceived security reasons – an example of which can be seen in the two US-led invasions of Iraq in 1991 and 2003.

Liberals do not just base their arguments on the spread of democracy. They also focus on two key elements of interaction between nation-states: trade and international organisations. For liberals trade is how states, and their peoples, interact during times of peace. They do this by exchanging products and services back and forth, often things that other states do not possess. This is a positive-sum interaction for both parties and inevitably also leads to the sharing of culture, ideas and the movement of people due to the literal and figurative pathways that are opened between nations. Positive-sum interactions are also important to liberals in a general sense as they prove that interactions between peoples and states can benefit both sides, rather than just one. As long as each party benefits to some degree (in the case of trade those states participating) then the result is a net positive for all. Everyone gains *something*. This may be that one side benefits financially from selling tea, and the other side benefits in a non-financial way by adding tea to their culture as tea leaves do not grow well in their climate or geography. In this sense, trade enriches all that come into contact with it, either directly, or indirectly. This positive-sum interaction does not have to be equal for both sides so long as something is gained by each party. For liberals, trade, being positive-sum, opens up communication links and shows the benefits of peaceful interactions across cultures that offer yet one more way to avoid war, as should a war occur then trade ceases between the warring parties and the benefits are lost.

The second element of interaction between states, international organisations, is a much newer phenomenon. Different cultures have been shown to have been trading since historical records began thousands of years ago. Yet we have only witnessed international organisations becoming a permanent structural component of the global system in the twentieth century, principally with the establishment of the United Nations in October 1945, although there were notable, and largely unsuccessful, earlier attempts at using organisations to establish order on a more limited scale. For liberals, international organisations provide a second element that underlines their theory. Simply by having a permanent 'big table' around which to interact and conduct diplomacy – and in the modern era there are many tables of this kind at regional and global levels – states can find ways to solve disputes. This lessens the need for war and provides a forum for diplomacy which, although rooted in compromise, can offer solutions that are acceptable to those who are in arbitration.

International organisations are, therefore, central to the modern liberal account of International Relations.

It is no surprise that the liberal account is one that points towards a world of peace and harmony, and this has always been the case for liberals, who see that as their desired end goal for the global system. Yet, for liberals this is not philosophical idealism, but a conclusion that comes by virtue of manifestly real phenomena such as trade, international organisations and the spread of democracy. Each of these provides proof for their central idea that alternatives to war exist. Of course, having read the prior chapters of this book, you will know that our world has seen a lot of war and that warfare has become more deadly. So it is clear that despite the evidence for their claims, liberals have opposition. To help explain this, we can track back to US President Woodrow Wilson who addressed his famous 'Fourteen Points' to the US Congress in January 1918 during the final year of the First World War. As he presented his ideas for a rebuilt world beyond the war, the last of his points was to create a general association of nations, which became the League of Nations – essentially a prototype for today's United Nations. Dating back to 1920, the League of Nations was created largely for the purpose of overseeing affairs between states and implementing, as well as maintaining, international peace. However, when the League was unable to prevent the outbreak of the Second World War in 1939, its failure became difficult for liberals to comprehend, as events seemed to contradict their theories. Indeed it was analysing this timeline that the phrase 'idealist' came to be used widely as a pejorative to mock liberals for their apparently misplaced optimism, most notably by Carr (1939).

6.2 – KEY TERMS: Positivism

Both realism and liberalism are shaped from the same building block – positivism – which is an approach that views the world as 'out there' waiting be observed and analysed by the researcher. Theories that are built on positivism see the world 'as it is' and base their assumptions upon analysing physical elements such as states and international organisations, which they can account for and ascribe values to. Positivism is therefore based on the study of facts and the gathering of physical evidence. It is related to the scientific view of the natural world as being one that operates via laws (such as gravity) that can be revealed by careful study and observation. Positivists assert that equivalent laws can be revealed about the social world.

Despite the efforts of prominent liberal scholars and politicians, liberalism failed to retain a strong hold and another theory emerged to explain the continuing presence of war. That theory became known as realism. Realism gained momentum during the Second World War when it appeared to offer a convincing account for how and why the worst conflict in known history commenced after a period of supposed peace and optimism between 1918 and 1938. Although it originated in named form in the twentieth century, many realists have traced its origins to earlier writings. Indeed, realists have looked as far back as to the ancient world to the writings of the Greek historian Thucydides (460–400 BCE) where they detected similar patterns of human behaviour as those evident in our modern world.

As its name suggests, advocates of realism purport it reflects the 'reality' of the world and more effectively accounts for change in international politics. Thomas Hobbes is another historical figure often mentioned in discussions of realism due to his description of the brutality of life during the English Civil War of 1642–51. Hobbes described human beings as living in an orderless 'state of nature' that he perceived as a war of all against all. To remedy this, he proposed that a 'social contract' was required between a ruler and the people of a state to maintain relative order. Today, we take such ideas for granted as it is usually clear who rules our states. Each leader, or 'sovereign' (a monarch or a parliament, for example) sets the rules and establishes a system of punishments for those who break them. We accept this in our respective states so that our lives can function with a sense of security and order. It may not be ideal, but it is better than a state of nature where chaos and anarchy (the lack of a higher authority) prevail. As no such contract exists internationally and there is no sovereign in charge of the world, disorder and fear rules international relations. That is why war seems more common than peace to realists, indeed they see war as inevitable. When they examine history they see a world that may change in shape, but is always characterised by a system of what they call 'international anarchy' as the global system lacks the kind of hierarchical order that we experience within our domestic societies.

6.3 – KEY INSIGHTS: Statism, survival and self-help

Statism helps us understand what realists mean by 'international anarchy' as it focuses us on the idea that the central actors in the global system are nation-states who compete on a technically level playing field. There is no higher power beyond a nation-state, and for any group of people to become a 'player' in international relations they need to secure their sovereignty and form their own state.

Once statehood is achieved, the next order of business is **survival**. As there is no higher power regulating the global system, states will frequently clash and seek to dominate each other. For this reason, for realists, whatever needs to be done to ensure the security of the state against the threats (actual or potential) is warranted.

Finally, realists argue that as a state pursues its survival over time, it can only ensure the best chances of surviving by understanding the necessity of **self-help**. Trusting in an international organisation like the United Nations, or relying on the promises of another state, is potentially perilous because it puts your fate in the hands of an external actor, which is unwise. So, each state must take the required steps to help itself. This may be in the form of growing its military, forming fair-weather (temporary) alliances, or by developing other attributes that may deter an attack by another state.

The best way to understand realism and how it views the global system is to break it into elements, as we have already done with liberalism. Dunne and Schmidt (2020) have helpfully described these as the three Ss of realism: *statism*, *survival* and *self-help*, as outlined in Box 6.3. These core elements are at odds with liberalism, as when a realist looks at the world, they see a world of danger. To go back to the liberal idea of positive-sum outcomes, realists invert this concept and see most interactions through zero-sum logic, where they are more concerned with the idea of relative gains. For example, a liberal would see trade as an interaction where all parties gain something, and in that sense a scenario of *absolute gains* when measured for its overall effect. Trade, then, gives all parties mutual enrichment – such as the trading of tea analogy from above. But, seeing this from a realist point of view, should that tea-rich state decide to use the profits of their tea trade to build a massive military and attempt to grow their power and territory by dominating other states, then trading with them actually enables them to (potentially) become a future mortal enemy. For reasons such as this, realists see most interactions between states as zero-sum. Any interaction where a rival state gains in a relative sense, even if they only gain something small, is a *loss* to your state as it has made a competitor richer, and potentially more powerful. And, as the global system is anarchical and based on self-help, that interaction may at some point prove to be one that is regretted.

6.4 – KEY TERMS: Isolationism

Realists are sometimes confused with isolationists – those who seek to put up barriers to interactions and pursue national self-sufficiency by removing themselves from international affairs. Realists are not isolationists. They simply caution that interactions should always be carefully entered into, always taken with a strong pinch of salt, and measured through the logic of their three Ss. Contrary to isolationism, realists recognise the necessity for all states to continually engage in international relations so they can assess their relative power and security against that of other states – which is constantly in flux.

Another central area that sets realism and liberalism apart is how they view human nature. Realists do not typically believe that human beings are inherently good, or have the potential for good, as liberals do. Instead, they claim individuals act in their own self-interests. For realists, people (and states by extension) are selfish and behave according to their own needs without necessarily taking into account the needs of others. Therefore, realists believe conflict is unavoidable and perpetual, and so war is common and inherent to humankind. Underlining this further, Hans Morgenthau, a prominent realist, is known for his famous statement 'all politics is a struggle for power' (Morgenthau 1948). This demonstrates the typical realist view that politics is primarily about domination as opposed to cooperation between states.

Here, it is useful to recall the idea of theories being maps. Realists and liberals see a similar global system, but they draw different conclusions from what they see. When viewing that system through realist eyes, it appears to reveal a terrain of domination and power. The realist worldview therefore magnifies instances of war and conflict and uses those to map out a certain picture of the world, one of an ever-changing dynamic of competing states of varying power and influence. Essentially, all that is on the realist map is terrain and spheres of influence divided among states. Liberals, when looking at the same world, adjust their view of the very same terrain to blur out areas of domination and instead bring areas of cooperation into focus. They do this by adding a transparent layer on top of the realist map that overlays additional features such as international organisations and global trade that sit above and between competing states. When that additional layer is overlaid, the map takes on a very different meaning. Leaving this analogy behind, you may realise the subjective nature of such worldviews. This may seem arbitrary, but these theories have significant real-world impact and often influence how leaders see the world. The reason that realism and liberalism have remained central to International Relations despite their age is that they remain relevant to policy and offer valid (albeit competing) roadmaps to politicians seeking to navigate their state's way through the global system.

It is important to understand that there is no single liberal or realist theory, and this will become apparent as you progress in your studies and engage with the primary works of the theorists. Each scholar has a particular interpretation of the world, which includes ideas of peace, war and the role of the state in relation to individuals. Furthermore, both realism and liberalism have been updated to more modern versions (neoliberalism and neorealism) that represent a shift in emphasis from their roots. And those updated versions each have themselves many subdivisions. Nevertheless, these perspectives can still be grouped into theory 'families'. For example, if we think of the simple contrast of optimism and pessimism we can see the familial relationship in all branches of realism and liberalism. Liberals share an optimistic view of International Relations, believing that the world order can be improved, with peace and progress gradually replacing war. They may not agree on the details, but this optimistic view generally unites them. Conversely, realists tend to dismiss optimism as a form of misplaced idealism and instead they arrive at a more pessimistic view. This is due to their focus on the centrality of the state and its need for security and survival in an anarchical system where it can only truly rely on itself. As a result, realists reach an array of accounts that describe a system where war and conflict are common, and periods of peace are merely times when states are preparing for future conflict.

Another point to keep in mind is that each of the overarching approaches possesses a different perspective on the nature of the state. In what may be a familial similarity rather than a difference, both liberalism and realism consider the state to be the dominant actor in the system – possessing ultimate power. This includes the capacity to enforce decisions, such as declaring war on another state, or agreeing treaties that may bind states to certain agreements. The traditional theories analyse, and also recognise, the basic structure that was put in place after the Treaty of Westphalia when the modern state system came to embody Europe, and later the world. Yet, digging a little deeper, differences soon present themselves when we consider how each theory considers international organisations and trade relationships in relation to states. In terms of liberalism, its proponents argue that the global governance capabilities provided by international organisations, and the opportunities offered by trade, are valuable. These assist states in formulating decisions, build relationships, and formalise cooperation that leads to more peaceful outcomes. Realists on the other hand believe states partake in international organisations and trade only when it is in their self-interest to do so.

The English school and constructivism

An increasing number of scholars have begun to reject the traditional theories because of their obsession with the state and the status quo. In doing so they have opened up a middle ground between realism and liberalism on the one hand, and between the traditional theories and a range of critical theories on the other hand (these will be explored in the next chapter).

The thinking of the English school is often viewed as the first attempt to establish a middle ground in International Relations theory, albeit in this case a middle ground between liberal and realist theories. The English school involves the idea of a society of states existing at the international level. Hedley Bull, one of the core figures of the English school, agreed with the traditional theories that the global system was anarchic. However, he insisted this does not mean the absence of norms (expected behaviours), thus claiming a societal aspect to international politics. In this sense, states form an 'Anarchical Society' (Bull 1977) where a type of order does exist, based on shared norms and behaviours.

The English school is useful to help flag up a general misunderstanding that students often have that anarchy means chaos. The work of Bull and others in the English school draws attention to how international anarchy has its own unique type of order. After all, the world is not in a state of perpetual chaos despite its state of anarchy. It is not unfair to describe this as *liberal realism*, as it essentially posits (in its basic form) that the global order – as anarchic as it is – is not as pessimistic as the realists make out, yet not quite as optimistic as the liberals assert. English school theorists continue to develop their arguments beyond these observations (see Murray 2015), but for our purposes the central importance was that it showed that theoretical development beyond realism and liberalism was both welcome and possible.

Constructivism is another theory that can be viewed as a middle ground, but this time between the traditional theories and the critical theories that we will explore in the next chapter. It also has some familial links with the English school. But, it goes further and offers up new tools and insights in our theory toolkit. Constructivists highlight the importance of values and shared interests between individuals who interact on the global stage, as well as social norms that bring them together. Additionally, constructivists are interested in emphasising the agency of individuals, which in other words refers to people's ability to seek and implement change. As you may have already picked up when recalling the themes of the previous chapter, this breaks theory out of its focus on the system and state levels of analysis and reaches into the group and individual levels.

Alexander Wendt, a prominent constructivist, described the relationship between agents (individuals) and structures (such as the state) as one in which structures not only constrain agents but also construct their identities and interests. His phrase 'anarchy is what states make of it' (Wendt 1992) sums this up well and helps to advance some of the points made by English school theorists. Another way to explain this, and to explain the core of constructivism, is that the essence of international relations exists in the interactions between individuals. After all, states do not interact; it is *agents* of those states – such as politicians and diplomats – who interact, leading to a greater likelihood

---

6.5 – KEY INSIGHTS: Anarchy is what states make of it

Alexander Wendt (1992; 1999) used constructivism to suggest that there are at least *three* types of anarchy observable in our global system – overlapping and coexisting. He referred to these borrowing the names of famous European philosophers, Thomas Hobbes, John Locke and Immanuel Kant, whose writings he found embodied the systems.

1 **Hobbesian** – the statism, self-help and survival anarchy documented by realists. As Hobbes was writing about the English Civil War (1642–51) where security, law and order and safety were absent, his interpretations are often mapped on to the global system, especially by realists.

2 **Lockean** – a tempered anarchy where rules and expectations regulate behaviour. A 'live and let live' system analogous to the ideas outlined in the English school. Locke's work is often highlighted for his more optimistic view of human nature and his opposition to authoritarian types of political order such as that advocated by Hobbes via his idea of a 'Leviathan' bringing an unruly nation to order.

3 **Kantian** – a liberal anarchy where pluralistic security communities are built based on friendship and shared interests between states and ideas of collective security dominate the system. The key to this idea is that it is only regional, with other arrangements and zones of differently comprised states existing outside the so-called 'Kantian' zone. Kant posited that such zones would grow as their benefits became clear and potentially could envelop the globe. This inspired many international organisations, especially the European Union.

of mutual cooperation. Since those interacting on the world stage have accepted international anarchy as its defining principle, it has become part of our reality. However, if anarchy is what we make of it, then states and their agents can perceive anarchy differently and the qualities of anarchy can change over time. International anarchy could even be replaced by a different system if an influential group of individuals (and by proxy the states they represent) accepted the idea. To understand constructivism is to understand that certain ideas, or 'norms' as they are often called once those ideas become expected behaviours, have power. As such, constructivists seek to study the process by which existing norms emerge, and then are challenged and potentially replaced with new norms.

To explore this issue in a more tangible way we can look at the basic idea of the existence of the nation-state. Sovereignty was an idea that was accepted in Europe in the mid-1600s, and then gradually took hold over the ensuing centuries until it became a global 'norm'. There is simply no other accepted way to organise peoples that is currently recognised internationally. Today, when we look at a world map, the entire landmass of the earth (with the exception of Antarctica which has no native population) is divided into sovereign nation-states separated by physical borders. Understanding the value of constructivism is understanding that all those things that we take for granted, like the states we belong to and where they end geographically and another state begins, are simply constructs of human beings: they were agreed upon and built at a certain time and they will endure for as long as we want to keep them and invest in them. If a better idea takes hold, then we will see systemic change as we adjust to it and adopt it.

Constructivists examine the process of how new ideas emerge from within the policy-making machines of states, and also sometimes from individuals that they call 'norm entrepreneurs'. Then they track when and how these ideas become adopted – or when they do not. It is even possible to see the construction of your own nationality this way. At some point, a sovereign established control of a defined territory (your nation-state), then created a flag, an anthem, adopted a national language and perhaps even a state religion – amongst other things. These were all choices made by someone, somewhere, that became meaningful over time and are usually taken for granted today. However, once you realise the constructed nature of everything in the political world, even your own nationality in which you may be very invested, you can appreciate the value of what constructivism brings to the table.

Identity is, then, another key component of constructivism. When individuals (agents) interact, usually on behalf of a state, they do so in a social environment. This is why constructivism is sometimes referred to as 'social constructivism'. Put simply, identity is social, it exists *between* people via their interactions. Think of it this way, you would not know much about who you were and what makes you distinctive unless you could compare yourself to others. That may be others within your own society, or other states. That awareness of identity as being socially constructed completes the basic picture of what constructivism offers. It also indicates why constructivists often find their attention drawn to international organisations. For example, if the United Nations can be pictured as a 'big table' around which representatives of states sit, this can be visualised as the place where the world's norms (expected behaviours) are constructed through social interactions between elite actors representing their respective states. Then those norms can be regularly tested, challenged and sometimes changed. If you want to look at this in a more human sense – people make, and then remake, our global system. Everything is built by individuals making their ideas reality. The only barrier is that an idea must become a norm, signifying it has been accepted by others in the system.

It is hopefully clear how constructivism diverges from liberalism and realism by opening up International Relations theory beyond a simple argument between optimism and pessimism broadly focused on the system and state levels of analysis. It moves International Relations theory into a more holistic position, which over time has become a middle ground that offers a message that can be more appealing than other theories. Namely, everything is socially constructed. So, if aspects of the global order are flawed or troubling, they are not fixed in place or inevitable – they can be remade. This disrupts the rather unchanging world that realists, for example, see. So, if, as for many students and scholars, realism and liberalism do not put enough variables on their maps, constructivism offers a welcome alternative.

CASE STUDY 6.1: Warfare – a bug or a feature?

Photo 6.2 Iran nuclear talks in Vienna, 14 July 2015

Credit: Hasan Tosun/Anadolu Agency/Getty Images

Realists and liberals are divided when it comes to understanding why war exists, and what can be done about it. Realists believe it is an ever-present 'feature' of our system as international anarchy drives conflict because security is scarce. As a result, states look to acquire territory and resources or to eradicate/absorb a competitor to enable them to feel more secure. Mearsheimer called this *The Tragedy of Great Power Politics* (2001) as the very nature of the global system appears to make this cycle perpetual. Mearsheimer's 'offensive realism' is one of the most pessimistic quadrants within the theory family, yet even its less pessimistic bedfellow, 'defensive realism', still includes war as a feature – albeit not occurring as often. Defensive realists, such as Jervis (1978), posit that states are incentivised to act moderately as they understand that aggression will lead to war, which reduces security and is therefore best avoided except when absolutely necessary.

On the other hand, liberals see war as more of a recurring 'bug' that can be addressed by the growing preponderance of democracy and the spread of organisations such as the United Nations. When goods, services, culture, laws and people are seen to be moving freely back and forth between and among states, liberals feel confident that the incentives for war are shrinking. Like a bug is reported and worked on by a developer when it does enough damage to draw the ire of users, liberals see evidence that people, and states, want to enjoy the fruits of a more peaceful global system. Liberals do not deny that the bug exists, or that it is pervasive and seems to pop up in unexpected times and places – but they believe that we have the tools to gradually reduce its damaging effects and perhaps, one day, to fully eliminate it with the right skill and effort.

To illustrate this, for realists, when conflict begins to materialise that poses a risk to national security (or 'survival', to recall one of realism's three Ss), states typically have only two choices: to 'balance' or 'bandwagon'. Balancing involves making alliances with other states to offset the growing power of a competitor. This allows for a better chance of success if war ensues (as you add the military power and resources of one's allies to your own). It also provides greater deterrence as states grouped together are a more formidable foe and their competitor(s) may decline to make an aggressive move, fearing defeat. On the other hand, states can bandwagon with their competitor, by coming into line with their wishes (give in, in other words), and thereby

Photo 6.3 Secretary Kerry shakes hands with Iranian Foreign Minister Zarif at the Iran nuclear talks in Vienna, 14 July 2015

Credit: US Department of State/Flickr

removing the threat of war. Liberals view stark choices such as this as remnants of a past world, now replaced by a world of 'complex interdependence' (Keohane and Nye 1977). This is a more optimistic world where states, and their fortunes, are bound together through a complex web of trade and the ever-growing rules and regulations developed by international organisations that act to constrain war and give us incentives to get along.

For liberals, there are tools available other than war to produce acceptable outcomes. Here, we can use the example of diplomacy between Iran and the United States, as part of a larger multilateral process between 2003 and 2015. When evidence leaked in 2002 that Iran was allegedly developing nuclear weapons, it came at the height of the US-led War on Terror, which was partly focused on so-called 'rogue states' that sought Weapons of Mass Destruction (WMDs). The United States had already invaded two of Iran's neighbours (Iraq and Afghanistan) and it seemed, based on US rhetoric, that Iran would also face invasion. Yet, war was avoided because diplomacy was pursued – ultimately culminating in a landmark 2015 agreement known as the Joint Comprehensive Plan of Action (JCPOA). Even though the United States and Iran later resumed a path of confrontation, watermarked by the arrival in office of the Trump administration in 2017, the power of diplomacy was still seen in this case to de-escalate a critical episode.

Liberals generally lamented the War on Terror as it saw the United States taking a unilateral posture. A war with Iran, and/or Iran's development of a nuclear weapon, would have thrown the world order into chaos for at least two reasons. Firstly, the United Nations' system of collective security – a pillar of the liberal account – would have been irreparably damaged as the United States had already ignored the will of the UN Security Council, which had *not* given prior approval for its invasion of Iraq in 2003. A second unilateral action by the world's only superpower would have swept the rug out from underneath any image of a world ruled by international law and left in its place a unipolar image that more resembled the 2004 parody movie *Team America*. Secondly, Iran's neighbours and competitors, such as Saudi Arabia, would have likely sought nuclear weapons to balance Iran's rising power. This would have set off a regional nuclear arms race and also damaged the Non-Proliferation Treaty – itself another hallmark of diplomacy.

Where realists would look at this case and see two competitors facing off against each other with Iran having the stark choice to balance or bandwagon, from a liberal vantage point the case shows how personal relationships were built during multiple years of negotiations and these helped transcend state rivalries. Wendy Sherman, the US lead negotiator, recalled how she and her Iranian counterpart, Abbas Araghchi, both became grandparents during their negotiations and shared videos of their grandchildren with each other. Personal relationships like this do not dissolve or change pre-set national interests on either side, but they were instrumental in both sides developing the resolve to work diplomatically. Similar relations were developed between officials at the highest level when they spent seventeen days locked in intense discussions in Vienna during the concluding phase – the longest continuous negotiations in history, featuring all foreign ministers of the permanent members of the UN Security Council. Following the announcement of the deal in front of the media (pictured in Photo 6.2), Sherman described the scene on the final day, when all the diplomatic personnel involved gathered together (pictured in Photo 6.3), as US Secretary of State John Kerry addressed the parties:

> Secretary Kerry was the last person to speak. He recounted that when he was 21 he went off to war in Vietnam. He made a commitment that he would do whatever he could in his life to make sure that there was never war, ever again. The room was absolutely still. There was quiet. And then everyone, including the Iranians, applauded. Because, I think for all of us we understood that what we had done was to try to ensure peace, not war. (Sherman 2016)

The diplomats laboured in the areas where agreement was possible and found a way to make it acceptable for both sides. For Iran this involved the removal of economic sanctions that had been sponsored by the United States and the removal of any direct military threat. For the Americans, the deal placed Iran under a strict regime of verification to ensure that it could not develop nuclear weapons, and if they appeared to be doing so there would be time to react before those weapons became a material threat. This result was a testament to the very principles that liberals espouse and brings us back to the analogy of how liberals see war as a bug in the system that can be bypassed with the right tools and understandings. The JCPOA and those aforementioned personal relationships, while damaged during the Trump years, offer a basis for future progress by proving that diplomacy can be a positive sum for both sides despite their ongoing enmity.

 CASE STUDY 6.2: Theorising the United Nations

Photo 6.4 Mahmoud Abbas (centre), President of the Palestinian Authority, with his delegation in the General Assembly, 29 November 2012

Credit: Stan Honda/AFP/Getty Images

From a theoretical point of view, the effectiveness and utility of the United Nations differs depending on which perspective we choose to adopt. Liberals tend to have faith in the capacity of international organisations, primarily the United Nations, to uphold the framework of global governance. Such organisations may not be perfect, but they help the world find alternatives to war through trade and diplomacy (among other things), which are staples of the liberal account. Realists, although they do not reject the United Nations completely, argue that states will eventually resort to war despite the efforts of international organisations, which have little real authority. Generally, realists believe that international organisations appear to be successful when they are working in the interests of powerful states. But, if that condition is reversed and an organisation becomes an obstacle to national interests, then the equation may change. This line of enquiry is often used by realists to help explain why the League of Nations was unsuccessful – failing to allow for Germany and Japan's expansionist desires in the 1930s, so both states left the League and invaded their neighbours.

On the other hand, constructivists see organisations like the United Nations as places where they can study the emergence of new norms and examine the activities of those who are spreading new ideas. If we can once more briefly recall the US decision to invade Iraq in

2003, constructivism would highlight that while it is true that a powerful state ignored the United Nations in pursuit of its own self-interest (as a realist would describe it), by doing so it violated the standard practices of international relations. To use constructivist language, the United States disregarded a 'norm' by invading Iraq illegally (in the eyes of international law) and even though there was no direct punishment, its behaviour was irregular and so would not be without consequence. Examining the difficulties the United States faced in its diplomatic relations after 2003, and the major shifts in its policymaking thereafter (including reluctantly, at first, joining multilateral discussions with Iran as mentioned earlier), gives considerable weight to this insight.

Constructivists study the emergence of norms at the United Nations, attempting to track and understand the process of how our world order is under constant change through the actions of individuals, groups and states pursuing different agendas. An example is Palestine, which is currently an observer state at the United Nations since it is not (yet) considered sovereign as it is presently part of the State of Israel. The United Nations does not have the power to rule otherwise by itself, nor do pro-Palestinian statehood activists and supporters who have been advocating for Palestinian secession from Israel for decades. To recall the benchmarks for sovereignty from Chapter two, Palestine has both internal and external challenges to its quest for statehood.

Looking deeper, this case allows us to consider the path that norms take and the importance of the United Nations as centre stage of that process. There are three steps in the 'norm lifecycle' (Finnemore and Sikkink 1998): *emergence*, *cascade* and *internalisation*. In the case of Palestine, we have seen norm emergence as the idea of statehood is clearly active as a project. We can also see the cascade as over two-thirds of the world's states have come to accept Palestinian statehood, causing a growing expectation for others to do the same. Importantly, this pressure is most visible in international arenas such as the United Nations. Despite this cascade, there are still powerful states who are resisting, most notably Israel and the United States. For Palestine to become a sovereign state it will need to overcome this resistance, allowing the norm to become internalised, and thereby complete the cycle. Should this occur, accepting Palestinian statehood would become an expected behaviour, one that became natural. When norms reach this stage, you can usually also recognise instruments/effects that serve to make them tangible. For example, if Palestine reaches statehood, we would see legal documents and physical elements agreed at the United Nations – such as internationally recognised borders – and material symbols of Palestine's existence (flags, nameplates, permanent staff etc.) permanently appearing alongside, and equal to, those of other states.

In this sense, constructivism adds layers to our understanding of how socially constructed elements of our system, such as sovereignty, works in practice. Of course, not all norms make it all the way to internalisation. Some come apart along the way if the case is not sufficiently well supported. So, it is unclear at this stage what lies ahead in Palestine's quest for statehood. What is clear is that constructivism gives us unique tools to detect, and to understand, this process as one that plays out internationally – with the United Nations centre stage. Additionally, it helps to lock in the realisation that all the features of our political world, including the existence of the United Nations itself, were once just an idea that subsequently went through the norm lifecycle and earned its place as a tangible part of our global system. It should also be clear that understanding this process is to understand that nothing political is forever, one day the United Nations itself may not exist if another idea supplants it. Ideas are always under contestation, development, debate and renewal.

Conclusion

This chapter has surveyed the traditional and middle ground approaches in International Relations theory, each of which possesses a legitimate, yet different, view of the world. Realism offers a pessimistic view of our world, while liberalism counters it with a more optimistic view. Constructivism and the English school offer a viable middle ground between – and beyond – the traditional approaches, arguing that the pessimist/optimist distinction is too restrictive. We hope that you see value in each of the theories covered so far and see that they provide the foundations for opening up ways to ask questions about International Relations. We also hope that you realise that it is not necessary to restrict yourself to a simple optimist/pessimist equation, nor is it necessary to adopt one theory as your own. The key is to understand theories as a toolkit that you can apply in your studies. Using a theory to gain insights into an issue, as this chapter did with the case studies of war and the United Nations, is to understand the reason why these theories exist – as a means by which to attempt to understand a complex world.

 END OF CHAPTER QUESTIONS

1. The traditional theories emerged many decades ago when the world was very different. In what ways do they still offer useful insights today?

2. Make a list/diagram of the key commonalities within realism, liberalism and constructivism. Consider how these elements form the basis of each theory family and make them distinct from one another.

3. Why do the traditional theories focus more on the system and state levels of analysis?

4. How is international anarchy characterised by middle ground theories such as the English school and constructivism?

5. Do you think warfare is a bug, or a feature, within the global system? How can you use International Relations theory to develop an answer?

CRITICAL THEORIES

Stephen McGlinchey, Rosie Walters and Dana Gold

Question: There are eight theoretical families within International Relations explored so far in this book, and many more beyond. Why do we need so many?

As our global system has grown in complexity, the family of theories that International Relations offers in response has grown in number. Recalling the previous chapter, a debate between realism and liberalism has been raging since the foundation of the discipline. We also learned that the English school attempted to open up a middle ground between these two duelling theory families, a trend that was expanded when constructivism emerged. While developments like these held court for much of the twentieth century, a growing number of voices began to enter the discipline expressing dissatisfaction with the range of possibilities that International Relations theory was offering. By the end of the Cold War in 1991 – and considering the resulting changes in world order – a range of theories emerged that were critical of the journey that International Relations had taken thus far. The uniting thread between these approaches was a perception that there was a need to examine alternative ways of ordering our world, and in doing so expose factors that the traditional theories have chosen to downplay or ignore. The critical approaches are to varying degrees 'revolutionary' in the sense that they seek material changes to the status quo. This chapter will deal with four of the most well-known critical theories – Marxism, feminism, postcolonialism and poststructuralism. To showcase the elasticity of the theory 'toolkit' approach, similar examples and case studies will be carried through from the previous chapter to show that any theory can be applied to any example and yield insights.

The evolution of theory

To help us understand why theoretical shifts take place we can refer to Thomas Kuhn's *The Structure of Scientific Revolutions* (1962). This book set the stage for understanding, in general, how and why certain theories are legitimised and widely accepted. Kuhn also identified the process that takes place when theories are no longer relevant and new theories emerge. For example, the vast majority of human beings were once convinced that the earth was flat. With the advancement of science and technology, there was a significant discovery that led humans to discard this belief. When such a discovery takes place, a 'paradigm shift' results and the former ways of thinking are replaced by new ones. Although changes in International Relations theory are not as dramatic as the example above, there have been significant evolutions in the discipline. This is important to keep in mind when we consider how theories play a role in explaining the world and how, based upon different time periods and our personal contexts, one approach may speak to us more than another.

Figure 7.1 Charting International Relations theory through a critical lens

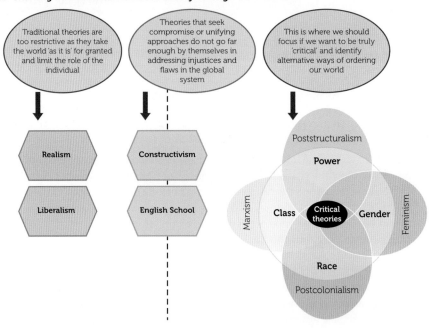

The critical theories often borrow from each other, or hybridise, making it harder to completely separate them. In practice, they are more representative of a Venn diagram – overlapping with each other in varying ways – than the relatively distinct theory families explored in the previous chapter. In addition, it is common for critical theories to incorporate, or develop, insights from constructivism.

When we discuss 'critical' approaches to International Relations theory, much as we did when we labelled the theories in the prior chapter 'traditional' and 'middle ground', we are using a simplifying device to refer to (and make sense of) a wide spectrum of theories that have been established. The theory families discussed in this chapter share one particular trait – they are critical of commonly held assumptions in the discipline that have been central since its establishment. To borrow a common distinction, the traditional theories are built on simply observing the world 'as it is' rather than reaching for images of the world as it 'ought to be' and putting many more variables and investigations on the theoretical map (see Figure 7.1).

For those with a critical approach, the altered circumstances of the global system since the end of the Cold War called for approaches that are better suited to understand, as well as question, the more complex world we find ourselves in. Such theories are valuable because they identify things that have typically been ignored or overlooked and also seek out ways to transform our world. In that sense, the critical approaches also generally reject middle ground approaches as they do not usually go far enough in providing a voice to individuals who have frequently been marginalised, particularly women and those from the Global South. The critical theories also typically reject positivism. Instead they build their theories with postpositivist and interpretivist approaches.

7.1 – KEY TERMS: Postpositivism and interpretivism

Postpositivism rejects the positivist approach that a researcher can be an independent observer of the social world. Postpositivists argue that the ideas, and even the particular identity, of a researcher influence what they observe and therefore have an impact upon what they conclude. Postpositivism pursues objective answers by attempting to recognise, and work with, such biases with the theories and knowledge that theorists develop.

Interpretivism (sometimes called 'anti-positivism') takes things yet further by arguing that objectivity is impossible. As an approach, this leads researchers to focus on gaining *subjective* knowledge through approaches where individuals, or smaller groups, are analysed in depth through detailed observations and discussions. This harnesses a broader framework of 'qualitative analysis' in which deeper sets of data are sought from smaller numbers of participants – such as through detailed interviews. This is a different approach to gathering data than the more positivist inclined 'quantitative analysis' where larger datasets are sought to gain broader insights – such as polls of hundreds or thousands of people asking them a small number of questions with only yes/no/maybe-type options for answers.

Marxism

Marxism is a good place to start with critical theories. It is a disparate theoretical family held together by one key point: the global system should be replaced. Therefore, Marxism is unabashedly a revolutionary theory. The theory is based upon the ideas of Karl Marx and consequently is the only theory of International Relations that is named after a person. Although Marx is a historical figure, his writings have lived on and inspired a modern vein of critical theories that relate directly to contemporary issues.

As Marx himself famously stated, philosophical writings typically only interpret the world rather than outline how to change it. Answering that call, Marxists today – and the wide range of critical theoretical families they inspire – are interested in understanding all the historical elements of today's global system. Taking that knowledge, which spans economic, political and social critique, they focus on how our global system empowers some groups (mainly the elite, or 'the 1 per cent') and simultaneously disempowers others (the everyday person, or 'the 99 per cent'). For this to change, the legitimacy of the state must be questioned and then it must be ultimately dissolved. In that sense, emancipation from the state in some form is the essence of the system change Marxists seek. Marxists believe that we are not *born free* – instead we need to *be freed* via the proliferation of revolutionary thinking that raises awareness of the injustices of the global system.

7.2 – KEY PEOPLE: *Karl Marx*

Photo 7.1 Karl Marx (1818–83)

Credit: Shawarsh/Wikimedia Commons

Karl Marx (1818–83) was a German intellectual who lived during the height of the industrial revolution in Europe. Based on his writings, the term 'Marxist' refers to individuals who believe that society is divided into two classes – the capitalist class of 'owners' (the bourgeoisie) and the working class (the proletariat). The proletariat are at the mercy of the bourgeoisie, who control their wages and therefore their standard of living. Marx hoped for an end to the class society and an overthrow of the bourgeoisie by the proletariat – whom he sought to inspire towards a communist revolution. Communism is a form of ordering society with (in principle) no private ownership, no rivalling political parties, and no hierarchies – such as class. Instead, an all-powerful state would ensure that all citizens would share more equal outcomes than they would in a capitalist society.

Inspired by Marx's ideas, many states worked towards adopting communism – most notably the Soviet Union, where the world's first successful communist revolution began in 1917. But, in the Soviet Union (and elsewhere) the system failed to work economically and succumbed to systematic political corruption (see Courtois et al. 1997 and the 2019 *Chernobyl* television miniseries). As a result, there are only a handful of communist countries left today. Those that do remain, such as China and Vietnam, are communist in name only and use a hybrid form of government that allows for capitalism and private ownership while holding on to communism's authoritarian political elements such as a one-party political system and tight controls over the flow of information. Such restrictive features of communist systems led to the mirror-image description of Western states in the Cold War as the 'free world' due to widespread features in the 'First World' such as multi-party electoral systems and a free press. Marxist theorists today argue that, contrary to the image of capitalism (which is now global) as a free world, the dominance of the nation-state in the post-Cold War system has led to ordinary people around the globe becoming divided and alienated, instead of recognising what they all have in common as a global proletariat.

This critique, and dismissal, of the central unit of International Relations – the nation-state – is what makes Marxism so relevant as the major underpinning critical theory. The traditional theories take a world of nation-states as a given and therefore fail to envision what a global order would look like if formulated differently. Worse, by taking the state for granted, there is little or no incentive to critique the role of the state and the negative effects it has. For example, the state has a monopoly on warfare, deciding how and when to conquer territory or kill another state's citizens. It also has the exclusive right to tax people, decide what 'the law' is and to demand allegiance from its citizens under penalties that range from fines, to imprisonment, to death. In addition, states partake in, and therefore legitimise, globalised capitalist trade systems that have led to ever-growing inequalities across the world. The rich seem to get richer, while the bulk of humanity remains exploited. Marxists believe this is a corrupt arrangement, and it is only with the dissolution of states from the world map that humankind will free itself of the chains of domination and inequality.

As the global system grew through the twentieth century to incorporate powerful international organisations in addition to states, such as the United Nations, Marxists saw further problems. In particular, Marxists view the globalisation project of the 1990s onwards as one that legitimised and locked in the very patterns of inequality that Marx had exposed more than a century earlier. This is because the United Nations, and the other organisations associated with it, only represent states, not people. To Marxists, the supposed grand projects within the United Nations – such as the establishment of human rights – are no more than band aids over a deeper corruption that has become all-encompassing.

It must be noted that modern Marxism does not have one clear idea of what a stateless world would look like. This is all the more complex as prior experiments with variants of Marx's own solution, communism, gradually fell apart in each of approximately twenty-five states in which it was tried during the twentieth century. Therefore, while the course of history and human experience has muted communism as a viable system, it did not kill Marx's longevity as the source of a body of work that provides the bedrock for critiquing the modern global system. In other words, the real-world failures of communism as a viable political and economic system did not take away from the vitality of Marx's theoretical critique that power is not fairly distributed.

Postcolonialism

Postcolonialism differs from Marxism by focusing its critique on the inequality between states or regions, as opposed to classes. The effects of colonialism are still felt in many regions of the world today as local populations continue to deal with the challenges created and left behind by the former colonial powers. Postcolonialism's origins can be traced to the Cold War period when much international activity centred around decolonisation and the ambition to undo the legacies of European imperialism. With the independence movements of the twentieth century, the peoples of the Global South rebelled 'against the false belief that providence created some to be menials of others' (Nkrumah 1963, ix). Central to postcolonial scholarship is the idea that the prejudices, biases, ideas and understandings that made colonialism possible in the first place did not disappear overnight with the granting of independence to former colonies. For centuries, Europeans believed they were best placed to rule the world, as was outlined in Chapter three. While they may have been forced to renounce most of their territorial claims, Western states are far from treating the former colonies as their equals – despite what the principle of sovereignty asserts. Postcolonial theory offers a way to identify these 'neocolonial' practices that create and then reproduce global inequalities.

For postcolonial scholars, an important endeavour is to highlight the colonial legacies that created current inequalities and the neocolonial power structures that reproduce them. Take, for example, a dominant image in the West of the continent of Africa as a place in need of financial aid, a moral burden, a drain on resources. Yet, Africa is also a place of great wealth and resources that have consistently been extracted (taken) by outsiders (see Box 7.3). Underlining the postcolonial critique further, while they may no longer be under direct colonial control, two-thirds of the world's poor live in states that

7.3 – KEY TERMS: Neocolonialism

From the sixteenth to the nineteenth centuries, Europeans enslaved millions of Africans, transporting them to the Americas to work on plantations. Millions died during the journey or as a result of brutal conditions when they arrived. When the transatlantic slave trade ended in the early 1800s, Europeans still needed raw materials to fuel their own economies. So instead of transporting Africans to work on plantations in the Americas, they brought the plantations to the newly colonised territories of Africa. Before colonisation, many African communities focused their agricultural efforts on subsistence – growing what was needed to survive. Under colonialism, however, African economies were restructured to focus on minerals and cash crops (such as precious metals, cocoa, cotton and coffee) that could be exported. Colonising powers created vast cash crop plantations and introduced punishing taxes on households so that those Africans that were unable to pay them were forced to find waged labour on the plantations or in mines.

Such fundamental structuring of economies – and the historical experiences of being colonised – cannot be undone overnight. As a result, many of the poorest states in Africa, while now independent, remain deeply conditioned by their past and subject to indirect means of influence and control, such as unequal global trading practices and the political power of large corporations. Postcolonialism gives us the theoretical toolkit to make a case that while the Global North (or what can also be referred to as 'the West') may often criticise developing states for their economic failures, the enduring legacy of colonialism and new forms of control – neocolonialism – are often much to blame.

are rich in natural resources. One of the main reasons for this is that cash crops and valuable minerals are still extracted and exported to the Global North – now by transnational corporations instead of colonial governments. Struggling economies of the Global South compete to attract transnational corporations for the employment and revenues they will bring. Yet in order to do so, they join a 'race to the bottom', pitting countries against one another for who can offer the lowest taxes and cheapest labour and thus the greatest profits.

Take, for example, Ghana, home to the so-called 'Gold Coast', rich in minerals and petroleum. Between 2004 and 2008, mineral exports from Ghana increased by 50 per cent and yet during that period its tax revenues from mining actually decreased (Besada, Lisk and Martin 2015). If a state increases its taxes on a corporation (thereby reducing its net profits), there is the danger that it will just move its business elsewhere – leaving thousands unemployed. The same structural scenario leads to a lack of incentive to fully regulate and monitor tax compliance and payments – which provides a fertile ground for tax evasion and corruption. One study found that the amount of money that leaves Africa each year through illicit tax practices by corporations based in the West is nearly three times the total amount of aid and grants the continent receives (Global Justice Now 2017). Another study shows that in 2010 alone, states of the Global South lost over US$1 trillion to illicit financial practices, mostly in the form of tax evasion (Hickel 2014). This discussion suggests that the exploitation of the Global South did not end with independence, it just took on different forms.

7.4 – KEY PEOPLE: Edward Said

Photo 7.2 Edward Said (1935–2003)

Credit: Bettmann/Getty Images

Edward Said's *Orientalism* (1978) explores how representations in poetry, literature, philosophy and political theory of the 'Orient' – predominantly North Africa, the Middle East and Asia – constructed it as a place waiting for Western exploration and domination. Said documented how the East was constructed by the West as an exotic and enchanting place, full of religious fanaticism, despotic leaders, irrational men and beautiful but oppressed women who could not speak for themselves. It was represented in a way that always implied an unfavourable comparison to the West, which was assumed to be a place of rationality and reason, Christianity and secularism, democracy and enlightenment. Said argued that these representations became dominant and it became almost impossible to think or speak outside of them.

Key works in postcolonialism have explored how representations of the Global South have fuelled imperialism by analysing enduring orientalism in Western discourse. For example, in Western depictions of the War on Terror, the depiction of the Eastern woman as a passive victim in need of rescue was used as part of the justification for certain interventions. This can be seen when US First Lady Laura Bush claimed that the War on Terror was 'a fight for the rights and dignity of women'. Orientalism divides the world into 'West versus East, us versus Muslims, cultures in which First Ladies give speeches versus others where women shuffle around silently in burqas' (Abu-Lughod 2002, 784); a world of 'white men saving brown women from brown men', as Spivak (1985) once put it.

In colonial times, Orientalist representations were made possible by the West's exploration into, and domination over, the Orient. They also made continuing exploration and domination possible by constructing the Orient in the Western imagination as a barbaric place in need of 'civilisation'. Present-day Orientalism is made possible by the cultural and political dominance of the West, and it makes possible continuing military intervention in the Middle East, in regions that are not seen as capable of governing themselves and protecting their own citizens – especially women – and are seen as a threat to the West. This is a crucial point in postcolonialism: that representations of former colonies can tell us much more about the West's power over them than they can about the societies themselves. Orientalism leads to the assumption that the West knows best and that any intervention by the West in the East will be not only benevolent, but also beneficial. Of course, as the example of Iraq shows – a state that has been marred by instability since the US-led invasions in 1991 and 2003 – this can often be far from true.

Postcolonialism therefore laments that the discipline has historically been dominated by flawed perspectives, principally written by white Western scholars and published in the English language. It challenges International Relations to reflect on the kinds of knowledge this produces. It shows that scholarship produced in the West that does not challenge centuries-old Western assumptions about the 'other' is in danger not only of failing to recognise the historical legacies of colonialism that influence current inequalities, but also of actually reproducing those inequalities. Postcolonial scholars are, therefore, important contributors to the field as their critique widens the focus of enquiry beyond International Relations' traditionally Western mindset and reflects the more diverse perspectives of our world.

Feminism

Another theory that critiques the inequality inherent in the global system is feminism. Feminism entered the field in the 1980s as part of the emerging movement critiquing the traditional theories. It focused on explaining why so few women seemed to be in positions of power and examining the implications of this on how international relations were structured. Recognising this introduces a 'gendered' reading of International Relations, where we place gender as the prime object in focus.

Photo 7.3 Leaders pose for a photo at the G20 Summit in Osaka, 28 June 2019

Credit: Brendan Smialowski/AFP/Getty Images

You only need look at a visual of any meeting of world leaders to see how it appears to be a man's world. The G20 represents the bulk of the world's people and economic activity through its membership of nineteen powerful states, plus the European Union. Yet, when embodied as a photograph of thirty-eight high-ranking officials taken in 2019, only *three* of the participants were female.

Once we have answered the question of where the women are (certainly not in political power relative to men) feminism will invite a deeper question that asks us to consider how we can reconstruct international relations so it can account for the experiences of all people. For some feminists this can be achieved by adding women to areas where they have been excluded, for example, all-women candidate lists in elections to ensure more women are elected, and some governments having gender-balanced cabinets. Developments like these, while a sign of progress, are often felt to not be enough to address what feminists refer to as a patriarchal culture – the male-driven environment that created such things as politics (and business) and led to the structural exclusion of women in the first place. In this sense, it is not men that are the problem per se, but a certain manifestation of the male gender that has enabled a distorted political and economic system to emerge across the world.

There are various different branches of feminism that each frame gender in different ways and place a greater emphasis on certain inequalities. Examples of early liberal feminists include nineteenth-century campaigners such as Mary Wollstonecraft and Harriet Taylor Mill and the early-twentieth-century suffragette movement, which used activism and civil disobedience to campaign for women's rights to vote in the United Kingdom (which was passed into law in 1928), and in doing so inspired movements elsewhere. Contemporary liberal feminists prioritise issues such as equal representation in political office, equal representation in corporate governance and equal pay – arguing that these will help to catalyse wider change. Marxist feminists, by contrast, are interested in how current economic and political structures depend on, exploit and undervalue women's labour, both in factories and workplaces and in the home. For example, Cynthia Enloe (1989) wrote about how women's labour is exploited everywhere from banana plantations, to military bases, to tourist beaches, and is essential to the global economy. Postcolonial feminists are interested in how new forms of colonialism impact women of the Global South. For example, Chandra Talpade Mohanty (1988) argues that white Western feminists frequently reproduce colonial discourses of rescue towards women of the Global South, as already explored above in the section on postcolonialism. Poststructuralist feminists are interested in how our understandings of what it is to be a man, or a woman, shape the different roles we are able to take on in the world and the very structures of power that govern us. Carol Cohn (1987), for example, analysed how sexist and sexualised language used by US defence intellectuals to describe nuclear weapons masks the potential atrocities these weapons could cause and even makes them seem desirable.

To bring our discussion of feminism back to its familial roots, whatever variant it may take, feminism at its core unites to challenge International Relations to reflect on its historical dominance by men and the exclusion, until recently, of the experiences, perspectives and qualities of women. Sometimes this is as explicit as the language used in many of the discipline's foundational texts, which refer to 'man' to describe all of humankind (mankind). It can also be seen in the qualities that traditional theories, especially realism, put forward as universal truths about the nature of 'man' – rational, calculating and aggressive to name a few – which have historically been perceived as masculine qualities in almost every culture in the world. Feminists ask why these have been valued above supposedly feminine ones such as emotion, compassion and pacifism – which are equally 'human' in their nature. Of course, most feminists would argue that these are not inherently masculine or feminine qualities, but rather that (to borrow constructivist terminology) they have been socially constructed as such for centuries.

The crucial point here is that only the qualities deemed to be masculine have been taken to be relevant to theorising about human nature and statecraft in the traditional theory families. This results in theories, such as realism, which not only ignore the experiences of large parts of the population, but also become self-fulfilling prophecies as they create the aggressive, competitive political system that they claim to be describing. As V. Spike Peterson (1992) argues, as long as gender remains 'invisible' it may be unclear what 'taking gender seriously' means. Ideas about what it means to be a man or a woman – the social construction of gender – permeate every aspect of international politics and of our daily lives. In seeking to understand how and why that happens, and with what effects, feminism hopes to make the world a fairer place for everyone. Here, you might again see some overlaps – with constructivism in this case, for example (see Figure 7.1).

Poststructuralism

Poststructuralism is perhaps the most controversial of the critical theories as it questions the very beliefs we have all come to know and feel as being 'real'. Poststructuralists do this by critiquing the dominant narratives that have been widely accepted by other theories. These, they believe, have evolved into *metanarratives* – complex accounts explaining how the world works that are unquestioned by most people, but are really just convincing stories created by those in power. For instance, liberals and realists both accept the idea of the state and for the most part take it for granted. Such assumptions are foundational 'truths' on which those traditional theories rest – becoming 'structures' (or metanarratives) around which they build their account of reality. So, although these two theoretical families may seem to be in opposition, they actually share a general understanding of the world. Neither realism nor liberalism in their modern forms seek to challenge the existence of the state nor attempt to think beyond it – they simply count it as part of their reality. Poststructuralism seeks to question these commonly held assumptions of reality that are taken for granted, such as the state – but also more widely the nature of power.

Jacques Derrida's contribution in this area was in how he showed that you could deconstruct language to identify deeper, or alternative, meanings in texts. If you can deconstruct language (expose its hidden meanings and the power it has), then you can do the same with fundamental ideas that shape international relations – such as the state. By introducing doubt over why the state exists, and who it exists for, poststructuralists unlock questions about central components of our political world that traditional theories would rather avoid. If you can shake the foundations of a structure, be that a word or an idea, you can move beyond it in your thinking and become free of the power it has over you. This approach introduces doubt to the reality we assume to share and exposes the often thin foundations that some commonly held 'truths' stand upon as we live in a world of metanarratives that can each be dissected, if so desired.

You might ask why someone would want to do such a thing, and for that we can turn to Michel Foucault. Through the 1960s to 1980s he wrote prolifically about the idea that power and knowledge are mutually constitutive – that is, they create and reinforce one another. Within societies, only some groups of people – elites such as politicians, journalists and academic experts – have the power to shape our common understandings of a particular subject. And those common understandings in society come to influence how we act on any given issue, who we trust as an expert on it and who we choose to govern us, thus reinforcing the positions of power of those elites. You might (again) be seeing some overlaps here, this time with Marxism – for example via the idea of how elites control society – but poststructuralists take critiques such as this to a deeper level and reach results that go beyond the critique found in Marxism.

7.5 – KEY TERMS: Discourse

For poststructuralists, supposedly common-sense understandings about a subject or cause do not simply describe the world around us – they reflect the power relations within it. And they also help to shape it. This is labelled as 'discourse'. The classic example is how language is used to give legitimacy to certain actions and to delegitimise others. We can see this in the labelling of somebody using violence for a political cause as either a 'terrorist' or a 'freedom fighter'. That labelling is almost always done by those in a position of power and it has profound consequences for the actions taken in relation to that person. For example, the labels of 'terrorist' or 'freedom fighter' don't simply describe a person, but instead reflect assumptions about a person's politics, the cause they are fighting for, the threat they pose to society and the supposed justification of the means they are using. Those assumptions are shaped by how we view other peoples, cultures, religions, ideologies and so on. And they can change with time and place. Many civil rights campaigners who are now celebrated were labelled terrorists in earlier times. An example of this would be Nelson Mandela, who became South Africa's first Black president in 1994. However, he had previously spent twenty-seven years in prison after being convicted of revolutionary acts of sabotage through his organised efforts against apartheid – an authoritarian system that governed South Africa via a system of anti-Black racial segregation from 1948 until the early 1990s.

Discourses – our shared understandings – shape how we as a society respond to issues. For example, da Silva and Crilley (2017) analysed comments on newspaper websites and social media by British people discussing the choice of some British citizens to travel to Syria and join Islamic State. They concluded that the majority of people posting believed foreign fighters were motivated primarily by religion and had been brainwashed into unwavering support for a violent ideology. Perhaps unsurprisingly, then, the most popular prescriptions for how the UK government should respond to these fighters were to revoke their passports and criminally punish them. Poststructuralists recognise this as evidence of a particular discourse that had become dominant in a society – in this case displaying an understanding of terrorists as being irrational and unable to be reasoned with. While that may be true in some cases, perhaps some of these foreign fighters were motivated by more complex causes such as disillusionment with British foreign policy in the Middle East, Islamophobia in the UK, unemployment, poverty, functional illiteracy, or boredom. Research suggests that media coverage of measures such as harsh legal punishments and revocation of passports only serve to deepen the feelings of exclusion, the very feelings that can make somebody vulnerable to radicalisation (Lister 2015).

Poststructuralism does not focus on ethical judgements about issues such as terrorism. Instead, it shows how dominant discourses close down the options available in responding to such issues. For example, the understanding of terrorists as irrational rules out any possibility of their rehabilitation and reintegration into society through efforts to better understand the causes of their radicalisation. This not only leads to lost human potential, but also to a more violent world as only military and security measures seem like rational responses to terrorism and these in turn exacerbate many of the causes of radicalisation. In turn, these measures enhance the power of the state by giving it yet more power over the individual in the name of counterterrorism.

For poststructuralists, we can never experience anything outside discourse – that is through shared understandings that dominate our societies. As poststructuralists seek to question universal truths and metanarratives, the core of their theory is to actively choose *not* to take ideas as we know them for granted, nor to see certain paths of action as inevitable. Above all, poststructuralism encourages us to question how those in positions of power frame a particular issue and how doing so might serve to represent their interests and to shore up that position of power. Again, you may see some overlap here with the other theories in this chapter, such as feminism and postcolonialism. In fact, all of the theories discussed in this chapter explore in one way or another how power operates in international relations to oppress certain peoples.

 CASE STUDY 7.1: Postcolonialism, feminism and the United Nations

Photo 7.4 Female soldiers from Rapid Action Force on 18 January 2007, ahead of their departure to Liberia on a UN Peacekeeping mission – the first UN-deployed all-female unit

Credit: RAVEENDRAN/AFP/Getty Images

Whereas most media and general coverage of the United Nations paints it as a well-intentioned international organisation, critical theories (as their description would suggest) offer a more nuanced take. Postcolonial scholarship allows us to focus on the UN Security Council – the most powerful organ of the United Nations where five permanent (P5) members sit, each of which has a permanent veto over anything tabled there. These five states are China, Russia, the United Kingdom, the United States and France – the nations that were (in their 1940s configurations) allied against Nazi Germany, Imperial Japan and the other Axis powers in the Second World War. Because these nations were victorious in the world's last major war, they were able to give themselves permanent seats in the post-war order that still endures today, of which the UN Security Council is a central element. Postcolonial scholarship points out that all the P5 states were former colonial powers (though to very different extents) and through the design of their veto can continue to wield

disproportionate power in the modern era. To further underline the structural problems at the heart of the United Nations, there are no states from Africa or Latin America permanently on the Security Council. This serves to implicitly, and sometimes explicitly, restrict Global South initiatives.

If we dig a bit deeper using feminism, we can see more critiques of the United Nations – but also acknowledge certain successes. A central issue with the United Nations is that, by itself, it has very little power or money. Both of those resources come from the goodwill and participation of the member states. As explored in the previous chapter, the United Nations is governed around the principle of sovereign equality where the ultimate decision-making rests with states – especially the P5. Essentially, nothing transformative can occur at the UN level without the approval of historically powerful states. This is the issue for many feminists, who believe that international organisations such as the United Nations should do more to raise awareness and push for change, especially in areas of gender inequality. But sovereignty raises barriers to progress.

For example, the World Economic Forum's Global Gender Gap Report of 2020 noted that worldwide gender parity was a century away, despite meaningful progress in landmark issues such as extreme poverty and maternal mortality. One of the most known nation-state offenders in the gender inequality category is Saudi Arabia, which, despite progress in recent years, continues to treat women within its society in ways that are deeply unequal. It was ranked 146th out of 153 states measured in the aforementioned report – amongst the worst. In Saudi Arabia women do not have equal voting or civil rights, undergo various forms of social segregation (including dress codes) and were only given the right to drive in 2017 after a lengthy campaign (Photo 7.5). Yet Saudi Arabia does not receive sanctions for this behaviour. Instead, in 2017 and 2018 Saudi Arabia was elected to positions on three principal women's rights bodies within the United Nations – including the Committee on the Elimination of Discrimination against Women (CEDAW). The irony of this is not lost on feminists and points to the deep structural gender inequities visible within international organisations such as the United Nations, and the thinly veiled patriarchal nature of their day-to-day operations.

The United Nations is not deaf to examples such as those above and has worked towards improving life for women across the world – and this is the point where the mixed picture becomes clearer. Feminists often harness the platforms available through the United Nations and secure progress that would not be possible without the playing field made available by international organisations. Perhaps the best example of this came in October 2000, when the UN Security Council adopted Resolution 1325 – a landmark in emphasising the value of equal participation of women, as well as their increasing involvement in the promotion and maintenance of peace and security. Furthermore, it recognised the disproportionate impact of conflict on women. The United Nations subsequently created several specialised groups, such as the Task Force on Women, Peace and Security, as well as the Task Force on Violence Against Women, to uphold its commitment to the protection of women's rights. Additionally, the United Nations has also provided women in impoverished countries with more access to resources and opportunities they would otherwise not have, for example through the UN Girls' Education Initiative. Further, a large number of the United Nations' Sustainable Development Goals (explored further in Chapters seventeen and eighteen) target issues pivotal to women in ways that are designed to be more nuanced in order to overcome some of the ineffective application of prior efforts, which tended to help some women more than others.

As with many things at the international level, progress in one area is often simultaneous with a perceived lack of progress in others. Despite efforts of the United Nations to push for more global gender equality, feminist scholars such as Tickner (2005) have argued that women suffer from discrimination that means they are still not being taken seriously at both an institutional and grassroots level. It is hard to read the case of Saudi Arabia vis-à-vis the United Nations as evidence of this changing. Discrimination and inequality for women remains, particularly in states that may be suffering from poverty, war or deprivation. And, when António Guterres became UN Secretary General in 2017, he continued an unbroken run of male leadership going back to the founding of the organisation in 1945.

As a result, and despite progress, feminists remain watchful over the United Nations and critical of its ability to achieve the results needed. A continued negative gendered perspective within the functioning of the organisation serves to slow or hinder structural change for women around the world. The critique seems to have caught on and Guterres (2020) has made commitments towards using his leadership to make this 'the century of women's equality'.

Photo 7.5 The logo of the Support Women to Drive movement

Credit: Women2drive/Wikimedia Commons

CASE STUDY 7.2: Marxism, poststructuralism and warfare

Photo 7.6 South Korean conservative activists during a rally denouncing North Korea's hydrogen bomb test, Seoul, 7 January 2016

Credit: JUNG YEON-JE/AFP/Getty Images

Marxists believe that war is one of the many tools utilised by capitalists to ensure their power persists by maintaining the status quo in a world where rich states continue to dominate the weak. For example, Marxists would argue that the United States-led invasion of Iraq in 2003 was a disguised attempt to control Iraq through the economic seizure and exploitation of its oil. Under US President George W. Bush, the United States invaded Iraq under the justification of searching for weapons of mass destruction as part of the US-led War on Terror. However, despite no such weapons being discovered, the United States remained militarily deployed in Iraq until 2020 when discussions finally began with the Iraqi government over their withdrawal.

Marxists would point to this situation as evidence of the often thinly veiled/hiding in plain sight motivations for war – which are typically for economic or political exploitation. Indeed, the original name for the 2003 war was touted to be *Operation Iraqi Liberation*, until it was quickly changed to *Operation Enduring Freedom*. You may not have spotted the relevance at first glance but abbreviating the former spells OIL. Some have dismissed this as an erroneous slip of the tongue by US Press Secretary, Ari Fleischer (2003), who used that phrase in a press conference at the height of the invasion. Yet, for Marxists, such things more likely represent a brief glimpse behind the veil,

highlighting the lack of accountability the elite feel towards legitimately explaining their actions to the general public.

While the above 'OIL' example may seem trivial, when added to other examples from the Iraq war it comes to embody the core of the Marxist critique. Often cited here is the awarding of substantial contracts to Haliburton (Rosenbaum 2004) for reconstruction and oil extraction in Iraq. Haliburton was the company of which Vice President Dick Cheney had been Chairman and CEO prior to taking office. Additionally, the following quote by a speechwriter for President Bush is instructive:

> The United States has been drawn into an ambitious campaign to undo and recreate the repressive and intolerant Middle Eastern status quo … If successful, this campaign will bring new freedom and new stability to the most vicious and violent quadrant of the earth – and new prosperity to us all, by securing the world's largest pool of oil. (Frum 2003, 282)

The idea behind statements such as this glorifies the capitalists of the West as agents capable of change in world politics whilst non-Western states – like Iraq – lack agency and are therefore prey to having their sovereignty violated and their regime 'recreated'. Such a world is, to Marxists, unethical and unequal – as is a system that allows such behaviour to go on without meaningful sanction or reprisal for aggressor nations like the United States and its allies.

Moving beyond Iraq and Marxism, nuclear weapons are a major component of warfare in the contemporary era. As explored in Chapter two, they have changed the equation when it comes to warfare, giving civilisation-ending power to those who wield them. Yet, only a small number of states have developed these devastating weapons. Addressing this very point, poststructuralism raises an important critique that further allows us to apply our theoretical toolkit to the issue of warfare.

Political leaders and publics are (mostly) content to tolerate quantities of nuclear weapons that could destroy the entire planet many times over, as long as they are in the hands of themselves or their allies (Hansen 2016). In the hands of enemies, however, even the capacity to possibly start developing a small number of nuclear weapons could be seen as reason for panic and action. The weapons undoubtedly exist and have very real destructive capabilities regardless of who holds them. However, from a poststructuralist perspective, discourse is key to how we understand them and act on them. If we live in a society with many such weapons, the dominant discourse may be that 'we' would never actually use them unless attacked, that 'we' are humane and peaceful, and these weapons may serve our peaceful cause by deterring other states from attacking 'us'. By contrast, if 'they' – that is a state that is not a trusted ally – start developing the capacity to make nuclear weapons, we may well perceive that as an act of aggression.

This can be seen in the examples of Iran and North Korea, both of which have pursued nuclear programmes in recent decades and faced resistance from the international community for doing so, including being referred to as 'pariah' or 'rogue' states – amongst other such descriptors. Despite material differences in their regimes, both share in common an antipathy towards what they perceive as Western dominance of the global system. They are thereby portrayed as untrustworthy and unfit stewards of nuclear weapons, despite the fact that the United States is the only nation to have actually used them in combat, neatly underlining the 'us' and 'them' hypocrisy that poststructuralists point out.

Conclusion

There are many more theory families in International Relations than the ones explored in this chapter and in Chapter six (see McGlinchey, Walters and Scheinpflug 2017). Yet, the theories covered in this book so far offer a solid starting point for achieving an understanding of where the most common approaches are situated and what they bring to International Relations. It is fair to say that the critical theories are usually regarded by students as more difficult to grasp than the traditional and middle ground theories. However, this is a reflection of the fact that today's world is much more complex than at any time prior and so we need more complex tools to deal with this. The critical theories open up the intellectual space to think about things like gender, class, race and power and in doing so explore the possibility of alternative world orders. Each of the theories explored in this chapter has put such issues on their theoretical maps for good reasons, and the result is that the discipline has become more holistic and more inclusive. So, while International Relations may have started its journey in the early twentieth century as a fairly limited discipline with only two operational theory families, it went into the twenty-first century much transformed.

END OF CHAPTER QUESTIONS

1. Using examples of international issues you feel are important, examine some of the ways the critical theories can be seen to overlap.

2. What is required in order to make international organisations, such as the United Nations, more inclusive or diverse in terms of class, power, gender and race?

3. Should International Relations theorists be focused on revolutionary and/or activist thinking about how the world 'ought to be', or should they be more focused on analysing the world 'as it is'?

4. Read through some of today's headlines on a news app/website or in a newspaper. Then, go back over the idea of 'discourse' as explored in the chapter. Read the same headlines a second time and consider how your impressions of those headlines may have changed.

5. What do the critical theories add to our understanding of the issue of warfare?

GLOBAL STRUCTURES

Although the global system has three key actors (nation-states, international organisations and individuals), too often International Relations has overly focused on the nation-state due to its prominence. In the second part of the book, we address this by exploring other structures that are intertwined throughout the global system that bring to the fore its non-state components. This is a more complex journey that unpacks the wide category of international organisations by exploring global civil society, international law and the importance of economics. Also, we explore culture, religion, gender and sexuality – which deepens our understanding of individuals, and groups, and some of the things that motivate them.

INTERNATIONAL ORGANISATIONS

Shazelina Z. Abidin

Question: In what ways do international organisations challenge, and complement, the power of nation-states?

An international organisation is an umbrella term that encompasses a broad range of organisations with an international flavour. Strictly speaking, it is an organisation that should have at least three members, has some sort of fixed membership, is governed by a set of rules or agreements, and has some kind of formal structure or routine by which it works. The organisation may be one of states (an intergovernmental organisation), or an organisation composed of other non-state groups that work internationally (an international non-governmental organisation), or an organisation composed of a mix of state and non-state groups (a hybrid organisation). International organisations increasingly complement – and sometimes challenge – the power of nation-states in the global system. For example, let us imagine stepping off a plane into a foreign country. As you disembark you switch on your phone to check your messages. You follow the sign that directs you to immigration, and then pick up your luggage at the designated carousel. You then walk through the 'nothing to declare' green lane to exit the airport. Those actions would have already brought you into contact with the work of at least four different international organisations. The aircraft that you arrived in would have been one of the many planes under the International Air Transport Association and regulated by standards set by the International Civil Aviation Organization; that you were able to use your phone would have been courtesy of the work of the International Telecommunication Union; and your customs clearance would have been aided by the Kyoto Convention set by the World Customs Organization. This is but a snapshot underlining that it is increasingly difficult to imagine a world in which states are the only actors that matter.

Intergovernmental organisations

An intergovernmental organisation (IGO) is an organisation with a membership of states only. The organisation is usually founded upon a treaty, or a multilateral agreement, and consists of more than two states. Member states determine the way in which the organisation is run, vote within the organisation and provide its funding. The United Nations (UN) is the prime example of an intergovernmental organisation thanks to its almost universal membership. Only states can be members of the United Nations and membership is valued because it confers upon the member state formal recognition of its sovereignty. There are currently 193 member states – but it is important to note that a small number of 'states' exist that are not members. Taiwan, for example, has repeatedly requested membership but has had its request blocked by China because it regards Taiwan as a part of its territory and does not recognise it as a legitimate state. Taiwan, of course, wants UN membership because this will mean that the international community fully accepts its sovereignty and can gain all the privileges that this would entail – principally protection (via international law) from any future Chinese attempt to take (back) control of it. The Taiwan example has gone unresolved for decades due to the major role that China plays within the United Nations as one of its most powerful members, yet it serves to illustrate the importance of sovereignty and the access it brings – in this case as the price of entry for membership of the world's premier organisation.

8.1 – KEY INSIGHTS: The six main organs of the United Nations

Photo 8.1 The Headquarters of the United Nations, New York

Credit: Steve Cadman/Flickr

Photo 8.2 The UN General Assembly

Credit: Patrick Gruban/Flickr

Photo 8.3 The UN Security Council

Credit: Neptuul/Wikimedia Commons

1. **The General Assembly** (Photo 8.2)

The main deliberative organ of the United Nations, composed of representatives from all 193 member states, each of which has one vote.

2. **The Security Council** (Photo 8.3)

Has primary responsibility for international peace and security. It has fifteen members, five of which – China, France, Russia, the United Kingdom and the United States – are permanent members who also hold veto power. The other ten are voted in by the General Assembly for two-year tenures. Under the UN Charter, all member states must comply with Security Council decisions.

3. **The Economic and Social Council**

Facilitates discussion and policy recommendations for the world's economic, social and environmental challenges.

4. **The Trusteeship Council**

This was established to supervise the transition to self-government or independence for a range of 'trust territories' mostly taken from defeated states during the Second World War. This work was completed in 1994 and the Council now only exists on paper.

5. **The International Court of Justice**

Located in the Hague, Netherlands, the Court is charged with settling legal disputes between states and giving legal advice to the United Nations and its agencies. Not to be confused with the International Criminal Court, which is an independent judicial body that prosecutes individuals – not states – for international crimes.

6. **The Secretariat**

Consists of staff drawn from around the world carrying out the work of the United Nations. The Secretariat services the above organs and administers the programmes and policies established by them. Staff are dispersed in multiple locations and offices around the world.

Of the six main organs of the United Nations, the General Assembly is the most democratic as each state gets one vote, no matter how big or small, rich or poor. It is also the place where, every September, world leaders give their address to the international community from behind a dark green podium with the UN crest clearly visible. The most powerful organ is the Security Council, which can impose sanctions on states or deploy military forces on behalf of the international community to keep the peace in a certain area, region or state. The United Nations itself does not have its own military force, but it can muster military and police personnel through contributions by its members.

In order to be inclusive, the United Nations has welcomed the participation (though not membership) of non-state civil society groups during some of its meetings, but never at the closed-door sessions of the all-important Security Council. From time to time, organisations are invited to give an address to the Security Council during the thematic debates that are held on their particular topic. These are in layperson's terms 'hearings', where each speaker presents a prepared text in turn. The real work of the Security Council is at the 'informals', where member states negotiate in earnest on a draft resolution that will later be tabled and circulated but not open for discussion to those outside the Security Council. This is why there are those who argue that the Security Council is unrepresentative, even perhaps elitist, as any resolution that is adopted by those fifteen states in the Security Council are binding upon all 193 member states of the United Nations. The first time that the Security Council consulted officially with another organisation was in 2007, when it decided to bring on board the African Union Peace and Security Council as a consultative partner due to the extent of security issues in Africa.

Organisations may speak as observers to the General Assembly, or as organisations with 'consultative status' with the Economic and Social Council, for example. There are civil society organisations on all issues, ranging from disarmament to oceanic noise pollution, and from mental health to refugees. We explore the actions of civil society organisations further in Chapter nine. There are also private individuals who are invited to speak at special UN meetings to give their accounts of sexual abuse, torture or discrimination. Yet, no matter how powerful these testimonies are, it is ultimately up to the member states to determine a course of action, if any. The Secretariat, including the Secretary-General who leads the United Nations, cannot take action on its own and can only appeal to member states to 'do something'.

Consequently, intergovernmental organisations are helpful in reminding us of the difference between 'global *governance*' (which international organisations in all their forms bring to the global system) and 'global *government*' (which does not currently exist). An intergovernmental organisation's power rests with governments (member states), not with the organisation. States are free to leave these organisations, or even in some cases to ignore them. There are usually consequences for both actions, but the fact remains that even in extreme cases – such as when the United Nations imposes sanctions, or authorises war, on a state – intergovernmental organisations do not rule over states. Such punitive measures are only possible when the member states of the UN Security Council are in accord, agree with such proposals, and a coalition of states agrees to finance and partake in the operation. Therefore, the power rests with the states themselves, especially the more powerful states, and there are regular examples of states rejecting a certain course of action because it was not in their national interests. Here, the failures of the United Nations to establish a coordinated response to the prolonged civil war in Syria comes to mind, despite hundreds of thousands killed and millions displaced since 2011. Another example, to recall from previous chapters, was when the United States ignored the Security Council and invaded Iraq in 2003. While the former describes a scenario of 'doing nothing' about a perceived injustice internationally, the latter highlights the fact that the United Nations is also unable to do anything material to restrain powerful states. Both examples serve to underline the point yet again (as it is important) that intergovernmental organisations – even those as powerful as the United Nations – do not signal an era of global government.

Leaving aside bigger organisations like the United Nations, intergovernmental organisations are typically more specific in nature – often dealing with just one particular issue or a specific geographical area. The work that they do is often clear from their names – for example, the International Whaling Commission (IWC) or the International Criminal Police Organization (INTERPOL). These are issue-based organisations and their members are worldwide. Then there are organisations of states in specific regions, such as the Association of Southeast Asian Nations (ASEAN) and the African Union (AU). These often emulate elements of the European Union, but none (as yet) feature supranational powers (see Box 8.2). Other organisations are neither geographically limited nor confined to a single issue. The Commonwealth of Nations, for example, is an organisation the membership of which is almost exclusively comprised of former colonies of the United Kingdom. Existing in its current form since 1949, the Commonwealth also has its own permanent secretariat.

An organisation that looks to be intergovernmental in nature might not even be classified as an international organisation. The Non-Aligned Movement (NAM) for example, has around 120 member states but is considered a 'forum' because it is a loose grouping of states that does not have a fixed secretariat or even a headquarters. There are many similar examples that do not fulfil the formal requirements and showcase further the nuance of the definition 'intergovernmental'. Some of these have ties to the United

8.2 – KEY TERMS: Supranationalism

Photo 8.4 The EU flag

Credit: Thijs ter Haar/Flickr

Photo 8.5 The European Parliament

Credit: Guilhem Vellut/Flickr

Photo 8.6 Euro currency

Credit: Images Money/Flickr

To have 'supranational' powers means that an organisation is actually able to govern its members and have a degree of independence in decision-making from its member states. The only clear example of an international organisation such as this is the European Union (EU). For that reason, it is often described as *sui generis*, or 'unique' in its own right. The European Union is unique because, unlike the United Nations and all other intergovernmental organisations, it can actually be said to exercise a degree of sovereignty over its members via law-making powers in certain areas that its members agreed to relocate to the supranational level. This was done by a series of treaties that each member state negotiated and agreed, with the aim of 'pooling' their efforts in certain areas to enhance their shared peace and prosperity. Considering Europe's warring past and the economic and social devastation that the Second World War brought to the continent, integration was seen post-1945 as a novel solution to breaking the patterns of past rivalries. This began with predominantly economic integration across its six original members and gradually grew to include political, social, legal and even military areas across its twenty-seven member states. It also has its own currency – the euro. Together with its other capabilities, elements like these give it some of the powers and features typically only seen in states.

The issue of supranationalism is not without controversy. There is a rising tide of discontent with the growing power of the European Union and a desire in some political circles to weaken, or even dissolve, the organisation so that more of the power returns to the states. The 'Brexit' debate, when the British public voted in a referendum to leave the European Union raised many of these issues and is an instance of the idea of supranationalism being challenged by more traditional sovereignty arguments. The United Kingdom's eventual exit in 2020 was the first time a member state had left the organisation.

Nations that are explicitly spelled out in the document that establishes them. Take the International Atomic Energy Agency (IAEA), for example. The founding statute of the Agency dictates that its reports should go to the United Nations so that the Security Council may take action against any states that fail to meet their obligations. This works out well for the international community – as the International Atomic Energy Agency monitors the use of nuclear technology while the UN Security Council enforces measures to ensure state compliance over nuclear safety and security.

The diverse types of international organisation

International non-governmental organisations (INGOs) are non-governmental organisations that either work at the international level or have international members. International non-governmental organisations are a mixed bag, best described as those organisations that are not international business entities (which are usually labelled transnational corporations), or terrorist and other criminal organisations who act across borders. Within this large category, you may be most aware of those international non-governmental organisations who commit headline-grabbing acts. For example, images of Greenpeace protestors chaining themselves to ships, or of anti-globalisation protestors blocking streets, have been well covered in the media. These are the organisations whose mission is to raise awareness among the general public on issues of concern. No less effective are those that carry out their missions away from the limelight. Mercy Corps, for example, helps disaster survivors in countries around the globe and Médecins Sans Frontières (Doctors Without Borders) is often the first highly skilled responder to a crisis.

One of the world's more visible international non-governmental organisations is the International Red Cross and Red Crescent Movement. This is the umbrella movement which is comprised of the International Committee of the Red Cross, the International Federation of the Red Cross and Red Crescent Societies and the National Red Cross or Red Crescent Society. Today, this movement is synonymous with work with victims of humanitarian crises, but before its founding there was no organisation to carry out such work and no guidelines for humanitarian concerns arising out of war and conflict.

8.3 – KEY PEOPLE: Henry Dunant

Photo 8.7 Henry Dunant, founder of the International Red Cross Committee

Credit: British Red Cross/Flickr

In 1862, Swiss businessman Henry Dunant published a book describing the aftermath of the 1859 Battle of Solferino, which he had experienced first-hand. He wrote how the soldiers were left wounded on the field with no medical care even after the battle had ended. Dunant managed to organise the local population into providing assistance to the sick and wounded. Many were moved by his account and in 1863 he founded the International Committee of the Red Cross. Dunant's efforts prompted a push to provide for the care of wounded soldiers and civilians caught in places of conflict. This was the start of the Geneva Conventions, which all UN members have since ratified. The Geneva Conventions form part of the international law that governs humanitarian concerns arising out of war and conflict and stand as testimony of how an international non-governmental organisation (in this case the Red Cross) can start a movement that later develops into international norms and standards.

Hybrid organisations are those international organisations whose membership comprises both states and civil society groups, explored more fully in the next chapter. The states may be represented by government departments or agencies; while civil society can be just about anyone or any organisation. One such hybrid international organisation is the International Union for the Conservation of Nature (IUCN), which deals primarily with the preservation of the environment and whose members include government agencies from countries such as Fiji and Spain and non-governmental organisations from all corners of the globe. Individual members are often experts and affiliated to one of the IUCN's six commissions. The number of hybrid organisations has increased as more partnerships are forged between states and civil society organisations. Hybrid organisations – where governments, non-governmental organisations and transnational corporations all have a say – can be highly effective because of the reach, expertise and funding that such groupings can command.

Thus far we have only considered those organisations whose members are from different parts of the globe, giving the 'international' flavour to these organisations. But there are many organisations that are not fully 'international' in nature. One of the examples that was already touched upon is the European Union. Technically speaking (so far) only states in Europe are allowed to be members. There is also the African Union, where only the states in the African continent and its surrounding waters are eligible to be members. These types of organisation can be described as 'regional organisations' because membership is based upon their geographical location. There are also issue-based organisations that are at the same time regionally specific. The North Atlantic Treaty Organisation (NATO) is an example of an organisation whose members are situated on either side of the Atlantic Ocean and are committed to a collective security arrangement. These organisations may not be 'global', but they do have an international reach and/or make decisions that sometimes have an impact on the system.

8.4 – KEY TERMS: ASEAN

Photo 8.8 ASEAN leaders pose during the opening ceremony, 35th ASEAN Summit, Thailand, 3 November 2019

Credit: Anton Raharjo/Anadolu Agency/Getty Images

The Association of Southeast Asian Nations (ASEAN) is an association of ten states of Southeast Asia – Brunei, Cambodia, Indonesia, Laos, Myanmar, Malaysia, the Philippines, Singapore, Thailand, and Vietnam. Created in 1967 with five members before growing to today's membership of ten, ASEAN was conceived as an economic intergovernmental grouping to raise the standard of living and the status of the region. It has aspirations to become a single market, following the example of the European Union, allowing the free movement of goods, services, people and capital between member states.

Regional organisations have emerged in all parts of the world. The Organisation of American States is the oldest example, with its roots going back to the 1800s. Every regional organisation, and indeed every organisation, is different in terms of its mandate and its structure. For example, even though ASEAN has a permanent secretariat based in Jakarta with a bank of civil servants attached to its offices, the ASEAN secretariat has very little autonomy when compared to a regional organisation such as the European Union or even an international organisation such as the United Nations. Even at the ASEAN Summit – the most important meeting within the calendar – the Secretary-General of ASEAN does not have a seat with the Heads of State and Government of the member states; they sit with the Ministers and the other VIPs of ASEAN off-stage. This can be explained by looking at ASEAN's mandate, which never began with the aim of establishing a supranational body to govern the southeast Asian region.

Unlike the European Union, which also started from an economic base but then later branched out into security, foreign policy and monetary union (traditional domains of the state), the driving force behind the establishment of ASEAN was a belief that creating the right environment for economic growth was the key to social and political regional stability (Roberts 2012, 36). This is perhaps why ASEAN member states never envisioned that its organisation's secretariat would grow to rival the member states in power and status – as the European Union's equivalent bodies have. Even more than five decades later, despite the adoption of the ASEAN Political-Security Blueprint and the annual ASEAN Defence Ministers' Meeting, ASEAN remains primarily an economic grouping, thereby making it an example of a 'soft' regional organisation (Ahmad 2012). Once again, compared to the European Union, which has an ever-growing level of executive and legislative power, ASEAN has followed a different course.

Examples such as ASEAN and the European Union should serve to underline that regional organisations – in fact all international organisations – are each unique unto themselves. They show that the strength and shape of an organisation is dependent upon the power invested in it by its member states, and the needs with which it was created to serve. These sometimes evolve over time, and not always with the end result of the organisation gaining more power and/or growing in size. Sometimes, regional organisations can fade away into relative obscurity, or collapse entirely when they are no longer needed. One example of this is the case of COMECON, an economic union of communist states which was dissolved when its patron (the Soviet Union) ceased to exist in 1991 and its member states were moving towards capitalism following the end of the Cold War.

How international organisations add to our map of the world

States were once the judge, jury and executioner of all matters related to the conduct of international affairs. Under the guise of state sovereignty, the state could act with impunity as far as its citizens and lands were concerned. Today, the pressure of outside interests, amplified through international non-governmental organisations, has eroded state impunity. Perhaps in no other area has there been such a major leap forward than in the development of norms involving human rights. It also used to be the case that monarchs, presidents, prime ministers and other state leaders held immunity from any kind of criminal prosecution while they were in power. That too, has now changed. The International Criminal Court, which sits in The Hague, now has the jurisdiction to hold individuals responsible for a range of crimes. The United Nations briefly discussed the idea of an international criminal court in the 1950s, but it took the efforts of a coalition of international non-governmental organisations, calling themselves the Coalition for the International Criminal Court, to realise the vision of a world court for heinous crimes. In 1997, the Coalition eventually managed to garner the political will, and within a few short years the Court had been established. Today, approximately two-thirds of the world's states are members and dozens of individuals have been prosecuted for war crimes, genocide and other crimes against humanity.

The fact that not all states are members of the International Criminal Court should serve to once again remind us that we are still not talking about global government, as states need to voluntarily opt into the Court. This is done typically by the formal signing of a treaty by each state (in this case the Rome Statute), which is then ratified (processed within that state's political/legal system), making the International Criminal Court's authority recognised within that state's legal structures. Three of the world's most powerful nations – the United States, China and Russia – have so far refused to take such a step, fearing that their multiple operations in foreign affairs may put their operatives at risk of prosecution. But this does not take away from what constructivists call the normative momentum that is building around human rights as pressure mounts for states that are holding out to join, and the repercussions and reputational damage of not joining appear to multiply over time. We explore further issues of international law such as these in Chapter eleven.

Building on the example of the International Criminal Court, there are many other success stories of how international organisations, once thought to be the tools of states, have come into their own and set the agenda for the international community. An example is in the area of environmental and climate activism. It took the combined efforts of vocal non-governmental organisations and the organisational might of the United Nations to bring states together for a watershed conference on the environment in Rio de Janeiro in 1992. Often called the Earth Summit, the UN Conference on Environment and Development was revolutionary because it emphasised the collective responsibility of states towards the well-being of the planet as a whole. Following the Earth Summit, states signed the UN Framework Convention on Climate Change, the Convention on Biological Diversity, and the Convention to Combat Desertification – treaties that became important milestones in the fight to save the environment from the harmful practices of humankind. The momentum the Earth Summit generated still has an impact today as states continue to work together, albeit often acrimoniously, to try to combat climate change.

For the average citizen, the most important international organisations might be those whose work is more local. The UN Development Programme has been a lifeline for many impoverished nations, helping to raise populations out of poverty and working to close the gender equality gap that affects many developing nations. In these cases, instead of states contributing to the organisation and keeping it financially afloat, it is sometimes international governmental organisations such as the World Bank that provide the means for the states to pursue development policies that would otherwise not be possible. However, the results of these programmes have been mixed and are often contentious, as they have sometimes left countries in significant debt or failed to improve their economies. This is a point that will be picked up and explored across several chapters in Part three of this book, as will the issues of climate and health movements internationally.

8.5 – KEY INSIGHTS: International organisations and International Relations theory

International organisations have contributed to shaping the discipline of International Relations itself, with many of its theories adapting to incorporate politics above the nation-state – as has been explored in Chapters six and seven. This is most visible in the debate between realism and liberalism, which we will briefly recall here. For liberals, institutions are created and designed primarily to increase cooperation between states and build a more peaceful world order. But realists, on the contrary, tend to see states as motivated by their own self-interests – using international organisations merely as a means to an end when convenient. Realists argue that these organisations are created and shaped by the most powerful states so that the status quo may be preserved, that is, the states' dominant role in the international system (see Mearsheimer 1995). This is why it may not come as a surprise when international organisations are accused of being unfair or undemocratic – as delving into the realist part of the theory toolbox suggests that these institutions were never established to create a level playing field. Liberals, on the other hand, look at the same data but maintain an account that posits that the existence of international organisations does not point to a flawless or perfect world, and argue that over time positive-sum logic will rise to the top of the agenda and the international order will be more just and less prone to realist-inspired zero-sum thinking – which typically leads to conflict. Of course, liberals are not utopians and such a system retains the means to keep 'rogue' nations in check through peer pressure (normatively speaking) or sanctions.

International organisations also help us to underline the difference between bilateralism and multilateralism, central features of how today's international relations work. Bilateralism refers to direct discussions between two states on any number of issues, sometimes culminating in summits involving leaders and senior officials. This all typically takes place outside the realm of international organisations. On the other hand, international organisations are the platforms by which most multilateral interactions take place as these refer to any form of relations that involve more than two states. While multilateral engagements are the very stuff that international organisations were created to facilitate, they can also sometimes create entirely bespoke structures beyond those of the more well-known institutions such as those of the United Nations. An example of this would be the Five Power Defence Arrangement involving the United Kingdom, Australia, New Zealand, Malaysia and Singapore, which is a series of longstanding defence relationships between the aforementioned states with a deployment of military resources and a headquarters in Butterworth, Malaysia. Hence, multilateral engagement can, and does, also produce many artefacts beyond the state and contributes to a significantly more complex map of international relations than the one recognised by realists, for example.

CASE STUDY 8.1: The 2014–16 West African Ebola pandemic

Photo 8.9 Dr Tom Frieden, Director of the US Centers for Disease Control and Prevention, exits the ELWA 3 Ebola treatment unit, 27 August 2014

Credit: CDC Global/Flickr

Covid-19 most likely comes to mind when the word 'pandemic' is mentioned. However, it was not the first, and will not be the last, pandemic we face. Between 2014 and 2016, the African continent saw a major outbreak of Ebola – a virus that causes hemorrhagic fever leading to organ failure. Ebola was first discovered in 1976, but it was the outbreak of 2014–16 – mainly in Guinea, Liberia and Sierra Leone – that showcased the full extent of its deadly nature. As Ebola rapidly spread across borders, the World Health Organization (WHO) declared a 'public health emergency of international concern' on 8 August 2014. This declaration officially classified the outbreak as a 'pandemic' (an epidemic spread across many countries) and legally obliged states to respond promptly. In order to understand how crucial an international organisation is to the international community, we can look at the steps taken by the WHO in partnership with states and other non-governmental organisations to contain the spread of Ebola, which had an estimated case fatality rate averaging around 50 per cent. Illustrating the danger of Ebola by way of comparison, Covid-19 had an estimated case fatality rate that was a fraction of 1 per cent in some states and rarely higher than low single-digit percentiles in most others – yet it still caused global devastation.

The first report of the West African Ebola outbreak was in Guinea in March 2014 by the World Health Organization Regional Office for Africa. By then, the WHO was already working together with the Guinean Ministry of Health as well as other partners, deploying teams to detect further cases, manage the existing ones and trace possible contacts to those infected with the virus. In the first few months of the outbreak, it did not help that at least 10 per cent of those infected with the virus were the frontline healthworkers who came into contact with the patients. The WHO then worked together with Médecins Sans Frontières, a non-governmental organisation, to set up isolation facilities and contain the spread. In parallel, the WHO mobilised laboratories across Africa, and in France, to help diagnose patients who were suspected of having the virus.

The World Health Organization Global Outbreak Alert and Response Network was despatched to Guinea towards the end of March to identify how to isolate the threat of the virus. This was followed by an international team of physicians whose expertise included infection prevention and control. Isolation units, renamed 'Ebola Treatment Units' for better reception by the local communities, were established across the countries concerned. The international community contributed financial aid to help the WHO and the states affected by the virus and medical experts from across the globe were brought in to help fight the pandemic.

The Director-General of the World Health Organization helmed the efforts, and in June 2014 declared a Level Three emergency of the Ebola virus outbreak, allowing the WHO to convene an urgent and high-level meeting to discuss steps to contain the outbreak. A number of meetings at the sub-regional and regional level ensued, and the presidents of the three main states involved met to coordinate their responses. Finally, the UN Security Council convened an emergency session on 18 September 2014 to discuss the pandemic – the first ever emergency sitting to discuss a disease. This meeting paved the way for the creation of the Emergency Ebola Response, which allowed other UN agencies and international organisations to also contribute towards a coordinated response.

Of course, the chronology of events as explained above are merely the tip of the iceberg. A great many other steps were also taken at both the macro and micro level by different entities in order to bring about an end to the outbreak. Only an international organisation could work, operate and marshall efforts on different levels: the community, states, and the wider international system. As if that was not enough, there was also a need to work both forward and backward; working forward meant working to contain the spread by treating those infected, while working backward meant sifting through all those who had come into contact with the patients to also test them for infection. This success was only possible through the coordinated efforts of a well-funded specialised agency such as the WHO, as the states where the Ebola had spread,

already battling poorly managed healthcare systems and widespread poverty, were ill-equipped to deal with the magnitude and severity of the virus.

The success was not without its challenges. When the Ebola outbreak began, efforts were hampered by weak laboratory and surveillance systems and a general mistrust of health-care workers who were despatched to help those areas where the outbreak was most virulent (US Congressional Report 2014). Traditional beliefs and inherent denials about the disease also factored into why it was at first difficult to bring the disease under control (Piot 2014). Precious time was therefore spent disseminating information about the outbreak to counter the mistrust and stigma related to Ebola. Indeed, when fast forwarding to the 2020s, and witnessing a similar proliferation of false information about Covid-19 and its vaccines and therapeutics, it it clear that a lot more work still needs to be done in this area across the world so that lessons are learned for future pandemics.

CASE STUDY 8.2: The question of Kosovo's sovereignty

Map 8.1 The dissolution of Yugoslavia

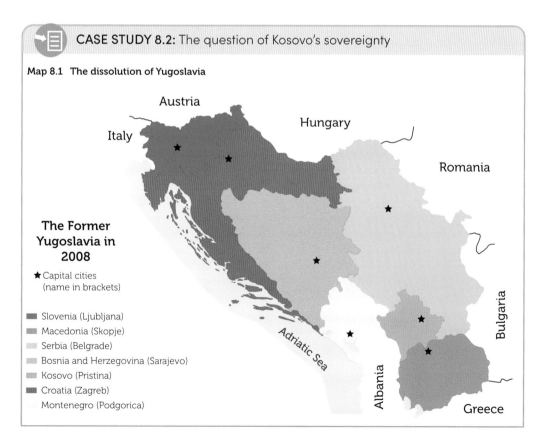

The Former Yugoslavia in 2008

★ Capital cities
(name in brackets)

■ Slovenia (Ljubljana)
■ Macedonia (Skopje)
▨ Serbia (Belgrade)
▨ Bosnia and Herzegovina (Sarajevo)
▨ Kosovo (Pristina)
■ Croatia (Zagreb)
▨ Montenegro (Podgorica)

The end of the Second World War saw the establishment of the Federal People's Republic of Yugoslavia, a communist state closely aligned to the Soviet Union. Yugoslavia was comprised of six republics – Bosnia and Herzegovina, Croatia, Macedonia, Montenegro, Serbia and Slovenia. In 1963, it changed its name to the Socialist Federal Republic of Yugoslavia. It was not long before Yugoslavia became unstable with demands for more autonomy from the central government in Belgrade. Most notable of these protests were in Croatia between 1970 and 1971, which eventually resulted in the Constitution of 1974 that reduced the power of the federal government in Belgrade and increased the autonomy of the two provinces in the republic of Serbia – Vojvodina and Kosovo. Things finally erupted in 1991, when Yugoslavia broke apart (Map 8.1). The Republic of Serbia joined forces with Montenegro and became known as the 'Federal Republic of Yugoslavia'. Almost a decade of civil war and instability ensued as the rival factions within the former state fought to establish their own claims on sovereignty.

Unrest in the autonomous province of Kosovo eventually manifested in the 1998–99 Kosovo War with the Federal Republic of Yugoslavia on one side, and the Kosovo Liberation Army on the other. At the height of the crisis, NATO intervened on humanitarian grounds, becoming a third party to the war. From the very beginning of the crisis, almost 200 humanitarian organisations were engaged on the ground, many of them under the coordination of the UN Refugee Agency (UNHCR) because of the number of people who had fled their homes due to the conflict. Mass killings, widespread rapes and pillaging were some of the allegations against the Yugoslav troops during the war investigated by the Kosovo Verification Mission of the Organisation for Security and Cooperation in Europe, a regional intergovernmental organisation based in Finland. These crimes were tried by the International Criminal Tribunal for Yugoslavia (ICTY), a UN Tribunal established in 1993.

The Kosovo War finally ended when Slobodan Milošević, President of the Federal Republic of Yugoslavia, accepted the terms of the international peace plan. On 10 June 1999, the UN Security Council adopted Resolution 1244, which established a peacekeeping force under the NATO umbrella, as well as the United Nations Interim Administration Mission in Kosovo (UNMIK). Despite the controversy surrounding the prior aerial bombardment by NATO, it was not until UNSC 1244 was adopted that states could accept a NATO-led peacekeeping force in Kosovo. The Kosovo Force was then established, comprising troops from both NATO member states and non-member states.

The establishment of UNMIK did not resolve the legal status of Kosovo, nor was it meant to. It was created to help the Security Council ensure the conditions for a peaceful and normal life for all inhabitants of Kosovo – which it did by beginning talks in February 2006 under the stewardship of UN Special Envoy and former Finnish President, Martti Ahtisaari. Negotiations stalled, however, and on 17 February 2008 Kosovo self-declared its independence as a sovereign state. The Republic of Serbia (which had since broken off from the Federal Republic of Yugoslavia, leaving it and Montenegro as distinct sovereign states) argued that the declaration was illegal and not in accordance with UNSC Resolution 1244 or the UN Charter. States around the world were divided – some recognised Kosovo's secession from Serbia, some did not. On 8 October 2008, pursuant to a request by Serbia, the UN General Assembly agreed to refer the matter of Kosovo's independence to the International Court of Justice.

Negotiations in the General Assembly that resulted in the resolution to send the question to the International Court of Justice only asked the Court for an advisory opinion, not a ruling towards the issue at hand which was whether the unilateral declaration of independence by the Provisional Institutions of Self-Government of Kosovo was in accordance with international law. The opinion of the International Court of Justice was that the declaration of independence was not in violation of international law since international law has no prohibitions on declarations of independence. The Court understood that the question of the independence of a state (and therefore its sovereignty) is a question of *political* recognition – as detailed in Chapter two.

Approximately half the world's states now recognise Kosovo. Yet, despite this, Kosovo is still not a member state of the United Nations as agreement at the Security Council cannot be reached, principally due to Russia's veto. This issue underlines the nature of power politics, but also the pressures of normalising the idea of breakaway states forming. States such as Russia also have regions that seek independence (Chechnya, for example) and as such Russia acts in its own self-interest to mute such claims, rather than amplifying them by agreeing to Kosovan independence. Russia is not alone in this stance, and other states who have secessionist claims within their borders, such as China (who also holds a Security Council veto) and India, take a similar stance on Kosovo. Therefore, international organisations such as the United Nations are only as strong as their member states allow it to be. For that reason, and by design, it cannot transgress the bounds of its mandate and recognise the sovereignty of Kosovo by itself.

Conclusion

When attempting to answer to what extent international organisations challenge, and complement, the power of nation-states, we can recall some of the results their contributions yield. This points us to the realisation that, like many things in International Relations, there is no simple answer. International organisations can be essential, such as in the case of Ebola – or largely ineffective, such as with the Kosovo question. Yet, there is no denying that on the whole, international organisations have become a major factor in how our world works, and therefore a key area of focus for International Relations scholars. Their growth, particularly through the twentieth century when the concept of global governance came of age, means that nearly every aspect of life is regulated in some way at the global level. And, as will be explored further in the next chapter, they are instrumental in advancing the rights and security of the individual across a wide range of areas. Going back to the airport analogy used at the start of this chapter, we may not always be aware of how international organisations affect our lives or how they play a role in assisting us during cross-border problems and international crises. But our lives would be materially different without them.

END OF CHAPTER QUESTIONS

1. What are the major advantages and disadvantages of states joining international organisations?

2. Keeping in mind a state's national interests, how can less powerful states use regional organisations to their advantage?

3. In what ways is the European Union 'supranational' and how does this contrast with all other IGOs, which are 'intergovernmental'?

4. In what ways are international organisations the most appropriate of the global system's three key actors to address major shared global issues, such as climate change and pandemic disease?

5. Consider some of the ways that what you have learned about international organisations reflects upon what you have previously learned about International Relations theory.

GLOBAL CIVIL SOCIETY

Raffaele Marchetti

Question: How do the actions of non-state groups change the nature of the global system?

As the previous chapter showed, international organisations in their wide array of forms have challenged the exclusivity of states in the global system. Among the non-state actors benefiting from this development are public-interest-orientated international non-governmental organisations, often known as civil society groups. The standard definition of civil society identifies it as the space outside government, family and market, a place in which individuals and collective organisations advance allegedly common interests. Civil society organisations can include community groups, non-governmental organisations, social movements, labour unions, indigenous groups, charitable organisations, faith-based organisations, media operators, academia, diaspora groups, lobby and consultancy groups, think tanks and research centres, professional associations, and foundations. Political parties and private companies can also be counted as borderline cases. The presence of civil society organisations has, therefore, become increasingly relevant within the global system, changing its nature due to their involvement across a range of areas.

Conditions for transnational activism

Different theoretical perspectives can be used to interpret global civil society. Liberals may understand it as the actor that provides a bottom-up contribution to the effectiveness and legitimacy of the international system as a whole. In essence, it is democracy in action as power is being held to account by the populace. Realists, however, may interpret global civil society as a tool used by the most powerful states to advance their interests abroad, often promoting and popularising ideas that are key to the national interest. Marxists may see global civil society as political vanguards that can spread a different world view that challenges the dominant order. Finally, some even argue that the concept of civil society as a sphere distinct from the family, state and market remains a Western concept that does not apply easily to societies where the boundaries between these spheres are more blurred. It is useful to keep these various perspectives in mind as you read through the chapter.

9.1 – KEY TERMS: Civil society

Civil society is a term that emerged in the 1980s after large-scale movements within certain states were detected. These were broadly anti-government/corruption movements in authoritarian regimes, and they involved a diverse range of actors such as labour unions, charities, and community and religious groups. These groups are sometimes also referred to as the 'third sector' in society – with the government (public sector) and for-profit businesses/transnational corporations (private sector) comprising the other two sectors. As these groupings became ever more international in both their support base and also their areas of action and funding, the term 'global civil society' came into use to describe a component of the global system that had unique characteristics.

The theoretical and empirical study of civil society sprung from specific historical, political and socioeconomic backgrounds. The early debates on civil society were firmly grounded in the West, having played an active role in issues such as state formation, nuclear disarmament, environmental sustainability, and gender and race struggles. Following the end of the Cold War the wave of civil society literature incorporated the wider framework of globalisation and began to enter the discipline more. This trend was part of the movement of International Relations scholarship analysing beyond just the state and system levels, towards appreciating the roles of individuals and groups – the very realm of civil society.

The activism of global civil society groups has been facilitated by a number of specific conditions. First, a number of international organisations have supported the inclusion of civil society actors within international decision-making. For example, the 1992 UN Earth Summit in Rio de Janeiro provided a means for previously scattered groups to meet and create common platforms and networks. The European Union has followed a similar approach by integrating different types of civil society organisations within its governance mechanisms. Second, the state's priorities for the allocation of resources changed in the 1980s and 1990s due to a trend towards the privatisation of industries. In that climate, it was common to see state-owned enterprises (such as utilities) being sold off to private companies. For that reason, in many Western nations, the state's overall role in public affairs was reduced. In this context, civil society organisations were able to subcontract many functions from the state and take up new roles as service providers. Third, the globalisation process has generated a sense of common purpose among civil society actors. This has been a trigger for internal unification – increasing the sense of solidarity among civil society organisations. It has also united the groups that want to highlight the negative sides of globalisation. Finally, through the internet, groups from different parts of the world have been able to familiarise themselves with other political realities, like-minded organisations and alternative forms of action. In this way, they have been able to increase their political know-how and their ability to join forces in addressing common targets.

Transnational advocacy networks promote normative change in politics through the use of transnational campaigns often within the framework of human rights defence. Many of these have had success in influencing policy on global issues, with significant past campaigns such as the anti-apartheid struggle gradually resulting in major changes in our world. Box 9.2 shows a list of examples, with further reading, of international agreements and structures that came to be at least in part due to the pressure and mobilisations of civil society groups. Beyond these, we can already see the roots of further change in the wider movement across a range of civil society groups towards environmental/climate action and in gender recognition and women's rights.

9.2 – KEY TERMS: Transnational advocacy networks

A transnational network can be defined as a permanent coordination between different civil society organisations (and sometimes individuals), located in several countries, collectively focused on a specific global issue. By forming transnational advocacy networks, civil society organisations have used their leverage at the international level to achieve notable results. Some notable examples, with further reading, are:

» The establishment of the International Criminal Court (Cakmak 2008)

» The Jubilee campaign on Third World debt, which induced creditor governments and the International Monetary Fund to take some steps towards debt relief for highly indebted poor countries in 1996 (Busby 2007)

» The international campaigns to ban landmines which led to the intergovernmental conference in Ottawa where the Mine Ban Treaty was signed in 1997 (Anderson 2000)

» The UN Convention on the Rights of the Child of 1989 (Brooks 2005)

» The UN Declaration on the Rights of Indigenous People of 2007 (Sargent 2012)

Global civil society as a response to transnational exclusion

In today's complex world, traditional institutions have struggled to provide effective and legitimate responses to global issues such as climate change, financial instability, pandemic disease, intercultural violence and global inequalities. As a response to these shortcomings, forms of so-called multi-level, stakeholder governance have been established that involve a combination of public and private actors. Civil society action at the international level is predominantly focused on building political frameworks with embedded democratic accountability. At present, most global governance bodies suffer from accountability deficits – that is, they lack the traditional formal mechanisms of democratic accountability that are found in states, such as popularly elected leaders, parliamentary oversight and non-partisan courts. Instead, the executive councils of global regulatory bodies are mainly composed of bureaucrats who are far removed from the situations that are directly affected by the decisions they take. People in peripheral geographical areas and in marginalised sections of society are especially deprived of recognition, voice and influence in most contexts of global governance as it is currently practised. An example of this that we will return to in the case study section was the struggle that people of the Narmada Valley organised against the project of a mega dam, which eventually led to an international mobilisation (Khagram 2002).

An apt depiction of such an international system is to describe it as characterised by 'transnational exclusion'. In recent decades most global regulatory bodies have begun to develop closer relations with civil society organisations precisely in order to fill this legitimacy gap. While the role of civil society organisations in these contexts is predominantly based on consultative status, they allow the civil society organisations to have a seat at the table. For example, the Committee on World Food Security within the UN Food and Agriculture Organisation has reserved seats for different types of organisation, including non-governmental organisations and social movements, research centres, financial institutions, private sector associations and private philanthropic foundations.

Given their need to balance a deeper impact on society with greater legitimacy, global governance institutions have been under pressure to be more inclusive and attentive to the political demands coming from below. Thanks to such dynamics, civil society actors have managed to increase their access to international agenda-setting, decision-making, monitoring and implementation in relation to global issues. Today it is almost common practice to hold public hearings not only at the United Nations, but also at many other major international institutions including the World Bank and the European Union. At the same time, the challenge to the inclusion of civil society actors in global governance mechanisms remains significant. New institutional structures are continually emerging and the challenge in terms of integration is therefore endlessly renewed. New institutional filters are created, and civil society actors have to constantly refocus and adapt to new circumstances. An example is provided by the G20, where civil society actors have become embedded.

9.3 – KEY TERMS: The G20

The G20 (also known as the Group of Twenty), founded in 1999, is a more diverse successor to the more Western-dominated G7 (formerly G8 before Russia was expelled in 2014) – although, the G7 still continues to operate in parallel. Together, the G20 members account for roughly 75 per cent of the world's trade and two-thirds of the world's population. In the early years of the forum's summits, civil society organisations struggled to find a voice in the proceedings. However, reflecting their importance, they are now included as one of the seven engagement groups of the G20. The seven groups are the 'B20' (Business community), 'L20' (Labour unions), 'S20' (Science), 'T20' (Think tanks), 'W20' (Women), 'Y20' (Youth associations) – and finally 'C20' which represents civil society organisations.

Values promotion and creating change

At the core of the dynamics leading to the emergence of transnational activism is the perception of the possibility of change in the area of one specific global issue. This might arise due to a new issue becoming significant (for example climate change) or the reinterpretation of a long-standing issue such as gender. Ultimately, the key feature of transnational activism in global governance is precisely its stubborn attempt to influence the normative battle on the right and legitimate interpretation of crucial global issues. From this perspective, civil society organisations should be seen not only as traditional problem solvers (providing solutions that governments are less suited to deliver) but also as problem generators (placing new problematic issues on the international agenda). While the perception of an unjust situation necessarily constitutes a precondition for action, it is only when the actor recognises the possibility of having a positive impact on such a situation that mobilisation may start. Two elements are necessary for such mobilisation: (1) conceptualisation and (2) political commitment.

Transnational mobilisation on global issues should be interpreted as the result of several steps. A crucial challenge for any transnational network is to present the issue at stake in such a way that it is perceived as problematic, urgent and also soluble. Think, for instance, of the case of feminism. Through the action of a number of feminist movements, beginning with the suffragettes in the late nineteenth century, the traditional role of women was challenged and eventually replaced in many states by a new egalitarian position entitling women to have equal standing in society. The first step in cross-border mobilisations is therefore the production of knowledge and the creation of 'frames' through which the issue at stake can be correctly interpreted.

A second step consists of the external dissemination and strategic use of such knowledge. This is a crucial stage as it is the point at which information acquires a fully public dimension – and therefore political significance. Global public opinion needs to be attracted and its imagination captured for framing the terms of the conflict in such a way that the issue at stake becomes the focus of a general interest requiring public engagement. Dissemination often passes through scientific channels. When networks become active players in the communities of experts on global issues (for example, the networks of disease experts at the World Health Organization), they tend to be perceived by public opinion as credible sources of information and this increases their influence on policymaking. However, dissemination can also be executed though other forms, including public action such as mass protests.

In order to successfully promote change, a third step is necessary. The task here consists in gaining a recognised role in the public sphere as a rightful advocate of general interests. To the question 'in whose name do you speak?', transnational networks need to offer a response that enables them to claim representation of interests that are wider than just those of a small group. Once transnational networks succeed in shaping a challenge associated to a particular global issue, the political opportunity for mobilising and network building arises.

Although success necessarily depends on international circumstances, conditions at more local levels often play an important role in the rise of global social movements. In national contexts, civil society organisations are rooted in a web of social relations and common identities. They have access to important resources (such as people and money) but operate in highly formalised political systems that shape and constrain their mobilisation and impact through a number of political filters. For instance, while democratic countries tend to leave space in the public square for activism, the room for manoeuvre in countries ruled by undemocratic regimes may be more limited – or even forbidden in some cases. At the global level, however, there are few such restrictions. This factor widens the options for political action. In fact, transnational networks may help increase the political opportunities that are present in national contexts; they often perform a facilitating role, providing space for actors who are usually voiceless and excluded. Transnational networks can also amplify local voices by setting them in the context of global issues and policies, thus strengthening local or national activism.

9.4 – KEY TERMS: Multistakeholder governance

Multistakeholder governance seeks to diversify decision-making from the usual state or international organisational centres, which tend to dominate global discussions due to their political and financial power. Instead it seeks to set up systems where ideas can pass through several different layers, and through multiple types of actor (both public and private) in order to gain a result that has more legitimacy than that of (for example) a decree or policy made by a government. The word itself is built out of components. Firstly, the 'multi' is related to the older term, 'multilateralism', and is an attempt to evolve that term from its origins of describing a global system where multiple states have influence. Multistakeholder governance reflects a system where 'stakeholders' (the second part of the term) comprising civil society organisations and other groups such as those who have expertise or lived experience of the issue at hand have a seat at the table next to states. The final part of the term 'gover*nance*' is a word that plays off the more formal idea of 'govern*ment*' – a word to describe the exercise of sovereign power. Governance, on the other hand, reflects the distributed nature of power and influence in the global system and the array of non-state actors who are available to help address shared problems and opportunities.

Transnational networks can be understood as organisational responses to the new global socio-political environment in which political opportunities on the one hand and scarce resources (finance, knowledge, etc.) on the other create conditions in which a network structure can perform better than other organisational forms. As this combination is inherently contingent, transnational networks tend to have a limited political life. On the one hand, networks are created in response to a specific issue; it is difficult to adapt them to a different issue and in many cases it is easier to simply create a new network. On the other hand, social movements and especially networks are cyclical phenomena. The interaction between the set of values shared by social movements and global political opportunities leads to the emergence of different projects of political change, reflecting also the heterogeneity of actors – for instance, balancing reformist with more radical attitudes. Individual networks, therefore, fit a specific set of conditions – internal and external to global movements – but when some of them change, the factors that led to their rise may dissolve, mobilisation may decline rapidly and networks are unlikely to maintain their significance unless they adapt their strategy and at times their own identity to the new political contexts.

Contested legitimacy

While it is clear that civil society organisations cannot aim to replace the traditional channels of political representation, it is recognised that they often play a key role in 'broadcasting' viewpoints that struggle to be included in the political agenda. From the activist perspective, the issue of political representation should not be interpreted as a matter of who they represent but, rather, what they aim to represent. It is the issues they tackle and the values they seek to uphold that are crucial – possibly more than their constituencies. Civil society organisations usually claim to advance the public interest. While it may not be clear what the public interest is with regard to many global issues, the ambition of civil society is, as argued above, to contribute within the normative battlefield of global public opinion.

To explore the issue of legitimacy we can look at the two extremes of the civil society spectrum – the divide between mainstream politics and radical groups. At one extreme there are the civil society organisations established by governments and international organisations. At the other we find civil society organisations that are typically considered criminal, such as terrorist groups and mafia organisations, despite their occasional social roles (Asal, Nussbaum and Harrington 2007). These represent the two extremes of co-optation and ostracisation. In other words, they are examples of groups' integration into, and exclusion, from the political system.

9.5 – KEY PEOPLE: Nelson Mandela and Yasser Arafat

Photo 9.1 Nelson Mandela in 2008

Credit: South Africa The Good News/Flickr

Photo 9.2 Yasser Arafat in 1987

Credit: Wojtek Laski/Hulton Archive/Getty Images

It is important to consider that the term 'civil' is normatively loaded and tends to be interpreted in line with the predominant ideology. For this reason, history is at times ironic: prominent political leaders such as South Africa's first Black president Nelson Mandela and Palestinian leader Yasser Arafat were long considered to be leaders of criminal groups, even terrorists, and yet in due course they were both awarded the Nobel Peace Prize for their political impact on their respective societies and the wider world. History teaches us that the move from criminalisation to normalisation (through co-optation or transformation) can be fairly quick when seen with the perspective of hindsight.

For groups closer to the mainstream of politics, or those groups seeking to enter the mainstream, there is always the risk of co-optation by the institutional system. Civil society organisations need financial resources, public recognition and political support – all of which can be provided or facilitated by the political system. At the same time, the political system may take advantage of the fragmentation and proliferation of civil society organisations by picking and choosing, on the basis of political convenience, the groups most inclined to cooperate with the current political agenda. In this way, there is a danger that some civil society organisations may find themselves used instrumentally to facilitate top-down representation of specific interests. On the other hand, issues of violence and resistance to political systems are always controversial, depending as they do on political interpretation. To borrow a common phrase – one person's terrorist is another person's freedom fighter. Consequently, those who take an oppositional stand to the status quo and agitate for material changes have often been criminalised and/or politically marginalised.

The attempt to influence the governments of foreign states is a key part of foreign policy, and another area we can explore when investigating perspectives over the legitimacy of civil society organisations. For example, supporting and funding non-state groups to promote democracy is welcome from a liberal perspective insofar as societies are conceptualised as open and expected to maximise the opportunity for their citizens to exercise their freedom of choice. However, this move can also be perceived as an illegitimate attempt to impose foreign influence on domestic state affairs, or even as an act of aggression. If the latter perspective is dominant within a state, it may deploy countermeasures that include censorship and limitations on foreign civil society organisations – or groups that are associated with foreign actors or states.

The first structured democratisation programmes were launched by the United States in the 1990s. After this, other similar programmes were initiated by governmental bodies in other Western states and by the European Union. These programmes have often worked in close cooperation with non-governmental organisations and think tanks (sometimes with very close links to the state) that have together played an important role in both funding and operating democracy promotion policies. The turning point towards supporting civil society organisations occurred during the Clinton administration (1993–2001). Under Clinton's presidency, new pro-civil society appointments were made to fill key offices in the main governmental programme for democracy promotion in the United States Agency for International Development (USAID). This generated a trickle-down effect with significant change in the actual implementation of such policies in other states as they emulated the American example.

The turn towards civil society organisations in democratisation efforts was due to two principal reasons. On the one hand, in the 1990s the fear of left-leaning (socialist or communist) political movements and ideologies had decreased due to the collapse of the Soviet Union and the end of the Cold War. This made it possible to replace the traditional American scepticism into open support for civil society organisations, including those groups situated on the left-liberal side. On the other hand, the failure of different types of older democracy promotion strategies during the Cold War led to a reconsideration of strategy. The Cold War strategies, being more top-down, had actually contributed at times to the emergence of so-called hybrid regimes characterised by the simultaneous presence of both formally democratic elements such as elections and oppositions and illiberal features such as concentration of power in the government. This reconsideration pushed for a move from formalistic to more substantive democracy promotion activities and led to the support for civil society organisations with the intent of challenging such hybrid regimes through elections and social pressure from within the state.

Aid provided from abroad to non-state groups was intended as a contributing factor to improve local capacity in several, mutually reinforcing ways. A primary focus was in strengthening the ability of local groups to conduct independent election monitoring, including the capacity to hold parallel vote counts to check for corruption. Fostering broad civil engagement in the electoral process and delivering voter education was also important. Advocacy and activism on political and civil rights was preferred to that on socioeconomic and cultural-identity issues. And finally, funding was also directed to provide equipment or other material assistance to opposition parties to help them campaign effectively and to encourage them to work together and build broad coalitions. This way pressure was indirectly mounted on governmental transparency and democracy enhancement.

In the present day we are witnessing a backlash contesting the legitimacy of foreign policy moves such as democratisation. Dozens of states now impose sanctions on foreign-funded civil society organisations, which creates a tense dynamic (see Dupuy, Ron and Prakesh 2016). From Russia and China to Ethiopia and India, foreign civil society organisations suffer a growing tide of governmental limitations at the local level due to nationalist fears over a perceived negative impact on the host governments. Other issues can arise, such as the receipt, amount, mechanisms, use, reporting, and taxation of the funding received from foreign donors. At the same time, civil society organisations with foreign funding create an opportunity for states to strike back and censor those organisations if they should come to operate in ways unfavourable to the political will of the donor state, or the host state. Such groups are therefore prey to shifts in political will on all sides and therefore not always fully empowered to set their own agendas, which raises an additional issue of legitimacy in cases where civil society is too closely tied, or too easily prey, to state agendas.

Civil society organisations and intergovernmental organisations

The transformation of the strictly state-based historical Westphalian system into today's more complex system of global governance is a process that has been going on since the end of the Cold War – as we have covered through the prior chapters of the book. Today's global system, in addition to states, is now populated by a wide variety of international institutions from purely intergovernmental to completely private ones. Between these two extremes, there are a number of hybrid institutions. These can feature both public entities such as states and private actors such as international non-governmental organisations or transnational corporations. And, each can have, in different degrees, a formal seat and the power to take part in the decision-making process.

There are signals that the United Nations itself is slowly moving from the one extreme of being a purely intergovernmental organisation to potentially becoming a more hybrid organisation that is progressively including in its proceedings a number of stakeholders, though in different forms. At least three mechanisms can be singled out.

The first by now well-developed mechanism for the inclusion of stakeholders adopted by the United Nations is the classical consultation with civil society organisations, whereby civil society may at times also include for profit actors (e.g. the Millennium Compact). Before any annual session of the UN General Assembly, for instance, a public hearing takes place with a number of non-governmental organisations engaged with the themes of the following session. In parallel to any world summit, there is often a civil society gathering sometimes sponsored by the United Nations. Notably, these typically involve consultations with civil society outside (before or parallel to) the formal mechanisms. Yet, a second formula has been implemented in recent years going one step further and formally including non-governmental organisations in the decision-making process of the United Nations. This is an innovative transformation that significantly erodes the once purely intergovernmental nature of organisations such as the United Nations. With this second mechanism, non-governmental actors move inside intergovernmental organisations. From an international relations perspective, this is revolutionary.

A third mechanism for engagement with civil society involves the subcontracting of specific functions to non-governmental organisations that have expertise or capacity in specific areas. The United Nations usually assigns through public tenders a number of tasks to civil society organisations, in areas such as public sector development, aid, or monitoring. This is an established practice that is adopted by many other international organisations. In this case, the non-governmental organisation would independently do the work it was tasked, and report back to the intergovernmental organisation along an established process. A related annex to this mechanism concerns an intergovernmental organisation actually founding, financing, aggregating or simply sponsoring a newly created non-governmental organisation. For instance, between 1946 and 1965, UNESCO, whose parent organisation is the United Nations, founded and financed no less than twenty-five new non-governmental organisations, outsourcing entire areas of its activity to them. This makes the links between civil society and intergovernmental organisations much closer, and much more top down, than in cases of subcontracting.

9.6 – KEY INSIGHTS: UNAIDS and the Committee on World Food Security

UNAIDS, the Joint United Nations Programme on HIV/AIDS, is a hybrid partnership striving to achieve universal access to HIV prevention, treatment, care and support. Since 2007, non-governmental organisations are included in the Programme Coordinating Board (PCB) – the governing body of UNAIDS. The programme pulls together the efforts of the UN system, civil society, national governments, the private sector, global institutions and people living with and most affected by HIV. The PCB of UNAIDS guides, reviews and makes decisions about the policies, priorities, long-range plans and budgets of UNAIDS. There are 37 seats on the PCB: 22 member states, 10 cosponsors and 5 intergovernmental organisations – one seat for each of the following five regions: Africa; Asia/Pacific; Europe; Latin America/Caribbean; and North America. Though technically non-governmental organisations do not have the right to take part in the formal decision-making process of the PCB, in practice they fully participate as essential stakeholders in decision-making processes. They do not, however, have voting rights.

The Committee on World Food Security (CFS) of the Food and Agriculture Organization was set up in 1974 as an intergovernmental forum for review and follow up of food security policies. In 2009 it went through a reform process that included a number of stakeholders. The vision of the reformed Committee is to be the most inclusive international and intergovernmental platform for all stakeholders to work together in a coordinated way to ensure food security and nutrition for all. The Committee reports annually to the Economic and Social Council (ECOSOC), one of the main organs of the United Nations (see Box 8.1). Participants can be from representatives of UN agencies and bodies, civil society, non-governmental organisations and their networks, international agricultural research systems, international and regional financial institutions, representatives of private sector associations and private philanthropic foundations. The Bureau, made up of a chairperson and twelve member states, is the executive arm of the Committee. The Advisory Group includes civil society and non-governmental organisations, particularly those representing smallholder family farmers, agricultural and food workers, women, youth, consumers and indigenous people. It helps the Bureau advance the Committee's objectives to ensure linkages with different stakeholders at regional, sub-regional and local levels and to ensure an ongoing, two-way exchange of information.

As evidenced by these three mechanisms, the most classical locus of intergovernmental action, the United Nations, is changing. More and more, non-governmental actors get closer to important decision-making processes at the international level. With this trend there also comes a redefinition of legitimacy that is now moving from a purely input legitimacy to an output legitimacy. From representatives whose legitimacy derives from a formal mandate, increasingly legitimate actors are perceived as those who have relevant expertise, sound moral principles or simply an ability to deliver on the ground. The notion of authority (who gets to make decisions) within and across every level of the global system is, therefore, changing.

CASE STUDY 9.1: The moratorium on the death penalty

Capital punishment is the practice of executing someone following a legal process, commonly known as the death penalty. Instances of using the death penalty are as old as recorded history, but in the modern era they have become more the exception rather than the rule as states favour imprisonment and rehabilitation. Those states that still use the death penalty typically reserve it for the most serious of crimes such as murder, terrorism, treason and sometimes also drug offences. Amnesty International's annual report (2020) cited China as the state with the most executions that year, having executed 'thousands' of citizens. Iran is second on the list with approximately 250 executions, and Saudi Arabia third with 184. These three states

have maintained the top three positions in the global execution figures for several years. The figures are often approximate due to the secretive nature of certain regimes, especially China, where death penalty records are state secrets.

The goal of abolishing the death penalty is a key aspiration of human rights activism (see Hodgkinson and Schabas 2004). It is a contemporary example of how initiatives backed by civil society organisations can have lasting impact. This mobilisation was only possible because a number of 'rival' civil society organisations decided to work together. Despite their differences, these organisations managed to find a middle ground on an operative basis. While the topic

Photo 9.3 Paris Die-in, 2 July 2008. A die-in is a form of protest in which participants simulate being dead

Credit: World Coalition Against the Death Penalty/Flickr

of the death penalty has been debated for centuries, it is only in recent decades that significant institutional changes have occurred, with a number of states removing capital punishment from their legal systems.

The anti-death penalty stance only managed to gain importance at the UN level due to the specific transnational mobilisation of civil society organisations (Marchetti 2016). While earlier activism contributed to creating the right political context at the national level, it was the campaign for a moratorium on the death penalty that specifically targeted the United Nations. This ultimately led to a UN General Assembly resolution in 2007, which was reconfirmed several times in subsequent years and today remains a significant human rights benchmark. The campaign not only contributed to having the United Nations pass a (non-binding) resolution with a global scope, but was also important in persuading a large number of states to abandon the death penalty.

In material terms, the campaign developed through a multi-stage process of normative promotion. It began in a specific place: Italy. It then became stronger by 'going transnational' via civil society organisations networking together and sharing resources and ideas. The campaign then returned to the national domains so that key target states could be persuaded to back it from within their own political systems. Finally, the campaign targeted the United Nations, where it successfully achieved the backing of the General Assembly. As for institutional strategies, between pressure (hard dynamics) or persuasion (soft socialisation), the main approach of this campaign consisted in lobbying local, national, European and global public institutions with soft persuasion initiatives. In terms of targets, the campaigning aimed principally at influencing public institutions and key actors within them. The selection of this specific strategy was dependent on the type of goal the campaign set for itself.

Affecting the very existence of citizens who risk execution (especially in cases where innocence is maintained, despite any legal rulings) the issue of the death penalty is by definition at the core of any legal system aimed at providing security to its members. Given such a nature, any change in its regulatory framework cannot avoid discourse and bargaining with the very public institutions that can carry out executions legally. As a consequence, this kind of activism intended to modify the legislative position within states and, in order to achieve that, it operated institutionally both at the national and international levels. While other kinds of initiatives aimed at the wider public were successfully developed and secured broader public support, public institutions who stood able to promote legal reforms were prioritised as targets. However, public institutions were not only targets, they also became partners. Most of the persuasive activities of the campaign were developed in synergy with public institutions, which provided financial, political, or procedural support due to a growing normative acceptance across multiple societies that the death penalty should be abandoned.

Two communicative moves had a particular importance in the campaign strategy: framing and storytelling. Beyond the strategic decisions to develop a transnational coalition and to enact multi-layered lobbying, the specific tactical decisions that most characterised this campaign were very much based on the nuanced combination of reason and emotion. On the one hand, there was the construction of a cosmopolitan frame mainly based on universal human rights, intended as a rational tool to challenge, from a legal point of view, the traditional understanding of the death penalty in terms of sovereignty. On the other hand, there were 'humanitarian missions' led by civil society organisations in swing countries, intended as an emotional tool to persuade institutional gatekeepers and veto players to change their position in favour of the moratorium.

The dynamics of the process cannot be fully captured without making clear the part played by persuasion tactics. Humanitarian diplomacy developed by civil society organisations through persuasion activities remains key. In this case the undertaking featured two main components. First, the idea of the right to life was communicated persuasively as a desirable outcome – something that attached well to several already popular international agendas. Second, an empathic process was generated by using powerful narratives drawn from individual cases. These were mainly stories told by people previously sentenced to death and now pardoned, or moving accounts by their relatives. In both cases, civil society organisations played a central role as either reason-based frame creators or emotion-based narrative disseminators. They played an important role as an alternative and/or adjunct to diplomatic politics and achieved a clear and lasting impact at the international level that has ensured that the death penalty increasingly becomes the exception rather than the rule.

CASE STUDY 9.2: Mega dams and the Narmada River

Photo 9.4 Sardar Sarovar Dam on the Narmada River, Gujarat

Credit: Rupeshsarkar/Wikimedia Commons

Damming a moving body of water, such as a river, slows down and materially changes the flow and the landscape around it. It can also create a large area of water behind the dam (a manmade lake, or series of lakes), which is managed in different ways. Larger dams, or 'mega dams' are built to generate electricity (hydroelectricity), divert water for irrigation of crops or for other uses such as to store in lakes in case of drought and to help prevent flooding. While these are worthwhile outcomes, damming is a controversial issue for those in proximity to the project as it can lead to communities being relocated and losing their land. It also has a series of environmental impacts that affect the ecosystems associated with the river and the land around it. Beyond these issues, it also impacts international relations, as when one state decides to dam a river that flows onwards to other states, it affects vital water flow downstream and can lead to disputes.

For example, the Nile (Map 9.1) has a drainage basin covering eleven African states. In 2011 Ethiopia began construction of a mega dam – the Grand Ethiopian Renaissance Dam – to provide hydroelectric power to address national energy shortages. Yet, downstream of the dam, which was completed in 2020, Egypt fears disruption to their shared water supply from the Nile – which accounts for 90 per cent of Egypt's fresh water. Disputes like this can lead to serious incidents, even war. Due to this, the dispute has drawn in the African Union, a regional international organisation, and major powers such as the United States who have diplomatic and economic influence over the states concerned. Access to fresh water is likely to be one of the pivotal international issues in future years as climate change and a growing global population causes stresses on water supplies in key areas. Yet, within this category an underappreciated element is the role of civil society organisations and their focus on highlighting the effects of such projects at the local level, which we can see in a long-standing dispute over a damming project in India.

Map 9.1 The Nile

The Narmada River is the fifth largest in India. Plans to build over three thousand dams on the river to provide hydroelectric power and divert water to provide irrigation to agricultural land were developed through several decades, with construction beginning on a series of dams in the mid-1980s. An opposition movement, Narmada Bachao Andolan, was set up to give voice to locals who stood to lose their land as a result of the reservoirs and higher water levels caused by the dam projects – but also due to

environmental concerns that would impact life at the local level. The movement used slogans such as 'development wanted, not destruction' and it quickly became a transnational network, drawing in international environmental and social non-governmental organisations. Working together, they put pressure on the project internationally and in doing so contributed to making it one of the world's most debated development projects (Cullet 2007).

This global civil society mobilisation not only raised awareness of the issue beyond India, but it materially impacted an international organisation, the World Bank. This occurred after local activists visited the construction area of the Sardar Sarovar dam (Photo 9.4), one of the larger dams on the river, and found violations of environmental regulations and a concurrent lack of transparency over the full environmental and social impact. The World Bank had earmarked approximately $450 million in financing for the project to the Indian government as part of its development activities. It soon found itself on the receiving end of questions from local activists, with these concerns amplified internationally by environmental groups. An independent review was held and the World Bank formally withdrew from the project in 1993, an unprecedented step, agreeing that environmental considerations were not adequate in the planning of the project.

Although the Indian government continued with the project in 1999 after several delays, the mobilisation materially impacted debates about global and local development policy, especially the social and environmental impact of mega dams and the effect they have on river systems and those who depend on them. Beyond being just a local example of activism, the long-running dispute showed how local actions could be upscaled using transnational civil society practices to advocate for, and promote, different structures for how development funding was apportioned internationally. Additionally, local voices, originally unheard in the debate and not consulted with by the Indian government in its original plans, came to have their concerns amplified.

On a broader scale, the debates held through this episode have become symbolic, materially shaping development debates on later dam projects – such as the aforementioned Ethiopian dam on the Nile. For example, the debates raised by Narmada Bachao Andolan and their wider impact inspired the creation of the World Commission on Dams, a group that involved civil society groups, experts and academics together with government and non-governmental figures who worked together to shape international guidelines for dam building. This was an example of multistakeholder governance, a practice that harnesses global civil society in order to gain a result that has more legitimacy than – for example – a non-consultative governmental decision such as that made by India over the Sardar Sarovar dam.

Conclusion

Over recent decades, the actions of non-state groups have indicated a move towards a dilution of state power, changing the nature of the global system. Civil society organisations have managed to influence decision-makers by giving voice to the voiceless and framing new issues. At the same time, they have managed to pressure international organisations so that the overall level of transparency, consultation, outside evaluation and efficiency is measurably higher than it was in the past. Nevertheless, the impact has been uneven. Most transnational activism has come from Western organisations, with significant exceptions in Latin America and some parts of Asia. Other parts of the world are still socially disconnected. Russia, China, most of Africa and the Arab world constitute islands that remain relatively isolated from the growth of global civil society. And, because civil society organisations are unevenly concentrated in the Global North, the political results they have achieved also exhibit an imbalance. The gains realised by political activism have mostly been in line with agendas framed in northern states and benefiting northern constituencies. However, this is unlikely to continue as agendas rise from the Global South and Western power and influence simultaneously declines. This will hopefully make the future of global civil society more 'global'.

 END OF CHAPTER QUESTIONS

1. In what ways do you see civil society organisations promoting agendas that challenge the traditional dominance of the state?

2. To what degree are global civil society organisations expanding the range of agendas visible in major international organisations such as the United Nations and the European Union?

3. Do non-state groups have the power and resources to play a meaningful part in solving key global issues such as tacking environmental degradation, protecting human rights and achieving gender equality?

4. How would a realist, a liberal, and a Marxist view global civil society's role differently?

5. In what ways do you think civil society can become more 'global' in the years ahead?

INTERNATIONAL POLITICAL ECONOMY

Günter Walzenbach

Question: Who gets what, when and how?

International Political Economy (IPE) studies the reciprocal relationship between politics and economics in the global system. Acknowledging the economic foundations of global order, it proposes a fusion of economic and political analysis to form a holistic approach examining the global system that both complements and transcends the family of theories explored in Part one of this book – whilst also recognising some of the global structures that reach throughout this part of the book. It explores a set of guiding questions that arise from areas such as trade, production and finance and their interaction with political pressures identified in richer and poorer states, in the strategies of transnational corporations, and in international organisations. Awareness of International Political Economy is central for students of International Relations as it shows the divisions in the discipline about how our global system might progress, and highlights whether who gets what can (or should) fundamentally change.

Actors and interests

International Political Economy theories suggest different answers to the question of meaningful system change that would influence who gets what, when and how. They build on some of the insights and the familial frameworks of the theories that have been covered in Chapters six and seven by linking political actors across states to international economic relations. The latter, economic relations, builds around markets as the location where trading occurs on the bases of demand and supply. Individual households and productive organisations meet as buyers and sellers, exchanging goods and services at agreed prices. For market participants, such as private enterprises or the people who sell their labour for wages, the direction in which the global system should be changed (if at all) is a matter of contestation.

10.1 – KEY TERMS: Transnational and multinational corporations

Transnational corporations (TNCs) are internationally operating firms owned and controlled by nationals of one state with production facilities in two or more states. These operations add value to the purpose of a business by conducting and controlling economic activities across borders, including marketing and distribution. This often entails a particular corporate strategy to establish permanent positions in foreign markets and to command a high level of investments in sectors such as services, manufacturing or commodities. In this way, transnational corporations have diversified from their old focus on agricultural production and extractive industries predominantly located in developing states. While they come with considerable variation in terms of size, resource endowment and management structures, there can be little doubt that such entities wield significant power and influence within the global system. The use of an alternative term, **multinational corporations (MNCs)**, puts emphasis on the merger of capital from more than one nation-state, and therefore, on the lack of a single home base. Here the geographic spread of a business is considered secondary in comparison to the diverse nationalities that make up its governing board. Both these terms, often used interchangeably, capture the activities of large businesses operating in competitive environments extending beyond the jurisdiction of any given state. Some of today's biggest corporations are US retailer Walmart, China's utility company State Grid, Japan's Toyota Motor, and the Netherland's Royal Dutch Shell.

In liberal IPE, free markets work best as mechanisms for the efficient allocation of resources. For liberals, wealth maximisation is the driving force behind IPE. Accordingly, state intervention in market processes should be kept to a minimum. The starting point of analysis is the individual actor with wants and preferences in a world of limited resources. Actor capacity is also extended to interest groups, private firms and a diverse set of state actors. Open markets are the best tool to generate economic growth, wealth and development across the globe. Importantly, all will benefit from an unrestricted flow of traded goods and capital across borders. The entire global system is characterised by interdependence and cooperation rather than anarchy. Given the diversity of international actors, competition, negotiation and bargaining results in positive-sum outcomes where all participants are able to benefit. For this reason, state actors are likely to cooperate for mutual gain through international organisations that form broader international regimes in specific issue areas such as trade and finance. Thus, international organisations exercise an independent role in the implementation of global rules as third-party mediators and honest brokers, providing a check on the exercise of state power and helping private as well as public actors to solve collective action problems.

For liberals, the international economy can be managed in a way that is comparable to arrangements at the national level. International rules and regulations can be designed so that international competition works for states as well as groups within society. The World Trade Organization, for example, must mediate between the interests of developed and developing states as well as the interests of importers and exporters of different types of goods. Overall, globalisation is seen as a force for good by liberals as it brings about prosperity and peace. Building on this, complex interdependence, a key liberal concept, identifies a growing number of interactions across borders. Firms, state actors and individual members of civil society use multiple channels of communication discussing a range of issues without preferential treatment of security concerns (Cohen 2008). Due to economic prosperity, less power is concentrated in just a few hands and more resources are available for individuals to engage in cross-border contacts, to join larger groups, and to enjoy social interactions. Liberals therefore emphasise the diversity of the global system and identify cooperative behaviour among all human beings regardless of their specific roles. What matters most is the sum of individual activities driven by rational motives and a desire for welfare maximisation.

In realist IPE, by contrast, the state is the single most important actor – pursuing its national interest in an environment defined by anarchy. International economic relations are important for the positioning of states in the global system because they significantly influence the definition of the national interest. For example, for oil-dependent economies good foreign relations with oil exporting states are of vital importance. Ultimately, however, national security concerns take priority over relations that maximise wealth through economic growth. In other words, for realist IPE, money is not everything. Instead, actors will always hold a preference for power rather than material gain.

10.2 – KEY TERMS: The Global Financial Crisis

The Global Financial Crisis refers to an extreme contraction in the availability of credit leading to a severe downturn in economic activity in 2007 and 2008. It had its origin in falling house prices in the United States and the inability of an increasing number of homeowners to repay their loans. In an environment where the regulation of the domestic market was lax and house prices were on a constant rise, many lenders made risky loans in ever larger numbers. In addition, mortgage contracts were used as a key component in 'derived' financial products (mortgage-backed securities) frequently bought, sold and resold for profit between banks, private investors, hedge funds and insurance companies. However, once several of the latter incurred heavy losses due to bad loans, panic set in. The willingness to buy derivatives declined sharply and almost everyone was trying to sell respective holdings, leading to the system collapsing like a house of cards. This was watermarked by the collapse of the US financial firm Lehman Brothers in September 2008 and virtually all banks significantly reducing lending activity thereafter in what was known as the 'credit crunch'. This cut into business activity and consumer spending, leading to a widespread global crisis as, due to the networked character of finance, events in the United States had a contagious effect on other economies.

While realists do not doubt that trade leaves everyone better off, their prime concern is the composition and subsequent (re)distribution of gains from trade. In other words, realists champion relative gains, and the precise motives that stand behind the pursuit of these gains by states. Realists therefore remain unconvinced by the argument that interdependence would reduce the prospects of a future war. Rather, international politics will continue to determine the pattern of economic relations, and international organisations ultimately serve states to assess the effects of their engagement with the global economy. According to realism, the state continues to be the maker and shaper of globalisation and qualifies the process as neither irreversible nor irresistible.

Marxist approaches to IPE challenge liberal and realist accounts by rejecting a harmony of interests among the owners of capital. They claim that material or physical conditions, rather than ideas, drive human behaviour towards seeking to dominate others. Over time, the necessity to accumulate capital creates inter-state rivalry and competition. Gradually a capitalist class in possession of the means of production develops organic linkages with state structures that severely constrains what is achievable in domestic as well as foreign settings. In particular, the transnational networks of social and cultural elites are attuned to the demands of large, internationally operating firms. Given the dependence of elected politicians on capital, the state is not a neutral entity, but an agent in the pursuit of policies favourable towards further wealth concentration.

For Marxists, capitalist states need to become active beyond national borders as states themselves are the most active parties in the competition for international market shares. As the nation-state internationalises it becomes part of a larger, more complex, political structure that aims to safeguard the capitalist mode of production on a global scale. Thus, a transnational capitalist class emerges that manages the global economy in line with the social division of labour. This entails, for example, the emergence of a unified form of hegemonic leadership through a single state, a group of states or global, quasi-state institutions, making it impossible to locate capital neatly within domestic political systems. Moreover, it conditions the way developing states are incorporated into a global capitalist system so that underdevelopment in some areas is the direct outcome of development elsewhere. Essentially, dependent relationships are extended from the local to the global and defined by an unequal exchange between leading industrial producers and peripheral states as suppliers of agricultural and natural resources. This global manifestation of capital for Marxists, however, is inevitably driven towards crises and marked by intense forms of social antagonism between those who own the means of production and those who don't. In resistance to exploitation on a global scale, the struggle by alternative transnational class alliances is seen as the main driving force that can instigate fundamental social change.

The process of global market integration has restated the central question of who gets what, when and how. Through the upscaling of economic activity, the relationship with national and transnational levels of politics has become more complex. After the end of the Cold War trade intensified and expanded geographically, international production chains multiplied and contributed to the growth of transnational corporations, while financial markets interacted with unprecedented speed. The specific challenges that globalisation poses for political authority and the difficulty to respond with governance arrangements beyond the state is still felt today. Until the 2007–08 Global Financial Crisis the sectoral manifestation (size and nature) of the global economy and its international division of labour appeared irreversible due to the belief in the ability of unregulated markets to generate economic growth (Polanyi 1957).

Trade

For liberals, free trade and the exchange of goods generates peace and prosperity by connecting people and fostering economic interdependence. According to the principle of comparative advantage, all states can experience positive welfare effects by concentrating their productive capacity on what they are best at and then purchasing other goods from foreign producers. This behaviour allows cost savings through specialisation and the satisfaction of domestic needs through the free exchange of goods. Accordingly, if China can cheaply produce textiles, whereas the United States has a similar advantage in producing grains, both can increase the total availability of products by trading with each other, with China exporting textiles to the United States and the United States exporting grain to China. The exchange of goods puts the two trading partners in a position where they use their specific resource endowment most efficiently. Indeed, acting upon this principle global trade has grown fast, especially since the 1990s. Concurrently, the World Trade Organization, founded in 1995, has ensured that trade flows as smoothly, predictably and freely as possible and has reduced the average import tariff among its member states to 5 per cent – as well as targeting non-tariff barriers.

10.3 – KEY TERMS: Tariff and non-tariff barriers

A **tariff** is a tax on imports between sovereign states. Typically, this trade instrument is used by governments to increase the price of foreign goods in domestic markets. Consumers will then be less likely to buy foreign goods as they become more expensive than local alternatives, which thereby become more competitive. For example, during the Trump administration, the United States imposed tariffs of between 10 and 50 per cent on imports such as solar panels, steel and aluminium entering its market. While this might be seen as a blunt tariff instrument, protectionist measures in the form of **non-tariff barriers** are also widely used. This is a summary term for a range of practices by which governments can restrict the free flow of goods and services by imposing domestic rules, regulations, bureaucratic barriers and customs, as well licences and quotas. Extreme types of non-tariff barriers are embargos and sanctions, where trade is cut off, in whole or in part, usually due to some political, diplomatic or military conflict. Trade can also be restricted when governments show reticence to award public contracts to foreign firms and mention security concerns as the reason for the exclusion of foreign competitors – such as in the case of Chinese company Huawei's mandated removal from the British 5G market in 2020.

Many observers question the economic purpose of trying to integrate poor states into global markets by selling their raw materials or cheap manufactured goods. Marxist IPE qualifies such attempts as the 'development of underdevelopment' to highlight the resulting dependency on the export of primary commodities at low prices. In the case of coffee beans, for example, the roasters, retailers and coffee shop owners in the developed world take 90 per cent of the revenues, whereas the farmers on plantations earn little more than 1 penny per cup of coffee sold. Moreover, liberal trade policy has frequently put some developing states in a cycle of instability and debt. At different points in time, Thailand, Argentina and Ghana (for example) have experienced balance of payments deficits, borrowing too much money to finance their development projects or to pay for their imports. All three failed in their attempt to use national assets to generate income that could pay back their debts. As a result, these states then faced general increases in price levels, reputational damage, and a continuing dependency on financial stabilisation measures by the International Monetary Fund (IMF).

In response, free trade supporters point to different examples such as China and India, which over time managed to achieve economic prosperity and growth by opening up to global markets. Part of their success stories is the use of capital, technology and management skills from abroad in support of their own development goals – although the control of the transferred resources and key decisions remained with companies in Europe or North America. This view holds that such step-by-step liberalisation can work through externally driven change, if the domestic economy is also supported by new administrative arrangements such as financial regulation, anti-corruption policies, labour market flexibility and social safety nets.

Illicit trade flows, however, constitute an increasing problem, even if one accepts the liberal idea of free markets. Increasing numbers of goods and services cross borders in breach of legal import and export requirements. For example, criminal behaviour has been widely observed with counterfeit medical and pharmaceutical products, making copies of highly valuable originals or using dangerous components, putting the health of consumers at risk. Pirated goods have amounted to more than 2.5 per cent of world imports and generated a global turnover of well over one trillion dollars (Lallerstedt 2018). Regularly, blame is passed on to emerging markets that have fewer safeguards. Not surprisingly, critical scholars have pointed to the reaction by firms themselves asserting their authority rather than waiting for official reform efforts by governments. To solve the identified problem, they resort to a variety of measures ranging from corporate strategies and patent policy to cartel formation and the collective management of market shares (Strange 1996). Such private protectionist practices are a constraint on the liberal market economy, ending up just as relevant as tariffs, quotas, subsidies and sanctions imposed by traditional economic statecraft.

Production

For realists, the state continues to set the rules that transnational corporations must follow in many areas. The domestic institutions and economic ideology of the home economy matters due to its direct impact on corporate strategy and the need to secure relative gains (Gilpin 2001). Arguably, the main advantage of a global firm is to be able to combine the strength of its home base with productive activities in a range of different geographic locations. In the 1990s, therefore, many business models looked to the territorial reorganisation of production processes into different stages, making room for single components and semi-processed goods floating around in highly specialised cross-border networks. In fact, transnational production has become the main economic activity on foreign markets, tying by far the largest proportion of global trade to exports and imports within the same corporate structure. For this reason, states work hard to create a political and legal environment that is conducive to foreign direct investment (FDI). While they are aware of the constraints this creates for economic policy, they also see opportunities from outsourcing – when production is located in cheaper overseas markets. For example, whenever a corporation such as Apple cuts down on costs and transfers part of its production process to the Taiwanese manufacturing firm Foxconn and ships its products to customers worldwide, the question arises in which jurisdiction major parts of the profits will ultimately stay. For a transnational corporation, this will invariably (at least historically) be the place where it pays the least amount of tax.

10.4 – KEY TERMS: Foreign direct investment

Foreign direct investment (FDI) is a cross-border investment by an individual, a group of people or a company to build a lasting interest in an enterprise resident in another state. Importantly, the control over the resources transferred remain with the direct investor. The investor has the intention of a long-term business relationship with the receiving entity that includes a significant influence on internal management and corporate decision-making. Typically this implies the ownership of 10 per cent or more of ordinary shares or voting power in the respective enterprise and the use of its productive capabilities for the maximisation of profits.

However, the idea of a global value chain that locates various stages of the production process across different sites works best when tariff and non-tariff barriers are low, and modern communication technology enables management processes from a distance. Apple, for example, has its headquarters in California but integrates different technical components coming from the United States, Japan, South Korea, China and Germany (among others) into its end products. From this angle it is not surprising that many powerful states have sought regional economic arrangements safeguarding FDI flows and combining technological advantage with cheap labour supply. Whether this in equal measure creates opportunities for developing states is a matter of intense debate (see World Trade Organization 2019). Different steps of building a smartphone, a television or a car can be carried out in different states – but developing states such as Vietnam or Cambodia might remain fixed in this process with labour-intensive assembly at low wages rather than with more advanced manufacturing.

Given the social embeddedness of economic networks clustered around individual product lines, development strategies count on a competitive upgrading of export-oriented industries. Yet the distribution of profits depends on the precise location of economic actors within a global network, that is, whether they are engaged in the provision of raw materials or the marketing of an end product. Although all participants in corporate governance arrangements have an interest in increasing their relative gains, the policies set by governments (and the international regimes they form) are an important constraint. China, for example, before joining the World Trade Organization in 2001, took various measures to ensure that foreign investors would agree to transfer their technologies, undertake joint ventures with domestic firms and work closely with local suppliers.

This gradual improvement and upgrading of specific roles in the larger production process has been endorsed by liberally minded international financial institutions, non-governmental organisations and development experts. By working on their competitiveness, firms can build up their position within a chain, allowing them to capture a greater market share of global production. It offers a welcome recipe for industrial development at the local level where direct state intervention has failed. Moreover, the larger development community sees the purpose of disseminating management skills in support of local producers especially when the access to high-end foreign markets is protected through social regulation in the form of certification schemes. The 'fair trade' label, for example, addresses the identified problem by offering consumers a third-party assurance that the product they are buying meets a minimum set of criteria. This may include a range of environmental and social standards addressed by minimum prices, safe workplace conditions and sustainable farming methods. Thus, civil society activism and corporate social responsibility are essential supplements to government action and legislation, especially as low productivity, poor infrastructure and child labour continue to undermine many global supply chains.

Problem-solving in this sector cannot do without broader partnerships linking up the business community with civil society actors to address these issues in a more sustainable way. Nestlé, for example, has tried to control better its exchange relationship with cocoa producers to address consumer concerns about unethical business practices. At the same time, members of the business community rallied at the World Economic Forum under a new set of guidelines. The Davos manifesto, a public declaration of the joint view of global business leaders, rejects the notion that corporate strategy is exclusively driven by shareholder value. Instead, global firms should be as concerned with employees, customers, suppliers, local communities and society at large. In response to long-standing criticism the World Economic Forum finally reconsidered its advice to business leaders, reminding them to pay their fair share of taxes, to respect human rights and to welcome new market entrants throughout the supply chain.

Finance

For Marxist IPE, the far-reaching power of the financial service industry reflects best the theoretical notion of a well-organised, transnational group of people holding a strategic position within global capital. Finance once had the limited task of supplying foreign currencies that facilitate international trade, but by the twenty-first century the amount of wealth held in paper form had exploded. A decade after the global financial crisis, financial markets had recovered to their previous strength, albeit with increased volatility. More importantly, the sector's stellar rise has had an impact on wider political and social relations. Across many states the desire for new financial instruments modified capitalism, resulting in the biased redistribution of wealth upwards to the executives and major shareholders of investment banks, financial firms and transnational corporations (Reich 2015). Accordingly, financialisation, defined as 'the increasing role of financial motives, financial markets, financial actors and financial institutions in the operation of the domestic and international economies' (Epstein 2005) became closely associated with neoliberal reform strategies. Through privatisation and deregulation, political power moves away from ordinary people to the owners of capital, creating stagnant wages and precarious employment. In this account, the IMF and the associated central banks are complicit in serving the interests of a transnational class of capital owners by championing price stability and low inflation over job security.

The excessive use of derivatives and their subsequent securitisation – a long-established though little-known financial instrument – carried the major burden of having caused the global financial crisis. In the liberal worldview, however, this behaviour optimises market performance and redistributes risks that only require light government regulation. Critical accounts, by contrast, contained repeated warnings about the dysfunctional and reckless behaviour of financial elites – reflecting a general situation where financial actors had become more powerful than politicians. Stiglitz (2010) put the blame on investment banks, regulatory authorities and the leadership of the US federal reserve consistently enabling markets to make more money with which to influence the political process.

The reaction to the crisis saw state intervention to bail out struggling banks and develop far-reaching reform packages including new government strategies for job creation and employability. While a radical alternative to capitalism in line with Marxist thinking did not emerge, key realist claims were confirmed. The rescue and reform efforts were coordinated internationally but relied on the ability of powerful states to improve the stringency of market regulation and generate additional currency reserves for the IMF at the domestic level.

Between global governance and deglobalisation

Why is purposeful reform and change so difficult? Firstly, interdependent relationships between developed and developing states have focused too much on market fundamentals such as growth rates, property rights, free competition and consumer behaviour. Historically, many of the elites in developing states accepted the call for trade liberalisation and restructuring, but the resulting terms of trade amounted to an unequal exchange. The geographic location of most transnational corporations in North America, Europe and East Asia also stands in the way of a more balanced global development. Not all transnational corporations want to embrace corporate social responsibility and contribute to basic health provision, education and sustainable food production. Instead they create artificial demand on foreign markets irrespective of social needs of populations or government failings in the Global South. Their leadership promotes a business culture, management concept and corporate governance structure inappropriate for states at different stages of development.

For interdependence to work better, liberals have proposed the 'post-Washington consensus', challenging the earlier policy proposals of the US Treasury and the main international economic organisations (IMF, World Trade Organization, World Bank), which suggested that fiscal discipline, privatisation, deregulation and open markets would work best for less developed states (Stiglitz 2008). Their new demands include a more active role for the Global South in policy formulation with a stronger emphasis on social policies to reduce poverty and inequality. The benefits of this reform project depend on the precise arrangements used for implementation. In other words, political choices matter when opting for a precise policy mix of liberalisation and protectionism. Intergovernmental organisations and non-governmental organisations, working together in public–private partnerships and reformed global governance arrangements are supposed to carry the reform burden. Complex interdependence cannot imply a 'one-size-fits-all' approach and needs to take seriously the challenges of biased policy transfers to the developing world. In short, developing states need policy space to explore what works best for them, and the opportunity to voice this. Although the global market can play an important role in development, it needs to be balanced by the involvement of domestic state institutions. The final assessment about success and failure of progressive development must draw on a broader set of indicators, including environmental and social sustainability goals.

Secondly, relative gains calculations fundamentally changed when it became clear that American hegemony within the global system was declining. While states such as Brazil, Russia, India and South Africa (four of the so-called 'BRICS') rose economically in the post-Cold War years, for realist IPE only China (the 'C' in BRICS) with its economic power and highly competitive manufacturing is the true contender for hegemonic leadership. Yet, not many can see a Chinese elite being able to convert material power (such as with their Belt and Road Initiative) into a socially acceptable form of global order and institutionalised hegemony (Danner and Martin 2019). Despite impressive economic achievements, neither the teachings of Mao nor of Confucius seem to be able to provide an ethical basis for global leadership (Zhang 2015). Furthermore, other major powers in Asia, principally Japan and India, appear unwilling to accept the idea of a 'Chinese Century', in contrast (for example) to the Western powers who largely accepted the idea of 'Pax Americana' in the twentieth century. The current structure of the global system suggests early evidence of a step in a different direction as no single power seems able to control the commercial, productive and financial centres of the system as the United States did in the twentieth century. As a result, global forums such as the G20 experience high levels of stress to fit the conflicting geopolitical and economic interests of their membership into a working system of decision-making.

10.5 – KEY INSIGHTS: China's Belt and Road Initiative

Map 10.1 The Silk Road

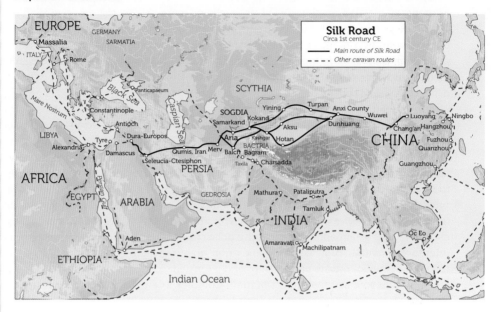

The Belt and Road Initiative is a global infrastructure plan that was developed in China and since 2013 has been implemented in more than a hundred states, mostly belonging to a group of emerging economies in Asia, Africa and Europe. Officially the project-based funding initiative has been promoted in line with liberal ideals and as an attempt to strengthen China's soft power by establishing networks of partnership, coordinating sustainable development strategies and facilitating people-to-people contacts as well as cultural exchanges. It involves the upgrading, or building, of land and sea trade routes as well as the creation of special economic zones along the old 'Silk Road' (Map 10.1). For realists, however, the Belt and Road Initiative represents the centrepiece of President Xi Jinping's grand strategy that achieved formal recognition in China's written constitution. Rather than following the depiction of a loose cooperative framework, they see the operation of debt-driven projects for the sake of specific foreign policy goals with an overarching intention to replace, or rival, the previously American-dominated global order. In this context, the Belt and Road Initiative is sometimes compared to the Marshall Plan of 1948 when the United States provided aid to help refinance Western European states following the devastation of the Second World War. This account neglects, however, that apart from the promotion of free democratic institutions most of the spending at the time went into the purchase of US agricultural and manufacturing products. Accordingly, Marxists point to the domestic workings of the Chinese economy showing very high savings rates and public investments that have led over time to huge surpluses in the availability of capital and labour. For them, the geographic expansion manifest in the Belt and Road Initiative is simply driven by state-owned enterprises seeking productive investments abroad.

The third reason that reform is so difficult is that transnational class alliances or transnational social movements of the scale necessary for a lasting system transformation are yet to emerge. Nevertheless, Marxist IPE was right insofar as competition for sales on international markets continues to pressure business owners everywhere to lower their costs. Typically, this implies a search for cheaper ways to source land, labour or capital as part of the production process. Historically, in agricultural societies this had focused on the search for new territory but was replaced by the search for cheap labour. This initially sparked economic growth in Asia as hundreds of millions of agricultural peasants – predominantly in China – were converted into urbanised factory workers. But this also entailed major social consequences as, given the access to a low-wage workforce in Asia, wage growth in developed countries has fallen and many industries have been outsourced, leading to the loss of manufacturing jobs. Any potential awareness by the Western workforce to share a common political cause with their fellow workers in China (as Marxism would suggest) is easily counteracted by a 'they took our jobs' narrative that is often harnessed by populist and nationalist figures.

In stark contrast to the free movement of capital, liberal IPE has often sidelined an analysis of the free movement of people (labour) across borders. A case in point is the United Kingdom's post-Brexit immigration scheme, which closes UK borders to most low-skilled workers. At the same time, skill shortages have been identified in many sectors, leading to advanced economies seeking to attract high-skilled labour from developing states. Accordingly, the UK outlined a fast-track 'global talent' immigration route specifically designed to attract scientists, engineers and leading innovators in the humanities and arts. Not surprisingly, qualifications and their transferability have become a key issue in the movement of skilled labour, and related to this, the recognition of international educational opportunities. While this may be positive for the individuals involved who are able to move abroad for higher pay and presumably a better life, they contribute to a brain drain that leaves developing states worse off.

In sum, the long-standing tension between global market integration and legitimate forms of political authority that may seek to interfere in, or restrict, global processes continues to be one of the defining elements of IPE. The ability of capital to organise on a global level without a simultaneous development of matching transnational policy reforms has led to unprecedented levels of inequality within and between states – as has been explored above. As global governance remains partial, fragmented and gridlocked, the only clear alternative is a protectionist model that questions the benefits of globalisation and the managerial abilities of an international political class. Whether driven by left-wing reform populism or right-wing authoritarian populism, parts of the general public across political systems find deglobalisation ideas appealing as it promises credible system reform much closer to home. Yet, history suggests otherwise as protectionism has invariably led to severe economic contraction, or disaster (such as war) as was seen in the 1930s.

 CASE STUDY 10.1: The Global Compact for Migration

When we think about a question such as who gets what, when and how – as posed at the start of this chapter – its remit includes all levels of analysis. For example, the labour movement and civil society organisations have frequently mobilised to secure enforceable labour rights in the global economy with the help of international organisations. Despite numerous UN conventions, declarations and frameworks aimed at protecting the rights of groups of people, migrant workers remain marginalised and vulnerable to exploitation, unemployment and poor social protections. The Global Compact for Migration is an attempt to use a diplomatic agreement on twenty-three common objectives to commit all UN member states to safe, orderly and regular migration in the context of globalising labour markets (United Nations 2018). It reflects the official approach to global

Photo 10.1 Silhouettes of migrants above the entrance to the international conference on the Global Compact for Migration in Marrakech, 11 December 2018

Credit: FETHI BELAID/AFP/Getty Images

governance, promising a better balance of social, economic and environmental standards with transnational labour rights.

Like many agreements made at the international level, the Compact relies on voluntary compliance by its signatories. This means that it will only impact to the extent that states decide to implement each of the agreed objectives in their national systems. Therefore, regular peer review of national progress reports forms the main mechanism to facilitate the spread of best practices and bring about a global policy change. For the liberal advocates of this approach, the plight of migrants can be improved by opening domestic labour markets and improving access for low-skilled foreign labour (Angenendt and Koch 2019).

The proposed international regime works with the idea of a 'compact' to streamline the domestic migration policy of all participating states. It has the overarching objective to acknowledge local employment needs while excluding exploitative behaviour towards migrants. Liberals see an opportunity for win–win cooperation through a global governance arrangement with shared policies and joint solutions, while noting very different migration challenges in countries of origin, transit and destination. Although negotiated by the foreign ministries of the UN member states, the Global Compact for Migration advocates this approach, asking for policy coherence across government departments. Canada, for example, has often been recognised as the

model for the comprehensive management of labour migration providing universal access to public services in education, health, housing and social security.

By drawing on multistakeholder partnerships, the official negotiators avoided an alleged bias in favour of business demands for flexible labour supply. Indeed, the Global Compact for Migration suggests in the implementation phase new forms of cooperative behaviour involving civil society actors such as migrants, diasporas, local communities, trade unions, philanthropic foundations, faith-based organisations and human rights groups (United Nations 2018). Thus, the emphasis is on societal activism and capacity building jointly with the private sector, strengthening the compliance and implementation efforts of individual UN member states.

Objective six of the Compact outlines a decent work environment and suggests variable partnerships with stakeholders to agree on regulations that enable the recruitment industry to monitor its own ethical standards. Migrant workers should hold written contracts, be aware of their provisions and be able to request legal assistance. In short, it advocates effective rights and obligations in complaints and redress mechanisms. However, the degree to which individual stakeholders will commit to this is an open question. This sector of the global economy consists of a diverse set of interested parties including money lenders, lawyers, recruiters, travel agents and even people smugglers. It also consists of employers seeking human capital. What unites them is the pursuit of financial gain by facilitating human mobility across borders. International recruitment agencies, for example, have become a one-stop shop for the demand and supply of foreign labour especially in low-wage sectors of the industrialised world with highly flexible job markets.

As many governments have liberalised their labour markets, risks and responsibilities connected with the flexible management of migrant job seekers have also changed. Objective 16 of the Compact addresses this by promoting inclusive labour markets and prioritising the full participation of migrant workers in national economies to achieve better social cohesion. In practice this demands the matching of existing employment opportunities with investment in skills development and the mutual recognition of qualifications among the migrant population as formulated in Objective 18 of the Compact. In this way it targets the dual structure of many domestic labour markets where a primary sector of secure jobs contrasts quite sharply with a secondary sector of precarious employment. In the latter – the sectors of construction, hospitality, healthcare and agriculture – demand fluctuates widely due to specific business cycles or seasonal variation. Also, subcontracting to smaller firms to stay competitive internationally often works to the detriment of the migrant population when outsourced contracts rule out trade union membership or the formation of work councils.

A further important goal, articulated in Objective 20, is the commitment of signatories to promote faster, safer and cheaper transfers of remittances. By enabling migrants to send money home from their employment, developing and emerging markets benefit from the availability of additional financial resources. With the help of stronger competition, regulation and innovation the remittance market has significant growth potential. New

technological innovations such as mobile payments and online banking can reduce costs, improve speed, enhance security and create new distribution channels. As a form of private capital, remittances have so far not acquired the same standing as FDI, official development assistance or private sources of development finance (O'Brien and Williams 2020). Yet, they should become part of a national development strategy as industrialised states absorb large numbers of the workforce from the capital-poor periphery. As it stands, remittance flows are too negatively affected by domestic legislation raising transaction costs, which push many providers into informal transfer methods, feeding financial shadow markets in sub-Saharan Africa, Eastern Europe and Central Asia. Finally, the use of remittances does not necessarily mean greater social security for the families of migrant workers as their flow can be unstable and unpredictable depending on the type of employment (Hennebry 2014, 372). As noted in Objective 22 of the Compact, UN member states need to establish further mechanisms to close the governance gap in the portability of social security entitlements and earned benefits once workers move between developed and underdeveloped states.

 CASE STUDY 10.2: The US–China trade war

Photo 10.2 President Donald Trump and President Xi Jinping at the G20 Japan Summit in Osaka, 28 June 2019

Credit: Shealah Craighead/Trump White House Archive/ Flickr

The strategies leading up to a trade war follow the principle of tit for tat or 'equivalent

retaliation', where one actor copies an opponent's previous action to inflict economic costs. This behaviour can lead to economic conflict in which states use extreme forms of protectionism such as high tariffs or quota restrictions to directly damage each other's trade. During the presidency of Donald Trump (2017–21), his administration took a mercantilist position in an increasing number of trade disputes with China. That approach asserts that given limitations on global wealth, a state must export more than it imports to secure an advantage over rivals. In the past, World Trade Organization rules have been respected by state actors eager to prevent mutually damaging trade wars. The Trump administration, however, escalated a trade conflict to address recurring annual trade deficits that the United States had amassed. It challenged the industrial policies implemented by Chinese authorities, such as the 'Made in China 2025' policy, which allegedly resulted in unfair competitive advantages on global markets (Qiu, Zhan and Wei 2019).

For some time, US–China trade did not match the expectations of win–win cooperation. In contrast to the idea of comparative advantage, state-directed investments, a non-market economy and widespread disregard for the rule of law in China created an atmosphere of suspicion. From the American perspective, Chinese companies gain an unfair advantage over foreign competitors seeking market access. Allegedly, in their own market, they engage in intellectual property theft, product piracy and the forced transfer of foreign technology. Consequently, the dispute between the two powers, which has continued in the post-Trump years, is not about trade as such, but about technology-induced job losses in the United States aggravated by a manipulated exchange rate policy. Moreover, there is a growing concern that China uses its FDI to access sensitive technology to outgrow US industrial capabilities. In line with realist thought, the acquired know-how from sensitive production lines could eventually create a security dilemma. The use of unfair trade practices including import restrictions such as tariffs and quotas, export subsidies and low interest loans as well as stringent local content requirements adds up to an image of a new economic superpower that needs to be contained (Liu and Woo 2018, 333).

Frequently, foreign firms find their access to Chinese markets conditional upon joint ventures with domestic, government-linked companies, even if the latter develop into competitors on global markets. The Trump administration chose to confront such practices bilaterally rather than through the World Trade Organization complaints procedures related to market access. Hence, relative gains considerations matter in terms of competitiveness as well as national security. The trade war, escalating on multiple fronts, reflected the hesitation of the United States to promote further economic globalisation to the detriment of its own hegemonic position in the system. The Belt and Road Initiative adds to these worries as China combines economic power with geopolitical interests and aspires to become the biggest aid donor in Africa and Asia.

For realists, a trade war is not an indicator of a failed foreign economic policy or of unreasonable demands from another state. Even if two states set out with a commitment to free trade, each partner still has an incentive to defect to a higher tariff. Under the assumption that the other party will not reciprocate, the dominant state always benefits from unilateral action at the expense of its counterpart, for example, by increasing the costs for specific imports to help its domestic producers. At the same time, being aware of the incentives (and domestic pressures) to deviate from free trade, retaliation is likely and mutual losses are anticipated. A case in point is American farm exports, which were targeted by China with a 25 per cent tariff rise. Within one year, the value of US sales fell by one third and the federal government resorted to publicly funded subsidies to bail out American farmers.

During the course of the trade war, both sides suffered significant losses in their bilateral export volumes with higher prices hurting consumers. Private and state-owned companies equally experienced increasing production costs that reduced their competitiveness on global markets and triggered job losses due to falling sales. Xi and Trump finally agreed to partially suspend their trade war efforts, eventually leading to the signing of a new agreement in January 2020. The so-called 'phase one' deal committed China to buy American manufactured goods, services, energy and agricultural produce worth an extra $200 billion over a two-year period. While ignoring World Trade Organization governance, the United States negotiated an outcome-based trade deal with verifiable trade flows and immediate market access. Yet, the voluntarily agreed import expansion by China failed to materialise and many retaliatory tariff measures remained in place or changed only slowly. The focus on export targets only briefly overshadowed other problems such as non-tariff trade barriers, FDI and the protection of intellectual property, which will likely remain on the agenda for years to come.

International Political Economy accounts sensitive to domestic politics point to the politicisation of trade relations, qualifying the 'phase one' deal as a fundamentally wrong approach to deal with the causes of the bilateral trade deficit between the United States and China. Indeed, assuming hegemonic rivalry, the tense US–China relations after the trade war generate further disputes over key economic policy issues, at least until the political leadership of both states can agree on a reform of the multilateral trade regime. For the United States this implies reviving collaborative efforts with the European Union and Japan to strengthen general World Trade Organization mechanisms especially as regards industrial subsidies, investments and market access. For China, an improving compliance record within a reformed trading system will only become viable in return for a formal recognition of its socialist market economy where state-owned enterprises and the Communist party continue to dominate.

Conclusion

There are regular attempts to change the world for the better and shape the patterns of who gets what, when, and how. However, once approached through the lens of complex interdependence, relative gains or transnational class, such efforts focus on the economic as well as social consequences of globalisation. Rather than looking at economic growth in isolation, singling out states or targeting the distributional consequences of capitalism, International Political Economy considers the varying capacity of political authority to deal with global market pressures. Thus, as seen in the case studies, the negotiations of the Global Migration Compact and the US–China trade war form two polar points in a spectrum of political responses to increasingly conflictual international relations. The identified tension between global governance and deglobalisation unsettles any neat distinction between small-scale attempts at problem-solving and more ambitious, transformative, reform efforts. Global problems in need of purposeful system change – such as economic development, power rivalry and labour migration – will be tackled much more convincingly if we manage to keep alive the dialogue between competing viewpoints.

 ## END OF CHAPTER QUESTIONS

1. Compare and contrast the key claims in the three classic theories of International Political Economy.

2. Identify globalised economic sectors and examine the major problems they face in terms of wealth creation.

3. How, if at all, can the international community address the marginalisation of migrant labour?

4. Who were the winners and losers in the trade war between the United States and China during the Trump presidency?

5. From the International Political Economy perspective what factors delay, hinder and undermine purposeful change in the global system?

INTERNATIONAL LAW

Knut Traisbach

Question: How do international legal norms affect the behaviour of actors across the global system?

International law is a system of norms, a social practice and a professional culture that remains open to change and contestation. It comprises learned techniques, traditions, institutions and ideologies that evolve. These add up to a unique form of law – one that is very different to the laws we each experience domestically. As shown through earlier chapters, there are numerous state and non-state actors that engage in the regulation and administration of nearly all aspects of international life. Yet, questions often persist as to what *kind* of law international law is. This is especially pertinent as we have already established that, technically, there is no higher power above the state due to the principle of sovereignty. This itself raises questions of not just how international law exerts influence, but why states comply with it and how effective it is. Appreciating the dynamics that these questions cause forms an important part of understanding how this central normative structure within our global system works and how International Relations understands it.

What law is international law?

To help understand international law we will start with a thought experiment. Imagine a small settlement with a number of properties on each of which stands one house where one family lives. This settlement has no common government, court system or police force. The internal affairs of each family as much as the borders of each property are respected as inviolable. The families have predominantly bilateral relations with each other and engage in commercial exchanges of goods and services. If the head of a family dies, the established promises and agreements towards other families need to be respected by the heirs. It is commonly accepted that one may have recourse to force to defend one's interest in family and property. Other families do not intervene in these disputes as long as their interests are not affected, or they have formed an alliance with another family.

Ask yourself whether you would call this settlement a legal system? Perhaps intuitively you would say no. Yet, consider for a moment which kind of rules and principles must exist even in such a setting. If you think a little deeper, you will encounter some of the foundational legal institutions that exist in most legal systems. The concept of property, title, territory and border are there; a principle of autonomy and authority seems to apply to the families; and the institution of contract exists. You will also detect rules in the form of established customs, and you might even identify a principle that 'agreements need to be kept'. Thus, even in such a rudimentary setting, some customary rules and principles exist even if they are not called 'law' or written down. You may also note that some characteristics essential to a legal order are missing. There is no authority above the families that makes laws for all, adjudicates conflicts or enforces laws and judgments. The rules and principles seem to stem from established practices motivated by the needs of cohabitation, pragmatism or mere common sense. Whatever rules exist in this settlement, their validity and effectiveness are exclusively rooted in the will of the families and their members.

If you translate the situation of the settlement to the global system and substitute the families with states, you will get a picture in which states hold supreme and exclusive authority over their people and territory and follow predominantly customary and contractual rules in their relations. Yet, they have no world government above them. The principle of sovereignty expressed and confirmed the supreme authority and equal status of all states – developing (as noted in prior chapters) through practice and the writings of scholars between the sixteenth and eighteenth centuries. This meant that the validity of any legal rule between states depended on the will of states themselves or, conversely, that states were only bound by legal norms to which they had consented.

Many observers still regard international law as caught in an enigma: how can international legal norms be effective if their existence depends on the will of states, the very subjects international law shall govern? Many answers have been given to this question, including that other examples of rules exist, such as traditions, that instil compliance (rule following) without any strict enforcement. Another argument is that enforcement can take forms other than coercion. Most frequently, however, observers point to international practice which confirms that states constantly produce, engage with and recognise international rules. Henkin (1979, 47) famously stated that 'almost all nations observe almost all principles of international law and almost all of their obligations almost all of the time'.

11.1 – KEY INSIGHTS: Reflections on international law

1 'The law of nations ... derives its authority from the consent of all, or at least of many nations. It was proper to add MANY, because scarce any right can be found common to all nations ... Nay, frequently in one part of the world, that is held for the law of nations, which is not so in another. Now this law of nations is proved in the same manner as the unwritten civil law, and that is by the continual experience and testimony of the Sages of the Law. For this law ... is the discoveries made by experience and time' (Grotius 1625).

2 'Law of Nations or International Law ... is the name for the body of customary and conventional rules which are considered legally binding by civilised States in their intercourse with each other ... The Law of Nations is a law for the intercourse of States with one another, not a law for individuals' (Oppenheim 1912, 1).

3 'It is my claim that sovereignty has already been relegated to the status of a second-order norm which is derived from and geared towards the protection of basic human rights, needs, interests, and security. When this doctrinal move has been completed, international law will be [an] "individual-centered system"' (Peters 2009, 544).

4 '[T]he weakness of international law results from the fact that it is international and not supranational, that it exists between nations which are, at the same time, the originators, interpreters, and enforcers of the law. More particularly there is no enforcement agency which can guarantee the observance of the law, especially against a powerful transgressor' (Morgenthau 1974, 333).

5 'The problem of how order may be established in the absence of an overarching sovereign ... has been, and continues to be, the problem which has preoccupied both mainstream and critical theorizing about the discipline ... [A]n exclusive focus on this framework cannot provide an understanding of the history of the relationship between international law and the non-European world. The non-European world, relegated to the geographical periphery, is also relegated to the margins of theory. The specific historical experience of European states is generalised and universalised by its metamorphosis into the defining theoretical preoccupation of the discipline' (Anghie 2005, 109).

Let us look at some of the five statements about international law from Box 11.1 in more detail. The first statement stems from Hugo Grotius who wrote one of the earliest books about international society and the laws *inter* (between) nations in 1625. These international laws depend on 'continual experience' over time, that is, some form of customary behaviour, supported by the consent of nations and dependent on identification by learned persons. Tellingly, Grotius also states that nations may differ in their identification of the valid rules.

The second statement is taken from a textbook published in 1912. You can see that 'conventional' rules appear now beside customary rules for the regulation of relations between states. These contracts (called treaties, conventions or covenants) can be concluded between two states (bilateral) or negotiated by numerous states (multilateral). International treaties are today the preferred means of agreeing on rules between states because as they are written down, they have the advantage of being more specific than customs. Of course, disputes about the interpretation of written provisions still occur, but codified rules provide a more stable grounding for law. Oppenheim's 'definition' of international law makes reference to 'civilised' states, which was a common formulation at the time and still appears in many treaties. International law, as we know it today, was developed mainly in Europe, and states did not grant the same status to colonies or other territories that were open for discovery and annexation. These 'civilised' states often used their power to make the rules they preferred in order to legitimise their interests.

The third statement highlights a more contemporary position about the changing character of international law. It posits that international law has developed towards a legal system in which the individual has acquired a central role and state sovereignty no longer shields the internal affairs of states. We will explore these and the other statements in the course of the chapter as we discuss different characteristics of international law. The brief analysis of just these first three shows that international law has evolved. Although there have been and continue to be diverging understandings of international law, the present chapter introduces you to the understanding of international law as a system of norms (legal prescriptions of expected behaviours), which is a term you should already be familiar with from earlier chapters. This approach reflects the professional techniques that international lawyers learn and apply (Kratochwil 2018).

11.2 – KEY TERMS: International legal order

Photo 11.1 Roman goddess Justitia

Credit: pixel2013/pixabay

International lawyers advise governments and assess the lawfulness of actions and situations. Lawyers learn how to identify precedent, interpret the law and balance conflicting rights and interests. These professional techniques constitute a practice. Ideally, this work would always be neutral and objective (the Roman goddess Justitia, pictured, is usually blindfolded) but international law does not establish a perfectly neutral and objective order – it is always influenced by power and interests due to the nature of the global system. International law consists of certain conventions on argumentation and modes of conflict resolution that some regard as a craft, others as an art. Most likely it is both.

The contents of international law

Domestic law stems from domestic lawmakers and regulates the life of the inhabitants of a particular state. Regional law, such as European Union law or the law of regional human rights mechanisms, stems from regional intergovernmental organisations and addresses the states and persons of a particular geographical region or legal regime. Then there is public and private international law. Private international law concerns conflicts of law that may arise in cases where the domestic laws of different states could apply, for example in cases of cross-border commerce, marriages or liabilities. Public international law, on the other hand, is the subject of this chapter and addresses relations involving states, intergovernmental organisations and non-state actors, which include individuals, groups, non-governmental organisations and transnational corporations. Within public international law, a distinction is traditionally drawn between the law of peace and the law of war (humanitarian law or the law of armed conflicts). The law of peace regulates peaceful relations and includes such subject matters as international treaty law and the law of diplomatic and consular relations.

11.3 – KEY TERMS: The laws of war

Under Article 2:4 of the UN Charter, the use of force by states is prohibited except in instances of self-defence (Article 51) or an authorisation by the UN Security Council. The legal regulation of the permissible resort to force (*jus ad bellum* – the law to engage in war) lies at the transitional points between the law of peace and the law of armed conflict. Some scholars also speak of the regulation of the transition to peace after the end of armed conflicts (*jus post-bellum* – the law after war) which includes questions over how to end armed conflicts, transitional justice and post-war reconstruction. International humanitarian law (IHL) is the law of armed conflicts (*jus in bellum* – the law applicable in war) and regulates the conduct of hostilities. It comprises a large body of customary rules and a series of important conventions and additional protocols adopted in more recent times, principally in The Hague and Geneva. International humanitarian law regulates, among other things, the methods and means of warfare and the protection of certain categories of persons – for example, the sick and wounded, prisoners of war and civilians. More specific treaties prohibit the use of certain types of weapon (such as chemical or biological weapons, mines or cluster munitions) or regulate the protection of cultural property during armed conflict.

The different legal spheres of domestic, regional and international law are not strictly separated but overlap and interact in many ways (Koh 2006; Walker 2014). European Union law, for example, is often directly applicable domestically, and domestic courts apply and interpret also international legal rules. Likewise, the strict distinction between the law of peace and the law of armed conflict has been somewhat blurred by the development of international human rights law and international criminal law. Human rights law builds on and develops fundamental principles of humanitarian law for the protection of individuals. On the other hand, human rights have considerably influenced the refinement of humanitarian rules for the protection of combatants and civilians in both international and non-international armed conflicts. Parallel to this development, international criminal law, which is addressed later in this chapter, has had a strong influence on the interpretation of humanitarian and human rights law.

As we have seen, traditionally, states were the principal subjects of international law and bearers of privileges and obligations. Still today, the status of a sovereign state implies full membership in the international society of states with all rights and obligations this involves. Privileges include equal legal status, immunities, jurisdiction or membership in international organisations, for example. Obligations towards other states arise from voluntary contracts, from the principle of non-intervention or from responsibilities for wrongful acts. Given the historic focus on states, individuals were not direct subjects of international law as statement two in Box 11.1 highlights. It was only as citizens of a state and through this state that they could promote their interests on the international level. For example, if foreigners were tortured by officials of another state, the individuals themselves could do very little according to the then prevalent international law. Even worse, if a state tortured its own citizens, this was an internal matter in which other states were not supposed to intervene.

Form the standpoint of international law, all states are equal in their sovereignty. This is not to say that they actually are equal in practice. Realists (for example) would note differences in power as the decisive criteria which determines the status, possibilities and behaviour of states. The speaker at the conference dinner, who made statement four in Box 11.1 about the lack of a superior enforcement authority was Hans J. Morgenthau. He and other realists were sceptical about the effectiveness of international law in a world of unequal power. For them, international law was inept at understanding the behaviour of nations. For realists, international law serves mainly as a tool in the hands of the powerful to be used (or discarded) in their own national interests. While realists do not necessarily see this as a problem, scholars of 'Third World Approaches to International Law' argue that fundamental principles of international law like sovereignty, the rules about statehood or the acquisition of territory reflect the interests of powerful nations. Statement five in Box 11.1 highlights how the interests of less powerful states, especially those outside the West, are marginalised. This is especially the case for contributions by cultures and groups of people that precede (or fall outside) the Westphalian system, such as indigenous groups, as detailed in Chapters three and four. Feminist scholars make a similar argument when they point out that international law deals mainly with traditional spheres of male power such as diplomacy, trade and war and has broadly neglected the concerns of women in the private sphere or during conflicts. Thus, enlarging the realm of recognised subjects of international law beyond sovereign states has given other actors the possibility to influence international rules.

The next question is, then, in what kind of rules international law manifests. Article 38(1) of the Statute of the International Court of Justice, the principal judicial organ of the United Nations, lists as sources of international law on which the court may rely in its decisions: treaties, customary international law, general principles of law that exist in most domestic legal systems (such as behaving in 'good faith') and, as a subsidiary means, also judicial decisions and scholarly writings. The first two statements in Box 11.1 refer to customary law, which derives from the established practices of states that are supported by a subjective belief to be required by law. If a customary rule exists, it is binding on all states except where a state has persistently objected to this rule. You can perhaps imagine that the deduction of legal rules from social practices and subjective beliefs poses many difficulties.

11.4 – KEY INSIGHTS: Torture and international law

The United States is a member state of the International Covenant on Civil and Political Rights, which contains a prohibition of torture, and is also party to the Convention against Torture and Other Cruel, Inhuman or Degrading Treatment or Punishment. After the attacks of 9/11, the CIA brought suspected terrorists to secret prisons in various countries where the suspects endured intense interrogations by local collaborators that included sleep deprivation, waterboarding (causing the sensation of drowning) and other measures.

How would an international lawyer analyse this? We neglect for the moment whether humanitarian law is applicable since the US government claims to engage in a global war against terrorism. An international lawyer would begin with the aforementioned international treaties that the United States has ratified and would determine whether the interrogation measures amount to torture as defined by these treaties. For this, the interpretation of torture in previous cases can give important guidance. In our example, the situation is complicated by the fact that both treaties stipulate that state parties have obligations regarding any individuals and territory under their jurisdiction. Hence one could argue that instances of torture on foreign territory and executed by non-nationals do not fall within the ambit of the obligations of the United States under these treaties. Yet also a counterargument is possible. One could make a case for the application of the treaty if the acts of torture on foreign soil were effectively controlled by the United States and are thus attributable to it. You could also examine statements and practices by states and other international actors in order to collect evidence that the prohibition of torture is today of such fundamental importance that no derogation from this rule is permitted under any circumstances (*ius cogens* – peremptory law).

You can see now how the work of international lawyers blends out questions of power and political interests. You will also note how the early idea of state consent as a necessary requirement for an international rule still permeates the above argumentations. For international lawyers, the main difficulty often consists in proving state consent or, at times, in constructing alternatives for it in order to confirm international legal obligations.

The international legal order is not static. After the Second World War, the United Nations was established with the principal aim to ensure peace and security through international cooperation and collective measures. Article 2 of its Charter confirms as guiding principles of the organisation the sovereign equality of its member states, the peaceful settlement of disputes, the prohibition of the use of force and the principle of non-intervention. On the one hand, it is an institutional setting for functional cooperation with the objective to set and attain common aims, for example, by establishing common normative frameworks through collective action. On the other hand, the hierarchy and composition of its main organs reflect the unequal distribution of power (see Fassbender 2020). This distribution is challenged by newly emerging or re-emerging powers such as the BRICS countries and by practices of block voting by countries of a geographical area. In addition, the internal bureaucracies of the Secretariat and the General Assembly have been successful in promoting international agendas such as the Sustainable Development Goals. Other UN agencies, such as the Offices of the High Commissioners for Refugees and for Human Rights, have made major contributions to the development of solutions and normative responses to global challenges. All of this never happens without setbacks, but, as constructivists have shown, the organisations themselves develop an 'identity' and can succeed in promoting wider change by learning from failures and adapting to changing realities.

Numerous principal and subsidiary UN organs and specialised agencies engage in the application, enforcement and development of international law. This work comprises, for example, classical legal work in the International Law Commission and in committees of the General Assembly, practical work in the field and diplomatic efforts by Offices of High Commissioners and their staff. All of these bodies, and many more international organisations, promote and shape international law in various ways (Klabbers 2015).

The existence of a global organisation, the legal prohibition of the use of force, the establishment of a system of collective security and the protection of human rights have caused fundamental changes in the international legal order. International lawyers and politicians speak frequently of the 'international community' that cooperates to pursue common interests which cannot be achieved by single states alone.

11.5 – KEY INSIGHTS: Non-state actors and soft law

Today there are countless actors that engage in the making, interpretation, use and enforcement of international norms. States remain the principal international actors. Yet the bureaucracies of intergovernmental organisations and their organs, numerous international, regional and domestic courts and tribunals, influential non-governmental organisations and even groups or single persons (so-called 'norm entrepreneurs') engage in the pronunciation, interpretation and dissemination of international legal norms, standards and other types of 'soft law' that is not expressed through binding treaties or custom. The UN General Assembly, for example, has created numerous standards and principles through its resolutions, such as the Sustainable Development Goals or the Guiding Principles on Business and Human Rights.

The development of the Responsibility to Protect is a pertinent example of 'soft' lawmaking and the role of the 'international community'. The military intervention in Kosovo by NATO in 1999 was widely regarded as illegal as the Security Council did not give prior authorisation for the use of force, but some observers nevertheless regarded it as a legitimate action to stop a genocide. In the aftermath, responding to a public call of UN Secretary-General Kofi Annan, a private expert group under the auspices of the Canadian Government (the International Commission on Intervention and State Sovereignty) prepared a report on 'The Responsibility to Protect'. The principle was included in the final document of the UN World Summit in 2005, but no international treaty exists that codifies the principle. Both the Security Council and the General Assembly have repeatedly referred to this doctrine, as have many civil society and non-governmental organisations, which use it as an argumentative tool in their advocacy. It is an example of how a non-binding policy initiative can gradually gain normative authority without an international treaty.

Yet, realists would assert that no powerful state needs to fear an intervention, or be obliged to intervene elsewhere in the name of human protection. States can not only ignore the Responsibility to Protect's supposed obligations, they can also harness it for legal justifications of military interventions they wish to pursue. For example, humanitarian reasons were invoked to justify the US invasion in Iraq in 2003 and for the NATO-led campaign in Libya in 2011. On other occasions – such as in the protracted civil wars in Syria and Yemen – the doctrine has had very little to no effect in protecting those affected as major states were unwilling to take substantive action. From this perspective, we can also see developments such as the Responsibility to Protect as another way that powerful states use international law as a justification for their national interests. This is not merely an issue of politics versus law. There are and will always be international lawyers (not only realist scholars) who provide legal arguments to justify the use of force on humanitarian or other grounds. Hence, even as international law continues to evolve, the realities of the global system and the prerogative of sovereignty are ever present.

The functioning of international law

The multitude of norms, legal regimes, actors and normative processes is reflected in more recent approaches that understand international law more as a pluralistic 'process' than a unified 'system' of norms. These approaches focus more on 'soft' lawmaking, socialisation and learning than on formal sources. This takes us back to the idea of the normative 'life cycle' that was first explored in Chapter seven where a norm first emerges, then a cascade begins, before it is finally internalised. Consider, for example, the development of an international legal norm prohibiting torture. For the first stage of norm emergence, the influence of so-called 'norm-entrepreneurs' (such as private individuals, lobbying groups, non-governmental organisations) is essential. Through a combination of means (e.g. persuasion, shaming etc.) and on different organisational platforms, the norm-entrepreneurs make their case to governments and in society. The new norm then starts to gain wider acceptance. States may follow the norm based on functional considerations because accepting the norm improves their reputation or brings other advantages, as rationalist scholars point out. Those state and non-state actors that have endorsed the norm engage in a process of redefining what qualifies as appropriate behaviour. Constructivists highlight how such a norm is regarded as good and appropriate and becomes part of the identity of actors ('torture is not what we do').

At this stage, regional and international treaties might be negotiated and adopted that make the norm binding. These treaties oblige member states to bring their domestic laws in conformity with their supranational obligations. Norms such as the prohibition of torture then exert normative force domestically through fundamental rights guarantees and criminal law provisions. In addition, the norms continue to be invoked in regional and international fora such as regional and international courts and organisations. Human

11.6 – KEY INSIGHTS: Interpreting the United Nations Convention on the Law of the Sea (UNCLOS)

Map 11.1 China's claims on territorial waters

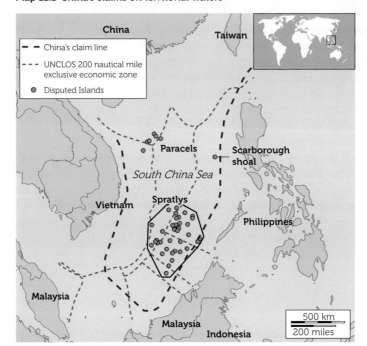

UNCLOS defines the rights and responsibilities of states toward the world's oceans. Starting from the coastline of a state, the treaty defines various zones for the exercise of sovereign power. The rights and control of the coastal state decrease with the distance from the coast. In the context of disputes over maritime zones between China and its neighbours (Map 11.1), consider the following two statements:

1 'Based on the practice of the Chinese people and the Chinese government in the long course of history and the position consistently upheld by successive Chinese governments, and in accordance with national law and international law, including the United Nations Convention on the Law of the Sea, China has territorial sovereignty and maritime rights and interests in the South China Sea' (Ministry of Foreign Affairs of the People's Republic of China 2016).

2 'We [the Heads of State/Government of ASEAN Member States] discussed the situation in the South China Sea … We reaffirmed that the UNCLOS is the basis for determining maritime entitlements, sovereign rights, jurisdiction and legitimate interests over maritime zones, and the UNCLOS sets out the legal framework within which all activities in the oceans and seas must be carried out' (ASEAN 2020).

rights treaties usually establish specific control mechanisms (such as independent expert committees) that ensure that treaty members comply with their obligations. The committees conduct, for example, state visits and review periodic reports from states. Thus, these norms acquire a transnational character through interactions between a variety of actors across issues and across historical public/private and domestic/international dichotomies. Eventually, norms can become internalised if they 'achieve a "taken-for-granted" quality that makes conformance with the norm almost automatic' (Finnemore and Sikkink 1998). Customary international law reflects, perhaps best, this last stage.

As we have seen, the potential internalisation of international norms does not necessarily mean that international law is a guarantor for a just global order. The internalisation is difficult to measure and apparent internalisation can also be undone. Much rests on the will and interests of the actors involved. International law itself cannot solve injustices and cannot impose solutions. Ultimately, many of the politically charged issues are simply expressed through the language of international law. Consider the two statements in Box 11.6 where China and the ASEAN governments refer to the United Nations Convention on the Law of the Sea, claiming that their differing interpretation of the treaty supports their respective claims. Importantly, neither of them argues that the treaty is irrelevant and has nothing to say about the matter. From the perspective of international law, the states could (and should) comply with the 2016 ruling of an arbitration panel that refuted many of China's claims. Yet international law cannot oblige them to do so.

Coming back to the question at the beginning of the chapter, we should recognise that international law is an imperfect law. But so is domestic law despite its stronger enforcement mechanisms. We have seen how international legal norms exert influence in many different ways. Enforcement, too, can take many different forms, comprising binding judgments by international and regional courts with which states overwhelmingly comply, sanctions imposed by regional and international organisations; or individual criminal responsibility.

CASE STUDY 11.1: From war crimes to the International Criminal Court

Photo 11.2 Exterior view of the International Criminal Court building in The Hague

Credit: Michel Porro/Getty Images

The International Criminal Court, based in The Hague, Netherlands, is the only permanent international court adjudicating on the criminal responsibility of individuals. This includes state leaders and other officials indicted for genocide, crimes against humanity, war crimes or acts of aggression (international crimes). Although the jurisdiction of the Court is conditioned on proof that local courts have been unwilling or unable to investigate the alleged crimes, which means that local courts have priority in investigations, the potential jurisdiction of the International Criminal Court is a notable restriction on state sovereignty. It took up its functions in 2002 when its founding treaty, the Rome Statute of the International Criminal Court, entered into force. Over 120 states have ratified the statute, but powerful states such as India, China, Russia and the United States are not yet parties. The International Criminal Court is not to be confused with the International Court of Justice (which primarily settles disputes between states). The law on individual criminal responsibility for the most horrendous crimes is an apt example demonstrating norm development as multiple actors contributed over time, and in many different ways, to the norms of international criminal law.

The idea that some acts, such as piracy and slavery, are criminal directly under international law goes back many centuries. In more modern times, the notion that war criminals could be held accountable before international tribunals was discussed after the First World War, but it was only after the Second World War that this came into being when the allied powers established international military tribunals in Nuremberg and Tokyo. The prosecution of political and military leaders before international tribunals complemented the numerous domestic trials of war criminals in many different states. The international tribunals contributed to the definition and application of the international crimes that we know today. The development of the relevant legal norms was furthered by the UN International Law Commission, which first elaborated the Nuremberg Principles on international crimes. After the Nuremberg trials, the UN General Assembly requested the Commission to begin work on a draft code of offences against the peace and security of mankind. The latter project led eventually to the elaboration of a draft statute for an international criminal court. This preparatory work not only influenced the statutes of the first two ad hoc international criminal tribunals for the former Yugoslavia and Rwanda in 1993 and 1994 respectively, but formed the basis for the subsequent negotiations of the Rome Statute.

An assessment of the effectiveness of the International Criminal Court depends on one's outlook on international society. Realists and other critics doubt its effectiveness and point to the low number of proceedings that have been initiated and brought to conclusion. They highlight that several of the most powerful states have not ratified the Rome Statute and stress the lack of cooperation from states in collecting evidence and securing witnesses. Liberals, on the other hand, argue that the Court is evidence of international cooperation to achieve greater global justice. It shows how wider social preferences in international society of what counts as unacceptable behaviour can shape decisions to create enforcement mechanisms. The International Criminal Court is, in this reading, proof of the regulatory power of international organisations. Critical theory approaches take issue with these liberal assumptions. They point to the impossibility of the Court to live up to its aspirations while operating in a flawed political landscape. They criticise the liberal professional culture of international criminal lawyers who claim to deliver judgments in the name of humanity and thus engage in the biased promotion of new standards of 'civilisation'.

For most international lawyers such theoretical discussions bring little to the practical problems they face. In their day-to-day business they focus in a more pragmatic manner on the tasks of securing witnesses, collecting evidence and preparing arguments. International criminal law, just like international law, has created a practice that builds on professional knowledge, learned techniques and a sense of legal obligation. There can be little doubt that these criminal tribunals have influenced the legal development of international criminal norms through their interpretation and use of these norms. In addition, numerous domestic trials as well as historical clarification and truth commissions in Latin America and South Africa contributed to the practice of transitional justice norms (Sikkink 2011). From a constructivist perspective, these norms develop slowly and are intrinsically connected to discourses and contestations between professionals and wider society of what is acceptable.

Institutions often play a crucial role in this norm development. Several actors during different periods have contributed to the development of these norms, including international and domestic courts, experts, regional institutions and (of course) international organisations. The acceptance and application of legal norms by an institution gives them content and meaning. If institutions with a high degree of binding authority, such as courts and tribunals, adjudicate and enforce norms, this contributes not only to the effectiveness of these norms. It also strengthens the normative and organisational context in which the acceptance of the norms becomes institutionalised through the establishment of professional networks and cultures.

However, the leaps in the development of international criminal law happened mostly as a response to crisis (see Charlesworth 2002), not because of a universal concern 'to fight impunity' or 'to improve the lives of vulnerable groups'. Even if depictions of normative developments can imply a continuous trajectory through history, these narrations of progress are often drawn with hindsight and do not convey all the breaks and setbacks that have occurred and are likely to occur again, which can be understood more fully by comparing Moyn (2010) with Sikkink (2017).

 CASE STUDY 11.2: The Trump administration's withdrawal from the JCPOA

Photo 11.3 President Donald Trump, accompanied by Vice President Mike Pence, signs an Executive Order sanctioning Iran, 24 June 2019

Credit: Joyce N. Boghosian/Trump White House Archive/Flickr

The Joint Comprehensive Plan of Action (JCPOA) is an international agreement reached between Iran, the five permanent members of the Security Council, Germany and the European Union in 2015. In response to fears about Iran developing a nuclear weapons programme, it agreed to specific nuclear non-proliferation measures. In return, a large number of sanctions on Iran were lifted, subject to a strict inspection regime led by the International Atomic Energy Agency. The UN Security Council formally endorsed the plan through Resolution 2231. Although the Trump administration withdrew from the JCPOA in 2018 and then passed a range of executive orders placing sanctions on Iran (Photo 11.3), this case study shows the normative environment that persists even in situations where an international agreement allegedly 'fails'.

The JCPOA is an apt, albeit complex, example of how diplomacy, politics and law interact. For realists in particular, the withdrawal of the United States was an example of how national security calculations and/or changes in domestic policy preferences take precedence over international law. By this reading, the United States and Iran entered the agreement when they had a political and security calculus that rendered the deal convenient. Then, when that calculus shifted, marked by Donald Trump's arrival in office in 2017, the United States simply withdrew without relying on the formal conflict resolution mechanism in the agreement and imposed new sanctions on Iran thereafter. For realists, the entire situation shows how quickly compliance with an agreement can change when a state's priorities change. Yet, there is more to the story. Diplomacy relies heavily on agreements, whether they are regarded as formally binding or not. The JCPOA was an example of this as it contained detailed provisions and specific commitments, in many ways resembling a contract.

When assessing the situation of the Trump administration's withdrawal from an international law angle, the first question would be to determine whether the JCPOA had any binding effect. If the US withdrawal was 'unlawful' under international law, then Iran's subsequent decision not to fulfil parts of its commitments could be qualified as a justified reaction. The Trump administration repeatedly stated that the JCPOA was a mere political commitment, not an executive agreement or binding treaty. But the JCPOA resembled an international agreement in many ways: it contained very detailed provisions about commitments of the parties, implementation, duration and dispute settlement. Under international law a treaty is any international agreement concluded between states in written form and governed by international law. Domestic designations and internal laws do not directly affect the validity of an international agreement. Neither does a change in leadership automatically imply that international agreements entered into by previous administrations can be easily terminated. Even if we assume that all parties to the JCPOA agreed that it was a non-binding political commitment, international lawyers would still consider whether the formal endorsement by the UN Security Council created any legal obligations for the states concerned (Mulligan 2018).

Perhaps recognising the legal weaknesses of its arguments, the Trump administration also spoke of alleged breaches of the JCPOA, accusing Iran of hiding enrichment activities over and above the agreement. If true, this would be one of the recognised grounds to cease performing the commitments under the JCPOA. Yet, the Trump administration gave no clear evidence of this, nor could any be found by third parties.

Understanding this case from an international law perspective would also lead us to consider the wider and long-term effects of the JCPOA, even despite its failures. Abstract concerns and areas of conflicting interests had to be negotiated and put in writing, requiring a general consensus on wording and meaning. More broadly, the agreement has given several states, and an international organisation (the European Union) a leading role in diplomatic negotiations with Iran. This represents a wider international will to find ways to continue engagements with Iran due to the economic and political benefits. Even when agreements seem to fall apart, they leave lasting effects and relations that are a basis for future negotiations. Indeed, that precise scenario was what allowed the successor Biden administration (from 2021) to swiftly resume negotiations with Iran after taking office. International law's intrinsic value is therefore firmly connected to a multilateral and multilayered understanding of international relations that are often invisible when looking only at the surface level.

Conclusion

Questions about how international legal norms affect the behaviour of actors across the global system will always persist. Realists will continue to point to instances when powerful nations use their political power to 'bend' international law or use it to promote their interests. International lawyers will emphasise instances of 'success' when disputes have been settled peacefully or a new international treaty has been adopted. Yet, as this chapter has shown, there is not one approach that can fully describe the social practices and the multitude of actors at the international level. That the individual has acquired such a prominent role in contemporary international law as a central subject beyond state confines is truly remarkable. Returning to the example early in the chapter about the families and their properties, today states are no longer regarded as monolithic blocks but each individual and groups of individuals have rights that permeate the international. They are fundamentally embedded in an (albeit imperfect) transnational system of laws. Additionally, international law is not static, but it is a form of law in a constant process of development. The normative force of international law lies in the delimitation of valid arguments, in the possibility to challenge established positions, in the institutionalised forums for conflict resolution and in the justificatory potential that rests in law.

 END OF CHAPTER QUESTIONS

1. How much does the assessment of the role and influence of international law depend on one's theoretical outlook?

2. Can you identify advantages in the alleged 'weaknesses' of international law?

3. How can state and non-state actors outside 'the West' shape the international legal order?

4. Considering how domestic, regional and international legal orders interact, do you think it makes sense to speak of a 'transnational' or 'global' law?

5. How has the international legal order changed, what provokes change and how do you see the future of international law? Are states any less important in this future outlook?

RELIGION AND CULTURE

John A. Rees

Question: How accurate is it to claim that there is little that concerns International Relations today that does not involve elements of religion or culture, or both?

Religion and culture are complex phenomena that have, unfortunately, traditionally been ignored by the bulk of International Relations scholars. Underscored by ideas such as secularisation theory, it was long thought by many in the discipline that these were lower order domestic matters that would lose their importance over time. This thinking built on observing the vast majority of Western, especially European, states, which had experienced a centuries-long decline in religion since its heyday pre-1648 when the church (directly or indirectly) had dominated much of Europe via the Holy Roman Empire. When taken together with another prevailing orthodoxy – globalisation – which was said to be synthesising cultural differences and bringing common understandings and experiences to all of humankind, you can perhaps understand why International Relations placed its attentions elsewhere. This began to change with the influence of the critical theories in the 1980s, but it was real-world events such as the Iranian revolution in 1978–79, the fall of the Soviet Union in 1989–91 and especially the attacks on 11 September 2001 (9/11), that marked a turning point. In this sense 9/11 can be viewed not just factually as a memorable religion-inspired terrorist event, but also thematically as a structural attack on Western culture and institutions – thereby signalling the need for International Relations to update its thinking and widen its horizons. Addressing this need, this chapter identifies religion and culture separately at first, before bringing them together to show how they interact to form religio-cultural identities.

Elements of religion

Following the al-Qaeda attacks on the United States on 9/11, studies of religion in world politics multiplied rapidly. In the words of Keohane (2002), the events provoked the realisation that 'world-shaking political movements have so often been fuelled by religious fervour'. Even a brief glance at everyday affairs seems to support the comment made by Berger (1999) that 'the world today … is as furiously religious as it ever was, and in some places more so than ever'. This view is also supported by the numbers. Whilst there are important variations and contrasts depending on location and religion, research by Johnson and Crossing (2019) suggests that the percentage of the world's population identifying as religious has risen from approximately 80 per cent in 1970 to approximately 90 per cent today.

12.1 – KEY TERMS: Secularisation theory

Secularisation theory was an orthodoxy in pre-2001 academic and policy debates. It posited that the pursuit of science and reason (characteristics associated with the European Enlightenment) had made religion largely irrelevant as it was a feature of a pre-modern era. Europe and North America's political systems had supposedly divorced themselves from direct religious influence through secular ideas such as the separation of church and state – reflecting the core characteristics of the Westphalian system. This was assumed to be a pattern that would replicate in other geographical areas as the Westphalian system grew to become global – especially after the end of the Cold War. Secularisation theory was widely practised and often taken for granted – especially by the United States. It shaped how diplomacy was conducted with more religious states, especially those of the Middle East and North Africa. Rather than discuss religious issues, negotiations were purposefully focused on political, economic and social issues – with the belief that over time those would become dominant and religious issues would fade. Madeleine Albright, America's first female Secretary of State, summed this up as follows, 'diplomats in my era were taught not to invite trouble, and no subject seemed more inherently treacherous than religion' (2006).

To identify with a religious group can mean many different things. Because of this, scholars argue about the relative value of big data (quantitative) studies on religion and seek to supplement this with conceptual approaches and contextual evidence. The following qualitative approach considers three elements of religion:

1. The framework of religious belief: this can be divided between 'fundamental' and 'contextual'
2. An understanding of religious practice through rituals and teachings
3. The place of religion in the dynamics of power

The first element of religion is the belief that divine beings and/or forces hold relevance to the meaning and practice of politics today and throughout history. These beings are sometimes understood as a knowable God or gods, sometimes as mythical and symbolic figures from our ancient past, and sometimes as spiritual forces beyond or within the physical realm. Encounters between humans and beings/forces so described could be considered a basic element across a vast array of religious practices and traditions. From this perspective, the intersection of religion and politics occurs when these believed encounters inform individual and group behaviour in the public realm.

Different religious traditions understand the influence of religion upon politics in different ways. Traditions that we might call 'fundamental' propose that politics is a matter of organising society according to divine commands. In Iran, for example, the highest political authority is a Supreme Leader guided by principles from the Shia branch of Islam – the second-largest Islamic tradition worldwide after the majority Sunni tradition. Likewise, in Myanmar, an influential group of religious monks started a movement intent on imposing Buddhist principles on society, including on non-Buddhist minorities. Thus, some religious politics is based on fundamentals that, in the view of adherents, cannot be changed without the standards of society also being compromised. This remains so even if those fundamentals are not embraced by all members of that society. And, in the latter case may be seen as repressive or intolerant of diversity of thought.

By contrast, traditions that adopt a 'contextual' approach hold that politics is a matter of influencing society according to divine principles, but as part of a wider tapestry of influences. For example, religious development organisations such as the Aga Khan Development Network (also from the Shia branch of Islam) work in areas of health care and education in countries in Africa and Asia without seeking to control entire political systems. Similarly, in Myanmar, the so-called Saffron Revolution of 2007 saw Buddhist monks standing with the poor against the ruling military dictatorship and supporting the beginnings of a period of multi-party democracy. In these examples, religious politics is adapted to changing circumstances and takes into account diverse interests and beliefs across society.

What is common to both fundamental and contextual religious traditions is an understanding that politics is in some sort of interactive relationship with the intentions of, or traditions associated with, gods (or God) and spiritual forces. In the case of Myanmar, for instance, we see a complex overlap between a religious group needing to adapt to changing context without losing religious identity and freedoms. This interactive understanding contrasts strongly with secular approaches that demote, and sometimes deny altogether, a role for religious encounter in political affairs.

12.2 – KEY TERMS: Religion

Religion is variously defined as (1) personal, communal and institutional practices based on believed encounters with transcendent realities beyond (or within) the material world; (2) the social dynamics created by the separation of sacred and mundane space; or (3) an idea rooted in Christian terminology employed to codify (and control) a wide variety of social and cultural practices. Elements of religion include: belief (or faith) in god(s) and/or spiritual forces in the public square; sacred rituals and stories shaping community life; and particular forms of dominant power and resistance.

The second element of religion involves rituals that reorder the world in collective imaginings, practices and sentiments. Although the word 'faith' can be associated with belief in unseen realities, as we have already noted with reference to 'encountering' the gods, humans throughout time have needed to see, touch and smell the sacred. Our senses are portals to the spirit. Therefore, rituals function as tangible symbols of the intangible realm. Importantly, religious ritual in public spaces, or in ways that are openly accessible to wider society, can be understood as a way of 'devising order' (Småberg et al. 2012). As such, they are a part of public political life. Of particular importance is the way religions practice ritual in ways that devise order at national, regional and international levels. These practices are key to understanding the importance of what Elshtain calls the 'really existing communities' of religion operating internationally (Elshtain 1999).

Alongside public rituals, religious teachings based on stories of significant figures, events and ideas from the past, beliefs about the future, impart truths about the meanings of existence and even of time itself – like predictions about the end of the world. For other religious traditions, time is an illusion and the main focus is living in the moment according to sacred ideas rather than the connection of past–present–future. These elements – interpreting the past, projecting the future, living in the 'now' – are basic to the development of political ideologies also. By locating the practice of religious ritual and storytelling in the public domain, we can observe how religion and politics become entangled in complex ways.

Importantly, by 'entanglement' we do not mean 'enstranglement' where the particulars of religious practice are disregarded or crushed under the weight of political interest. Hibbard (2010) argues instead that secular states and religious traditions both 'deal with issues of normative content, collective identity, and legitimate authority', and these overlaps place religion in a unique position to sanctify or stigmatise a particular political agenda, imbue political action with moral or spiritual meaning, and provide felt responses for mobilising popular sentiment. Importantly, this complex interaction redefines religious participation as based on competing ideas of society, often uniting some religiously oriented citizens with secular-oriented citizens on an issue, and in opposition to fellow religious citizens from the same tradition who adopt a different social and political view. For religious citizens, these competing positions can be determined by the different ways sacred rituals and storytelling are enacted and imagined because 'different renderings of religious tradition underwrite differing visions of social life and hence differing politics' (Hibbard 2010).

Thirdly, and for a significant number of scholars, religion is understood to be an agent of dominating power. Long before this view took hold in the study of religion in International Relations, it gained traction with thinkers and movements fighting for independence from colonial rule who associated religion with Empire. Thinkers such as the postcolonialist Frantz Fanon (1967, 28) wrote of 'the pacification of the colonized by the inescapable powers of religion'. The negative postcolonial depiction of religion in International Relations is particularly aimed at Christianity, not only because of the violent colonial practices of Christian-oriented empires, but also because the very language of 'religion' could be traced to Christian roots, thus equating the use of categories such as 'religion' and 'secular' to the practice of colonial control. In this way, religion could be defined as an idea rooted in Christian terminology employed by hegemonic (dominating) Western Christian powers to codify (and control) a wide variety of social and cultural practices (Hurd 2017).

Three additional viewpoints on religion and colonialism are also worth noting to complete the picture of religion in a world of dominating power. The first of these is that Christianity and colonialism are linked in complex and diverse ways. For instance, Casanova's study (2019) of Jesuit missions from the mid-sixteenth to late eighteenth centuries argues that the Jesuit idea of 'accommodation' helped to develop an early form of globalisation characterised by 'a world system of religious pluralism' and contributed to the rise of humanitarianism and global human rights regimes. Second, religions associated with colonial conquest have often been received, adapted and re-indigenised into the soil of post-colonial societies. For instance, when the World Bank surveyed over 60,000 of the poorest people on earth – many of whom live in former colonial territories around the world – in an attempt to hear their core concerns, religion emerged as a significantly positive factor. Contrasting the low status of postcolonial state authorities, the Bank reported that 'churches and mosques, as well as sacred trees, rivers, and mountains, were mentioned time and again as important and valued by poor men and women' (Narayan 2001). Third, religions associated with colonial rule also produce resistance movements *against* colonial violence shaped by 'liberation theologies' drawn from their religious tradition, as resistance movements within Christianity suggests (Hovey and Phillips 2015, xiii).

Importantly, none of the above is intended to let off the hook Christianity, or indeed any other religious tradition, when it comes to legacies of violence. Rather, it is to come into line with many other scholars, policymakers and practitioners on the ground, that religions are just as disposed towards peace-making and to the causes of liberation and resistance as they are to acts of oppression and domination.

Elements of culture

There are many proposed meanings of culture, and these vary from the simple to the complex. While each approach has value for understanding the social world around us, we will opt for a simple version that still gives us plenty to work with. We can begin with an understanding of culture as the combined effect of humanly constructed social elements that help people live together over multiple generations. As with religion, we will explore three elements of culture, illustrating each element in ways that are relevant to the study of International Relations:

1. Common or shared life
2. Symbols of identity
3. Debates over the meaning of 'a good life'.

12.3 – KEY TERMS: Culture and tradition

Elements of culture include binding experiences of common life; symbols and stories of collective identity; and collective agreement and divergence on what is 'good'. Incorporating an understanding of culture involves appreciating how it generates a broader category of 'cultural and religious actors' as religion itself is often embedded in culture. These are individuals, communities and organisations motivated by identity-forming elements of religion and culture operating at local, national, regional and international levels. No account of culture is complete without an understanding of 'tradition'. This involves the individual and communal practices of religion and culture developed over time, often adapted to answer challenges posed to belief and association in social context, that can both reinforce and challenge social norms, and which are intended for the purpose of strengthening community through memory reinforcement and ethical purpose.

The first element of culture has to do with common or shared life. While media reporting seems to constantly prioritise stories of war, conflict and controversy – as the saying goes about the news cycle, 'if it bleeds it leads' – it is equally the case that local, national and international society requires a remarkable degree of cooperation. In political analysis and commentary about Western societies, for instance, we can fall into the trap of presuming that conflict is rife in society when some studies show that common bonds between citizens are often stronger than the forces of polarisation. Common bonds can sometimes be forged through family, economic interests or security concerns (through such idioms as 'the enemy of my enemy is my friend'). Yet, there are other bonds that are forged at the social level as peoples of difference find ways to live together across times and spaces by forging common beliefs, habits and values. It is from this practice of common life that culture often emerges, including at the global level through the networks of cultural interconnections and interdependencies brought by globalisation (see Steger and Wahlrab 2017).

Sport provides good examples of culture as common life. Let us think about football/soccer. Local clubs can be founded on distinct community identity. For example, local Australian players from a Greek background can play for a team sponsored by the Hellenic Association. Yet clubs can equally represent a locality rather than a particular group. For example, the Smithfield Stallions of Sydney (a fictional team) might have individual players from Greek, Ethiopian, British and Turkish backgrounds. Regardless of background, at the international level all players in these clubs have a loyalty to the Australian football team. Football is the common bond – a sporting pastime but also cultural practice. Beyond local culture(s), think about the way entire nations can be said to embody the activities of its national sporting heroes or generate a common bond despite other differences. That bond is an expression of culture.

The second element of culture is symbols of identity. Constructing and interpreting 'signs' is a basic activity in any society. The kind of signs we are referring to in this case are those constructed as tangible 'identity reminders' in modern societies. They include styles of architecture (such as bridges or religious buildings), land or waterscapes depicted as central to the activity of life (such as in harbour cities), monuments, flags and other identity banners, styles of clothing, and distinctive food and drink. These signs are much more than tourist attractions, but ways for community members to imagine, enact and feel who they are as a group and in ways that help the group live together cohesively.

12.4 – KEY INSIGHTS: Flags

Photo 12.1 Peshmerga throw away the ISIS flag and hang up the Kurdish flag, 11 September 2014

Photo 12.2 Taiwan Pride March, 29 October 2011

Credit: MARWAN IBRAHIM/AFP/Getty Images

Credit: Carrie Kellenberger/Flickr

Flags are an easily detectable, yet not always examined, cultural artefact. The flags that each nation-state displays are symbols so powerful that citizens are often prepared to die for them on the fields of battle because the flag represents their way of life or ultimate values and interests. On the other hand, persecuted or minority communities within a state spread across a region might see a national flag as a symbol of oppression rather than freedom. In this sense a flag symbolises a dominant way of life that excludes them. Such groups (for example the Kurds) typically maintain their own flags as signs of independence or defiance to rally their people around a common symbol. Even terrorist groups such as Islamic State have adopted flags. The phenomenon goes yet further when considering the use of the rainbow flag by LGBTQ+ groups worldwide as a symbol of collective identity and pride across borders.

Societies need to tell stories, which form another element of symbology. Such stories are told to reaffirm and refashion ideas of where that society belongs in relation to the wider world. As such, we could understand such stories as performances repeated over generations that are designed to influence what we understand to be real. Sometimes cultural difference can be most starkly understood by the different stories societies tell about themselves. It is no surprise that 'culture change' often involves a society accepting a different story about itself (or struggling to do so) in order to embrace a new social reality or accept a new view about its own history. Likewise, what is sometimes referred to as a 'culture war' occurs when different stories clash and compete for public acceptance.

This could be seen, for example, in the United Kingdom during the Brexit debate in 2016 when two competing stories were told about the nature of British life as either being independent, or as part of a common European culture. Although a referendum settled the issue politically, both stories still compete and continue to cause significant social stresses. Another example is that First Nations peoples readily, and with significant justification, contest the stories of settlement in the United States, Australia, Canada and elsewhere. In such places, national holidays can instead be mourned as commemorating invasion and dispossession. Even in the case of New Zealand, where the Treaty of Waitangi was signed in 1840 between the British colonisers and Māori tribes, the terms of the Treaty are still debated, particularly in relation to the lack of Māori contribution to those terms (Toki 2010). In all cases where First Nations peoples seek to affirm their cultural rights in modern law, established power interests have also been challenged. These depictions of preservation, loss and the struggle for self-determination serve as specific illustrations of the importance of language, ritual, place and tradition, and the role that each plays in

---

 12.5 – KEY PEOPLE: Malala Yousafzai

Photo 12.3 Malala Yousafzai at the first Girl Summit, 22 July 2014

Credit: Russell Watkins/UK Department for International Development/Flickr

Malala Yousafzai lived in northwest Pakistan. When she was twelve, and inspired by her father who was a teacher, she began to speak out for the right to education. This was something that was becoming increasingly restricted due to the influence of the Taliban (a fundamentalist Islamic movement) in Pakistan and in neighbouring Afghanistan. In 2012, she survived an assassination attempt at the hands of the Taliban and, on her recovery, became an advocate for the many millions who were being denied education due to certain cultural perceptions about girls and their place in society – especially those advocated by groups such as the Taliban. In 2014, aged seventeen, she was co-recipient of the Nobel Peace Prize. She used the prize money to set up a non-profit organisation (the Malala Fund) to invest in, and advocate for, education in a number of states where girls often miss out on secondary education – such as Pakistan.

telling stories at the heart of culture, that can be replicated at the national, regional and international levels.

The third element of culture is the way a society decides what it means to have 'a good life'. Like living organs, societies experience growth and decline, health and decay, fitness and injury. Extending the analogy to mental well-being, we could say that culture is a way to measure the psychological and emotional health of a society. The United Nations Development Programme regards 'well-being' and the 'pursuit of happiness' as fundamental to the sustainable health of a society, whilst the United Nations Educational, Scientific and Cultural Organization regards 'building intercultural understanding' via the 'protection of heritage and support for cultural diversity' to be a priority for international peace and stability. These descriptors reflect understandings of a healthy culture from the perspective of international society. As such, culture involves agreement on the kind of things that are good for society and can make it flourish. Combing the 'local' and 'global' levels, these views translate into debates concerned with what can be described as 'global ethics in a glocal context' (Hutchings 2018, 188–209).Images of a good life can also lead to an international 'culture clash' when different societies prioritise different understandings of what those 'good' things are. One of the leading frontiers of culture clash worldwide involves the campaign for gender equality in areas such as education, employment, reproductive and marital rights. The story of Malala Yousafzai reminds us of the power of one individual to inspire an international response on the vital issue of education for girls. It reminds us that culture is about the way individuals and societies define what the ideal 'good' is, and the extent to which global citizens like Malala Yousafzai, the global networks inspired by her story and those who violently oppose it are willing to go to uphold their beliefs and pursue their interests.

Religio-cultural identity: The both/and approach

Whilst it is important to consider religion and culture separately at first in highlighting the ways that they influence international relations, scholars have long drawn interlinkages between them. For example, Geertz described religion as a 'cultural system' composed of myths, rituals, symbols and beliefs created by humans as a way of giving our individual and collective lives a sense of meaning (cited in Woodhead 2011, 124). Consider the similarities between the elements of religion and culture we have described above, such as the role of symbols and stories in both accounts. By drawing these linkages, we might turn our distinct concepts into different descriptors for the same phenomenon such as 'religious' and 'cultural' rituals, 'religious' and 'cultural' symbols and so forth (Table 12.1).

An important question to ask is whether 'culture' should be necessarily understood as the larger, more significant category, with 'religion' as a subset within it. Such a view makes sense because no single religion encompasses an entire society in the world today, and no society lives entirely according to one set of sacred rules and practices. On the other hand, in some contexts religious authority and identity can be more significant than any other cultural element. For example, when American soldiers moved into the Iraqi city of Najaf in 2003 to negotiate security arrangements, it was not the town mayor or the police chief that had most influence. Rather, it was the religious leader Grand Ayatollah Ali al-Sistani, whose authority influenced not only the city but much of the fracturing state itself. Taking another example, when Communist authorities confronted striking dock workers in Poland in the 1980s, it was not only unions that opposed them but also the Catholic Church, whose priests performed sacred rituals and stood in solidarity with strikers in open defiance of the government.

Table 12.1 Religion and culture's overlapping themes

Elements of religion	Overlapping themes	Elements of culture
1. God(s) and spiritual forces in the public sphere	Personal and collective encounter	1. The binding experiences of common life
2. Sacred rituals and stories shaping community life	Signs and practices of identity	2. Symbols and stories of collective identity
3. Forms of dominant power and resistance	Contesting ideas and interests	3. Agreement and divergence on what is 'good'

In both these examples, the elements of religion are equally – if not more – prominent than the elements of culture. Perhaps the most useful approach, therefore, is to see the elements of religion and the elements of culture in constant interaction with one another. Table 12.1 summarises the elements we have examined. Each element relates to some of the deepest levels of human experience, both individually and collectively. Because of this, researchers are interested in whether the powerful energies of what we can refer to as 'religio-cultural identity' can be released to serve the common good, or alternatively, whether they unleash forces that impede attempts to build cohesive local, national and regional global societies.

Religio-cultural identity inhabits a space somewhere between the problems of conflict and the possibilities of cooperation. This approach can be seen as an adaptation of the idea of the 'ambivalence of the sacred' (Appleby 2000) in which the elements of religio-cultural politics we have explored have a dual and simultaneous capacity for both conflict and cooperation orientations. The usefulness of this approach is that it helps us to break free from the restrictions of an 'either/or' logic about religion and culture (i.e. *either* conflict *or* cooperation). Instead, we can focus on a 'both/and' analysis which allows individual and international examples of each (i.e. *both* conflict *and* cooperation) to inform us about the politics of religion and culture at the global level. Therefore, applying a 'both/and' logic we can consider comparative examples of religio-cultural identity that emphasise conflict and cooperation respectively.

12.6 – KEY INSIGHTS: Samuel P. Huntington's 'Clash of Civilizations' and Francis Fukuyama's 'End of History'

In a 1993 article and a 1996 book, Samuel P. Huntington argued that cultural and religious – rather than political, economic or ideological factors – define humanity. He envisioned this as a global system split up into nine different 'civilisations' (as shown in Map 12.1). Where one civilisation met another on the world map, this would create a fault line where conflict would likely break out, triggered by cultural or religious disputes. Huntington's ideas became prominent following 9/11 as they offered a framework to move beyond ideas such as secularisation theory. Huntington was also writing directly in response to Francis Fukuyama's 'End of History' thesis. Fukuyama had built

Map 12.1 Huntington's civilisations

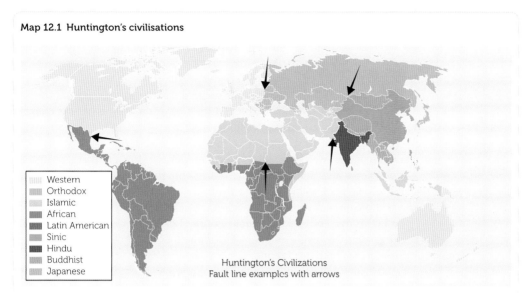

Western
Orthodox
Islamic
African
Latin American
Sinic
Hindu
Buddhist
Japanese

Huntington's Civilizations
Fault line examples with arrows

further on secularisation theory to argue that religious and cultural issues would diminish in importance as the world's states gradually moved towards one common form of government – liberal democracy, undergirded by global capitalism. Huntington felt that Fukuyama's liberal optimism was misplaced as (common to the teachings of realism) the world had not changed much, if at all, structurally following the end of the Cold War and patterns of conflict and rivalry (rather than harmony) would always drive an anarchical system.

The contribution of Huntington's theory and the controversy that surrounds it to this day usefully illustrates how religion and culture entered the mainstream debate in International Relations. His work in identifying geopolitical fault lines also continues to be insightful in examining where today's conflicts are occurring. Yet he also came under criticism from scholars for a perceived anti-Islamic bias and ethnocentrism in his writings. This was predominantly due to the painting of what he called the 'intolerant' Islamic civilisation as the likely trigger for a major global conflict. This was due to how (as he saw it) Islamic leaders viewed globalisation as a Western cultural imposition, and therefore a threat, that needed to be resisted.

After the end of the Cold War, Huntington (1993; 1996) suggested that world politics would no longer be shaped by a clash of ideologies (e.g. capitalism and communism) but rather by a 'clash of civilisations' that were drawn along religious and cultural lines. Beyond Huntington, contemporary scholars frame religion and culture as disruptive conflict-laden elements of world politics in a variety of ways. Juergensmeyer (2008) explicitly depicts religion and the secular state as clashing 'ideologies of order'. Scholars of global studies see a conflict between the interests of 'justice globalism' and 'religious globalism' (Steger and Wahlrab 2017, 75–9), thereby adopting a clash of ideologies framework. Rather than assuming the continuation of a conflict-driven world as Huntington did, others saw the new post-Cold War world order as an opportunity to redesign the way states and peoples interacted internationally. Religio-cultural voices were increasingly considered an important part of this conversation. Illustrating this, a UN consultative group known as the World Public Forum began an initiative in 2001 called the Dialogue of Civilisations. In stark contrast to the clash of civilisations assumption that religion and culture are causes of conflict, the Dialogue of Civilisations deploys the same broad elements as resources for building bridges between individuals and peoples in the development of sustainable peace and cooperation.

Applying a both/and logic to these examples, we can show that elements of religion and culture contribute to *both* clash *and* dialogue, to *both* conflict *and* cooperation. The benefit of this approach is twofold. First, it encourages us to look closely at specific elements of religion *and* culture – as we have done in this chapter – instead of forcing such complex phenomena into a singular assumption about conflict or cooperation. Second, applying a 'both/and' logic requires us to consider specific examples – as we have attempted throughout the chapter – without stereotyping religious and cultural traditions by pinning them to singular events. When the shortcomings of religion were once brought to the attention of the Hindu mystic Ramakrishna, he remarked that 'Religion is like a cow. It kicks, but it also gives milk' (Tyndale 2006, xiv). For every cultural symbol of hate, we see as many symbols of healing and peace. For every religious movement of violence, we see as many religious movements for reconciliation.

The 'both/and' understanding of religion and culture has become influential among policymakers working with individuals, local communities and national, regional and international organisations, marking a significant shift in our understanding of world politics as a whole. Beyond the issue of peace versus violence, it has also helped us understand the need for particular consideration about the extent of religious and cultural influence on politics throughout the world. For example, on religion Fox (2008) writes:

> A fuller picture of the world's religious economy would show secularisation – the reduction of religion's influence in society – occurring in some parts of the religious economy, and sacralisation – the increase of religion's influence in society – occurring in other parts.

Cultural factors are similarly dynamic, both in influence and in the forms they take. As Clifford once wrote, '"cultures" do not hold still for their portraits' (1986, 10). As such, the influence of culture on individual and global politics requires precise thinking in order to understand its many dynamics.

 CASE STUDY 12.1: 96-day church service to protect a refugee family

Photo 12.4 Bethel Church community undertaking a non-stop 96-day vigil, December 2018

Credit: KOEN VAN WEEL/AFP/Getty Images

Since 2010 regional and domestic conflicts, and the crises in human security that they generate, have placed European states under scrutiny for the role they play (or do not play) in answering the humanitarian challenge of forced migration. It was in this national and continental context that the Tamrazyan family found themselves facing deportation from The Netherlands back to Armenia in 2018. The Tamrazyans, who are Christian, fled Armenia in 2010 after the family's father Sasun received death threats for his political activism. The family sought refuge in The Netherlands and remained there on a temporary visa for nine years. In September 2018, the family was notified that they would be facing deportation. Efforts to retain an emergency pardon failed in keeping with an overwhelming rejection rate of such appeals by the Dutch government.

The small Protestant community of Bethel Church in The Hague lobbied for the Tamrazyans, entering the immigration debate in The Netherlands at a time of growing support for anti-immigration political parties in Europe. In a statement the church based its support for the Tamrazyans on the ethical tension between obeying Dutch law and living the principle of hospitality toward the vulnerable that is central to its religious tradition.

In grappling with this ethical impasse, the church found a radical middle way to uphold the practice of its faith and citizen loyalty to the state simultaneously. Taking advantage of an obscure Dutch law that prevents police from entering premises of worship during an ongoing religious service, the Bethel Church community undertook a non-stop 96-day vigil (pictured) in order to shelter the Tamrazyan family and stop their deportation (Kingsley 2019). The vigil service included prayer, reflection and singing, and attracted more than 12,000 visitors, one thousand preachers, and 150 volunteers from across the continent. The service extended until the Dutch government agreed that 700 families previously listed for deportation, including the Tamrazyans, would have their cases reassessed.

The case of the Bethel Church and its advocacy for the Tamrazyans can be examined in numerous ways. The Bethel vigil, for instance, can be interpreted through the lens of each element of religion from Table 12.1. The first element – god(s) and spiritual forces in the public sphere – associated 'fundamental' and 'contextual' interventions of religion in public life within the same religious tradition. The actions of the Protestant Church of The Hague could be understood as contextual in the first instance, though also grounded in a public commitment to religious fundamentals. As a local case transferable to transnational contexts, it highlights the role of faith communities engaging in humanitarian action as 'exemplars of affected persons and local organisations at the nexus of refugee crises' beyond secular-only responses (Ager and Ager 2017, 38).

The second element of religion – sacred rituals and stories shaping community life – helps to explain the interior substance of the Bethel vigil and the unique resources that religious communities bring to a commitment to justice. When analysing Pope Francis's 2013 visit to refugees on the Mediterranean island of Lampedusa, for instance, it may be inadequate to see this only through the generic lens of activism without first understanding the Pope's priestly authority to practice religious rituals of solidarity and mourning that gave his mission such impact (Rees and Rawson 2019). In the same way, it is important to view the Bethel Church action as a religious vigil sustained by religious practices of community prayer, preaching and worship, rituals and symbols. Hibbard suggests that religious communities hold a unique position to sanctify or stigmatise a particular political agenda (Hibbard 2010, 26) and, to this end, we might understand the Bethel action as a public stigmatisation of the Dutch Government's refugee policy expressed in uniquely religious ways.

The third element of religion – forms of dominance and resistance – feature in the Dutch case in interesting ways. Religious views in support of societies that are more parochial have informed the refugee debate in Europe, notably parties and leaders (including those in the Netherlands) that have shaped their ideologies with appeal to Christian identity and 'civilisation' frameworks notably pitted against constructions of Islam. This has had a dominating effect, not only on religious 'others' such as the Muslim populations of Europe, but also on Christian 'others' such as the Tamrazyans. The present case study also highlights, however, that religious counter-responses to domination also feature in the political space. It is important to note, in the view of its participants, the humanitarian intervention embodied in the Bethel vigil could be enacted in solidarity with refugees from any faith. Bethel minister Rev. Axel Wicke stated that although the Tamarazyans were Christian, their religion was not a consideration. 'We would've done it if they were Muslim' (Robertson 2018).

CASE STUDY 12.2: Reading Kim Jong-un's face

Photo 12.5 US President Donald Trump with North Korea's leader Kim Jong-un at the Sofitel Legend Metropole hotel in Hanoi, 27 February 2019

Credit: SAUL LOEB/AFP/Getty Images

In June 2018 a much anticipated US–North Korea agreement pledging peace and the denuclearisation of the Korean Peninsula was signed by Chairman Kim Jong-un and President Donald Trump at a summit in Singapore. However, the Agreement soon faltered, and a second summit was held in Vietnam in February 2019 (Photo 12.5). Mr Kim travelled to the Vietnam summit via train, a journey that would take up to sixty hours and involve multiple stops, thereby creating high media exposure. The unusually high degree of coverage for Kim outside the borders of North Korea was not only of interest to a watching world, it was also of strategic interest to the National Intelligence Service of South Korea. The train journey from Pyongyang to Hanoi created opportunities for a forensic examinationof images of Kim by the National Intelligence Service in order to gain insights into his health.

Methods employed by the National Intelligence Service arguably included several techniques derived from prominent cultural practices in South Korea and neighbouring states that would be considered unorthodox by Western states. Specifically, it is suggested they worked with palm-readers to analyse images of Kim's hands in order to determine his lifespan, and with experts in physiognomy to gain insights into his character and fortune by reading Kim's facial features (Bong 2019). Both practices are linked to a broad array of cultural phenomena associated with shamanism, where human agents (shamans) control or cooperate with spiritual entities or forces to gain insights beneficial to the community. Shamanism is considered to be 'the enduring core of Korean religious and cultural thought, exercising a profound influence on the development of Korean attitudes and behaviours as well as cultural practices' (Kim 2005). Even Christianity, which is more prominent in South Korea in contrast to other East Asian states, has only succeeded via a protracted negotiated cultural settlement with shamanism. Shamanistic practice has also adapted to Korea's shifting power alliances, such as the dominant presence of US interests in East Asia since the 1950s following the Korean War of 1950–3.

Placed in this dynamic cultural context, the actions of the National Intelligence Service seem less controversial than they might first appear. Physiognomy, for instance, remains widely practised in Korea and thus the elements of culture previously considered in this chapter can help us better understand these attempts to study Kim Jong-un's character via physiognomic readings.

A connection can be drawn to the first element of culture from Table 12.1 – the binding experiences of common life. State security entities such as the National Intelligence Service are mandated to safeguard the national community that they serve. We might think of this securitised space as a culture-free zone, but, viewed through a lens such as constructivism, with an emphasis on the role of identity and values in shaping political action, strategic action can be understood by regarding the National Intelligence Service as an agent of Korean cultural values (normative structures) and Korean cultural identity, including shamanistic identity.

The second element of culture as symbols and stories of collective identity takes us deeper into understanding the National Intelligence Service's methodology. An emphasis on strategic culture – defined as the differing security preferences of states as actors that 'are influenced to some degree by the philosophical, political, cultural, and cognitive characteristics of the state and its elites' (Johnston 1995) – interprets the specific actions of palm and face reading as attempts to gain a strategic advantage over its rival via the forensic deployment of cultural practices. The National Intelligence Service might act like a state security bureaucracy similar to its Western allies in every other sense, and certainly will attempt to produce data that is transferable across all cultural contexts (e.g. Kim's lifespan in years or his psycho-social temperament), but the modes through which some strategies are undertaken might also be understood as uniquely derived from the deep roots of Korean culture. The same could be said of other, if not all, states if culture is to be considered an influence on strategic practice.

Finally, this chapter has emphasised the overlapping elements of culture and religion, and sought to apply these dynamics in International Relations. It could be argued that Shamanistic practice sits within the elements of culture and religion as we have previously described, by understanding the National Intelligence Service's strategic method as dependent on *encounter* (via the shaman), the reading of *signs* through cultural *practices* (to produce shamanistically derived knowledge), and the upholding of *ideas and interests* (in the politico-spiritual service of the state and national community).

Conclusion

As the various examples throughout the chapter and the two case studies have shown, it is clear that religion and culture exist at the heart, or on the surface, of the many events and issues that concern International Relations. Consequently, religious and cultural factors must be included using the 'both/and' approach if we want to deepen our understanding of how the global system works. This is especially the case when considering the emergence of non-Western influences and positions that challenge the idea of the emergence of a globalised, or secular, world. In a real-world facing sense, understanding and including the impact of religio-cultural identity will help us better navigate and explain our ever more complex and seemingly divided world. It may also unlock insights and understandings that can serve to unite people, resolve disputes through more informed dialogue and lead to a more peaceful global system rather than to a clash of civilisations.

 ## END OF CHAPTER QUESTIONS

1. Do you believe religion can be a positive, negative or neutral influence shaping the future of the society you live in?

2. If you were asked to present an item representing your national culture, what item would you choose and how would you explain its significance?

3. Which is more important: preserving the cultural rights of a society or upholding the universal rights of all peoples? Can there be a middle point between these?

4. List the following identity markers in order of importance to you: nationality, gender, sexuality, racial and ethnic heritage, religion, citizenship, and one other category (anything you feel is important to who you are). Compare and contrast your list with three other people. Where are the points of overlap and contrast?

5. In what ways do you think Huntington's idea of the 'Clash of Civilizations' represents today's world?

GENDER AND SEXUALITY

Rosie Walters

Question: Should the 'personal' shape our understanding of the 'political'?

No matter where we live in the world, our daily lives are influenced by the gender we identify with and who we fall in love with. Norms around gender and sexuality shape the roles we take on in society, our freedoms and rights and even whether we live or die. As was the case with culture and religion (as explored in the previous chapter) gender and sexuality were once seen as unimportant in the study of International Relations – too 'personal' to be 'political'. However, in recent decades, scholars have drawn attention to the overlooked role of women and of LGBTQ+ people across the global system. Despite progress in some areas, many states block women and LGBTQ+ people from equal participation in politics, fail to recognise their contribution to the economy, prevent them from serving in the military, limit their access to basic rights such as health care and fail to keep them safe. Looking more deeply and widely at issues such as these indicates that socially constructed norms about gender and sexuality are important structures and processes that criss-cross throughout the global system. Together with our understanding of religion and culture, this final chapter of Part two reveals further insights about how certain individuals and groups feature in both our understandings of International Relations and of the global system, and how these dynamics impact upon many of the global issues that will be explored in Part three of the book.

Gender, sexuality and International Relations

Socially constructed norms around how male and female, straight and queer bodies behave dominate in every state and they shape our understandings of who should govern us and how. Even using terms such as lesbian, gay, bisexual and trans reflect Western ideas about queer identities as somehow 'deviating' from the heterosexual norm. In some cultures, such as Native American communities (especially before the arrival of European colonisers, who preached Christianity and heterosexuality), masculine women and feminine men were celebrated and seen as having been gifted with two spirits instead of one (Robinson 2017). Studying gender and sexuality means paying attention to how our understandings of people, bodies and relationships are all tied up in social norms and those norms themselves reflect global power relations.

13.1 – KEY TERMS: Gender, sex and LGBTQ+

Biology has historically placed humans into two **sex** categories – male and female – according to differences in chromosomes, reproductive organs and hormones. Yet, those who are biologically 'intersex' show that people do not always fit so easily into these two categories. **Gender** on the other hand refers to the social roles associated with male and female bodies. Many people do not conform to supposedly masculine and feminine roles, or identify with ones that do not necessarily map onto their birth sex.

LGBTQ+ is an initialism that joins the words Lesbian, Gay, Bisexual, Trans and Queer/Questioning. The '+' is added to represent the diverse number of other identities that do not have heteronormative and/or cisnormative expressions of their gender or sexuality. Heteronormativity is a belief that heterosexuality (relations between a man and woman along a gender binary) is the 'normal' or 'natural' state of affairs. Cisnormativity is a belief that a person's gender identity should match the biological sex category (male or female) they were assigned at birth.

Socially constructed norms tend to link qualities such as strength, aggression, leadership, rationality and intellect with masculinity and weakness, passivity, subservience, irrationality and emotion with femininity. That is not to say that men cannot show weakness or women cannot show aggression, but that to do so in many societies means to risk being seen as non-conformist or unnatural. For example, in many societies, women and girls have traditionally been linked to the domestic sphere with women's role seen as focused on taking care of their families and husbands. Patriarchal power relations are based on the idea that this is the 'natural' state of affairs, due to women's ability to bear children and the supposed nurturing qualities that gives them. Meanwhile, men are seen as breadwinners, who go out into the public sphere to earn money, to educate themselves and to take on positions of leadership. But when girls are given relatively equal access to education, they frequently equal or outperform their male counterparts, exposing the fact that policies or traditions limiting women's roles and rights are not based on biological facts, but rather on socially constructed gender norms. Often these norms serve to shore up power relations that keep men in power. Nothing about gendered power relations is 'inevitable' or 'natural'; rather it takes a great deal of time and effort by those in positions of power to maintain them (Enloe 2001).

While Photo 13.1 represents the sharp edge of the equation of how a patriarchal system affects women, a more routine example is the issue of women serving in the military. For centuries, women were excluded by a certain reading of the biological differences between men and women. This is not just in terms of physical attributes such as average height and strength, but also in terms of psychological attributes such as aggression. Women would not make good soldiers, this logic argues, because they are too physically weak and too emotionally caring to kill their enemies. But that understanding of gender cannot account for the countless women who have taken on roles as soldiers, military leaders, revolutionaries, suicide bombers and willing participants in some of the bloodiest armed groups to have existed. And, if military prowess really does come from the fact of having been born with male biology, why do so many militaries around the world still have restrictions on gay men and trans women? This is where we begin to see that military participation has everything to do with gendered norms about how the sexes should behave socially.

Photo 13.1 Notice to epicene women, 1902

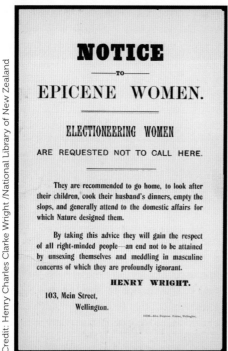

Credit: Henry Charles Clarke Wright /National Library of New Zealand

This poster, issued by Henry Charles Clarke Wright in 1902 in Wellington, New Zealand, clearly demonstrates the idea of gender roles. According to Wright, women were 'designed' by nature to carry out domestic work and 'meddling' in the masculine concerns of electioneering was tantamount to 'unsexing themselves'. In fact, New Zealand was the first self-governing state to give women the right to vote in 1893 and is one of the few states in the world to have had three female heads of government. This example shows just how dramatically ideas about appropriate roles for men and women can change over time and between contexts.

In an interview in 1982, General Robert Barrow, former commander of the US Marines, stated:

War is a man's work. Biological convergence on the battlefield [meaning women fighting alongside men] would not only be dissatisfying in terms of what women could do, but it would be an enormous psychological distraction for the male, who wants to think that he's fighting for that woman somewhere behind, not up there in the same foxhole with him. It tramples the male ego. When you get right down to it, you have to protect the manliness of war (quoted in Hartsock 1984, 199).

Here we see that the very nature of war has traditionally been defined in masculine, heterosexual terms: it is about 'our' men protecting 'our' women against 'their' men. It is about the male ego. The soldier is a manly man and he would not be as effective a soldier if he felt his manliness was under threat, whether from association with gay fellow soldiers, or from the realisation that a woman alongside him, who has been given military training and a weapon, is perfectly capable of defending herself. So, some feminists (Peterson and Runyan 1999) are left wondering, if the 'manliness' of a soldier is so natural – an inevitable result of his biology – then why is it so fragile that it would seem to be threatened even by association with femininity?

This leads us to ask further questions, such as: why is war 'manly'? What would it look like if states resolved their disputes through 'womanly' means? What would happen if leaders were valued for their ability to compromise and negotiate, not their aggression? These questions are not about counting males and females. There have been plenty of aggressive female leaders and compassionate male ones through the ages. This is about considering how the very structures of power that govern the relations between states are built upon gendered norms that value masculine traits over feminine ones. Those norms shape who gets elected (or selected) to lead states and, in valuing aggression over compassion, may make conflict more likely. This draws on the view of the world that the realists perceive. Yet as the various critical theories (especially feminism) have asserted, war does not have to be seen as inevitable or natural. It is only when we expose the fragility of so-called common-sense claims, such as those about male bodies in war, that we begin to understand how they shape the global system and our interpretations of it.

Political representation

It is not just the military that is seen as a masculine domain. In many societies, our very understanding of politics is based on the public, masculine sphere. People around the world prioritise issues such as security, the economy, and law and order when selecting a leader. Men are more often perceived as better on these issues because they are seen to be 'strong, tough, experienced and knowledgeable', while

13.2 – KEY INSIGHTS: Disparities in politics

Statistics help us reveal the extent of gendered and sexual orientation disparities in politics. In 2019, women made up 24.3 per cent of parliamentarians worldwide. Out of 193 nation-states, eleven women were serving as a head of state and twelve as head of government. Digging deeper, women made up 21 per cent of government ministers and their most commonly held ministerial portfolios concerned issues such as social affairs, family/young people/the elderly/disability, the environment, employment and trade and industry (UN Women 2019). It is hard to estimate the number of LGBTQ+ leaders and high-ranking officials, given that in so many societies people are still forced to conceal their sexuality for fear of reprisals or for social reasons. Exacerbating this, homosexuality is illegal in approximately seventy states, twelve of which prosecute it with the death penalty. However, there have been a handful of openly LGBTQ+ world leaders. These include Leo Varadkar, who became Taoiseach (prime minister and head of government) of Ireland in 2017 and Ana Brnabić, who became Prime Minister of Serbia in 2017.

women are seen as 'kind, compassionate, sensitive, understanding, honest and trustworthy' (Bystrom 2008, 61). Women in particular are not typically seen as able to take on the role of head of the military that most premierships and presidencies require (Carroll 2009). Analysis of the political campaigns of women in the United States (Carlin and Winfrey 2009; Kahn 2003) has shown that the media consistently reports on female candidates' families, appearance and personalities, focusing on their domestic roles as mothers and wives. By doing so, they give less attention to their policies than they do to male candidates and report disproportionately negatively on their likelihood of victory.

If the role of head of government is seen as a heterosexual, masculine domain, then it may be a reasonable suggestion to ask an aspirational female candidate to simply adopt masculine traits in order to win an election. The problem is that in order to do so, she would need to go against gender norms and in doing so, would go against deep-seated expectations about her behaviour. As women adopt harsher, more 'masculine' stances on issues such as security and law and order, and frame themselves as tough leaders, opinion polls show that they become less likeable to the electorate, who expect their female candidates to be approachable and friendly (McGinley 2009). A small number of women have succeeded in gaining support for a more 'feminine' style of leadership, such as in the example of Jacinda Ardern, as explored in Chapter five. In the specific setting of post-conflict Liberia in 2005, for example, Ellen Johnson-Sirleaf capitalised on the perception of women as peacemakers, not warmongers, in her successful presidential campaign. However, for every successful female leader able to show feminine characteristics and still be trusted by the public to run a state, there are multiple men like Recep Tayyip Erdoğan, Vladimir Putin and Viktor Orban, who have risen to power and won multiple elections off the back of a 'tough guy' image.

One widespread indicator of the gendered nature of the role of leader is in perceptions of the role of a male leader's wife – often referred to as the 'First Lady'. While a male leader hosts complex negotiations, a First Lady does the emotional and social labour of entertaining visitors and representing the cultural values of the state. She must support her husband's policies or negotiating stance and not meddle too much in political discussions. It is a passive role that resonates strongly with gendered norms around femininity. Meanwhile, when Leo Varadkar became Ireland's first openly gay head of government he spoke publicly about how he did not expect his partner Matthew Barrett to take on a 'First Gentleman' role by attending public events because, 'he has his own career' and, 'while that has been the tradition in politics, it doesn't necessarily have to be' (quoted in Manley 2017). Female partners of world leaders who have their own successful careers are typically still labelled 'First Ladies' and judged on their ability to 'turn heads' (see Photo 13.2). Yet, by definition, male partners of world leaders do not fit into the gendered role of 'First Lady' and as a result, it appears to be easier for them to break free of the expectations that come with it.

Human rights

While the Universal Declaration of Human Rights of 1948 states that 'everyone is entitled to all the rights and freedoms set forth in this Declaration, without distinction of any kind, such as … sex', scholars have shown that the rights enshrined in the Declaration ignore the experiences of women and LGBTQ+ people and are based around the experiences of male household heads. The initial focus in international human rights law was on protecting civil and political rights, although subsequent treaties have also dealt with social and cultural rights and the rights of groups. Yet in every case, feminists argue, they

Photo 13.2 Partners of the G20 leaders pose for a photo at the G20 summit in Kyoto, 28 June 2019

Credit: Pool/Getty images

In June 2019, when the G20 met in Japan, the leaders' partners posed for a photograph, as was highlighted in Chapter six. An article in the *Daily Mail* (Morgan 2019) praised the women for bringing a 'touch of glamour to proceedings', 'turning heads' and looking 'elegant'. It then adds, 'they were all joined by British Prime Minister Theresa May's husband Philip, 61, who looked smart in a black blazer, white shirt and tie as he gave a wave to the cameras'. Philip May is set apart from the others, not one of the 'all', or one of the 'wives' mentioned in the headline. His presence is described as 'awkward'. While the journalist could have used the term 'partners' to describe the whole group, that would not have fitted well with the rest of the content of the article, which focuses on how a group that comprises a successful businesswoman, investment banker, teacher, doctor, nurse (and so on) successfully navigated the fashion choices necessary to represent their countries as 'First Ladies' on the global stage. The article is one example among many that shows that a leader's partner is still a role that is inherently tied up in perceptions of femininity, with deviations socially 'awkward' to countenance.

are 'built on typically male life experiences and in their current form do not respond to the most pressing risks women face' (Charlesworth 1994, 58–9). Indeed, while to many women around the world, the greatest threat to their fundamental rights is a violent or controlling male partner or family member they share their home with, Article 12 of the Declaration states that 'no one shall be subjected to arbitrary interference with *his* privacy, family, home or correspondence'. While protecting 'his' rights to life, liberty and freedom from torture, to freedom of movement, to own property and to freedom of thought and speech, the Declaration focuses largely on rights in the public sphere, relating to politics, employment and finances. In doing so, it and subsequent treaties ignore the experiences of women in the private, domestic sphere. It is often within the family that women face the biggest struggles for their rights, such as freedom from physical and sexual violence, freedom of expression, equality in decision-making and the right to ownership and/or control over their finances.

Some efforts to redress this situation have been made, most noticeably in the form of the Convention on the Elimination of All Forms of Discrimination against Women

(CEDAW), which sets out specific rights that women are entitled to. However, the concerns raised by more conservative states during the drawing up of this Convention resulted in states being allowed to ratify it while stating reservations to particular articles. For example, in relation to an article asserting men and women's equal rights within marriage, Algeria entered a reservation on the grounds that this would contradict the Algerian Family Code, in other words stating it had no intention of bringing this particular right into Algerian law. Under Article 29(1) of the Convention, other states can dispute such reservations, and several European states tried to do so. However, Algeria had already entered another reservation declaring that it did not consider itself to be bound by the arbitration process set out in Article 29(1) and so little could be done. In short, 'Algeria stated its willingness to implement CEDAW so long as nothing needed to be done to implement CEDAW' (Neuwirth 2005, 28). Such examples raise questions about the will that exists to enforce the rights contained within the Convention compared to other human rights treaties.

Sexual and reproductive health and rights have also been historically overlooked, disputed or minimised. In the absence of clear language in any human rights treaty setting out individuals' rights to make decisions about their bodies, to be free of sexual violence, to have the information and resources to prevent unwanted pregnancy and sexually transmitted illnesses, and access to safe and legal abortion, lawyers have had to creatively draw on other human rights – such as the rights to life, freedom from torture and to physical and mental integrity – to make the case for women and LGBTQ+ people. But wording matters. Without specific reference to the very real dangers these groups face, their fundamental rights can all too often be ignored. Millions of girls around the world give birth each year either as a result of rape or of a lack of information about, and access to, contraceptive methods. A report by UN Women (2018) found that only four in ten states worldwide have actually criminalised rape within marriage, and twelve states still have laws that allow a rapist to be immune from prosecution if he marries his

13.3 – KEY INSIGHTS: HIV/AIDS and PrEP

Large numbers of HIV/AIDS cases first emerged in the 1980s and the virus rapidly became a global pandemic. Over 30 million people have died from the virus and some 38 million are believed to be living with it today, 25 million of whom are in sub-Saharan Africa (UNAIDS, 2020). The virus disproportionally affects LGBTQ+ people and communities in sub-Saharan Africa. There are a number of biological, social and political reasons for this, including social stigmas, sexual violence, poverty and a struggle for public resources and attention. Pre-exposure prophylaxis (PrEP) is a medication (in pill form) that, when taken correctly by a HIV negative person, virtually eliminates their risk of contracting HIV. PrEP is often compared to the female contraceptive pill that first emerged in the 1950s. Just like the contraceptive pill, it gives individuals control over their own bodies, regardless of their partner's behaviour or willingness to take other precautions. It is not only life-saving, but has the potential, alongside other treatments, to eliminate the pandemic altogether. During the Covid-19 pandemic, we saw how quickly resources can be mobilised to find treatments and vaccines against a virus when its impact is felt in states and communities where the majority of global power and wealth is concentrated. Yet, decades into the HIV/AIDS pandemic, many of the communities most affected, which are often underrepresented, still struggle to gain access to life-saving drugs such as PrEP.

victim. In addition, pregnancy and childbirth is still the leading cause of death of 15–19-year-old girls around the world (World Health Organization 2018). Meanwhile, tens of thousands of women die every year from unsafe abortions in states where abortion is illegal.

Calls by women to tackle the prolific rates of violence against them, especially where it most occurs, in the home, are often met with claims that the state cannot regulate people's intimate relationships. Faced with this, there are very few avenues internationally to mitigate this due to the power of sovereignty. Yet, when it comes to regulating the relationships and the bodies of women, non-binary and LGBTQ+ people, the state can and frequently does intervene. What could be more intimate than laws dictating you can only have sex with members of the opposite sex, regardless of who you are attracted to or fall in love with? Or laws dictating how a woman's health care should proceed if she finds herself pregnant? These kinds of question highlight the cracks in the international human rights apparatus, and the shortcomings in their development due to their historical lack of focus on gender and sexuality. As such, much work remains to be done to develop more inclusive human rights norms.

Gender and the global economy

A lack of understanding of women's realities and responsibilities, as well as policies and norms that exclude them from the formal economy, are costing women their rights and costing the global economy trillions. Women are much more likely than men to be found doing informal work, such as rearing livestock or growing produce in the garden, nannying or babysitting. In many societies there is a great deal of financial and social pressure on women to take up this kind of work in addition to doing unpaid domestic labour such as cooking and cleaning within the home, on which they spend 2.5 times more time than men (UN Women, no date). In so many cultures this work is seen as part of women's 'natural' role as homemakers, caregivers and nurturers. And when something is seen as 'natural', it is not seen as needing payment or recognition. Yet the global economy would collapse without it.

Women typically end up in informal or unpaid work because somebody needs to do it. And if men will not take on more of this responsibility, then it is impossible for many women to commit to formal employment. There are few policies addressing this because many states are hesitant to intervene in how labour is divided up within a household because it is perceived as too personal to be political. So women continue to take that unequal burden and also find creative ways to boost household income through informal work such as growing vegetables in the garden, cleaning the house of a neighbour and making things to sell at the market. As informal or unpaid workers, they typically are not factored into economic policy or considerations and are therefore not protected by labour rights, do not have access to pensions and have no protection from harassment, abuse or arbitrary dismissal. Even when women do take part in the formal economy, they face many obstacles.

13.4 – KEY TERMS: Queer theory

While feminism has spent decades putting the issue of gender on the map in International Relations, and in wider society, representing sexuality has been less prominent. However, queer theory has gradually emerged within the critical theory movement. Its central theoretical contribution goes beyond more straightforward LGBTQ+ activism to critique binaries in society (such as heterosexual/homosexual or male/female). Not only do these binaries oversimplify human experiences, they also imply a sort of hierarchy in which one side of the binary is seen to be better, or the 'natural' or 'moral' state of things. Queer theorists have explored how such simplistic binaries shape our thinking about war/peace, security/insecurity, public/private, democratic/authoritarian and so on. The historic (and ongoing) persecution of LGBTQ+ people shows that societies cannot so easily be divided into either/or categories, and that a state that is supposedly at peace, secure and democratic can still be violent, dangerous and oppressive towards some of its citizens.

A global economy that took women's work seriously would acknowledge and compensate the essential work that women already do. It would recognise that this work keeps us alive and keeps our global economy functioning. It would also involve policies that recognised women's experiences and the responsibilities placed upon them, helped them to manage those responsibilities alongside work and encouraged men to take up their fair share of the burden. And it would involve establishing global norms that allow women to train for and participate in every sector of the job market, regardless of their location. It would also ensure that women have equal participation in financial decision-making processes and equal ownership of the land and resources they work with.

CASE STUDY 13.1: Sexual violence and war

Photo 13.3 UK Foreign Secretary William Hague and Special Envoy to the UN High Commissioner on Refugees Angelina Jolie at the launch of the Preventing Sexual Violence in Conflict Initiative (PSVI), 29 May 2012

Credit: Foreign, Commonwealth & Development Office/ Flickr

Sexual violence has for centuries been seen as an inevitable by-product of war. Although rape is seen as a crime that invading male fighters commit against women, states and international organisations fail to fully understand the gendered power relations that cause rape. As already explored, states are built around gendered norms that see strength, aggression, leadership, rationality and intellect as masculine traits and weakness, passivity, subservience, irrationality and emotion as feminine. This is crucial to our understanding of sexual violence in conflict. It is not a 'deviant' behaviour sparked by the extreme situation of war, but rather a continuation or escalation of gendered violence towards women and men in peace – much of which takes place inside the home. Three aspects in particular are frequently neglected:

1 Rape is often committed by men against men

2 Women also commit sexual violence in war

3 The most prevalent form of sexual violence against women in conflict is domestic violence by a partner or relative.

The crucial point here is that sexual violence is about power, control and humiliation. For men – and sometimes women – to subject their male enemies to sexual violence is seen as the ultimate humiliation, because it forces them into the passive, helpless, feminine role of victim, stripping them of their masculinity and/ or 'contaminating' them with homosexuality. According to gendered norms, men have power as the head of the family, and they dominate women and children in the public and private spheres. Becoming a victim of sexual violence for some men – as well as a physical and psychological trauma – is a devastating loss of that control. A survey in the war-torn Democratic Republic of Congo found that 24 per cent of the men interviewed had experienced sexual violence (Kirby 2015). Rape, then, is systematically used in some conflicts as a means to humiliate enemy combatants and this is tied up with how we see the roles of aggressor and victim.

Initiatives to combat sexual violence in conflict have largely missed these gendered power relations. Take, for example, the United Kingdom's 2012 Preventing Sexual Violence Initiative (PSVI), which was launched by Foreign Secretary William Hague and UN Special Envoy Angelina Jolie (Photo 13.3). It brought together the UK's Foreign and Commonwealth Office (FCO), Department for International Development (DFID) and Ministry of Defence (MoD). While the initiative did try to engage with feminist analysis of sexual violence, a report by the Independent Commission for Aid Impact (ICAI) (which reviews UK government aid spending) found that the PSVI had no coherent strategy for how to tackle its root causes – the gendered power relations that already exist before conflict. For example, the

ICAI reports that while DFID incorporated PSVI initiatives into its programmes tackling violence against women and girls, attempting to address the causes of intimate partner violence in both peacetime and war, it neglected the issue of sexual violence against men and boys. Meanwhile, the FCO attempted to address sexual violence against men, women, boys and girls, but focused only on conflict zones, thus neglecting how it is linked to gendered power relations in peacetime. It concludes that 'from the beginning, there was no strategic vision or plan driving the work of the initiative' (ICAI 2020, ii).

A further blind spot in this initiative is how qualified the UK is to lead it. For example, the UK's initiative included sending a team of British police, forensic experts and lawyers to war zones to help investigate sexual violence and bring perpetrators to justice. Yet, the UK government's own statistics from 2019 showed that just 3.5 per cent of sexual offences reported to UK police in the previous year and just 1.5 per cent of rape cases resulted in a charge or court summons (Home Office 2019). If we start to think of wartime sexual violence as a continuation – or escalation – of peacetime sexual violence, we begin to question why states and organisations based in the Global North think that this is a problem they can solve on behalf of people in conflict-affected countries in the Global South, when they cannot control it within their own borders. Here we see that sexual violence is also understood in racialised terms. From the first European voyages of exploration to the Global South, through colonisation and decolonisation – and then recent understandings of poverty, famine and conflict – men in the Global South have consistently been represented in the Global North as violent, primal and prone to acting on basic instincts, while Southern women have been depicted as helpless victims of these men. Claims to be saving women of the Global South from their men has been used to justify any number of interventions, from colonial domination to the invasion of Afghanistan in 2001, despite the many horrific cases of abuse of those same women by militaries and peacekeepers from the Global North.

A focus on the threat of invading forces and sexual violence also speaks to nationalist and patriarchal views of women's bodies. In many cultures and religions, a great deal of importance is placed on the sexual purity of women (especially before marriage), their sexual monogamy once married and men's certainty that their children are indeed their children. The sexual activities (or lack thereof) of women are understood to reflect the honour of entire families. That is why the punishments can be so severe when women break the rules, such as in the case of honour killings. In nationalist discourses, women's bodies are seen to represent the honour of an entire nation. Rapes by invading troops, then, are seen as an attack on the honour of the nation, an insult to individual men whose partners' or daughters' purity has been tainted, and a threat to the ethnic, cultural and religious purity of the next generation. Here we see the real problem in focusing only on sexual violence in conflict and

neglecting the issue of domestic violence both in peacetime and conflict: there is only widespread concern for the safety and rights of women when violations of those rights are perceived to affect men and the nation as a whole. This consideration also builds more layers into the understandings of religion and culture explored in the previous chapter.

Returning to the ICAI report, it concludes that the main success of the PSVI initiative has been in 'making the UK a leading voice in the international effort to address conflict-related sexual violence' (2020, 15). This resonates with a feminist and postcolonial analysis of the UK's Preventing Sexual Violence in Conflict Initiative, which might lead us to question whether the whole outcome has been to position the UK as a protector of Southern women on the global stage, without much evidence to suggest that position is justified. The UK certainly succeeded in gaining attention for its claims to be combatting sexual violence against women. What it actually achieved in terms of protecting women, and men, is less clear.

 CASE STUDY 13.2: Sexuality and borders

Photo 13.4 Two asylum seekers pose with placards during the 'Not Gay Enough' demonstration in The Hague, 26 November 2019

Credit: NurPhoto/Getty Images

States in the Global North are often keen to proclaim their support for LGBTQ+ rights at an international level and to admonish those states that do not respect them. But, in some cases their treatment of LGBTQ+ migrants would suggest they have some way to go

before they can live up to the ideals they espouse. Many governments place the so-called 'gay conditionality' on aid donations to states in the Global South, dictating that they must end bans on homosexuality and the persecution of LBGTQ+ people in order to receive aid. It is a move that resonates with colonial ideas about bringing civilisation and liberal values to the peoples of the Global South (Kahlina and Ristivojecić 2015).

Queer theory offers useful insights here. 'Gay conditionality' sets up a simplistic binary between the West and the rest, modern, civilised, liberal values and outdated, barbaric homophobia. Yet, scholars of the Global South note the irony in the fact that in many former colonised states, laws banning homosexuality were drawn up by the very same powers of the Global North that are now trying to force their retraction (Chankia, Lwanda and Muula 2013). For example, while institutionalised homophobia in some African states is frequently presented as the result of traditional and cultural values that date back centuries, present-day attitudes towards sexuality were heavily influenced and shaped by Christianity as preached by colonial missionaries. Gay conditionality could be seen as one example in a long history of states of the Global North violating Southern states' sovereignty by attempting to impose policies and legislation, change attitudes and social norms, this time as a condition of aid that they can ill afford to forego (Velasco 2019).

Despite the Global North's claims to be protecting the rights of minority groups, when LGBTQ+ people from states in the Global South seek safety from persecution in the Global North, they rarely meet with success. For example, in the UK in 2009, some 73 per cent of all claims by asylum seekers for any reason were rejected at the initial decision-making stage, but for claims made by lesbians and gay men who were claiming fear of persecution in their own states on the grounds of sexuality, the rejection rate at the initial stage was between 98–99 per cent (Giametta 2017). Again, this challenges simplistic binaries that see the Global North as a safe and tolerant place for LGBTQ+ people to be, free from the danger and intolerance of the South.

Unlike those applying for asylum because of their ethnicity, religion or political views, LGBTQ+ asylum seekers face a double burden of proof. First, they must prove to their host state that LGBTQ+ people as a group are not safe in their home state and second, they must prove that they themselves are a member of that group. This process can be extremely invasive and can expose them to institutionalised homophobia and ignorance about LGBTQ+ identities. In the United States, there are documented cases where immigration judges initially denied the asylum applications of gay men because they did not seem effeminate. Others were asked to provide letters of testimony from former lovers, even though the lovers were still living in a state where homosexuality is a crime – and so to write such a letter would put them at risk (Gross 2018). Often, the fact of having lived their life up until now in a state where homosexuality is illegal means that LGBTQ+ asylum seekers have little

evidence of their sexual orientation to support their application as they (to borrow a common term) lived 'in the closet'. Similarly, if a trans person has lived their entire life in a state where trans people are persecuted, they are very unlikely to have transitioned and be able to show 'evidence' of their gender identity.

While acceptance rates for gay men and lesbian women's asylum applications are low, acceptance rates for bisexual people's asylum claims are even lower. Here again, institutionalised homophobia and misconceptions about bisexuality result in a lack of understanding of the experiences of this group and the dangers they face. A bisexual asylum seeker might have lived as heterosexual until now to avoid the dangers that 'coming out' as bisexual might cause them in their home state. In moving to a new state to finally live in their true identity, by definition, they have no evidence either of their sexual orientation, or of the persecution they have faced at home. There is also a perception that they can easily return to their own states and continue to live as heterosexuals, ignoring the trauma that this would cause them and the danger they would face if their true identity was discovered. Some bisexual asylum seekers therefore choose to apply for asylum as gay or lesbian, but they then face the consequence that if they do gain permission to remain in their chosen new home, should they ever wish to marry a member of the opposite sex in future, they could be arrested for fraud and deported (Gross 2018).

Lesbian and bisexual women are particularly disadvantaged by needing to prove their sexuality during an asylum claim because the persecution they face is so often in the private domain. Again, the public/private binary is important here. While the typical image of persecution is of someone being harassed in public or threatened with arrest, in many of the contexts around the world where homosexuality is illegal, conservative social norms also confine women to the domestic sphere as has been outlined earlier. The danger to them then is not from the state, but rather from their husband or family members who may act violently if they discover their sexual orientation. These women will have little evidence to show of the dangers they have faced, other than in their own memories and retellings. The same states that preach LGBTQ+ equality on an international level regularly deport these women to states where they risk death because they fail to understand the persecution they might face in the private sphere because of their sexuality. Here, analysing events from a queer theory or postcolonial perspective, and looking beyond simplistic binaries such as modern/traditional, safe/unsafe and public/private, allows us to see how the claims of states in the Global North to be promoting LGBTQ+ rights around the world can serve to mask those same states' violations of the rights of LGBTQ+ people from the Global South.

Conclusion

For a long time, gender and sexuality were seen as below 'high politics' – too personal to be political and not worthy of the attention of states*men*. As the case studies have demonstrated, claims that a given problem is too 'personal' or 'private' often mask the way that states already regulate the personal lives of women and sexual minorities, most commonly by not intervening to protect them from the greatest dangers they face. Gradually, these issues are beginning to gain visibility across the global system, and within the discipline of International Relations. However, as this chapter has shown, this is done from within existing frameworks that all too often reflect a heterosexual male point of view. The resulting practices therefore risk at best ignoring, and at worst perpetuating, unequal power relations that endanger women and LGBTQ+ people throughout the world. Only by paying attention to those power relations and by working towards redressing them can the global system become a place where every individual can access equal rights and security.

 END OF CHAPTER QUESTIONS

1. What kind of issues dominate media coverage of politics in your home country? Are they typically viewed as 'hard'/masculine or 'soft'/feminine issues?

2. In what ways is the use of quotas to ensure women and LGBTQ+ people are fairly represented in national parliaments an effective measure to address gender and sexuality disparities?

3. How has the global response to the HIV pandemic differed to the response to Covid-19? How might this be linked to perceptions of the communities most affected by each virus?

4. How can governments across the world recognise the essential contribution of domestic, unpaid and informal labour to the economy?

5. Can you think of other examples beyond those outlined in the chapter where states in the Global North claim to be 'rescuing' women or LGBTQ+ people in the Global South, even while they may be failing to secure basic rights within their own borders?

GLOBAL ISSUES

This part of the book deals with some of the world's most pressing global issues. What unites them is that each poses a security challenge to the state and/or to people that also involves activity at the international organisational level. In other words, they are the very issues that the discipline of International Relations is uniquely poised to offer insights on. Students often want to dive straight into learning about issues such as these as they likely reflect whatever sparked their interest in International Relations in the first place. Yet, as noted earlier in the book, it is impossible to work effectively at unpacking and understanding such issues in their full complexity without having first understood the history, theory and the structures of the discipline and the global system itself – which have been covered in the prior two parts of the book. Beyond simply presenting information that diagnoses the problem, the chapters show how International Relations thinks deeper and wider about how these issues can be addressed. In doing so, these chapters also serve as a reminder that International Relations is not just an academic subject, but its various debates reflect upon, and also impact upon, the real world.

CHAPTER 14

INTERNATIONAL SECURITY

Natalie Jester

Question: Who or what should be 'secure' in the global system?

Security is a natural place to start with this third and final part of the book as it is a unifying component in each of the global issues we face, and for that reason a central theme in International Relations. It is also a contested concept that has occupied minds for thousands of years. The central debate explored in this chapter is whether security should be about protecting the state or the individual – or both. Extending that, another question emerges as to who, or what, should provide security. For example, should this power remain with states or should it be relocated in whole, or in part, to international organisations? Key questions such as these ensure that security takes centre stage in International Relations. Exploring it allows us to recall many of the themes explored earlier in the book and also to point towards the global issues explored in this part of the book.

Traditional approaches to security

Traditionally, security has been focused upon conventional military threats to the continued existence of a state. This approach is captured well in Max Weber's definition, outlined in 1919, whereby the state is the apparatus 'that successfully lays claim to the monopoly on legitimate use of physical violence within a particular territory' (Weber 2004, 33). Reflecting this, the traditional conception of security emphasises the survival of the state through the maintenance of its current borders and sovereignty. It is helpful at this stage to recall that the principle of sovereignty in International Relations is most commonly argued to have originated in the Peace of Westphalia, which guaranteed the right of states to decide how to govern within their own borders, as was first explored in Chapter two. Whilst such principles are a material reality, they are filtered through human experience and shaped by power relations. For reasons such as this, sovereignty is not a straightforward concept and has come to mean slightly different things at different times as discourses have changed.

14.1 – KEY TERMS: The Declaration of Principles of International Law

Article 2 of the Charter of the United Nations (1945) asserts the right to member sovereignty. The Declaration of Principles of International Law (1970) later reinforced this as follows:

a. The principle that States shall refrain in their international relations from the threat or use of force against the territorial integrity or political independence of any State, or in any other manner inconsistent with the purposes of the United Nations,

b. The principle that States shall settle their international disputes by peaceful means in such a manner that international peace and security and justice are not endangered,

c. The duty not to intervene in matters within the domestic jurisdiction of any State, in accordance with the Charter,

d. The duty of States to co-operate with one another in accordance with the Charter,

e. The principle of equal rights and self-determination of peoples,

f. The principle of sovereign equality of States,

g. The principle that States shall fulfil in good faith the obligations assumed by them in accordance with the Charter.

If we are to focus on borders as a security marker, we must then ask who enforces sovereignty. States want the ability to make decisions about the governance of their own lands without interference. But what happens when an external force interferes? The United Nations is perhaps the most obvious arbiter in this case. Whilst the United Nations can intervene to prevent one state becoming involved in another's affairs, the organisation has been criticised as lacking the ability to hold states to account – especially the most powerful states in the system. The argument follows, then, that states exist within a system of anarchy whereby an external, overarching power cannot be relied upon to enforce the rules. Further, the landscape of global security is shaped by the number of states with significant power, how they perceive themselves and others, and how they interact with one another.

The concern with states, borders and militaries means that traditional security takes us back to realism. As has already been explored in Chapter six, a debate exists within realism over how states can best achieve national security. Defensive realists make the case that states will seek security through stability. There is little desire to upset the status quo because this will simply result in actions taken against you by other states, which in turn prompts another set of actions, and so on – resulting in greater overall insecurity. This series of ripple effects means that expansion is not typically seen as a desirable or viable strategy. Offensive realists argue on the other hand that the situation of anarchy results in uncertainty, which is especially problematic when you cannot be sure of the intentions of other actors. This means that states will seek security through the expansion of their power, upsetting whatever global or regional order exists at the time. As Mearsheimer (2001, 33), a key proponent of this approach explains, 'states quickly understand that the best way to ensure their survival is to be the most powerful state in the system'.

States certainly do seek to ensure their own survival, but this can be done through means other than war, as it is not always in a state's interest to engage in conflict. At this point it is useful to recall another theme outlined in Chapter six, liberalism's democratic peace theory, which directly relates to discussions about security. In order to go to war, states must commit to increased military spending, which will either come at the cost of other elements of the budget, such as education and health, or via rises in taxation. War also requires people to fight and even if military personnel are not killed, they may return with physical injuries and/or mental health concerns – such as post-traumatic stress disorder. It is therefore often a hard sell for a democracy to convince the public that war is in the best interest of the state. In addition, war poses a significant disruption to the economy, which compounds the above issues. Where democratic states disagree on a particular subject such as security, resources or territory, it is common for both parties to resolve the matter using the well-established tools of diplomacy.

To illustrate the democratic peace theory we can look at contrasting examples. Firstly, a brief comparison of an incident between two democratic states, Switzerland and Liechtenstein. One evening in 2007, 170 Swiss troops accidentally crossed the border into the neighbouring state of Liechtenstein before realising their mistake and quickly returning to Switzerland. Although this was technically an act of war on Switzerland's behalf, the situation was quickly resolved with good humour on both sides, neither seeing the other as a threat to security. The bombing of Libya in 2011 provides a contrasting example – one that allows us to recall that, while democracies do not go to war with each other, the democratic peace thesis does not eliminate war with a non-democracy. Muammar Gaddafi came to power in Libya following a 1969 coup and quickly cemented his power as a dictator. In 2011, in the context of the Arab Spring pro-democracy movement that was sweeping across North Africa and the Middle East, the Gaddafi government viciously cracked down on anti-regime protests. As news of the atrocities spread, the United Nations Security Council issued Resolution 1973 and a coalition including France, the United Kingdom, the United States and Canada (among other democracies) undertook airstrikes and enforced no-fly zones.

14.2 – KEY TERMS: 'National' and 'human' security

Traditional views on security emphasise both the preservation of the state and the existence of a military-type threat to its borders and sovereignty. This is broadly referred to as **national security**. However, in more recent times, other interpretations have emerged that focus instead on non-state actors and emphasise human pain and suffering. By stressing the individual level as opposed to the state level, this interpretation is referred to as **human security**. The central debate within defining security therefore is one that has at its origins a levels of analysis issue, recalling the themes in Chapter five.

While the examples above are helpful, they should not give the impression that the debate is simply one between the more optimistic account of liberalism with its democratic peace theory, and the more pessimistic debates within realism about how often states will go to war. Since the bulk of International Relations' history as a discipline mirrored the twentieth century's world wars and the Cold War it is perhaps not surprising that these state-based formulations of security emerged as they did. Both realist and liberal theories of security are therefore not designed to incorporate other elements and actors as their focus is built around the state and system levels. In the modern era, with a variety of non-state actors posing challenges to both domestic and international security, there is clearly a need to expand the realm of what we mean by security.

Moving beyond the state

Contemporary thinking on security does not do away with the focus upon the state entirely, but rather asks whether other actors might also help or harm security. It also allows us to consider critiques, such as those from Vitalis (2015), asserting that International Relations has historically been a white, Western-centric discipline. And, as the ideas of sovereignty and the nation-state were European creations exported to the rest of the world, state-based national security understandings became dominant as that was the world predominantly white Western theorists saw. But it was not necessarily helpful or correct in every context. Henderson (2015, 149), for example, makes a case that as African state systems have been established in a way that replicates the structures of their colonial past, foreign policy is conducted in a way that is 'accomplished through orienting the post-colonial state's foreign policy practices towards those that were acceptable to the major [global] powers'. This, he asserts, is why there must be a greater focus upon civil wars and non-state actors as agents of insecurity in Africa rather than focusing on instances of state-on-state war across the continent.

 ### 14.3 – KEY INSIGHTS: 'New wars'

Mary Kaldor coined the term 'new wars' in 1999 to describe types of warfare that are proliferating in the contemporary era. These largely revolved around four areas, all of which are analysed within the context of globalisation and the conditions it has introduced (or exacerbated) within the global system:

1   Violence between dynamic combinations of state and non-state networks

2   Fighting in the name of identity politics (such as religion) as opposed to ideology (such as communism)

3   Attempts to achieve political, rather than physical, control of a population through fear and terror

4   Conflict financed through non-state means and channels, thus continuing violence.

The conflicts engendered by Islamic State, although driven out of the territory it once occupied in Syria and Iraq, are a contemporary example that embody the criteria for new wars. Islamic State is a non-state transnational terrorist group (criterion 1). They seek to create a new type of state based upon religious identity centring on a new interpretation of Islam (criterion 2). They sought and exercised political control over the sovereign territory of at least two nation-states (criterion 3). In Mosul, northern Iraq, over 15,000 pages of documents written by members of the group were recovered after they were driven out, showing that they operated as a government, issuing formal documents such as birth certificates – as well as running a police force. It also employed some of the same revenue streams discussed above (criterion 4) by taxing people and businesses within its conquered territory.

The concept of 'new wars' is instructive here to unpack further the focus on actors, goals, methods and finance. Firstly, states are not the only actors on the world stage. Rather, if we are to consider security in the most relevant, holistic terms, we must also think about non-state actors. To borrow the words of Kaldor (2013, 2) 'new wars are fought by varying combinations of networks of state and non-state actors – regular armed forces, private security contractors, mercenaries, jihadists, warlords, paramilitaries, etc.'. In addition to posing a threat to security, non-state actors can also be security providers. For example, private military and security contractors (sometimes referred to as mercenaries) are not directly employed by a state but by a private company. Their use, sometimes subcontracted by states to provide security in war zones or post-conflict situations (such as in Iraq after 2003), has become a controversial debate in recent years (Chisholm 2014) due to concerns over the legality of state use of private armies.

Secondly, the goals of war are changing. Whereas wars used to be fought in order to maintain territory or for ideological reasons relating to the maintenance (or propagation) of a particular style of government – such as fascism, communism or democracy – new wars are often fought on the basis of identities such as religious, ethnic or tribal identity. Indeed, the mobilisation of identity is the desired outcome within new wars and not simply a side effect. One example is the civil war in Sudan, which raged in two phases between 1955–2005. It eventually resulted in the state splitting in two in 2011 along religious lines, with the Christian-majority South breaking away from Muslim-majority North to form the new state of South Sudan.

Thirdly, the focus upon military security and traditional 'battles' is becoming less common. Instead there is greater emphasis upon the political control of territory, including through the use of violence directed at citizens. This often occurs through some sort of population displacement aimed at those who are not signed up to the same ideology or have what is considered an undesirable identity. Boko Haram are one example of this. Their campaign of violence, bombings and kidnappings has displaced approximately 2.4 million people in north-eastern Nigeria and the surrounding region.

Fourthly, whilst wars were typically only financed by traditional state sources of income (taxation, government debt, etc.), new wars have a much greater variety of funding sources. These include smuggling, diaspora donations, looting or kidnap and ransom. This necessitates a blurring of boundaries and, as a result, it may be necessary to consider organised crime and wider human rights violations within analyses of security. The Taliban and al-Qaeda, for example, have raised funds through the opium trade (primarily derived from Afghanistan) and through credit card fraud schemes. This final point, when taken together with those above, shows that the nature of war is clearly no longer about state versus state conflict. It draws in a variety of actors and issues, often in complex permutations that cannot be easily resolved.

Elements of human security

Concepts such as new wars confirm that the traditional focus upon states, as opposed to human beings, has painted only a partial picture of security. This has led to criticism at several levels. Feminists, for example, point to the issue of rape as a weapon of war – which is not taken with the gravity it should be. Instead it is invariably seen as a regrettable, yet expected, wartime issue sometimes faced by women. Postcolonial theorists argue further that history is vital in understanding the imperial violence enacted by Western states upon colonial subjects, which sustains unequal power relations between states and peoples even to this day. Critiques such as these have been gathering steam in recent decades and have transcended academia to become a persistent theme debated in the public sphere.

The 1994 United Nations Human Development Report (UNHDR) drew a line under the issue and argued that too much emphasis had been placed upon conflicts between states, weapons of mass destruction and foreign policy. The UNHDR helpfully lists the threats to human security under seven categories:

1. Economic security

2. Food security

3. Health security

4. Environmental security

5. Personal security

6. Community security

7. Political security

The Report argues that these concerns are universal and that they often compound upon each other, leaving some people in dire situations. These threats encompass a wide range of dimensions and consider both deliberate acts designed to provoke instability and acts of nature such as earthquakes. Yet, it should also be noted that the latter also covers climatic events which could also be indirectly attributed to human beings – such as floods or droughts caused (or exacerbated) by climate change.

Personal security is taken to be the most important element of human security and the Report lists the following as threats: the state (physical torture); other states (war); other groups of people (ethnic tension); individuals or gangs against other individuals or gangs (crime, street violence); threats directed at women (rape, domestic violence) or children based on their vulnerability and dependence (child abuse); and threats to self (suicide, drug use). At each level, from local government to state parliaments to international organisations such as the United Nations, women are under-represented and shut out from decision-making indirectly or deliberately. Thus, issues affecting women especially are often omitted from security discussions because those making policy decisions view them as personal problems, or isolated incidents, and are therefore not treated with urgency. Feminists argue that such examples signify a patriarchal system that functions at a local, national and global level and underpins acts of violence of many different kinds (Enloe 2001). Rape, for example, can be connected to wider systems of misogyny that can be drivers of war and conflict, as well as being used as a weapon against local populations, as noted above.

Political security relates to freedom from human rights abuses and focuses especially upon people's ability to express their political beliefs freely. To illustrate this we can use the example of Augusto Pinochet, who ruled Chile from 1973 to 1990 after taking power in a military coup. Tens of thousands of people considered dangerous to the regime disappeared or were tortured, sexually assaulted or killed. Unfortunately, such examples are not confined to history and people in many states still face a wide range of different political security challenges today.

Community security emphasises the support and identity gained from group identity – for example the family or an ethnic group. Insecurity arises in this category when threats occur due to membership of a particular group. For example, the Rohingya are an ethnic and religious group of approximately one million people. They became stateless when they underwent a genocide in Myanmar starting in 2016 that resulted in them being forced to flee into neighbouring states. Issues such as these, of groups and individuals being forced from their homes, will be explored further in Chapter sixteen.

Economic security is concerned with absolute poverty – the inability to maintain a basic standard of living, which in turn endangers the life of the individual concerned and their family. Poverty is a pervasive issue in our world, and it is present within richer and poorer states – something further explored in Chapter seventeen. Related to economic security is food security whereby people should have access to food that they can grow or buy themselves, or obtain from government programmes. In the UK, for example, food banks and related charities distribute millions of food parcels each year to people who cannot feed themselves or their families. Food insecurity can be made by human conditions, but it can also result from environmental issues, whereby crops might be destroyed by flooding or insects.

Environmental security can be threatened globally and locally. As of 2020, the Amazon rainforest has been reduced to 80 per cent of its 1970s area, due to factors

14.4 – KEY INSIGHTS: Emerging norms of human protection

Bellamy (2017) outlines eight norms that have emerged within the global system, each of which shows evolution in the broader category of human security.

1 **International humanitarian law**. This forms a normative standard of civilian protection via written (codified) forms of international law that regulates the conduct of soldiers in war and seeks to protect non-combatants. Landmark components are the 1948 Genocide Convention and the 1949 Geneva Conventions.

2 **Protection of civilians**. A series of normative developments focusing on ensuring the United Nations both considers, and acts on, areas involving the protection of civilians – not just states. In that sense, this category embodies the mainstreaming of human security in the United Nations' everyday language and actions. It involves an interpretation of the UN Charter to be used in a way that overrides the will of states – such as Resolution 2165, which authorised humanitarian aid into Syria in 2014 without the consent of the Syrian government.

3 **Addressing specific vulnerabilities**. This category involves the identification of groups that are especially vulnerable, and the frameworks built to mitigate these. For example, refugees have been granted a worldwide right to claim asylum, a system overseen by a dedicated UN High Commissioner.

4 **Human rights**. A norm that has been constantly building since the 1948 Universal Declaration of Human Rights. Today, multiple mechanisms have been developed to monitor and assess how states perform in human rights categories – including using reports to name and shame states.

5 **International criminal justice**. Best illustrated through the example of the establishment of the International Criminal Court, which tries individuals for the most serious crimes, such as genocide. Although not all states are members, the Court's existence provides a normative deterrent effect, shaping behaviour across the global system.

6 **Humanitarian action**. This category principally refers to peacekeeping and humanitarian missions, typically coordinated by the United Nations, to deliver aid in wartime scenarios. This can be done through using force (when authorised by the Security Council) or through peaceful means with the agreement of the parties on the ground.

7 **Regional initiatives**. This takes the form of peacekeeping and humanitarian efforts undertaken by regional organisations, such as the European Union and the African Union. When adding to the work done by the United Nations, it adds normative and operational momentum to human protection and also diversifies the actors undertaking such moves.

8 **Responsibility to Protect**. Since 2005 this term has become part of the working language at the United Nations, significantly adding to and clarifying some of the developments in category 2 above. It has been referred to in a range of resolutions directed at reminding states of their responsibilities.

including illegal logging and encroaching agriculture. Animals and plants are destroyed, making this a problem for the local ecosystem, but the rainforest also absorbs two billion tonnes of carbon dioxide each year, meaning that its loss also causes worldwide problems for mitigating climate change. Environmental insecurity also threatens people's health, causing health insecurity. These debates are explored fully in Chapters eighteen and nineteen.

It should be obvious by now that formulating security at the human level is significantly more expansive than traditional approaches. Human security perspectives are better placed to account for the violence and suffering that impacts people's day-to-day lives and detect when these issues become international. Human security, however, is not without its detractors. Paris (2004), among others, has argued that the concept of human security is too broad, making it harder to assign responsibility for particular policy areas. The very question of who, or what, should be tasked to solve security problems – especially as the term becomes ever more complex – has become a major debate.

Protecting people

Momentarily going back to traditional conceptions of security, these set out that states experience insecurity when borders are breached and their sovereignty jeopardised. The solution provided in this case would often be to petition the United Nations for a collective security response and/or directly defend themselves in a war. Human security, however, is much broader and its emergence has coincided with a series of developments over when and how action should take place. Consequently, when insecurity occurs and the subject under threat is not a state, it is much less obvious what the solution might look like and who is responsible for providing it. Furthermore, it can be difficult to apportion blame, especially when these threats interact with one another: how, for example, might we hold a subject accountable for global warming that causes food insecurity? As a result, human security and the categories therein, as outlined earlier in the chapter, are perhaps best described as a diagnostic tool but not always a treatment. Yet, at a certain point, an argument can be made that the threat to life is so great in some cases that there is a need for an intervention of some kind.

Humanitarian intervention of different forms to protect individuals has been practised and debated for decades at the international level. Typically it has been regarded with scepticism due to conflicts over how and why certain principles are applied by states. For example, the overarching reason given by the United States for the invasion of Afghanistan in 2001 (the first 'war' in the War on Terror) was a standard national security case. It centred on militarily removing the Taliban regime who were harbouring al-Qaeda – a so-called 'regime change'. Yet an additional emphasis in the narrative for war focused on the need to 'liberate' or 'save' women from oppression under the Taliban regime. As Abu-Lughod (2002) notes, this presumes a helplessness that many women did not necessarily attach to themselves. This representation is underpinned by Said's Orientalism, which refers to the assumptions made by Western states about the nature of Eastern states as exotic, or in this case barbaric – as first explored in Chapter seven. As a result, it can be argued that when states use such apparently moral justifications for interventions it is not only problematic conceptually, but it can also obscure other more strategic (and presumably questionable) reasons for invasion such as implementing foreign policy doctrines of democratisation, or a desire to control natural resources. Critical approaches therefore highlight well the controversy over intervention. They suggest that use of certain language sometimes enables states with ulterior motives to make a case for interfering in the sovereign affairs of another state that may not otherwise be justifiable to the international community (Shepherd 2006).

The 'Responsibility to Protect' is, in part, an attempt to reset this debate by setting out clear written terms for intervention. As already covered in Chapter two, it was adopted in 2005 as a principle of the United Nations, aiming to prevent genocide, ethnic cleansing, war crimes and crimes against humanity. The Responsibility to Protect has three pillars:

1. states have a responsibility to avoid this kind of mass suffering
2. the international community should encourage states to fulfil this responsibility
3. if the state fails to protect its people or actively perpetrates violence, it is the duty of the international community to intervene.

 14.5 – KEY INSIGHTS: The Rwandan genocide

Map 14.1 Rwanda

In the early 1990s, Rwanda (Map 14.1) was comprised of two ethnic groups: Hutu and Tutsi. The minority Tutsi (approximately 15 per cent of the population) had historically dominated Rwandan politics, causing tension that on occasion turned violent. On 6 April 1994, the plane of president Juvenal Habiyarimana – a Hutu – was shot down, prompting a wave of violence. Over 100 days in 1994, 500,000–800,000 people were killed, mostly Tutsis by Hutu extremists. In human security terms, this threatens personal safety, and targeting by an ethnic group threatens community safety. Indeed, it is this systematic attempt to wipe out a group that makes this a genocide. The United Nations had forces in Rwanda at the time but no mandate to prevent killings. This recalls earlier arguments that the global system exists in a state of anarchy, with no overarching sovereign body to uphold norms and ensure accountability. Yet events in Rwanda and elsewhere in the 1990s did build momentum for the development of the Responsibility to Protect.

One way such an intervention occurs is through approval by the UN Security Council, typically conducted by a group of states working together to rally the necessary consensus and ensure no veto is cast by one of the permanent members (P5). The idea of such intervention is, perhaps obviously, to avoid large-scale loss of life and prevent serious harm, which are admirable aims. The United Nations adopted this principle in part upon reflecting on shortcomings over the responses to the 1990s genocides in the former Yugoslavia and in Rwanda. Beyond the immediate human suffering, the ripple effects of events like these last for many years, negatively impacting a wide range of areas from domestic security to community relations to democratic processes.

The 2011 Libyan civil war was the first time the UN Security Council authorised a foreign military intervention by explicitly referencing the Responsibility to Protect. In 2011 as part of the cascading events of the Arab Spring, mass resistance against the Gaddafi regime had reached a critical point in Libya. There were credible fears that the sitting government would turn the full extent of its military power on the people, resulting in bloodshed. International airstrikes on military facilities and equipment, and tactical support, contributed to the downfall of the government. Importantly, no foreign ground troops were placed in Libya due to the lack of political will for such a measure – and it should be noted that one state risking its own lives for those of another state for purely humanitarian motives is always beset with a strong risk-averse logic.

In practice, the Responsibility to Protect is mentioned much more frequently than it is employed. Overriding sovereignty is deeply controversial due to the continuing state-centric nature of the global system. When certain cases are discussed, there is often disagreement as to whether the threshold for the threat to life is significant enough to compel states to consider intervention. This is no small matter considering the political and financial costs of taking intervention measures – all of which are borne by states as the United Nations does not have any direct security means of its own, drawing all such funding and personnel from voluntary state contributions. Further complications arise when such action may involve a state that is allied to one of the P5 nations. An example of this is multiple Russian vetoes at the Security Council regarding various international actions on Syria which neutered any large-scale intervention in its civil war. This is despite the Syrian civil war being one of the most substantial generators of human security concerns in recent times with several hundred thousand deaths and several million displaced. However, such obstacles are not always insurmountable, and as mentioned before, consensus was formed over an intervention in Libya. This demonstrates that the expectations to use such measures as the Responsibility to Protect may be gaining normative power.

The Responsibility to Protect is also sometimes extended into peacekeeping. The argument is that it is not enough for foreign forces to simply arrive, prevent loss of life and then leave. Often particular structures that enabled the violence in the first place will remain, and therefore present a need for post-conflict interventions. As a result, it is considered more sensible to place peacekeepers on the ground in order to prevent violence from recurring in the short and medium term, perhaps until solutions to the underlying problems can be found. This practice can, however, be problematic, as these forces themselves sometimes commit acts of violence against local populations. There are multi-dimensional power structures in place in peacekeeping situations, with peacekeepers both highly likely to be male and paid significantly more than local populations, bearing in mind that the places they are sent to have often seen their economy negatively impacted by conflict. For example, UN peacekeepers arrived in Haiti in 2004 with a mandate to tackle political instability and organised crime. This remit was extended in 2010 following a severe earthquake. During this time, many peacekeepers paid local women and girls – some as young as 11 – to sleep with them, exposing some to sexually transmitted diseases, and fathering children who they then abandoned (Lee and Bartels 2019). The Responsibility to Protect, then, and debate around intervention, is complex. In contrast with traditional approaches that seek to ensure the continued existence of the state, human security makes the case for a significantly broader conceptualisation of security.

 CASE STUDY 14.1: The Gulf War

Photo 14.1 Saddam Hussein in Amman, Jordan, 11 November 1987

Credit: Chip HIRES/Gamma-Rapho/Getty Images

Tensions had been building in the Gulf throughout the 1980s, exacerbated by the Iran–Iraq war (1980–8). In the hope of weakening the revolutionary government of Iran, several nearby Arab states backed Iraq, including Saudi Arabia and Kuwait, who lent Iraq large sums of money. Iraq–Kuwait relations deteriorated after the Iran–Iraq war, with debt being a key reason: Iraq argued that other states had benefited from a weakened Iranian regime and that debt should be forgiven because Iraq could not repay it. Unsurprisingly, Kuwait did not agree. During this period there was also a global oil glut, with supply outweighing demand, driving down the

oil price. As a result, the Organization of Petroleum Exporting Countries (OPEC) – an intergovernmental organisation and sometimes also referred to as a cartel – restricted production quotas to increase prices, straining the finances of oil-producing states like Iraq and Kuwait. With Iraq already in a precarious financial position, this was seen by its government as a serious problem. Iraq accused Kuwait of producing more oil than permitted under OPEC rules – pushing down prices for everyone – and once again the two states were at loggerheads. The Kuwaiti decision to continue selling oil above its OPEC-ordered quota was taken as an act of aggression by Iraq, which had also staked a claim to Kuwaiti territory, though this was not taken seriously internationally.

Iraq invaded Kuwait on 2 August 1990, crossing the border with tanks, aircraft and approximately 100,000 troops. The decision to move the military across the Iraqi border and subsume one state into another violated Kuwaiti sovereignty because Iraq was not recognised as having authority over Kuwait. While the global system is said to be one of anarchy, in which no global body ensures obedience to the rules, the UN Security Council demanded that Iraq withdraw from Kuwait immediately. Iraq's leader, Saddam Hussein (Photo 14.1), refused. In late November, the United Nations authorised the use of military action resulting in a multi-state offensive, led by the United States. Iraq was driven out of Kuwait in what was known as Operation Desert Storm. In order to ensure that Iraq did not attempt to encroach on Kuwait territory again, the United Nations established a demilitarised zone between the two states under Resolution 667

Map 14.2 Gulf War no-fly zones

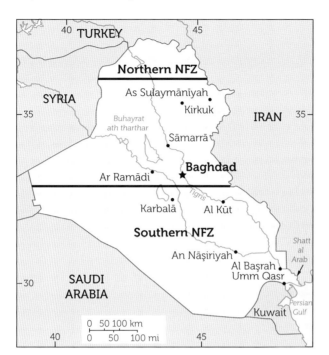

(1991). The UN mandate was expanded after Iraqi incursions onto Kuwaiti territory between 1991 and 1993 and an infantry battalion and no-fly zones (Map 14.2) were installed to prevent this occurring again.

Liberals often use this example as a case in point of international law and multilateralism working precisely as they were designed to. The United Nations system of collective security has seldom (perhaps never) worked so well as in this case – perhaps because the aggression was so obvious and allowing it to go unchecked (not using military force) risked undermining the system itself. This was especially pertinent as ideas of a 'New World Order', to quote US president George H. W. Bush (1989–93), had begun to replace images of Cold War bipolarity around this time. In a world that was rapidly growing together with globalisation and increasing democratisation, violations of this kind should not, and in this case did not, go unpunished. This was especially pertinent as advances in technology around the same time had made it possible for news reporters to present images live anywhere in the world, 24 hours a day. The media presence within these spaces was both a showcase of the injustices against Kuwaitis (who had lost their sovereignty) and simultaneously a driver of public support for subsequent intervention in overseas conflict to repair the damage and restore order. This has been labelled 'the CNN effect', borrowing the name of the US Cable News Network.

Realists would not accept the judgement of liberals that this intervention was a success of the collective security model. At first glance it appears true that there was an injustice and the UN system worked to redress it. However, the key issue for realists was that this episode did not directly involve any major powers' national security and was thereby uncontroversial and relatively simple to authorise. Neither Iraq nor Kuwait is a permanent member of the Security Council, so no veto was possible, and although Iraq was previously aligned with the United States (due to their shared opposition to Iran) it was not such a major alliance that would preclude the United States taking action in the way it did.

If we contrast the Security Council's lack of response to a similar instance in 2014 when Russia invaded and annexed part of Ukraine

(Crimea), the realist critique becomes evident in that security really does lie with the powerful states who take actions as they deem necessary in the hope they will get away with it. Gaining control of Kuwaiti territory and oil reserves might add up to a realist-inspired strategy – principally via a reading of offensive realism – as an attempt to ensure the survival of the Iraqi state. By this logic Iraq could be seen to have had dwindling financial reserves due to its past war with Iran and the subsequent oil price slump, which would make it difficult to maintain living standards and defend its borders. However, Saddam Hussein miscalculated his relative power and influence and suffered inevitable backlash via military attack – which a defensive realist would have cautioned was the likely outcome. To the contrary, in the later example Russia's President, Vladimir Putin, calculated correctly that Russia would not suffer the same fate as Iraq as any effort to remove Russia from Crimea at the United Nations could simply be vetoed – making it dead on arrival if so tabled.

Due to insights and contrasting interpretations such as this – many of which can be drawn far beyond the events themselves – the Gulf War is often used as a pertinent example of the utility of International Relations' theoretical toolkit in unpacking core issues of how security is interpreted, both at the state and system levels.

 CASE STUDY 14.2: Gun violence in the United States

Photo 14.2 Student lie-in at the White House to protest gun laws, Washington DC, 20 February 2018

Credit: Lorie Shaull/Flickr

On the morning of 14 December 2012, Adam Lanza shot and killed his mother Nancy, a teacher, before packing an assault rifle, two handguns and a shotgun, and driving to Sandy Hook Elementary School in Newtown Connecticut. Lanza shot his way into the school and killed twenty children and six adults, before turning the gun on himself. This was not the first mass shooting to happen in the United States, but its victims were among the youngest. In total, fewer than 4,000 people have been killed across all recorded terrorist incidents in the United States. In comparison, there are tens of thousands of deaths as a result of shootings each *year*, including even children, as the example above shows. A statistic like this raises the question as to why terrorism is one of the most hotly contested security issues in the United States and often dominates political debates, yet it kills far fewer people than gun violence. When we grapple with this question, we can ask whether US gun laws and controls should then be considered a security issue, given that guns kill more people than terrorists.

Rather than dwell on the domestic side of this issue, something within the remit of the American legal and political systems, we can look to International Relations for some answers and analysis. For example, applying the Responsibility to Protect, the United States has arguably failed to take responsibility for widespread suffering and loss of life (pillar 1) and has not protected its citizens (pillar 3). This means that, if we read the Responsibility to Protect literally and seek to apply it evenly, the international community might be in a position to intervene in the United States. However unlikely it is that another state would bring such an issue to the United Nations, adopting a human security framework does suggest that their endemic gun violence is a security problem. To break down this issue, gun violence in the United States occurs within several domains of human security. Under human security definitions, perhaps most obviously, guns pose a threat to personal security, which emphasises bodily threats. We might argue that gun violence comes under the concern for children, based upon their vulnerability, as so many incidences occur in schools. Moving beyond schools, in situations of domestic violence, women are more likely to be killed by a gun than by any other method, and gun ownership increases the likelihood of murder in this situation. In many cases, the men who obtained these guns did so legally, which raises questions as to whether existing US law is sufficient to ensure human protection.

Human security also contains a provision for the security of the community. Beyond the school context, threats to community also include the disproportionate harm caused to Black people by police shootings. In 2014, for example, a 12-year-old Black boy named Tamir Rice was killed by police in a playground. At this time, Rice was holding a toy gun; he was shot by police as soon as they exited their vehicle, with no time taken to obtain further information. Ohio, the state in which Rice was killed, is an open-carry state in which citizens are permitted to have guns on display in public.

From 2013, the United States has seen widespread protests and demonstrations under the Black Lives Matter banner, which seeks to raise awareness of the extent of police killings of Black citizens – as first explored in Chapter three. Here, the state is seen to be responsible for harm to its people due to the acceptability of guns as a law enforcement tool and how this escalates all police encounters. This disproportionately impacts some communities who often fall under unequal suspicion, or profiling, and thus have a higher level of encounters with police. When adding the undercurrents of racism often evident in policing and justice in the United States, the precarious nature of life for some groups within US society certainly reaches territory marked out by human security debates.

The examples above help us think about how it is that some issues have historically been perceived as security problems while others have not. For example, why is it common to perceive as a greater problem tanks crossing borders than large-scale loss of life due to guns in the United States, especially amongst schoolchildren and Black civilians? After yet another school shooting in 2018, Wayne Lapierre, head of the powerful lobbying group the National Rifle Association (NRA), addressed the calls for gun regulation and said:

> they care more about control, and more of it. Their goal is to eliminate the second amendment and our firearms freedoms so they can eradicate all individual freedoms … They hate the NRA, they hate the second amendment, they hate individual freedom.

Lapierre is not the first to represent attempts to restrict the sale of guns as an assault upon freedom and he will likely will not be the last. Helping to unpack this, constructivists argue that interpretation is what really matters when we are thinking about security because this shapes what we decide to do about problems that arise. Two constructivist concepts are useful here: articulation and interpellation (Weldes 1996). Articulation is the process through which ideas about different subjects (such as 'the NRA' or 'Americans'), objects, and ideas are linked together. In this case, the concepts of freedom and gun ownership are linked together. Interpellation is the way in which people are 'called into' particular identities. Here, this is accomplished through Lapierre's use of the term 'our', which assumes that there is an 'us' of some kind. Insights such as these help to open up the theoretical space for a more nuanced debate on the issue.

Conclusion

Traditionally, International Relations emphasised the security of the state, marking a clear preference when answering the question of who, or what, should be 'secure' in the global system. Repeated episodes of human suffering have caused scholars and practitioners to take stock and ask whether human suffering might be more important. When attempting to draw up an internationally recognised framework to answer such problems, such as the Responsibility to Protect, there comes embedded within such initiatives an unavoidable challenge to sovereignty. This is controversial considering that sovereignty is the bedrock of the global system. Yet it also indicates the gradual evolution of how sovereignty works, inspired in part by debates around the changing definitions of security that have been explored in this chapter. Security may still be about bombs and borders, but it can be about bodies too.

 END OF CHAPTER QUESTIONS

1. Consider, and reflect upon, the key attributes and the key differences in 'human' and 'national' security. Do you think these categories are compatible, or in conflict?

2. In the global system, who (or what) is responsible for protecting people and are the measures for doing so robust enough?

3. In what ways can it be considered morally right and/or broadly legal for one state to violate another's sovereignty?

4. With respect to human security, which groups of people are most likely to face insecurity?

5. Recalling your International Relations theory toolkit, what does an understanding of the debates around security add to what you already know about how we can reach answers and develop critiques about who (or what) should be secure, and why?

TRANSNATIONAL TERRORISM

Katherine E. Brown

Question: In what ways does terrorism expose the dark side of globalisation?

The interconnected nature of the global system has brought with it not only unprecedented opportunities and progress in human development, but also greater risks. A shadow side of globalisation gives criminal and violent groups the ability to spread their message and widen their operations. The impact of this alters not only the organisation, resources and methods of such groups but also their reasoning and motivations. Under these conditions we have seen the proliferation of terrorist groups with agendas and operations that go beyond the states where those groups originated and principally operate. International Relations concerns itself with transnational terrorism as it poses risks, and questions, that are not easily addressed through domestic (or disconnected) law and order solutions. In recent decades, transnational terrorism has also generated some heated debates, both in scholarship and in public and political spheres, due to 9/11 and the subsequent US-led War on Terror. It remains one of the foremost global issues in our world.

What is transnational terrorism?

Terrorism is a contested concept. Disagreements emerge over the purpose and function, the perpetrators, the victims, the legitimacy and the methods and targeting of terrorist actors. Therefore, how we define terrorism is important but not 'fixed'. Yet it is broadly understood as the use or threat of violence by non-state actors to influence citizens or governments in the pursuit of political or social change. This is not only a semantic or academic debate; the label gives states considerable power to act and use violence against a group and it significantly guides how a state should act. Misapplied definitions can lead to flawed counterterrorism strategies. Moreover, as states cannot agree on the definition, they argue over both the nature and the cause of terrorism as well as who can be called a terrorist, leading to international ramifications. With no agreed international law governing state responses, they struggle to work together to remove the threats. Perhaps the most widely accepted attribute of the term 'terrorism' is that it is derogatory and a sign of disapproval. Typically, labelling a group as terrorist negatively affects perception of the group's legitimacy, legality and how it should be addressed.

15.1 – KEY INSIGHTS: Defining terrorism

Much as transnational corporations originate in one place and develop operations that span the local and the international, those terrorist groups with goals, activities and organisational forms that reach beyond their point of origin can also be referred to as 'transnational'. This draws an important distinction from non-transnational terrorist groups such as the Tamil Tigers (LTTE) in Sri Lanka and the Euskadi Ta Askatasuna (ETA) in Spain whose goals, membership and activities are focused on state politics, even if they receive international support. While defining transnational terrorism is therefore relatively straightforward as it denotes when the issue is one for International Relations' concern, defining terrorism itself is the subject of much debate as seen in the definitions below:

» 'Terrorism is an anxiety-inspiring method of repeated violent action, employed by (semi-) clandestine individual, group, or state actors, for idiosyncratic, criminal, or political reasons, whereby, in contrast to assassination, the direct targets of violence are not the main targets' (Schmid and Jongman 1988).

» Violence with 'intent to threaten the unity, integrity, security or sovereignty of India or to strike terror in the people or any section of the people' (Indian Prevention of Terrorism Act 2002).

» 'Act of terrorism = Peacetime Equivalent of War Crime' (Schmid 1992).

» 'The deliberate, systematic murder, maiming, and menacing of the innocent to inspire fear in order to gain political ends ... Terrorism ... is intrinsically evil, necessarily evil, and wholly evil' (Johnson 1986).

The ability of terrorist goals, groups and terrorist activities to stretch beyond state borders is not new: from the Knights Templar fighting in crusades, nineteenth-century anarchist movements that sought to overthrow the monarchies and feudal systems of Russian and European Empires, to revolutionary support across South America in the twentieth century and Sunni mujahideen fighting in Africa and the Middle East in the late 1980s to the present day. Rapoport (2002) helpfully divided the history of terrorist groups into four successive waves, each characterised by the global politics of the day and culminating in a religious wave following the 1979 Islamic revolution in Iran:

1. An 'anarchist' wave beginning in the 1880s

2. An 'anticolonial' wave beginning in the 1920s

3. A 'new left' wave beginning in the 1960s

4. A 'religious' wave beginning in 1979.

Today it can be argued that a fifth wave of modern terrorist groups has emerged that is both a product of and challenge to key ideas associated with globalisation. It is important to note that some terrorist groups in the past had transnational goals, but they lacked the tools of the modern world to widen and deepen their message. Contemporary transnational terrorism operates in many states, utilising the 'shadow globalisation' flows of people, weapons and information to further their cause. The causes of this new type of terrorism reflect the deepening of human interconnectedness worldwide. Yet almost paradoxically, another characteristic of fifth wave terrorism is the idea that terrorists are operating in a 'leaderless resistance' with a form of 'DIY violence', and while terrorists may associate with particular groups, their affiliations are more akin to loose networks of association rather than collective group action of older style terrorist groups. Combined, it means that we are seeing terrorism as transnational in cause, action and effect.

Motivation and goals

Terrorist groups exist largely due to underlying root inequalities or perceived and real injustices, and the belief that violence will resolve these. Individuals join terrorist groups for a variety of personal and political reasons. This may be because they empathise and identify with the group, because their friends have joined, or due to a feeling that membership of the organisation brings benefits. Research suggests that some women joined Boko Haram willingly because they saw the possibility of better treatment within the organisation: they describe their husbands as well-off and generous; they personally receive their bride-wealth payments directly from their husbands, and they are expected to remain in purdah – seclusion from public contact – where they occupy themselves with household duties and childcare. This frees them from back-breaking agricultural labour and harkens back to practices of purdah involving upper-class Muslim wives in Lake Chad Basin societies in the precolonial and colonial periods (Matfess 2017). This contrasts with the media image of girls being kidnapped by terrorist groups to work for them. Both of these accounts are true; some women were coerced, and some chose to join for a better life, their diverse experiences and motives showing that we must be cautious about generalising 'why women' or 'why youth' join.

Another way of understanding why individuals join and remain part of transnational terrorist groups is radicalisation theory. Radicalisation is understood to be 'everything that happens before the bomb goes off' (Neumann 2013). It suggests that there are pathways to becoming radicalised and that it is a dynamic and individualised process. Because of its individual nature, there is no single (or accurate) terrorist profile. The New York Police Department produced one of the early guides for 'spotting' radicalisation, which led to some seemingly bizarre characteristics – such as an inability to grow pot plants and enjoying camping out – being identified as 'signs' of radicalisation (Silber and Bhatt 2007). The signs were problematic because they were so broad that almost everyone was potentially a suspect. What radicalisation research shows is that a quest for identity and greater significance in the world together with empathy for those who are suffering make an individual more vulnerable to terrorist messages that appear to offer solutions (Silke 2008). Research also shows that an individual with friends or family involved in terrorism or supportive of terrorist views is more likely to join a terrorist organisation than someone with no connections at all (Wiktorowicz 2006). As a result, lone-wolf actors are rare despite their high profile and the media attention they receive.

Indeed, one factor is that individuals join groups in order to 'belong'. This may be because they feel they 'don't belong' in their society, and seek alternatives, or because belonging to an organisation is normal within their network of friends and family. Shane Paul O'Doherty, who received thirty life sentences for his letter-bomb campaign in Ireland and the United Kingdom, but now renounces violence, said of his radicalisation journey that he did not belong to a 'republican family'. As a young boy, though, he read history books highlighting the injustices against the Irish people because of British rule, but: 'my actual joining, though, was very spur of the moment. I was walking home from school and a friend said he was doing it the next day and asked if I wanted to. I said I would. A rapid decision that had horrendous consequences' (Breen 2019). A survey of former fighters in Somalia revealed 27 per cent of respondents joined al-Shabab for economic reasons, 15 per cent mentioned religious reasons, and 13 per cent were forced to join through intimidation and threats of violence (Botha and Abdile 2014). Therefore, for radicalisation research it is important to understand how extremist beliefs, behaviours and belonging combine and lead to violent terrorist activity.

15.2 – KEY INSIGHTS: Islamic State

Perhaps no transnational terrorist group has gained as much attention and notoriety for its activities as Islamic State (also referred to as ISIS, ISIL and Daesh). While it was al-Qaeda that brought transnational terrorism to the centre of international relations following their 9/11 attacks, it was Islamic State that came to dominate attention over the longer term due to their desire to create a 'caliphate' (an Islamic empire) and more importantly their short-lived success in doing so. This is where their name originates, via their intention to annex territory and self-declare statehood. Capitalising on the chaos of the Syrian Civil War and ongoing instability in Iraq post-2011, Islamic State took control of large areas of territory. At one point it held approximately 30 per cent of Syria and 40 per cent of Iraq. By 2018, coordinated international action had pushed them out of most of this territory. Yet, looking at their designs for their 'caliphate' which were self-published online in 2014 gives a sense of the scale of what Islamic State was attempting to build (Map 15.1).

Map 15.1 The ambitions of Islamic State

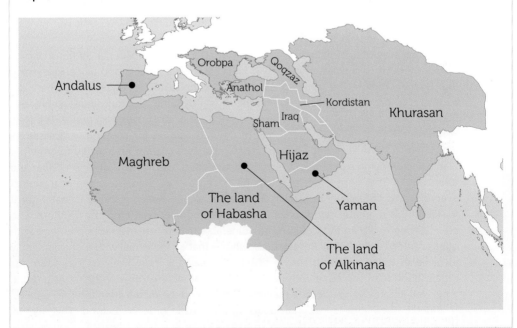

At the group level, goals are also transnational. This is illustrated by looking at al-Qaeda and Islamic State. These groups utilise religious language to create an understanding of global politics that divides the world in two. On one side is the world of Islam. This is a place of goodness, where religious laws are upheld, and Muslims are not oppressed. On the other side is the world of war where Muslims are oppressed by unjust and tyrannical leaders. They argue that, because of the global connection Muslims have with each other as a community of believers (*Umma*), all Muslims should join them in their fight against the 'Oppressors', regardless of where they live. They also argue that because the 'Oppressors' are everywhere and attack Muslims everywhere, their cause and fight is global. They refer to the 'near enemy' (local governments) and the 'far enemy' (global powers) as possible aggressors against whom a member of their organisation might fight. This enables them to tap into local political grievances – such as seeking to remove Western influence from Middle Eastern governments, or class inequalities in rural Afghanistan and Pakistan – and give them a global religious veneer, or to highlight global incidents and claim that they are related to their local cause.

Although most of the coverage of terrorist events seems to focus on high-profile events in Western states, the majority of those killed in terrorist attacks worldwide since 2001 have been Muslims living in Muslim-majority countries. Why? First, it is easier to target less well-protected sites and infrastructure in poorer Muslim-majority states, and the Muslims who die become 'martyrs' to the cause – regardless of whether they were victims or perpetrators. Second, Muslims who resist violent jihadist groups are demonised ideologically as 'unbelievers' so they can be killed too. This was partly what occurred in the territory that the Islamic State seized across Iraq and Syria. Finally, violent actions are often designed to alter the relations between governments and citizens in the Muslim world (Mustafa and Brown 2010).

Terrorist activities

Despite the consequences of transnational terrorism primarily being felt in Muslim-majority states, fear and awareness of the threats are felt strongly in Europe and North America. Terrorism is a 'communicative act', by which we mean it seeks to send a message that goes beyond the actual destruction caused to life and property. That message is to be heard by three groups of people: (1) civilians, who witness the events either locally or globally; (2) governments, which are called upon to respond to the terrorist violence; and (3) potential supporters, who are attracted to join by the terrorist actions. We will look at the different characteristics of terrorist activities in turn (Table 15.1).

Transnational terrorist groups focus on the location of attacks as much as, if not more than, who is attacked in order to generate a wide message. The importance of location was demonstrated by the attacks in Paris in 2015 by the Islamic State group. Paris is one of the most visited cities in the world and the group targeted 'everyday' places such as bars, a football stadium and a concert. This signalled that anyone and anywhere is a target, increasing fear of and publicity for the group's actions. This targeting strategy is in contrast to that of groups that may act across borders, but for whom the local political scene remains key. For example, the Tehrik-e-Taliban – while linked to a global cause of jihad – are local. They target beauty shops, police stations and market squares because they see these as opposed to the way of life they want to establish in their lands. The Tehrik-e-Taliban tried to kill the activist Malala Yousafzai because of her support for girls' education, and schoolgirls are targets because such groups wish girls to have an Islamic education that focuses exclusively on domestic responsibilities and learning the Quran. Malala Yousafzai has gone on to campaign against this understanding of Islamic education and promote women's schooling the world over, winning a Nobel Peace Prize for her efforts.

Table 15.1 Types of terrorism (adapted from Martin 2019)

ORGANISATION	OUTLINE	CAUSE/MOTIVES	OPERATIONS
STRAIN ONE: ANARCHIST			
NARODNAYA VOLYA	Founded in 1879, and dissolved ten years later, the Narodonaya Volya was organised in small groups (cells) but with a central committee that oversaw the group's main activities. It published newspapers and pamphlets illegally.	It sought to overthrow the Tzarist autocratic regime in Russia because the elite and bourgeoisie exploited the working classes. It never sought public office/government for itself.	Nardodnaya Volya is most known for the assassination of Tsar Alexander II in 1881. It believed terrorist actions would incite a general revolution by destabilising society.
Earth Liberation Front (The Elves)	Founded in the United Kingdom in 1992, the ELF is now an international organisation. It is widely regarded as descending from *Animal Liberation Front* and has close ties with *Earth First!* In 2001 the FBI classified the ELF as a terrorist threat in the USA.	Biocentrism is a belief that organisms on earth are equal and deserving of moral rights and considerations. They see biodiversity and wilderness as absolute goods. Belivers in deep ecology favour a rollback of industrialization and return to a simpler way of life.	Activities include economic sabotage (ecotage) against a wide variety of corporate and human actions that exploit the Earth, its environment and inhabitants. Over $42 billion dollars of damage to property in the USA alone is attributed to the ELF. To date no deaths have been attributed to the ELF.
STRAIN TWO: NATIONALIST/ANTI-COLONIAL			
Irish Republican Army (IRA)	The IRA is a paramilitary organisation in Ireland. It called a final ceasefire in July 1997, which preceded the Good Friday Agreement in 1998. It is a hierarchical organisation with a cell-like structure.	British rule over Northern Ireland is viewed by the IRA as an occupation and a militarised state that discriminates against Catholics. The IRA seek to unite the island of Ireland as one nation-state.	The IRA's tactics were to wage a war of attrition to wear down the British and force them to leave Northern Ireland. This was conducted within Northern Ireland and England through bombings, assassinations, kidnappings, extortion, armed robbery, hunger strikes and protests.
FLN (National Liberation Front)	Operating in Algeria and in France, the FLN was established in 1954. In 1962 it became a political party. It was divided into guerrilla units fighting in Algeria and in France as part of the 'café wars' between expats there; and another component more resembling a traditional army.	The FLN sought the end of French control of Algeria and identified as Arab Nationalist in ideology. Aside from claims of self-determination and self-rule, their determination and willingness to use violence was further incited by French use of torture and extrajudicial killings in the mid-1950s.	Most famously during the 'Battle of Algiers' (1956–57) they attacked French authorities in an urban guerrilla warfare strategy. After the ceasefire of 19 March 1962, the FLN killed between 60,000–70,000 *harkis*: Muslim Algerians who had served in the French army.

STRAIN THREE: NEW LEFT/MARXIST

Sendero Luminoso (The Shining Path)	Formed in Peru in the late 1960s. It has been in decline since the 1990s, but there are questions about whether it is resurging. 50 per cent of the combatants and 40 per cent of the commanders were women.	Rooted in Andean mysticism, and Maoist and Marxist ideology, it called for the abolition of a national market economy, industry, the banking system, all foreign trade and for the establishment of a communal, village-oriented economy based on a barter exchange system.	Sendero Luminoso conducted bombing campaigns, ambushes and assassinations. By 1991, it had gained control of much of the countryside of the centre and south of Peru and had a large presence in the outskirts of Lima. Remnants now focus on drug-trafficking and production activities to obtain funds to carry out attacks.
Brigate Rosse (The Red Brigades)	Mostly an Italian organisation that formed in 1969 and disbanded in 1989. It consisted of 400–500 members. A second group of up to 1,000 Brigatisti lived a normal existence as members of Italian society.	Group leaders advocated for the creation of a revolutionary state through armed struggle in order to create a split between the Italian Government and other Western Alliances. Marxist-Leninist ideology became more prevalent as the group grew. Its manifesto argued it fought for the working class against the capitalist system and the state.	The Red Brigades attacked factories and the offices of right-wing targets such as political parties or certain trade unions. Initial attacks were against property. It later targeted individuals through kidnapping, kneecappings and assassinations – including of the Italian Prime Minister, Aldo Moro, in 1978.

STRAIN FOUR: RELIGIOUS

Aum Shinrikyo- (Supreme Truth)	The movement mostly exists in Japan and Russia. It was founded in the late 1980s and was most influential during the 1990s. In 2007 it split into *Hikari no Wa* and *Aleph*. These two groups are viewed as cults by state authorities.	Under Shoko Asahara's leadership the aim was to seize control of Japan and then the world. The core belief is that Armageddon is imminent. Asahara, who was executed for his crimes in 2018, claimed to be the reincarnation of Jesus Christ and Buddha.	Most known for the Tokyo Subway Nerve Gas Attack on 20 March 1995. Twelve were killed and thousands injured. Its splinter groups are still active in Japan and Russia. Members are encouraged to arm themselves and seek out chemical and biological weapons to survive the predicted Armageddon.
Lord's Resistance Army (LRA)	The LRA operates in Uganda, Sudan, Democratic Republic of the Congo and the Central African Republic. It was formed in the late 1980s. By the 1990s it had around 3,000 combatants. This figure is likely in the low hundreds today.	The leader Josef Kony blended Christianity, Islam and witchcraft into a mystical foundation for his movement. Kony proclaimed that he would overthrow the government, purify the Acholi people, and seize power and reign in accordance with the principles of the Bible's Ten Commandments.	The movement destroyed villages and towns, drove hundreds of thousands more from the land, abducted thousands of children, and routinely committed acts of mass rape and banditry. Between 2008 and 2011 around 2,400 people were killed by the LRA.

Thus, while these may be seen as 'local' causes and local targets, they are also transnational in their wider effects.

The second feature of transnational terrorism is that activities are sometimes designed to provoke states into action as well as generate fear. Attacks are frequently symbolic in purpose and often have a high casualty rate for maximum shock value. It was inconceivable, for example, that the United States would not respond to the 9/11 attacks. By provoking states into doing something (usually military) to prove they are protecting civilians, terrorists hope that states' claims to live by particular moral, political or human rights standards are undermined, or that state actions end up being so costly that support for the government is eroded. This terrorist strategy was first formulated by Che Guevara, a leader of revolutionary communist movements in Cuba against the US-sponsored Batista government. The approach is known as focoism, whereby terrorists imagine themselves as the 'vanguard' of popular revolutions. Uyghur ethno-separatist groups (which have links to regional Islamist terrorism) operating in China's western provinces have also implemented this strategy. Their attacks have provoked ever greater Chinese crackdowns on the civil liberties of people living in the affected provinces – including mass detention of at least one million Uyghurs in internment or 're-education camps' since 2017 (DeHahn 2019).

As Muslim communities disproportionately feel the negative effects of the kinds of policy highlighted above, critics allege that government actions are somewhat counterproductive as they can provide more propaganda for terrorist recruitment campaigns. This plays to a common expectation of many terrorist groups that, in time, ever greater numbers will realise they are oppressed and join resistance groups – or that, with sufficient coverage, the international community will come to support their cause. The example of Palestine underlines this well since, despite decades of political struggle that have included terrorist tactics to establish Palestinian independence from Israel, the Palestinian cause remains popular internationally. On the other hand, rather than creating something (an independent Palestine), this tactic may also be used to destroy something. Here, we can point to the 9/11 attacks as bait to lure the United States into engagement in the Middle East, as a means of undermining their political and economic stability. By this logic, al-Qaeda pursued a strategy that aimed to grind down the global power and image of the United States so that over the longer term it may no longer be willing or able to interfere in Muslim lands.

In the past, states have managed to resist reacting to these sorts of violent actions by terrorists. Consider Italy's reaction to the assassination and kidnapping of the prime minister Aldo Moro in 1978 by the socialist Red Brigades. During the investigation, General Carlo Alberto Dalla Chiesa reportedly responded to a member of the security services who suggested torturing a suspected Brigade member, 'Italy can survive the loss of Aldo Moro. It would not survive the introduction of torture' (Dershowitz 2008, 134). However, with public and media scrutiny operating at speed and levels not previously encountered, the ability of governments to resist pressure is significantly reduced today. Influencing governments so that policies are changed is seen as a key activity of transnational terrorist groups, but they may also be influenced by governments directly through 'state-sponsored terrorism' and 'state-terrorism'. Iran is labelled as a 'state-sponsor of terrorism' for its support of Hezbollah in Palestine and Lebanon; so too Russia, especially for its 'cyber hacking' and military activities in Ukraine and the Caucuses.

Finally, the third reason for terrorist violence is to recruit members and reinforce loyalty and cohesion among existing supporters. Violent or highly technical attacks demonstrate the capability and will of the group carrying out the attack and amplifies its overall support. Support for Islamic State has come from citizens across every region because their media-attention-grabbing attacks raise the profile of the group and demonstrate their military mastery. Mandaville (2007) calls this 'the myth of success'. Islamic State propaganda frequently dehumanises its opposition, treating it like cattle who are easy to kill. The use of videos that mimic computer game imagery is supplemented by Islamic State creating its own 'skins' or 'maps' for popular games. Its version of Grand Theft Auto is situated in Baghdad and the people opposing the gamers are Iraqi police and Western militaries. Members say how they will 'respawn in Jannah' — 'respawn' being a gamer word for 'reincarnation' or 'being reborn', and Jannah is 'paradise' in Islam (Klausen 2015).

Organisation and resources

Managing a transnational organisation and connecting to multiple locations and identities requires considerable logistical and organisational capability. The practice of tapping into the local and the global can be described as a 'plug-and-play' approach. Transnational terrorist organisations have not only an ideology that 'plugs' into local grievances; their organisational structures and resources also operate in this manner.

15.3 – KEY INSIGHTS: The leaderless jihad

Reflections on the organisational structures of transnational terrorist groups led Sageman (2008) to talk about a 'leaderless jihad'. This describes the phenomenon of terrorist organisations becoming increasingly decentralised as they take advantage of new technologies, forms of communication and other aspects of globalisation. Consequently, communicating with transnational terrorist groups can be difficult. Negotiators cannot be sure the people they are talking to are representative of the group or have sufficient leverage to influence other members of the group, and splinter groups are more likely under these conditions. There are risks and vulnerabilities for terrorist organisations associated with this approach, notably in relation to information and operational security, coordination issues and resilience. There are also advantages in terms of longevity: the lack of central leadership gives them a greater scale and scope of operations and makes opposing or destroying them very difficult.

One of the main claims about transnational terrorist groups is that they are not hierarchical in structure but rather cell-like and even anarchical, lacking a formal leader. The evolution of the environmental movements towards 'fifth wave' terrorism indicates this. The Environmental Liberation Front (ELF) in the United States is quite distinct from the ELF in the UK or Mexico, in terms of operations and focus despite drawing on the same global ideology of bio-centrism and Deep Earth ecology, and having the same roots. In the United States property destruction is their *modus operandi* (destroying a ski resort, for example), while in the United Kingdom protest and 'occupying' sites to protect them from development are preferred modes of action. In Mexico, the ELF has targeted banks that support the expansion of the railway system through environmentally sensitive and protected lands. Rather than focusing on individuals and individual action, it is more helpful to focus on processes. One of the key processes within transnational terrorist organisations is the distribution and acquisition of money and equipment. Here we see the connections to transnational crime that can provide terrorist groups with whatever they require, provided the price is right.

Failed states (where governments have collapsed in some or all areas) also offer opportunities for mutually supporting connections between terrorism and criminality. The US government's National Strategy for Combating Terrorism (2006) contends that terrorists exploit failed states, using them to 'plan, organize, train, and prepare for operations'. However, some scholars disagree, noting that few international terrorists emerge from failed states (Simons and Tucker 2007) and most failed or failing states are not predisposed to exporting terrorism (Coggins 2015) – though they do generate significant security problems for their own citizens and neighbouring states. What is worth noting is that states that are weakly governed, rather than failing, are implicated. Pakistan is one such example. It was where al-Qaeda's leader, Osama bin Laden, was living when he was killed by the US military in 2011. This occurred, incidentally, without Pakistan being informed because the United States could not have assumed that he was there without intelligence and support from elements of Pakistan's government.

Countering transnational terrorism

Transnational terrorism represents a non-traditional type of security concern for states because the risk of attack does not just come from other states (in the form of war) but from mobile criminal groups. States perceive this as threatening core elements of their sovereignty, which has led to a range of law and order responses at the domestic level. Considering the transnational elements, states have also sought closer cross-border cooperation between government agencies, most notably in policing and intelligence. States have also reacted by seeking to prevent or disrupt the emergence of ideas that might support terrorist violence through anti-radicalisation initiatives. These are sometimes referred to as 'soft measures'. Overseas, these include supporting development goals of other countries to facilitate their stabilisation and the production of moderate voices in politics. Within domestic jurisdictions, 'soft' counter-extremism policies include placing greater emphasis on challenging specific extreme ideas in schools and universities, monitoring citizens for signs of radicalisation and criminalising the ownership and distribution of material that glorifies violence. These forms of intervention bring the state more directly into contact with the everyday lives of citizens, often regardless of any laws broken. Such developments demonstrate how terrorism is a concern for human security as well as national security.

The type of approach used depends in part on how 'victory' is defined. If victory is understood as the elimination of the terrorist threat, then there is a tendency to prioritise militarised and armed responses, with success measured in body bags. In contrast, if victory is understood as the prevention and prohibition of terrorism, then there is a tendency to prioritise criminal justice models in general, with success measured in prosecutions and low rates of recidivism. Where victory is measured as establishing positive peace, success is measured by addressing the 'root causes' of terrorism – which are often seen to be around unequal access to political, economic and social resources.

15.4 – KEY INSIGHTS: Counterterrorism

Counterterrorism consists of actions or strategies aimed at preventing terrorism from escalating, seeking to eradicate terrorism in a given context and limiting the negative effect of any attack. Counterterrorism can be classified according to four theoretical models: Defensive, Reconciliatory, Criminal-Justice, and War (Pedahzur 2009). Each model contains differences in threat perception, how to guard against that threat, how to frame terrorism legally and which agents effect counterterrorism. A state's strategy is usually a combination of some or all of these models (Table 15.2).

To attempt to harmonise responses, the United Nations has developed a global counterterrorism strategy (United Nations General Assembly 2006) that takes the form of a resolution with an annexed plan of action comprising four pillars:

Table 15.2 The four theoretical models of counterterrorism (Pedahzur 2009)

	Defensive model	Reconciliatory model	Criminal-justice model	War model
General features	Terrorism is a physical and psychological threat	Terrorism is a political problem	Terrorism is a criminal problem	Terrorism is an act of war
Goals/ methods of the state	Protect potential targets and victims	Address root causes	Arrest and punish terrorists	Eliminate terrorist threats
Legal aspects	Corresponds mostly to the rule of law in liberal democracies – except where practices override human rights and civil liberties	Corresponds with the law	Corresponds with the rule of law; judicial oversight of measures	Corresponds with the law of war; largely outside ordinary civilian laws
Agents (who)	Police, private security companies, firefighters, paramedics, local municipal authorities	Politicians, policymakers, brokers and diplomats	Police, criminal justice system	Intelligence units, military and paramilitary agents

1 Addressing the conditions conducive to the spread of terrorism

2 Measures to prevent and combat terrorism

3 Measures to build states' capacity to prevent and combat terrorism and to strengthen the role of the UN system in that regard

4 Measures to ensure respect for human rights for all and the rule of law as the fundamental basis for the fight against terrorism.

Some Western states have intervened internationally in order to prevent the emergence of terrorist groups or minimise the efficacy of existing terrorist groups. Such intervention comes in the form of international aid, military advice and training, and financial and military support to governments. This has entailed the risk of supporting undemocratic governments and engaging in militarised activities in contested spaces. The use of drones by the United States to attack terrorist targets in Pakistan is one instance that has given rise to considerable controversy, because it potentially undermines Pakistani sovereignty. A second point is that it imposes a state of fear on civilians, who find themselves under threat of strikes termed 'surgical' or 'targeted' by those operating them but which are perceived as random by civilians in these areas. Such operations can actually help terrorist groups by giving them a narrative around which to spin their agenda, reinforcing local fears of an unwelcome Western intervention in their societies.

A parallel approach has been to intervene at home by increasing state powers to minimise the effects and capability of terrorist groups to attack societies. The consequence, however, whether at home or overseas, has typically been to reduce civil liberties and restrict human rights. Indeed, the human experience of counterterrorism and counter-radicalisation policies and processes has often been negative. For example, we can see this in the crackdown on protestors in Egypt, including journalists and civil rights groups, in the name of fighting terrorism. Human Rights Watch (2021) has reported that Egypt is undergoing the most serious human rights crisis in its modern history. Similar patterns are seen in Turkey, especially following a failed coup attempt in 2016. Moreover, these security-driven efforts are criticised as counterproductive to the long-term goals of peace.

In Western states, attempts to impose security have often disproportionately affected certain groups – especially Muslims. Blackwood, Hopkins and Reicher (2013) found there was a 'prototypical' Muslim story of travelling through airports that was characterised by discrimination, humiliation and fear because of the actions by airport and border authorities. The ability of states to use violence so that a 'state of fear' is produced for (a section of) a population in the name of countering terrorism has even led some to call for the definition of a terrorist actor to include states. For example, when the Israeli military attacks a Palestinian group this is commonly seen as 'defence' or 'national security'. But when a Palestinian group attacks an Israeli troop convoy, which they perceive as invaders or occupiers, they are commonly deemed 'terrorists'. If we remove the binary of state and non-state actors, we might see this instead as a conflict between two opposing forces – both sharing legitimate aims and objectives. Due to examples such as this, complex and emotive as they are, there is often a failure to fully examine state actions that critical scholars blame for a significant cause of human insecurity worldwide. It is also important to look beyond the state towards civil society and everyday acts of resistance. International peacebuilding activities and efforts to stop violent extremism in protracted and complex conflict zones, such as Israel and Palestine, are often led by non-governmental organisations, who take on risks to support an end to violence.

 CASE STUDY 15.1: InCels as transnational terrorists?

Photo 15.1 People march to a vigil for the victims of Alek Minassian's van attack in Toronto that left ten dead, 29 April 2018

Credit: Cole Burston/Getty Images

When Merger (2018) wrote 'when is terrorism not terrorism? when the political motivations are misogyny' she was reacting to the reluctance to label Alek Minassian a terrorist after he drove a van into a group of people, killing ten, in Toronto in 2018. He had posted a video on YouTube just minutes before his attack, referring to an InCel rebellion. Like Elliot Rodger before him, who killed seven of his fellow students in 2014 because he was repeatedly denied sex, Minassian was part of a broader community of like-minded individuals who hold misogynist views so extreme that they justify and advocate for violence against women. They have built their own world of online men's groups united in their belief that sex and level of attractiveness determine your place in society, which excludes men who are not regarded as good-looking enough to form any romantic or sexual relationship. Hence, they are 'involuntarily celibate' (InCel). They proclaim that feminism has ruined the world such that they are unable to get what they are entitled to – status and power through sexual relationships with women.

The InCel community claimed and celebrated Minassian's violence, arguing that had women had sex with him, then lives would have been saved – something they think would have been possible prior to the sexual revolution of the 1960s. InCels consequently glorify mass violence. As one said, 'I'm happy to see a few normies die … We need to see a little bit of variety. I'm tired of the same ol' death count. How 'bout a rape count or an acid-in-her-fucking-face count?' InCels regularly use language like this to minimise the significance of their violence in comparison to the perceived injustices that they face – as, for example, there are high rates of InCel suicide (see Baele, Brace and Coan 2019).

Members of the InCel community tend to be men under the age of thirty, who self-identify as introverts and cover a range of socioeconomic groups. Their numbers are hard to calculate, with reports ranging from tens of thousands to hundreds of thousands. The movement is heavily inflected with white supremacy, with their ideal 'Alphas' exhibiting finely chiselled jaw lines, white skin, 'roman noses' and a toned physique. This worldview is justified through a distorted appropriation of evolutionary psychology and evolutionary biology, relying on eugenic theories that were most commonly associated with the Nazis. The globalisation of communications has facilitated the spread of this ideology and a minority of non-white men beyond North America also identify as InCels – accepting this presumed racial hierarchy and their place within it.

InCel attacks appear to have been mainly confined to North America, with at least four mass murders linked to InCel activities and six other associated killings. A January 2020 report by the Texas Department of Public Safety warned that InCels are an 'emerging domestic terrorism threat'. In February 2020, a German man gunned down nine people near Frankfurt before killing himself and his mother and in doing so appeared to be the first InCel attacker outside North America. He posted a manifesto online in which he called for the 'complete extermination' of many 'races or cultures in our midst' and specifically targeted Muslims. He also wrote. 'for my whole life, I haven't had a wife or girlfriend, for the last 18 years exclusively because … I know I'm being surveilled.' Some terrorism experts linked him to the InCel movement, as have a few InCels – claims that British and American (but less so German) media have seized upon to glorify his violence and minimise his neo-Nazi links. However, he never identified as an InCel, and did not appear to blame women for his lack of intimacy – but blamed governments. This highlights that caution is needed before categorising these events – in the same way that it is important to remember not every public act of violence by a Muslim is an act of Islamist terrorism.

The ubiquity of misogyny and the persistence of sexism and domestic violence worldwide make the label of 'terrorism' hard to stick to InCel violence. The violence is disorganised, not spectacular and rarely sustains media attention. Individual acts of violence lack a strategic purpose as there is no symbolic or material value in the locations of their attacks. Often those who die are not those they purport to hate, and to date there has been no disproportionate state response against young white men (the majority of InCels). Additionally, the lack of organisation or structure to InCels outside the online space makes their 'real world' justifications – 'martyrdom videos' and rambling manifestos – weak attempts to glorify their self-interested violence. The personal connections of these attacks to their life narratives blur the line between the public and the private, but also render suspect their claim that they are seeking to change the world or sacrificing themselves for a grander cause. Instead the quest for significance and motive can be seen as a destructive manifestation of the quest for celebrity. The risk with labelling InCels as terrorists is that it gives more 'real world' power and credence to their ideology and online hatred than it may deserve.

Minassian certainly wants us to believe he belongs to a movement. But his actions raise more questions than answers. For example, is it possible to negotiate with InCels? Additionally, might identifying InCel violence as terrorism render the term 'terrorism' too elastic and subsequently empty of content and lacking utility? In other words, by doing so, it becomes impossible to differentiate between domestic violence, gang crimes, smuggling and terrorism. As such the specifics of the forms of violence get missed and consequently overgeneralised (and therefore less effective) countermeasures are adopted. For example, accepting InCels as terrorists instrumentalises violence against women. It suggests that violence against women only really matters, and is only taken seriously by governments and police, when it is given the status of 'terrorism', but also that such statements are symbolic yet not actioned, because the structure of counterterrorism is already hyper-securitised and hyper-masculine. We can see this in Australia, where the Victoria Police Department publicly declared it would treat domestic abusers as terrorists, and acknowledged the link between terrorism and domestic violence, yet when they opened up a $30 million centre a few months later to combat terrorism, it lacked experts on violence against women (Diaz and Valji 2019).

CASE STUDY 15.2: Women and children returning home from Islamic State

Photo 15.2 Iraqi refugees and displaced Syrian women, living in al-Hol camp, which houses relatives of Islamic State group members, 28 March 2019

Credit: DELIL SOULEIMAN/AFP/Getty Images

In 2018 there were approximately 260 women and over one thousand children actively seeking repatriation, or who had already been repatriated to their home countries, following military successes against Islamic State that had seen it lose its territory (the so-called 'Caliphate') across Iraq and Syria. There were another four thousand women and three thousand minors in refugee camps or detention in Iraq and Syria (Cook and Vale 2018). Some women used the chaos of 2018 to escape, having been trapped there. Others were forced to flee but remained committed to the jihadi cause. The women and their children often experienced violence and exploitation and faced ongoing risks while detained in camps because of their proximity to members of Islamic State who had also fled. However, as a matter of countering terrorism and in the name of 'public safety', a number of European countries have stated that women and children will not be assisted in their quest to return home, and in extreme cases will have their citizenship revoked.

Shamima Begum left London for the Islamic State when she was fifteen and spent the next four years affiliated to the group through marriage and by publicly tweeting about her decisions. In 2019 she appealed for assistance to return to the UK for the sake of her unborn child after her two other children had died of disease. Five days later, not only did the UK government decide that they *could not* (it was too dangerous to extract her) and *would not* assist her (her situation was her own making and she 'deserved' to be there), the Home Secretary also revoked her citizenship. Her new-born baby later died of a respiratory infection. The government decision was based on the claim that she posed a threat to national security should she return.

Beyond membership of a proscribed organisation, it is not clear what charges would be levied, as women are unlikely to have participated in armed violence on behalf of the Islamic State. However, successful prosecutions of returnees have occurred. Samantha Elhassani, an American woman repatriated from the Islamic State, was convicted for financing terrorism in 2020. In court she gave a 'victim' narrative, pointing to an abusive husband and saying she was 'duped' into joining, which drew some sympathy from the judge. However, the FBI agent leading the investigation argued that 'she knew exactly what she was doing and why. She was an active participant in this heinous activity and is now facing the consequences' (Justice News 2020).

The 'hardline' approach refusing repatriation and depriving citizenship is a logical extension of the response to global terrorism. The EU Radicalization Awareness Network manual for managing returnees noted that a range of terrorist attacks in Belgium and France were all perpetrated to some degree by returnees from the Islamic State (2017, 15). With this presentation of returnees as a threat, the refusal to assist in repatriations is presented as a reasonable precaution to keep citizens safe. This reflects a critical argument that the counterterrorism response organised around the War on Terror has centred on the idea of 'exporting Western (in)security' – that is to keep the terrorists, and their fights, overseas – and this is simply a continuation of this externalising logic. However, it is not clear that this depiction of those affiliated to so-called Islamic State is accurate. Women are more likely to have been coerced into joining the group, or have been in violent and abusive relationships, opening up doubt about their autonomy and agency. Second, this approach conflates marriage to a member of a terrorist organisation with

evidence of guilt. Additionally, as a strategy, it undermines other efforts to deradicalise and rehabilitate 'formers', by suggesting that these women are beyond redemption and cannot be successfully reintegrated into society (Brown 2019).

The hard-line strategy also has international repercussions. First, it leaves insecure and vulnerable states at risk of more terrorism and instability – as those who cannot return 'home' will have to go somewhere. Second, it sets a dangerous precedent for revoking citizenship. Until 2012, this power was rarely used, but by 2019, 139 people who held dual nationality were deprived of their British citizenship – mostly individuals linked to violent Islamism. The revocation of citizenship is seen as the ultimate act of sovereignty, although human rights lawyers argue that it is the abdication of sovereign responsibility as it leaves individuals stateless, and therefore should be seen as an act of last resort (Masters and Regilme 2020). Third, the strategy suggests that being British is conditional upon 'good behaviour' in a way that is not the case for other citizens. This is highly problematic as dual nationality is often connected to former colonial states with large diasporas who have citizenship. As a counter-narrative strategy, it also has significant flaws as it confirms the extremist narrative that the 'West' is racist and does not care about the lives of Muslims. It enables the women and children to become 'martyrs' of the cause – regardless of whether or not they are still radicalised and members of the group.

Conclusion

Terrorism and terrorists can be transnational in three ways: through their goals, their actions and their organisational form – each of which exposes the dark side of globalisation. Furthermore, while examples of transnational terrorism since 2001 may appear to be mostly religiously inspired, one cannot conclude that there is anything inevitable about this, or that Islam specifically is the significant factor. Rather, it is in this instance that Islam provides a framework for some marginal groups to construct a convincing worldwide counter-narrative to that of a world dominated by Western political, social and economic models. For that reason, it is perhaps no surprise that Islamic transnational terrorism, over and above other types of terrorism, has become a sustained issue of concern. An important note on which to conclude is that countering terrorism does not fall exclusively to the state: civil society and everyday acts by ordinary people also have a role. These can include examples of popular culture, inter-faith dialogue and moments of solidarity that break down the oppositional and binary worldview that dominates terrorist ideology. This also means that state actors must be held to a higher account than terrorist groups by balancing their militarised, criminal-justice and socioeconomic counterterrorism responses. Finally, it is worth remembering that terrorist groups are products of their time and, just like us, live in a globalised world. They are both shaped by the globalised nature of our system and contribute to it by their actions.

 END OF CHAPTER QUESTIONS

1. Transnational terrorism defined one of International Relations' eras – the post-9/11 era (2001–19). Consider why this was the case, and then consider the extent of the threat that still endures from groups such as Islamic State.

2. Should governments be able to counter terrorism by any means possible? If not, what are the acceptable limits to government power, and should this be agreed (or regulated) internationally?

3. What can the international community do to counter violent extremism and terrorism, and the effects these have on individuals, states and groups?

4. The former UN Secretary-General, Kofi Annan, once said that extreme poverty in any part of the world was a threat to people in every part of the world. In what ways can the same be said for terrorism?

5. Reflecting on different definitions of terrorism, do you think InCels are terrorists?

MIGRATION

Anitta Kynsilehto

CHAPTER

16

Question: Why does the act of people moving from one place to another sometimes become a crisis?

Migration is a part of everyday life. People move for a wide range of reasons: to look for new opportunities, earn better salaries, reunite with loved ones, escape from social or political difficulties, or to study – amongst others. Indeed, several states, such as the United States and Australia, have themselves been built on migration. Others have been impacted by large-scale emigration events in their history (citizens leaving a state) such as Vietnam, Cuba and Ireland. Such events highlight that migration is not always voluntary and can instead be forced. This can even be as a result of mass movements of people as borders are drawn, and redrawn, such as when India and Pakistan split in 1947 along largely religious lines, displacing 14 million people in the process. In 2020 there were 82.4 million forcibly displaced people worldwide (UNHCR 2021) – underlining the extent of this truly global issue. By way of establishing scale, this number is within range of the total death toll of the Second World War. Yet it remains evident that tens of millions of displaced people across the world, often living in dire conditions, have not garnered the sense of international urgency and action that major instances of state-on-state warfare has, for example. This chapter explores these issues by investigating how migration is understood within state relations, international law and International Relations scholarship.

The International Relations of people's mobility

The first major reason people move is due to security concerns. In this case, moving is an act undertaken to save one's life: people move in order to flee war and persecution, or perhaps because the place of birth has become uninhabitable due to environmental conditions or climate change. If this takes place within the borders of their state, these people are labelled as internally displaced persons (IDPs). If they cross an international border, they become refugees. Accessing the formal status as a recognised refugee is a complicated process involving refugee status determination (RSD), by the host state or the UN Refugee Agency UNHCR. In recent years, there has been a multiplication in the number of people forced to flee their homes and a large majority of these people reside within the Global South. One of the states with a considerable number of IDPs and from which a large number of refugees have been forced to flee over recent years is Syria. Another is Venezuela, which we will return to later in the chapter.

16.1 – KEY INSIGHTS: The Syrian Civil War

The Syrian Civil War has raged since March 2011 and was exacerbated by the emergence of Islamic State, who operated across large parts of Syria and Iraq. The combined effects of the brutality practised by the Islamic State and the effects of the war resulted in over 10 million Syrians leaving their homes – either moving internally or leaving Syria entirely. It is the largest displacement in decades, and the very definition of a migration crisis. Most people who flee across borders stay in neighbouring countries, and this is evident in the Syria case. This is despite media attention and certain political figures often indicating the opposite by highlighting instances of refugees who attempt to go further afield – such as to European states. The largest number, approximately 700,000 Syrians, were given asylum in Germany, proving an exception to most other European states, which had attempted to pursue restrictive policies. Of the approximately 7 million Syrians who left, 83 per cent had come to reside in neighbouring states by 2019. Of those, Lebanon had hosted the most refugees from Syria per capita, whereas Turkey was among those hosting the most in absolute numbers with between 3 and 4 million Syrian refugees (Todd 2019).

The second major reason people move is due to work. These may be employees of transnational corporations, diplomats who represent their countries, experts posted in peacekeeping and crisis management missions or humanitarian workers engaged to alleviate suffering in complex humanitarian emergencies or protracted refugee situations. Migratory movements of these high-skilled populations are perceived as an integral part of the globalised world. Thus, their mobility is usually facilitated and their settlement is sought to be made as smooth as possible on behalf of both sending and receiving states. This selective facilitation is one example attesting to the classed character of the regulatory frameworks conditioning international migration where the above-mentioned globally mobile groups are often referred to as expatriates, not migrants.

Migration is often intuitively considered as movement from poorer states to richer ones. Here states located in the Global South are perceived as places from which aspiring migrants move towards Global North destinations. While this has been true in the past, much migration now takes place *within* the Global South, which will be explored further in this chapter's case studies. At the same time, many sectors such as agriculture, construction and maintenance rely on workforces that are often not as prominently discussed, or as well paid – namely undocumented migrants without a valid residence permit.

It is hopefully clear, then, that global mobilities in their diverse manifestations are an integral part of our global system. Despite this, some forms of mobility are more visible than others. International migration continues to make headlines as states, especially in the Global North, mount administrative obstacles and concrete walls in order to impede the entrance of those they do not want in their territory – as was seen with the bulk of European states in the Syrian example. Usually these headlines concern emergencies that erupt with the outbreak of war, or a sudden natural disaster, and the interest often fades after the most acute phase of the emergency is passed. When conflicts become prolonged – such as the war in Syria, ongoing conflicts in Central Africa, the exile of Rohingya Muslims from Myanmar or gang violence in Central America – more people flee from those conflicts and they become more visible again in the international media.

International Relations has often approached international migration from the perspective of states' attempts to control and manage migration to their territory and the role of international organisations in regulating regimes of rights related to human mobility. Yet these approaches focus more on migration as a category than on migrants themselves and have thereby come under scrutiny from critical perspectives. Critical scholars have reversed that trend by unpacking the processes by which some populations' migratory movements are presented as a problem and a threat to national security or cohesion (Huysmans 2006; Vaughan-Williams 2015). Feminist scholars have focused further by considering the gender of the international migrant and continued by examining and pointing to the multiple relations each migrant embodies and inhabits (Penttinen and Kynsilehto 2017; Piper 2008). In these analyses, the role of the human body is analysed as one of the concrete grounds on which global entanglements play out – as Penttinen (2008), for example, argued in analysing the global sex industry and trafficking of women for sexual exploitation. Finally, postcolonial approaches have pointed out how migration control and management processes are racialised (Bilgiç 2018), often selecting particular populations for closer scrutiny and confinement, and how issues like this keeps scholarship on migration overly focused on the Global North.

Structuring and categorising mobility

Over time, migration studies have emphasised pull and push factors to explain global mobilities. These factors refer to the reasons why people leave their place of birth and go to particular destinations, and less so to others. Push factors incorporate wars and conflicts, lack of possibilities to access paid work or continue studies, and natural disasters or environmental changes that render homes uninhabitable. Pull factors include, for example, personal or family safety, better employment opportunities and a healthier environment. Think, for example, of recruitment campaigns for seasonal workers in the agricultural sector. This type of work relies on migrant labour in different parts of the world. It is usually considered as short-term, circular mobility in order to meet temporary, seasonal labour force needs – the pull factor – in the receiving area, and the necessity for income-generating activities – push factor – in the sending area. It is also politically regulated as such, enabling access to short-term residence permits without the possibility of accessing social rights and benefits reserved for citizens and permanent residents.

16.2 – KEY TERMS: 'Voluntary' and 'forced' migration

Migration is caused by push factors (issues that would make one want to leave one's home state, such as hunger or war) and pull factors (elements that would attract one to a foreign state, such as safety or an employment opportunity). When these push–pull factors are weighed up by a particular individual, and occur together with an available opportunity or a means to move, they result in people moving from one state to another. This can be temporary or permanent.

Although a complex phenomenon, migration can be split into two broad categories: **voluntary migration** and **forced migration.** Voluntary migration categorises those who could have stayed, albeit sometimes with difficulty, but decided to move abroad. Forced migration is a more contested category as it involves movements of people displaced by war, conflict or oppression – essentially comprising a significant push factor. When this happens in such a way that people are moving from state to state, this is widely recognised with the status of 'refugee' and leads to such persons being able to apply for asylum in any foreign state in which they arrive. This category has begun to widen to include people displaced due to climate events and other natural disasters. Yet, there is no clear agreement on what a 'climate refugee' is – especially as many of such examples are internally displaced people (forced to move within their own state), which adds more complexity into finding definitions that better match the needs of the global issues of the twenty-first century and can be added to our international legal and normative framework.

The division between push and pull factors builds on the model of a rational actor who makes calculated choices in life. It has been criticised for presenting human mobility as unilinear and mechanistic, as it draws on the assumption of human action and mobilities that would depend on simple causes and effects and rationally calculated choices (Peterson 2003). Later migration research, drawing especially on feminist scholarship and life-story approaches that look at migratory moves as part of the migrant's overall life course and the meanings they assign to these moves, has shown how decisions on whether or not to move are more complicated than as suggested by the push-and-pull model (e.g. Erel 2007). While the need and will to move from one state to another, and conditions that render certain destinations more attractive than others bear upon this decision-making, these reasons cannot explain alone the multiplicity of mobilities at the global scale. This diversity has, however, proved to be difficult to identify and deal with in state-level regulatory mechanisms that recognise only one cause or ground for a residence permit.

Migration studies utilise categories such as economic or labour migration, family migration and student migration to classify and situate these reasons for moving across international borders. Looking at individual stories of people on the move, however, several reasons often occur simultaneously. For example, student migrants at the university level often work alongside their studies to supplement their living costs. Regardless of their field of studies or expertise, they usually get employed in low-wage, part-time jobs that do not require extensive skills and constitute a supplementary labour force that fills up vacancies in the state of residence. Traditionally, migration studies tended to operate from the premise of migrant understood as a man moving from one state to another. He would move in search of work opportunities abroad, often through organised recruitment channels or less formal networks of kin and friends. He would leave his spouse and children behind and send money back home. As for recruitment in sectors such as construction and mining, this continues to be the case. However, in some other sectors, such as domestic work, care and health professions, recruitment has targeted largely women, who would then become migrants supporting their families staying in the state of origin. Feminist researchers were early to point out the gender bias in migration studies (Morokvaśic 1984), and they have also worked on what have come to be called transnational care chains (Ehrenreich and Hochchild 2003). These denote the diverse relations of care connected with human mobilities: migrants who come to perform care duties such as caring for children, the sick or the elderly. As they do so, they leave behind children or ageing parents (for example) who in turn need to find other people to care for them in order to fill a care deficit.

Feminist scholars have drawn attention to the diversity of migration trajectories within and outside regulated channels of global mobility. Ethnographic explorations of irregular or clandestine mobilities have shown how people make choices and cross borders despite the attempts to seal the borders from those considered not worthy of access to global mobility (Khosravi 2010). Additionally, they may be (and often are) accompanied by citizens or permanent residents who do not agree on the political closure of borders undertaken in their name (Doty 2006). These mobilities are far from linear, and they necessitate not only hope and luck but also require keeping oneself informed on the changing practices of border regimes. Collyer (2007) has defined the travels of people moving northwards from different Central and Western African states as 'fragmented journeys'. With this he refers to the non-linear character of migrant trajectories where journeys are shaped by changing access across borders and the necessity to work where labour is needed in order to collect money for continuing to the next location.

Indeed, the routine practices of mobile individuals across borders call principles such as state sovereignty into question. Brigden (2016) illustrates this with examples drawn from Central American migrants seeking to transit through Mexico in order to reach the United States. Due to the tight border control not only at the actual border but also along the journey within Mexico, these migrant trajectories often include lengthy stays along the way while the aspiring migrants try to pass as Mexican nationals. However, despite various dissuasive elements on the way, they go about their journey, thereby challenging the border regime and forms of politics it entails.

16.3 – KEY TERMS: Ethnography

Investigating a complex phenomenon like migration represents something where positivist approaches (large-scale surveys, or theories that draw on the system and state levels – such as realism and liberalism) are often unhelpful as they fail to reveal the complexity of the situation. Ethnography, as a method, allows researchers to get on the ground and gain insights by gathering detailed accounts directly from individual migrants. Such knowledge is more detailed and also more likely to help the researcher gain an understanding (or awareness) of complex cultural, religious, gendered or social factors within the migrant community under investigation. Ethnography, then, focuses itself at the individual (and sometimes group) level of analysis. It is often used in conjunction with a range of critical approaches (such as feminism) to offer insights and potential solutions to particular migration cases.

A unique form of global mobility, made possible by the very nature of the global system, consists of diverse professional groups who are posted in different international missions – sometimes under the auspices of certain UN humanitarian missions or in non-governmental organisations. Feminist researchers have shown how these often create shadow forms of mobility such as sex trafficking as people who have been pushed into poverty congregate around an international mission to provide a service to deployed personnel with money and free time. Many examples of this exist, one of the most well known of which happened during the mass international relief effort that took place in Haiti following a devastating earthquake and subsequent state failure in 2010. In this particular case, employees of Oxfam were revealed in 2018 to have been sexually exploiting victims internally displaced by the earthquake in return for food and aid supplies, revealing a practice that had become somewhat endemic in similar missions worldwide.

Controlling migration

States seek to control the entry, exit and stay in their territories. This mostly concerns the entry and stay of non-nationals through visas and other similar conditions that set limits on how long a person may stay and what activities they may partake in. In some cases, internal movement of a state's own nationals is also restricted. For example, in China this is done by the hukou system that establishes residence permits within a certain region. Those moving to a different area within China without an official permit to do so face many difficulties, such as the impossibility for the migrant children to access education in the new place of settlement.

Based on a comparative study between different states across time, de Haas, Natter and Vezzoli (2018) argue that, while it seems that migration policies have become more restrictive in recent years, they have instead transformed in a different way. What has been perceived as an era of free mobility at the beginning of the twentieth century was, in fact, a highly racialised reality and concerned largely white Europeans. In Australia, this was explicitly stated in the 1901 Migration Restriction Act that excluded all non-white people from migrating there. This racial restriction was only annulled in 1973. The US Migration Act of 1917 similarly excluded all entrants from 'the Asiatic barred zone'. Contemporary migration policies are increasingly selective in terms of the high-skilled educational backgrounds of the aspiring migrant. Moreover, the liberalisation of migration policies has been coupled with tightened visa policies that severely curb international travel possibilities of nationals of states whose passports offer only limited access to other states without a visa. These factors combined have transferred migration from a racialised system to one that has made it easier for wealthy and educated Africans and Asians (for example) to move to Europe or North America, whilst possibilities for regular mobility have been extensively curbed for the poorer and less educated. This, in turn, calls for more nuanced policy analyses that consider various intersectional dimensions that include social class, for example.

One way of regulating migrants' access to territory and their stay in a host state is organised through private sponsorship regimes. People move between states through these channels with a specific job waiting for them upon arrival, and their residence status is tied to a specific employer. These channels have been under critical scrutiny as they can lead to exploitation as a result of the structures and policies in place that render it difficult for workers to escape and denounce exploitative conditions, their migration status being bound to their job. In many cases – especially those involving construction and domestic workers – it has been common in many states for employers (or employment agencies) to hold the passports of migrant workers, effectively binding them to their work and removing their freedom to leave without restriction.

Alongside individual states, regional organisations have sought to find ways to ease the mobility of labour from one state to another. These processes have aimed at free movement within their respective economic area and defining measures through which the moving person should be considered when applying for a job, which social security scheme to apply for and what happens to the family members of the worker. While these rules have been possible to agree on rather extensively as regards the mobility of labour *within* the European Union, for example, they have proven to be very difficult when it comes to agreeing on shared measures on the matters of forced migration *into* the Union, namely the issue of asylum seeking. Such debates amounted to what was known as the European migrant crisis of 2015 as a large number of displaced persons made their way into Europe across various land and sea routes. Within Latin America, by contrast, irregular migration has been addressed through regularisation campaigns targeting particular nationalities or, more universally, undertaken by different states since the establishment of Mercosur in 2002 (Acosta Arcarazo and Freier 2015). In Argentina, for example, migration policymaking since 2003 has explicitly rejected the focus on the removal of irregularly residing migrants – contrary to the approach in the European Union.

16.4 – KEY INSIGHTS: The European migrant crisis

Although the European Commission declared that the European migrant 'crisis' of 2015 was over by 2019, the conditions that caused it still endure. They also embody many of the push and pull factors that can lead to forced migration in general. The European continent has always been a destination for migrants due to its high levels of economic development and political stability post-1945. In tandem, such good fortune is rarer in neighbouring North Africa and the Middle East, which are separated from Europe by multiple navigable land and sea routes. In 2015 the number of migrants arriving into Europe more than doubled from already high levels, resulting in over 1.2 million asylum requests. The bulk of migrants were Syrian –

Photo 16.1 Irish naval personnel rescuing migrants as part of Operation Triton, 15 June 2015

Credit: Irish Defence Forces/Wikimedia Commons

due to its civil war – but significant numbers also came from Iraq, Afghanistan and several African states. Greece and Italy, being at the land and sea frontiers of entry routes, quickly saw their ability to deal with the situation overwhelmed and a crisis ensued as European leaders argued over how to distribute the asylum seekers. Meanwhile large camps were erected to temporarily house those who had arrived.

The crisis demonstrates the truly international effect of today's civil wars and instances of political instability within states – which cause displacements in ever more significant ways. Much of the same conditions of political instability and economic lack of opportunity that drove millions towards Europe also drove the American migration 'crisis' that led to Donald Trump's infamous promise to build a wall on the border between Mexico and the United States in 2016 as he campaigned for presidency. Cases such as these also highlight the difficulty in categorising those who are seeking entry. Are they economic migrants looking for a better life (emphasising pull factors), asylum seekers who cannot go home for fear of their safety (emphasising push factors), or are they some combination of the two – with yet more additional categories besides?

Far from being an academic debate, perceived 'crises' such as these shake the foundations of ideas of sovereignty and international obligations, such as providing asylum. They have also materially impacted the domestic politics of states who host such migrants, especially in Europe and America, such as through the rise of nationalism and populism. There is also the associated longer-term impact for those states who have lost large numbers of their able-bodied citizens who would presumably otherwise have been vital to the social and economic recovery from whatever problems affected that state.

Finally, social class is an important factor not only for regular forms of mobility but also in defining access to permanent settlement. An extreme form of how this plays out at the global scale is the way in which it has been possible to access citizenship of a given state in a fast-track manner after investing a set amount of money there. In the context of the European Union, Malta is a frequently cited example of this practice. Such privileges are only available to the wealthy, leaving those lower down the social ladder to invariably resort to joining those moving through the established land and sea routes noted above.

Governing forced migration

The 1951 Convention Relating to the Status of Refugees, or the UN Refugee Convention, is the main international instrument that regulates international protection. It was a product of its time: drafted shortly after the end of the Second World War, it was founded on the experience of the events, namely the Holocaust, that took place on the European continent. With this backdrop, it defined as a refugee someone who had been forced to flee because of events that occurred in Europe before 1 January 1951. This definition was amended by the 1967 Protocol Relating to the Status of Refugees that lifted time-based and geographical limitations as regards accessing refugee status, thereby opening up refugee status to any person internationally.

16.5 – KEY TERMS: The UN Refugee Convention

The 1951 Convention Relating to the Status of Refugees defines as a refugee someone who has been forced to flee due to persecution, war or violence through five criteria that need to be met in order to qualify for refugee status:

1 Persecution due to race

2 Persecution due to political opinion

3 Persecution due to nationality

4 Persecution due to religion

5 Persecution due to belonging to a particular social group.

It also outlines the rights pertaining to that status and defines states' obligation to protect

Photo 16.2 Ilhan Omar speaking at a campaign event, 4 October 2016

Credit: Lorie Shaull/Flickr

refugees who may seek asylum in their borders. It defines the core principle of international protection, the principle of non-refoulement, which means that the refugee cannot be returned to a state where their life or freedom would be threatened. For example, like hundreds of thousands of others, Ilhan Omar fled Somalia's civil war. After spending four years in a refugee camp in Kenya she was eventually given, along with her family, refugee status in the United States in 1995. In 2019 she became the first naturalised citizen of African birth to be elected to the US Congress.

However, some state parties that had ratified the 1951 Convention, such as Turkey, currently one of the top five refugee-hosting countries globally, kept the geographical limitation outlined in the 1951 Convention. Therefore, only persons fleeing Europe can officially qualify for refugee status in Turkey. What this means in practice is that a person from Syria, for example, who arrives in Turkey and applies for asylum, will not qualify for the international protection that refugee status provides. Since 2012, Turkey has applied a special protection scheme for Syrian refugees, but that scheme is dependent on the goodwill of the state, not on international law. As such, it is one example of the context-dependent dimensions of forced migrants' access to safety and the increased precarity of protection status if a person is not formally recognised as a refugee. Even if the Convention's status can be lifted from an individual or a group – or rejected following due process – it provides the strongest form of protection as these measures can only be taken according to strictly defined and internationally agreed criteria.

The Convention definition of a refugee has been criticised for not corresponding to the multiple reasons why people flee in the contemporary world, and for requiring a very individualised account of persecution (see Betts 2013). As a major default, the definition of refugee encompasses only those who have crossed an international border and are seeking safety in another state. This omits all those who are forcibly displaced within a state's borders. Moreover, feminists pointed out how the definition does not directly recognise persecution based on gender as one of the central criteria. Owing to this criticism, gender-related persecution was later identified under the criteria of belonging to a particular social group (Freedman 2007). While this category has grown to become the most encompassing among the five, it is but one more example of how gender gets allocated to a subordinate position in important international debates.

However, it would be difficult to amend the Convention completely, as it would be difficult to establish a consensus among states for a similarly strong renewed convention. Attempts towards renewing the international protection regime and establishing one on migration have been undertaken through the UN Global Compacts. However, despite the goodwill on pushing the process through, the Global Compact on Refugees, signed in December 2018, does not fulfil that aim due to its non-binding character. The same concern applies to the simultaneously negotiated, drafted and signed Global Compact for Safe, Orderly and Regular Migration, which would have bridged the needs and responsibilities related to those people who do not, for one reason or another, come within the category of a recognised refugee but who need to be recognised by the international community. Their non-binding character makes them both declarations of intent without establishing actual regulatory regimes at the international level that states would need to comply with and that would thereby provide migrants with a trustworthy regime under which their rights would be guaranteed.

Successive crises around the Mediterranean make constant headlines in the international media. In terms of refugee populations, over recent years, the forcibly displaced from Syria have been the biggest concern for major international donors that seek to organise and contribute to conditions that would permit the stay of the forcibly displaced in the neighbouring states. At the same time, large-scale forced displacement in other locations, such as long-term persecution leading to the genocide of the Rohingya in Myanmar and their escape into Bangladesh and Thailand have been addressed to a much lesser extent. In turn, far fewer donors exist to continue supporting those regions hosting hundreds of thousands of forcibly displaced – who are likely to stay. This is an example of how refugee movements that are geographically far away from potential Global North destinations are often deemed (directly, or indirectly) as less important in terms of a declared 'crisis' for the international community. Once again, the lack of modern frameworks at the international level (and sometimes a political will at the state or regional levels) to sufficiently deal with these instances and their ever-growing complexity is striking.

While the Rohingya crisis refers to a refugee situation that fits under the criteria of persecution due to ethnic origin and religion, there are reasons for forced displacement that are not yet recognised by any international protection framework. One such example is those who are forced to flee due to environment-related reasons and climate change. Questions such as whose responsibility it is to receive people who have no other choice than migrate when large areas become utterly inhabitable, due to drought or floods, for example, remain unanswered. Additionally, inhabitants of islands in the Pacific and Indian Ocean, such as Fiji and the Maldives, that risk disappearing under water as sea levels rise are left to ponder where they should they go, and under which regulatory framework. As noted earlier, a climate refugee as an internationally recognised category does not currently exist, primarily because it was not foreseen in the 1951 convention and 1967 protocol. And, to date, no successor with the equivalent force has been agreed.

Finally, lack of access to drinking water is already a major issue, and a source of conflict, in different parts of the world. Those who have the means can afford to buy water or will move to a place where such basic rights can be guaranteed. Those who are not able to use regulated channels to look for greener pastures, quite literally in this case, will be bound to find ways to do so for the simple reason of staying alive. Examples like this illustrate the discriminatory way in which access to global mobility is ordered in the contemporary world, here highlighting again its classed character. Moreover, this set of concerns highlights some of the problems that will need some form of collective responsibility in the near future. Yet, resolving these will require moving beyond nationalistic discourse and thinking collectively about the future of humankind.

CASE STUDY 16.1: The Venezuelan exodus

Photo 16.3 A nurse holds a sign against President Nicolas Maduro during a protest to demand better salaries and working conditions for teachers, Caracas, 5 October 2020

Credit: Leonardo Fernandez Viloria/Getty Images

Venezuela's economy gradually collapsed between 2010 and 2015. As a major oil producer, the falling price of oil in 2015 hit an economy already beset with political repression, human rights abuses and the endemic corruption of the Chavez and Maduro regimes. Hyperinflation and economic mismanagement made food and medicine unavailable, or unaffordable, to most people. This has resulted in large-scale protests and the collapse of social order to the extent that the state has functionally failed. Approximately five million people have left Venezuela through different channels as a result of the aforementioned issues. This is all the more disturbing as, in the past, Venezuela actually hosted large numbers of refugees due to its location and former prosperity. Therefore, as a case study, it illustrates how migration within the region is shaped by contextual and shifting dynamics.

Those who were the first to leave Venezuela were those who had the means to choose their place of resettlement. This was either due to accumulated wealth, or by their professional skills that gave them opportunities work abroad, or by a combination of these factors. Others with less ability to plan ahead later fled to the nearest border to seek safety in neighbouring states, such as Colombia. The extent of the numbers moving led Freier and Parent (2019) to describe it as an 'exodus' – second only in scale in modern times to the mass displacement caused by the Syrian Civil War. While Colombia has the longest land border with Venezuela and thus provides the easiest access for Venezuelans on the move, it also served as a transit state for those who wished to continue their journeys southwards.

The plight of Venezuelans and the questions over how to best offer a regional response to this displacement crisis have been addressed in the Quito Process, a multilateral regional forum. As part of this initiative, in 2018 representatives of eleven states from Central and South America signed a declaration to provide a collective response. The outcome of this was the continuation by individual states to provide Venezuelans specific channels to regularise their stay as well as apply for family reunion measures in order to provide family members safe access to the receiving state. However, despite this affirmed collective will, the signatory countries later began to restrict the entry of newly arriving Venezuelans. In August 2019 Ecuador, for example, began to require a specific humanitarian visa from incoming Venezuelans, despite the practical difficulty of applying for such a document and this being in breach of international human rights obligations.

The crisis in Venezuela has also pushed different categories of migrants to reverse their migratory trajectories. For example, a large group of people who left Venezuela during the crisis consists of Colombians who had moved to Venezuela to seek work. This underlines the dramatic reversal of Venezuela's situation as a state that once attracted economic migrants and offered safety from long-standing conflicts in Colombia that had raged between the Colombian government and criminal drug cartels and terrorist groups for decades. Yet, with the situation reversing and a spiralling crisis unfolding in Venezuela, many people understandably reversed their tracks.

In Chile, a reverse movement of a different kind was seen, once again partly related to shifting dynamics of regional security. Chile introduced a process in 2018 to facilitate access to a residence permit for Venezuelans. The process, however, was slow and did not give an initial right to work as people waited for their permit. This meant that many sought work on the black market, without access to social rights connected to the regular labour market status. That led to some calculating that leaving Chile would be a better solution. Added to this, widespread political protests within Chile broke out in 2019. While Chile is undoubtedly much safer than Venezuela, those with pending residence permits faced being stuck in a slow-moving bureaucratic process with uncertainty over how the political context might evolve – especially as Chilean society faces its own problems and shifting priorities. When adding the Covid-19 pandemic to this situation after 2020, making decisions became ever more difficult for each individual – and this uncertainty resulted in some going back to Venezuela. This serves as an example of how a simple model of push and pull factors determining human mobility is limited in its capacity to explain why some move, others stay, and yet others decide to return even if the conditions pushing them to leave their home in the first place have not changed.

Overall, the crisis in Venezuela shows how large-scale population movements change destinations depending on global and societal contexts at a given time, how mobilities are multiple and dynamic from a sending state to a receiving one, and how the regional reception dynamics change when the crisis prolongs over many years. In such a scenario, neighbouring states need to make policies that reach towards longer-term settlement and integration, which is not an easy task, especially when these states may be undergoing societal upheavals of their own (as with Chile) that pose additional challenges to policymaking. Long term, the only real solution to such a crisis – and this is true in any similar case – is the re-establishment of good governance within Venezuela itself.

 CASE STUDY 16.2: Morocco

Map 16.1 Ceuta and Melilla, Spanish territories in the African continent

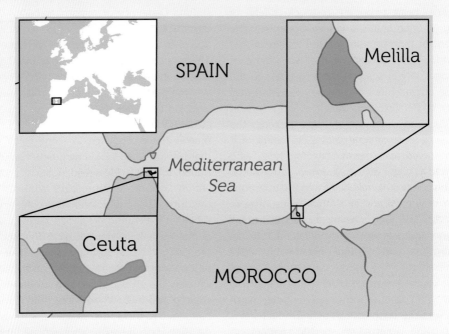

The Mediterranean Sea has been a prominent stage for a range of migration crises in recent years. These usually concern the attempts of people from different Central, Western or North African states to access the European continent by irregular means. This is paralleled with European quests to stop these attempts and push the responsibility to control borders and host people further down the African continent. The border between Morocco and Spain was the focus of international attention in 2005 when several migrants were shot at the fences of the land border separating the Spanish exclave of Ceuta in the African continent from Moroccan territory (Map 16.1),

and in 2006 with a record number of arrivals to the Canary Islands. Since then, international attention has become more focused on other routes such as the border between Greece and Turkey or between Italy and Libya – as mentioned earlier in the chapter. This European-centred discourse has obscured the large-scale migrant mobilisation on the ground in Morocco and highlights some of the ways in which the European Union has sought to outsource its migration management and border control.

The efforts to keep out migrants by various European states in 2015 and beyond were well documented in the media through images of migrants behind fences or facing armed border forces. Less well documented were increasing pressures by the European Union on the Southern Mediterranean countries, such as Morocco and Tunisia, to develop their migrant hosting capacities – with European states financing at least part of these efforts (see Andersson 2014). At the same time, Morocco developed a migration policy of its own for internal and external reasons. Externally, the pressure of a major economic player, the European Union, together with pressures from other African states opened up possibilities for forging good regional relations through economic exchanges and political support. Alongside these, internal pressures emanated from global civil society organisations and migrants' rights movement within Morocco.

In the regional migratory landscape, Morocco has performed several roles. Long considered as a place of emigration only, transit migration became visible in Morocco from the early 2000s onwards. This was coupled with persistent migrant activism within which migrants from various Central and Western African countries announced their presence by organising demonstrations and sit-ins calling for formal recognition as part of Moroccan society (Üstübici 2016). These mobilisations were amplified through rights-based activism by Moroccan nationals, causing the government to slowly realise that Morocco had turned into a place of immigration, not just a transit state.

In 2013 Morocco's King Mohammed VI announced two successive campaigns in order to provide migrants access to residence permits. Regularisation was accessible to those who fulfilled one of five criteria, the most important of which being residence in Morocco for at least five years. It was expected to benefit nationals of different Central and West African countries who are perceived as the large majority of undocumented migrants in Morocco. When the first campaign was launched, however, the number of those applying for a residency status remained below 30,000 and

included people in diverse positions such as foreign spouses of Moroccan nationals and refugees from Syria, who should have benefited from international protection status rather than this specific campaign.

A question posed by migrant individuals, associations and rights groups concerned the follow-up of the regularisation process. This includes the criteria for the renewal of one-year residence permits and the broad question of formal integration into society, which has become again more difficult in the Covid-19 context. For most migrants, the major issue is finding employment and a decent income. The integration process has thus far largely consisted of professional training provided by civil society organisations, but access to the formal labour market remains limited. These circumstances influence the ways in which especially younger migrants see their future: whether they can think of staying in Morocco or whether they decide to try and continue their journeys onwards – presumably to Europe.

Harsh forms of violence from border officers and police against those perceived as migrants have been part of the everyday life in areas close to the northern borders before and after the shootings in 2005. This has meant the dismantling of makeshift campsites near the Spanish exclaves of Ceuta and Melilla, and moving those without residence papers to central and southern locations in Morocco in order to deter migrants from approaching Spanish borders. Many migrants' rights activists have contended that there are two realities in Morocco since 2013. One is the changed landscape, especially in the capital city Rabat, where migrants became an integral part of the urban environment. The second is in the northern border areas, where migrants are harassed on a daily basis (Kynsilehto 2019). All these contribute to the evolving migratory dynamics that add nuance that goes beyond common understandings of the 'European' migrant crisis.

Conclusion

The fact that a range of mass movements of people from one place to another have become crises is emblematic of the porousness of today's global system in more ways than one. Migration demonstrates the erosion of the idea of the 'solid' Westphalian state built around a common nation of people with shared history and values. It also reminds us that widening definitions of security to the human level compels states to participate in finding shared solutions to crises, which do not stop at national borders. Finally, understanding migration involves appreciating a multiplicity of lived experiences of people on the move that are shaped by gender, race, social class as well as their migration status. The issues that are likely to shape migration (both internal and external) in the future are related to other planetary challenges, many of which are covered in this part of the book – especially climate change which stands to make large areas uninhabitable due to drought or flooding. A challenge for the global system will be to determine where these displaced persons should go and under which regulatory framework. These challenges require creative solutions at the international level that better correspond to contemporary conditions and proceeds in a way that will not set back the progress achieved thus far.

END OF CHAPTER QUESTIONS

1. Consider some of your family and friends who have moved from one state to another and discuss their journey with them. Which categories can you identify in their migration trajectories?

2. What migration 'crisis' is the most visible in the media now? Which people are moving and what do you consider to be their 'push' and 'pull' factors?

3. In what ways did the Covid-19 pandemic affect the wide range of global mobilities?

4. How should 'climate refugees' be protected, and by which entity within the global system?

5. In what ways, and for what reasons, do states seek to control migration of all types?

POVERTY AND WEALTH

James Arvanitakis and
David J. Hornsby

Question: In a world full of riches why is there a seemingly endless cycle of poverty?

Poverty and wealth are often found side by side. They are two dimensions in our world that are interrelated because they affect each other and influence both the willingness and capacity of states to ensure a stable global system. Traditional approaches to International Relations are premised on the notion of state sovereignty. But sovereignty as an absolute concept that reinforces separation between states has been tempered through the many processes of globalisation, including economic agreements and the establishment of international organisations. It has been further eroded by the emergence of human rights, which suggests that the sovereignty of a state can be challenged if a government does not respect or maintain these rights. In relation to poverty, globalisation raises the question of the obligation the wealthy owe to the poor. This thinking advances on what Singer (1972) called the 'rescue case' – a hypothetical obligation for someone to assist an infant drowning in a shallow pond if the child can be saved with minimal danger. In the context of global poverty, the logic flows that developed states have an obligation to help poorer states because they can, with minimal effort. However, the obligation of developed states to help alleviate poverty is not just relevant because they *can* assist; it is also because they are very often implicated in creating the conditions for its existence in the first place due to both the way they have structured the system historically and how they operate in it today. These perspectives confirm that poverty is a global issue on many levels.

Defining poverty

When measuring extreme poverty, it is most often thought about in terms of income. The World Bank has defined a global baseline as people living on US$1.90 or less a day. However, it is just as important to include quality of life in our thinking as a life of poverty is one of struggle, scarcity and deprivation. This takes shape through the lack of access to essential services such as affordable health care, electricity, shelter and food. In the poorest states people living in poverty typically also lack access to clean water and sanitation. As Box 17.1 shows, however, measuring poverty is more complicated than just an income expressed in dollars. Therefore, we must also understand poverty as *relative*, something that can (and does) happen in just about every community where people cannot afford to participate in everyday life due to their lack of financial means.

17.1 – KEY TERMS: Extreme poverty

Until the arrival of Covid-19 and its associated economic and social impacts, rates of poverty had been declining globally. The World Bank estimates approximately 700–730 million people live in extreme poverty in 2021 – approximately 9 per cent of the global population. While this figure may seem high, by comparison, this figure was 35 per cent in 1990. In 2018, the World Bank (2018a) presented the following scale in US dollars defining the level an individual's income would need to reach to meet their basic needs, relative to the cost of living in their society:

» $1.90 per person per day — in low-income states

» $3.20 per person per day — in lower-middle-income states

» $5.50 per person per day — in upper-middle-income states

» $21.70 per person per day — in high-income states

Now that we have defined poverty, we need to reflect on the conditions that prevent regions, states and peoples from having access to wealth. Though there are many elements to this, there are four key conditions to consider:

1. History of exploitation
2. War and political instability
3. Structural economic conditions
4. Inequality

Firstly, many of today's poorest states were historically exploited through colonialism, imperialism and/or slavery. These actions have had a lasting impact through entrenching inequalities between socio-ethnic groups within states. A prescient example is South Africa under British and Dutch rule. Both the British and Dutch restricted the rights of indigenous African groups in the areas of education, land ownership, access to capital and basic human rights. This resulted in the concentration of wealth in the hands of the white colonising minority and led to the development of deep disparities between socio-ethnic groups that still pervade today. Whilst colonialism and slavery were eventually abolished, the effects of the colonial policies and actions persisted, enabling the creation of the apartheid system of racial segregation in 1948. Even since the dismantling of apartheid in 1994, inequalities persist with the white minority population holding the vast majority of the economic wealth and the Black African population comprising the vast majority of those living in poverty. This is driven by the fact that capital and land continue to be concentrated in the hands of a select few.

This means that even after colonialism ended, the after-effects remained profound. This is not just because of a history of exclusion as described in the South African example, but in poor state building efforts by former colonisers. For example, as decolonisation unfolded in the second half of the twentieth century, many new states, particularly in sub-Saharan Africa, were left with inadequate or weak political structures that soon gave way to other types of exploitation via neoimperialism, dictatorship or corruption. In some states, these problems still persist. Of course, some former colonial states have become some of the world's leading economies – consider the United States, Canada and Australia. Yet this should not be viewed as a result of overcoming exploitation or a rejection of colonial policies, rather the continuation of colonial dynamics towards indigenous peoples in these spaces.

Secondly, when thinking of the fundamental conditions for economic development to take place in a state, security, safety and stability often come to mind. This is because peaceful conditions permit a government to focus on developing human capacity, natural resources and industrial capabilities. War and political instability act as significant disturbances to economic development and nation building as efforts are directed at combating violence or insecurity. For example, think of the conflict in Syria that began in 2011 where millions have been displaced. This mass flow of refugees and internally displaced persons leave behind a war-torn state that lacks the human and economic capital to govern its territory effectively. Likewise, in Yemen, where a civil war began in 2015, the United Nations Development Programme (UNDP 2020) estimates that a quarter of a million people have been killed directly by fighting and indirectly through lack of access to food, health services and infrastructure: of the dead, 60 per cent are children under the age of five. The social and economic consequences of examples like these will be felt for generations to come even should the violence end. This is a familiar pattern. In the 1990s in Somalia, for example, where 500,000 people died in a civil war, instability still persists as it is still widely regarded as a failed, or fragile, state.

17.2 – KEY TERMS: Failed and fragile states

When a state (the body that rules a nation) has disintegrated and no longer functions as a government, the term **failed state** is often used. In such scenarios widespread lawlessness typically follows, causing human security concerns for citizens, but also national security concerns in the wider region as refugees typically flee, seeking safety, and border areas become dangerous – the precise scenarios that can lead to war and other types of violence, such as terrorism. While the term failed state is widely used, scholars generally prefer a more nuanced term, **fragile states**, to describe states that are vulnerable due to deteriorating social, economic or political indicators. In this case, they may be descending towards crisis (such as Yemen) or recovering from crisis, but still in a fragile situation (such as Somalia).

This condition can also be seen in the developed world, though to a different degree. Consider the United States: it has spent upwards of $6 trillion (and counting) on its War on Terror since 2001. Yet, simultaneously, poverty and inequality increased within its own society – in part due to the government prioritising public spending on warfare rather than health care and welfare. It is no surprise, then, that when surveys on citizens' qualities of life are undertaken, high income nations that do not typically engage in warfare – such as Switzerland and Denmark – are often top of the list.

Thirdly, the way in which the international economic order is structured can either reinforce or ease poverty. Institutions such as the World Bank, the International Monetary

Fund (IMF) and the World Trade Organization (WTO) are dominated by wealthy nations and have come under scrutiny for the rules they establish and maintain that often place developing countries at a disadvantage. The World Bank provides loans and grants to the governments of developing states. But, before the World Bank issues a loan to a low-income state, certain conditions must be met. These are known as 'conditionalities' and they include austerity (a severe cutting of government spending), privatisation (the sale of government-owned assets) and financial liberalisation (opening up the economy to global trade). Imposing such conditions, or 'structural adjustments' as the World Bank calls them, have frequently been shown to cause more harm than good. In a detailed analysis, Brown (2009) found that many Latin American nations that have been exposed to such conditionalities experienced unequal growth, political discontent and a backlash against democratic institutions.

In other contexts, however, developing countries are doing more to try and assert their interests in international decision-making. For example, China and India play an increasingly dominant role in the WTO, taking advantage of coalitions of other developing countries to counter the influence of the traditionally dominant developed states in negotiations and dispute resolution processes (Narlikar 2020). This may be seen as an evolution away from, or a backlash to, conditionalities of a different sort that have sometimes been set by Western economies when trading with developing states. This is best seen in the European Union's practice of only trading with certain third parties in return for action to reduce domestic corruption and/or to promote human rights. Trade is used in this sense to push, or pull, states towards the dominant Western political model. In China's case, it makes a case of avoiding such conditionality entirely as a way of offering something distinctively non-Western to its trading partners.

Fourthly, inequality is an important contributor to poverty as it can reinforce divisions between the so-called 'haves' and 'have-nots'. In a relative sense, it can result in certain elements of a population lacking the tools and resources needed to counter the challenges they face. In an absolute sense it can render a whole state unable to rescue its citizens from dire circumstances because it lacks the financial resources. For example, in 2017 the United States had approximately 16 million children living in poverty. The financial cost to lift these families out of poverty was calculated by West (2017) as being US$69.4 billion per year. Compared to the entire US budget, West argues that this is comparatively small. For example, it is only approximately one-tenth of what the United States spends on defence per year. Yet it is still a staggering amount to provision even for one of the richest states in the world, not just financially but in terms of political will in a competitive system of government spending priorities.

The 'Gini Coefficient' is a statistical measure developed to gauge inequality by looking at income distribution. The higher the Gini Coefficient, the higher the level of inequality that is present. Wilkinson and Pickett (2009) found that societies that experience high levels of inequality are more likely to also experience violent crime, high levels of drug use and instability. This means (perhaps paradoxically) governments cannot focus on the longer-term structural human and economic development as they are preoccupied with responding to such social ills. Indeed, the United States is one such example of this. As a state with a Gini Coeffient that has steadily risen over the past few decades, it is perhaps unsurprising that it has come to experience precisely the problems outlined above. A more extreme example, and one that will be returned to later in this chapter, is South Africa, which consistently sits at the top end of the Gini scale. The nature of the problem is thus extensive since it is something that exists at both the domestic level (inequalities within states) and the international level (inequalities between states). Although there is a vibrant international charity system and a range of international assistance programmes, inequality remains a key structural condition associated with poverty.

Reducing poverty

Since the end of the Second World War states have come together to find ways to reduce poverty through prompting economic growth. As noted earlier, underpinning international poverty-reduction strategies is the notion of a moral obligation, which gives focus to approaches that seek to enhance the rights of the marginalised. The extent to which these efforts have been successful is debatable. Yet, the intent has certainly been there as states have attempted to address the challenges of poverty at a global level in four key ways:

1. Official development assistance (aid)
2. Trade and investment
3. Money lending
4. United Nations' goals

Aid is one way in which wealthy nations have attempted to meet their obligation to assist poorer nations. Developed countries have spent a great deal on official development assistance over the years. In 2018 alone, states spent US$149.9 billion on aid (OECD 2020). However, the success of such efforts has been inconsistent, and in some cases poverty has actually become worse. Some aid has come from developed countries or international institutions with specific conditions for use ('conditionalities') that have only served to make things worse. As already mentioned, such aid requires the receiving state to restructure its economy in ways that may not benefit the most vulnerable people. For example, during the structural adjustment programmes of the 1980s in Latin America, income per capita fell in eighteen countries. During similar programmes in sub-Saharan Africa, income per capita fell in twenty-six countries over the same period (Stewart 1991).

17.3 – KEY INSIGHTS: Aid and loans

Typically, aid comes from developed states and is either channelled bilaterally (or directly) from one state to another or diverted multilaterally through international organisations such as the United Nations. An important distinction is that aid is a gift and does not have to be repaid – whereas credit given by a state or via an international organisation (money lending) is different as these loans need to be paid back with interest. This can cause budgetary problems for the borrowing state, exacerbating their poverty problems, as they are unable to afford to invest in domestic programmes such as education and health care due to the burden of their debt repayments.

Aid does not always have the desired effect, proving a cliché that money cannot solve every problem and sometimes can even make it worse. First, inappropriate types of aid can be sent. Instead of sending money that a developing state can use to address poverty, developed states sometimes provide goods that may not be helpful. For example, in Gambia a number of oxygen devices were donated to a hospital, but unfortunately, they were not compatible with the local electricity voltage. This rendered the devices unusable, highlighting how aid needs to be both properly thought through and distributed in close consultation with the recipient nation. Second, corruption in some countries has seen aid syphoned off into the offshore bank accounts of the political elite. For example, around US$1 billion in foreign aid intended to help Bosnia rebuild itself after years of war in the 1990s was stolen by its leaders for personal gain. Third, aid has also been used for the political purposes of the providing state. For example, during the Cold War, the United

States and the Soviet Union used aid to prop up states that were sympathetic to their own political cause. In many of those places, this did little to address poverty; rather, it helped fund regional wars that led to further instability and poverty. For example, the 1975–2002 civil war in Angola saw the Soviet Union and the United States provide aid in the form of military assistance to opposing forces.

A second means of reducing poverty is by way of trade in goods and services together with foreign direct investment by private corporations. One of the ideas behind free trade and reducing barriers to investment between countries is to provide opportunities for states in the international system to grow economically. International trade in goods and services has risen exponentially since 1945. Investment between states, or so-called foreign direct investment, has been a major source of that economic growth. While many nations have benefited, these global activities frequently hide an inconvenient reality: developing countries are often only involved in a minor way in global trade and investment activities. Although nations such as China and India are investing heavily in an attempt to level the playing field, they are more fortunate than others due to their comparative wealth and high historic levels of economic growth. Despite some notable exceptions, the general picture is that trade and investment have not assisted poverty reduction to any significant extent. This is due to a number of reasons ranging from inadequate infrastructure such as roads, rail and ports to limited access to financial capital. Some aid has been used to address such infrastructure problems, but this has also come with conditionalities, including using the products and services of the donating state. In this case, Otor and Dornan (2017) found that for every Australian dollar spent on aid, it received $7.10 in export increases.

The Global Value Chain processes also illuminate how initial investment by wealthy nations does not always benefit poorer nations. Often developing states contribute to global economic processes by acting as sources for primary products or input materials in the production and manufacture of goods. These primary products then contribute to the production and manufacture of goods elsewhere – which then increase in value. This is often seen in the export of oil. For example, oil is extracted from the ground in a less developed state and a levy (or tax) paid to the state. That oil is then taken to overseas refineries and turned into petroleum (gas) and petrochemicals such as plastics because those facilities and the high-skilled workers needed are not easily found in that developing state. Finally, those refined products are sold back to the original state for its consumer market, but the price of those goods is many times higher than the proceeds it originally received for the extraction of the oil it took to make them. By maintaining a global approach to production and manufacturing of goods, inequities can be reinforced by keeping some economies in a low-value contribution cycle (see Lee and Gereffi 2013). This can distort the impact of international trade and investment activities and highlights how, in comparison to developed nations, many developing countries have a higher proportion of lower skilled or undereducated workers in their workforce. As a result, investment opportunities that require high-skilled and high-income employment are more often found in developed states and investment by corporations in developing nations typically targets a low-skilled and low-wage workforce. This reality is difficult to overcome.

A third poverty-reducing strategy is lending developing states money, or capital, so that they can invest in areas that will help them develop economically. Loans can be provided for key infrastructure projects such as bridges, roads, electricity lines and power plants. These can typically act as catalysts for economic development, but they require significant access to capital. In fact, it was the importance of access to capital that resulted in the establishment of the World Bank in 1944. Its mission was to lend developing states money at below market interest rates and also provide expert advice on the establishment of sound economic policies. On paper, the idea was a good one. However, the practices of the World Bank are not without controversy – something outlined above when discussing historical conditionalities. Although the most criticised of those policies have been abandoned, the damage has been done.

We must also consider that many of these debts may be identified as being unfair to the current people and governments as past loans (still under repayment) were often subject to large-scale corruption and misuse by prior regimes or administrations. Over recent decades issues like this have sparked calls to cancel the debt of developing countries and allow them a fresh start. This included the Jubilee 2000 community campaign that in May 1998 saw 70,000 people form a human chain around a meeting of global leaders in Birmingham, UK. The protesters demanded debt forgiveness for the poorest of nations. The campaign was successful, to a degree, resulting in the cancellation of US$100 billion of debt for thirty-five states. Despite this relief, a 2018 report by the IMF has found that the debt burdens are making poor nations more vulnerable than ever as debt repayments continue to hinder economic growth and investment in their citizens – the very things that would allow them to generate the wealth to remove themselves from debt.

Fourthly, and in response to some of the failings noted above, an approach emerged in 2000 when the United Nations set a goal to eradicate extreme poverty by 2015. The United Nations Millennium Development Goals (MDGs) consisted of eight categories, or areas of focus. A cross-section of approaches was employed for achieving these goals, including harnessing elements of the first three strategies outlined above: aid, trade and loans. A defining objective, however, was to have a coordinated approach to a set of agreed targets. The initiative proved a mixed bag in terms of results. For example, some goals related to education and child mortality saw real – if uneven – progress; while rates of hunger and malnutrition actually worsened in some cases. Exacerbating this further, the aftermath of the 2007–08 financial crisis reduced the projected amount of money (and jobs) available to many governments. Anthony Lake, Executive Director of the United Nations Children's Fund (UNICEF), accounted for the mixed picture of success and failure as follows:

> In setting broad global goals the MDGs inadvertently encouraged nations to measure progress through national averages. In the rush to make that progress, many focused on the easiest-to-reach children and communities, not those in greatest need. In doing so, national progress may actually have been slowed. (UNICEF, 2015)

Given these unsatisfactory results, the international community agreed that a more robust initiative was needed and the Sustainable Development Goals (SDGs) were adopted in 2015. They have 169 clear targets spread over 17 priority areas, all to be achieved by 2030.

Like the MDGs, the SDGs can be described as aspirational. Nevertheless, one reason they may offer greater hope in reducing poverty is that the planned interventions are more detailed. The target is not only reducing poverty but addressing the many conditions that feed and cement conditions of poverty, including poor (or negative) economic growth and meagre infrastructure development. Furthermore, the most vulnerable are now being targeted proactively – addressing one of the criticisms of the MDGs. We are again seeing mixed results emerge. Considering the unexpected economic shock due to Covid-19, concerted action will need to be taken to ensure these targets do not disappear off the international radar.

Photo 17.1 UN Secretary-General Ban Ki-moon on the CTBT20 Panel, 27 April 2016

Credit: Marianne Weiss/Flickr

Ban Ki-moon, born in South Korea in 1944, was the eighth Secretary-General of the United Nations (2007–16). Under his leadership, the Sustainable Development Goals were set out in 2015 (Table 17.1) – the first of which is eradicating poverty, which he saw as a moral and historical responsibility. You can follow the progress towards these goals on the SDG Tracker: https://sdg-tracker.org/

Table 17.1 The UN Sustainable Development Goals

1. No poverty	2. Zero hunger	3. Good health and well-being	4. Quality education	5. Gender equality	6. Clean water and sanitation
7. Affordable and clean energy	8. Decent work and economic growth	9. Industry, innovation and infrastructure	10. Reduced inequalities	11. Sustainable cities and communities	12. Responsible consumption and production
13. Climate action	14. Life below water	15. Life on land	16. Peace, justice and strong institutions	17. Partnerships for the goals	

Globalisation and the wealth–poverty dynamic

Globalisation is an important concept in the discussion of global wealth and poverty. It refers to both the integration of national economies as well as a perception that the world is increasingly being moulded into a shared social space by economic and technological forces. From changing interest rates to war and displacement, technological development to environmental disasters, what we see is that developments in one region of the world can have profound consequences for individuals, communities and cultures on the other side of the world. Like poverty, globalisation is also best thought of as multi-dimensional. For example, globalisation is more than the goods that flow between geographically diverse communities. Globalisation includes not only the what, but also the how and the why, the frequency with which something occurs, the social consequences of this process and the range of people involved.

Although the concept of globalisation is contested and subject to many different interpretations, the global interconnectedness it highlights is fundamental in reducing poverty. The World Bank (2018a) argues that globalisation has improved the material circumstances of those who have engaged in the global economy – with China the most obvious example, as is detailed further in the second case study. Though such an analysis is accurate at one level, it fails to account for the structural conditions that influence poverty. An alternative view highlights how globalisation can actually cause poverty by further entrenching inequality and concentrating any gains in the hands of those who are already wealthy and powerful. Another example we can use is the internet, which has allowed individuals to establish successful businesses and sell their goods all over the world. But how can you take advantage of this technology if you live in an area without internet access due to poor infrastructure, poverty or war? These citizens get left further behind and the inequalities that already exist are aggravated. Certainly, any analysis of the impact of globalisation on the wealth–poverty dynamic must recognise both of these perspectives and contradictory dynamics rather than slipping into an impression that globalisation is either 'good' or 'bad'.

17.4 – KEY INSIGHTS: Globalisation as 'Americanisation' and 'hybridisation'

A common critique relevant to our discussion on poverty is that globalisation is another word for **Americanisation** (Daghrir 2013). According to this critique, many of the economic policies that supposedly 'open up' international markets are of benefit to US-based transnational corporations and create fertile ground internationally for American foreign policy objectives. On the other hand, globalisation can also be seen as **hybridisation** (Pieterse 1994). This view was initially based on the creation of 'new' cultures and identities due to colonisation and the destruction of traditional indigenous groups. Applied to the processes of globalisation, hybridity has taken on a more positive character – framing globalisation as a series of processes that serve to benefit all sides involved in the exchange by promoting intercultural development and harmony.

One reason that poverty has remained a key characteristic of the globalised economy is a suite of policy initiatives based on the economic philosophy of neoliberalism that have arguably failed the world's poorest and most vulnerable. This pushes states to retreat from many of the services they once provided, such as transportation and utilities, whilst simultaneously deregulating markets and privatising essential services. Stiglitz (2002) provides a number of examples that highlight how free market neoliberal policies have driven the agenda of international institutions such as the IMF and the WTO since the 1970s. This has seen trade deals and reforms that minimise the role of government, the removal of trade barriers – even ones that protect workers' rights – and a reliance on a belief that economic growth and increases in wealth will eventually 'trickle down' to all segments of society. Such policies have fundamentally altered the traditional role of the state, whose priority has been to provide essential services for its citizenry and cushion the domestic economy from global economic shocks. States focused on the market as a priority often fail both to meet the needs of the majority of the population and address poverty. Hence, the philosophy of globalisation, if viewed through the lens of neoliberal policies, has resulted in the welfare of citizens being diminished at many levels while benefiting many transnational corporations based in wealthier nations. In this way, despite decades of increasing trade and global economic growth, poor nations have been captured in a cycle of poverty.

This challenge of globalisation in addressing the poverty issue was highlighted by the 2007–08 Global Financial Crisis. This event began in one state and quickly reverberated across the world, as covered in Chapter ten. Efforts to reduce poverty were impacted as recession and wealth contraction led to less money being available in the years during, and after, the crisis as the bulk of governments – especially in Western states – grappled with their diminished finances. States prioritised spending at home and foreign direct investment fell as corporations delayed or cancelled projects and governments reduced spending on overseas aid. While the many events associated with the Global Financial Crisis had negative outcomes with regard to poverty levels in developed nations, the impacts were even more significant for citizens in developing states. Even modest reductions in employment or income levels can tip families on lower income states into poverty, and, added to that, such states tend to have less extensive social welfare systems to assist people if they fall into difficulty. With significant economic events like this occurring periodically, the risk always remains that in an interconnected global economy the poorest will suffer the most when shocks occur, as has again been shown with more recent economic impacts caused by the Covid-19 pandemic.

 CASE STUDY 17.1: South Africa's cycle of poverty

Photo 17.2 Gift of the Givers donate food hampers, blankets, and Covid-19 and baby-care packs to a group of families at Mesco Farm in Stellenbosch, 7 July 2021

Credit: Gallo Images/Getty Images

As we have discussed, rising poverty levels and inequality between and within states have become an increasingly notable phenomenon. We have also explained how poverty is exacerbated in contexts where there is political instability and corruption – both examples of government ineffectiveness. Brady et al. (2016: 123) extrapolate the poverty and institutional linkages further by contending that contemporary poverty is impacted by previously established rules, policies and practices that are slow to evolve over time. This hypothesis is well illustrated in South Africa, where despite more than two decades of efforts to reduce poverty, levels of inequality rank amongst the world's most extreme.

The nature of poverty in South Africa largely stems from the enduring legacy of colonial and apartheid policies, but also the prolonged low levels of economic growth in more recent times which have been insufficient to generate the economic resources necessary to alleviate poverty. Under colonialism the indigenous population was used as slave labour for the Dutch and British settlers. This was expanded with the arrival of slaves from the Indian sub-continent. Despite the abolition of slavery in the early 1800s rights and economic resources were still demarcated racially. Apartheid, which emerged officially in 1948, entrenched the inequitable and racially defined distribution of rights to social services and access to economic resources to the minority white population and further marginalised the majority Black population.

Another element of the poverty dynamic in South Africa and a direct effect of apartheid-era segregation policies can be observed geographically. This is seen in inequities between urban and rural spaces, but it has also fundamentally reshaped gender dynamics related to household responsibilities and work opportunities. As a result, contemporary poverty in South Africa is characterised as mainly Black South Africans who are disproportionately economically inactive, less educated and living in rural areas. Additionally, incidences of poverty increase under scenarios where there are female-headed households and households with a large number of children (World Bank 2018b).

Poverty alleviation in post-apartheid South Africa has been articulated in a number of national policy documents such as the Reconstruction and Development Program (1993) and National Development Plan (2011) and supported by the use of fiscal policy to facilitate redistributive measures. These measures primarily include social wage expenditures such as investment in education and health, transportation, housing and local amenities as well cash transfers. Relatively strong economic growth in the period after 1994 helped sustain these measures and resulted in poverty levels falling significantly in the period leading up to the Global Financial Crisis in 2007–08. The impact of the crisis on South Africa was a sustained period of low economic growth, insufficient to generate the revenues necessary to support social wage expenditures. As such, between 2011 and 2015, the population living in poverty increased from 27.3 million to 30.4 million (Oxfam 2019). More important than the increase in poverty in numerical terms is that current levels of poverty in South Africa are deeper and more unequal when assessed against poverty indicators – building on the point made earlier in the chapter about the thin margins that people close to the poverty line often live on in developing countries.

For South Africa, poverty indicators are categorised into four dimensions: health, education, standards of living and economic activity. Addressing redistribution under these four dimensions has been restricted by systemic and historical inequities, particularly in the area of education and health. Under apartheid, poor access to education opportunities, skewed government spending in favour of White learners and policies such as job reservations for specific racial groups meant that the majority of the population suffered from unequal distribution of skills and training. This in turn negatively impacted their vertical mobility within the labour market and massively skewed income distribution in South Africa (Woolard 2002). Such a deeply structural issue as this takes time and effort to overcome otherwise it exacerbates over generations. Even if the playing field is technically levelled for a child today through a redistribution programme, these structural issues within their family situation leave them in a vastly different starting position than the child of a more historically wealthy, presumably White, South African.

Despite investments in education that amount to approximately 20 per cent of the government budget in the post-apartheid era, the groups that were previously denied educational opportunities are still the same groups that suffer from educational inequity today. The historical legacy of underfunded Black and mostly rural schools has made it difficult to redress deficits in schooling infrastructure and teacher training, implying that the 75–80 per cent of South African learners that depend on the public schooling system have poorer educational outcomes, thus exacerbating inequality further (Mlachila and Moeletsi 2019). A similar bimodal system prevails in the public health-care system, on which more than 80 per cent of South African households rely. A study by Ataguba, Akazili and McIntyre (2011) showed that despite the lowest socioeconomic groups bearing the largest burden of illness, this group also recorded the lowest level of health service utilisation and derived the least benefits. Research has shown that the relationship between health and poverty is inextricably linked, and that ill health prevents individuals from actively engaging in labour.

The engagement of the international community in South Africa's efforts to address poverty and inequality has been primarily focused on multilateral trade and foreign direct investment. Until recently, South Africa had been able to avoid seeking assistance from international financial institutions such as the World Bank or the IMF, instead engaging in multilateral trade and promoting foreign direct investment. However, the South African government was eventually compelled to enter into discussions with the World Bank and IMF around the development of an economic assistance programme due to the significant economic impact of the Covid-19 pandemic. As a middle-income state, South Africa has been a recipient of Official Development Assistance particularly since international sanctions were lifted at the end of apartheid in 1994. That said, contributions have remained relatively low in relation to the overall budget – amounting to approximately 0.2 per cent of total government spending. National Treasury (2020) data notes that in 2019/20 South Africa received approximately US$300 million in contributions from foreign governments and international organisations.

The inability of the current government to lift South Africans out of poverty and allow them to become economically engaged and active citizens reflects trends elsewhere in the Global South where current manifestations of inequality are deeply rooted in pre-colonial and colonial political and economic systems. The inability to break away from this trajectory has been worsened by the effects of the Global Financial Crisis and more recently the Covid-19 pandemic, which have brought about deeper and wider cuts to social welfare and support services, thus pushing more people into poverty.

 CASE STUDY 17.2: Views of China's Belt and Road Initiative

Photo 17.3 Workers of a Chinese construction company and stewardesses of the Addis Ababa–Djibouti Railway after the arrival of the first commercial train from Addis Ababa at Nagad railway station in Djibouti, 3 January 2018

Credit: HOUSSEIN HERSI/AFP/Getty Images

Throughout this chapter, we have discussed the way some poorer states have not been able to break cycles of poverty. One glaring exception is China. As China started to shift to a market economy in the late 1970s, the vast majority of Chinese citizens were living in poverty, having borne the brunt of Mao Zedong's failed communist economic policies. Today, that figure stands below 1 per cent. China has thus become a global economic superpower, while at the same time retaining dimensions of a developing state due to the speed of its transformation. For example, while its annual gross domestic product was US$14.3 trillion in 2019, second only to the United States, it falls below the World Bank threshold for gross national income (GNI) per capita to qualify as 'developed' as its new wealth has not (yet) dispersed amongst its population to the extent seen in developed states.

To illustrate the growing power and influence of China, and relate this to the issues outlined in this chapter, we can examine two views of China's Belt and Road Initiative. Driven by Chinese labour and financed through Chinese government loans, the size of the project is vast, as explored in Box 10.5 (Chapter ten).

The first view of the Initiative is as one that overturns established development patterns. This is China's preferred image – promising that the benefits will be shared, a win–win for those participating. The initial focus on infrastructure does mean that in the short term, little will be done to directly address poverty – but in the longer term, the benefits will be many. These can already be seen emerging. For example, in Ethiopia, the 70 per cent Chinese-funded Addis Ababa–Djibouti Railway began construction in 2011. China argued it would improve the internal productivity of the state and yield longer-term economic benefits that will help alleviate poverty (Photo 17.3).

Habib and Faulkner (2017) note that many partner states appreciate the minimal political conditions that come with Chinese finance and do not replicate the North–South, top-down, conditionality-focused aid. Hence, they are more able to access opportunities, such as the Chinese investments, and use those to develop their societies further. Indeed, the remarkable experience of China in reducing its own poverty levels are a testament to its record and expertise on the issue. But there still remain many questions over whether the aid, loans and investment laid on as part of China's Belt and Road Initiative will result in similar problems to that of traditional donor states. Loans have to be repaid and concerns have been raised whether recipients will face debts that will again place them in spirals of poverty.

This critique gets us to the second view, which draws on lessons learned from historical experiences of development and the lines of thinking these have established amongst politicians and scholars. This is best located in a 2019 World Bank Report that assessed the benefits and risks to seventy states along land and maritime corridors that connect Asia, Europe and Africa that will be affected by China's ambitions. It reported that the programme's success when measured at the human level depends on the implementation of policy measures focused on three broad categories: transparency, country-specific gaps and multilateral cooperation. In other words, it expresses a desire for China to add conditionality to its dealings with third-party states. In addition, the World Bank argues that many states need to strengthen environmental standards, adopt social safety nets, and improve labour conditions – matters on which the Chinese government do not typically insist. Such conditionalities would prove beneficial in the long term and ensure the programme is an economic as well as a poverty reduction success whilst not repeating the same mistakes of development projects of the past.

The report proposes a series of policy recommendations to help developing countries maximise the benefits and mitigate the risks of partaking in China's plans. It is estimated that China's programme could boost global trade by up to 6.2 per cent and global income could increase by as much as 2.9 per cent. However, in order for these statistics to be realised the World Bank asserted that complementary policy reforms are essential for the third-party states in question to unlock the potential gains of the Chinese initiative. In addition, stronger labour mobility and protection would ensure gains are more equally shared. The analysis by the World Bank also found that the programme has some significant risks that will be exacerbated by a lack of transparency and weak government institutions in participating economies – opening the way for corruption and the direction of funds to benefit the few, repeating an age-old tale. The World Bank report may not be welcomed as it can be interpreted as seeking to add the conditionalities of past aid – the very ones that have been heavily criticised earlier in the chapter. The difference is, however, that the World Bank argues both the donor (China) and the recipient states must focus on such reforms, moderating some of the power relationships.

Building further on this second view, some evidence is emerging that the Belt and Road Initiative reflects the kind of one-way, or exploitative, trade relationships that were outlined earlier in the chapter. For example, since a highway linking Pakistan to China was completed, Pakistani exports to China have fallen while imports have increased (Ridgwell 2017). Examples like this are causing concerns that China's 'new Silk Road' will not lead the to the benefits promised and that developing states must avoid the risk of once again being exploited, though this time by a rising China with hegemonic ambitions.

Conclusion

It is one of the major conundrums of our world that extreme poverty still exists in a world full of riches. Economic processes have helped lift many out of extreme poverty, but they have also largely failed to mitigate income and wealth inequality. And, in the aftermath of Covid-19, inequalities within and between states are being exacerbated whilst the world's billionaires continue to get richer. This poses a series of deeper moral and ethical questions that go to the heart of our global system – such as how to better distribute resources. What cannot be disputed is that the interdependence of our economies is best accompanied by an equal measure of ethical concern. That is, we owe each and every person a debt of responsibility for the actions we take and the policies we promote within our own states. Hopefully the recognition of this, perhaps best marked out by the SDGs, will lead to a more just world in the years ahead, which in turn will enhance the security and prosperity of all the world's people.

END OF CHAPTER QUESTIONS

1. Given the role of globalisation in creating the wealth–poverty dynamic, what needs to change in our approaches to it?

2. This chapter lists four key ways to reduce poverty. Are these the only ways?

3. What role should reparations from former colonial powers to those they colonised play in addressing global disparities in wealth?

4. Can international organisations be reformed to help address poverty more explicitly? How?

5. The UN's Sustainable Development Goals maintain real and tangible metrics that aspire to address a range of challenges, including ending poverty. To what extent do you think these goals are likely to be achieved by 2030?

GLOBAL HEALTH

Mukesh Kapila

Question: Since diseases cross borders indiscriminately, can health be an issue that unites us?

A spate of epidemics and pandemics has demonstrated the fragility of human health when diseases spread across borders. Their destructive social and economic impacts create political disturbances within states and disrupt international relations. The idea of global health connects an individual's private concern over their own well-being to the shared necessity to secure the health of everyone, everywhere. It is a modern concept that is a construct of the interconnected world we share. But at its roots are fundamental ideas that rely on innate human values that go back several millennia. Amidst the unprecedented turmoil of the effects of Covid-19 as it swept across the world, global health suddenly came centre stage in 2020. With 100 million infected within the first year and high death rates among vulnerable groups, states reacted by imposing unprecedented social restrictions and border controls. The situation grew more complex later in the pandemic due to a series of more infectious variants of the virus emerging. Few events in peacetime (if any) have so deeply affected the daily lives of so many individuals across the world. The impact of one virus has shaken our ideas of what a globalised world is, considering how quickly it can become an isolated one. Yet, it also allows us to explore whether such an event can act to unite us to some extent.

The values underpinning global health

Global health's roots lie in the innate universal values ascribed to health across cultures. It can also be found in the theologies of virtually all faiths. Underlying this, the Hippocratic Oath's code of medical ethics stems from 500–300 BCE and its essence has since been incorporated within every health-care system. In the modern era there are four basic moral principles of biomedical ethics:

1. Autonomy (respect for the patient, including their right to make choices)
2. Beneficence (an obligation to make contributions towards a patient's welfare)
3. Non-maleficence (harm must be avoided or minimised)
4. Justice (the fair and equitable distribution of health).

If we focus on the fourth moral principle, 'justice', this is applied by weighing each principle against the other, according to the context. In a world that is perpetually competing for limited resources, the only efficient way to practice health care is in a way that produces the greatest good for the greatest number of people. That implies making choices and how that is done is at the heart of modern debates on global health.

18.1 – KEY TERMS: Global health

A comprehensive definition (Koplan et al. 2009: 1995) calls global health:

> an area for study, research, and practice that places a priority on improving health and achieving equity in health for all people worldwide. Global health emphasises transnational health issues, determinants, and solutions; involves many disciplines within and beyond the health sciences and promotes interdisciplinary collaboration; and is a synthesis of population-based prevention with individual-level clinical care.

Global health bridges the individualised focus of a doctor–patient relationship with a worldwide concern for collective health, thereby recognising their interdependence. This is succinctly put by one of the many slogans developed around Covid-19: 'no one is safe until all are safe'. At its root, it is a construct of globalisation – the hallmark of which is the intensification of interactions between people at all levels across the world. As people mix and travel, or copy each other's habits, impacts on health status are inevitable. This could be through effects on the underlying determinants of health, for example, the spread of obesity and diabetes as certain diets and lifestyles become popular around the world. Or they could be because of the generation of new disease risk patterns, such as Ebola. Global health is projected as a public good but inherent in it are elements of both selfless benevolence towards others, as well as selfish self-interest. For example, when parents allow immunisations, they are concerned to keep their own children safe as much as protecting the children of others.

Moral values around health were traditionally centred on the duties and obligations of humans towards each other. While human rights concepts have been developing over centuries, the central instrument of protection for the right to health was eventually located in the 1966 International Covenant on Economic, Social and Cultural Rights. This United Nations treaty recognised 'the right of everyone to the enjoyment of the highest attainable standard of physical and mental health'. Nevertheless, a culturally nuanced debate continues. For example, the protection of health is typically seen in Western Europe as an individual human right but in China (for example) it is conditioned by duties and obligations to others. These political and cultural differences can create tensions when states must cooperate to stop diseases spreading across borders.

Over time, a global norm has emerged that all states have a duty to provide health services for their populations, who have thus acquired a right to health care. But this is not the same as the entitlement of a person to be healthy. For example, someone who takes up smoking cigarettes, despite public health advice not to do so, has given up their 'right to be healthy' even though they retain the right to receive treatment for the smoking-related diseases they may get. Furthermore, the right to receive health care is conditioned on the state having sufficient resources to provide such services. Thus, in poorer states, the latest therapies for lung cancer may not be available as national policymakers, guided by the principle of doing the greatest good to the largest number of people, may judge that chemotherapy for lung cancer is a lesser priority than, for example, maternity services. This may even be exacerbated by global target setting such as the Sustainable Development Goals, explored in the previous chapter, which can focus governments on certain higher impact areas like child mortality. Meanwhile, citizens of richer states typically expect to be able to access all types of services, with none of them rationed, or de-prioritised. There is also an unresolved tension between those states such as in Western Europe that consider the receipt of health care to be heavily subsidised or fully covered by their state, and others such as the United States that considers this a conditional privilege that is privatised and provided via insurance companies.

Distribution and determinants of global health

If the global health notion asserts that everyone deserves to live a healthy life, the practical challenge is achieving this. To start with, appropriate policies and resource allocation are essential to deliver the best possible health outcomes. Essential for that are accurate and accessible data on disease patterns and determinants. However, getting reliable data from states is a sensitive business. And subsequent validation, analysis and publication are even more fraught. For example, many states are reluctant to announce cholera outbreaks because of the economic implications for trade and travel. Beyond deliberate obfuscation by governments, the way health data are collected can often exclude coverage of difficult-to-reach populations such as refugees, minorities and other marginalised groups. This deepens inequalities by rendering the neediest 'invisible' (Davis 2020).

Billions of dollars of health sector investments are data dependent. This impacts the choice of diseases deemed more worthy of priority funding from limited national health budgets. It also impacts on research focus to find new medicines and vaccines. The transparency of world health data and objectivity of analysis, therefore, become paramount. Thus, the 'Global Burden of Diseases, Injuries, and Risk Factors Study' (Institute for Health Metrics and Evaluation 2016) has become vital. It is an international collaboration masterminded by an independent body, producing comparable annual estimates of national disease. The global picture shows a pattern of convergence that challenges our traditional notions of rich and poor or developed and developing. For example, today, more poor people live in rich and middle-income states than in the poorest states. Furthermore, over recent decades the traditional communicable disease killers of poor people, such as measles and tuberculosis, have become better controlled. Yet non-communicable diseases such as diabetes, cancers and heart disease, along with mental health problems, have come to the fore. Thus, non-communicable diseases now affect both rich and poor in all states.

18.2 – KEY INSIGHTS: Vaccines

Vaccination is the most effective known medical method to prevent infectious diseases. There are various types, but all have the same basic idea in common. They are an agent that is introduced into the body (by injection, for example) that stimulates the body's immune system to recognise and remember that agent and any others associated with it as a threat and destroy it – thus preventing the recipient from developing the infectious disease the vaccine was designed for. Vaccines undergo rigorous testing regimes before being made available to the public and most states have a public health vaccine regime for citizens to cover a range of preventable diseases. Smallpox was successfully eradicated in 1977 due to a global vaccine campaign, and vaccines have substantially mitigated the spread of other pervasive diseases such as measles and polio. Yet the complex and evolving nature of some infectious diseases – such as HIV and malaria – have made finding effective vaccines elusive in some cases.

However, the poorest still face traditional scourges such as malaria, diarrhoea and neglected tropical diseases. They also continue to have low access to reproductive, maternal and child health. But the poor must also contend nowadays with the 'double whammy' of non-communicable diseases because globalised advertising and wide-scale availability of cheap mass-produced food products have influenced many of them to adopt the high-fat, high sugar diets and sedentary lifestyles of richer people. Therefore, even as many disease vulnerabilities have globalised and converged, overall health outcomes have diverged within and between states. A good example is deaths from heart disease, which have accelerated across sub-Saharan Africa, even as they have trended downwards in Europe. Such deep inequalities stem from the social determinants of health. These are the conditions in which people are born, grow, live, work and age, and the systems (health institutions and financing) put in place to deal with illness. In turn, they are shaped by political decisions and the associated distribution of power and resources in a state or a community.

Setting goals for health

Closing the health gap needed precise metrics and this was first attempted with the Millennium Development Goals (MDGs). Made possible by the end of the Cold War in the 1990s, the Millennium Declaration of 2000 was a landmark proclamation by the United Nations that placed human development at the centre of international relations. States that differed on so much else managed to find common ground over the eradication of worldwide poverty through a roadmap of eight goals and eighteen targets to be achieved by 2015. The MDGs prioritised health because this was the least politically contentious area. No less than three goals were dedicated to the sector: to reduce child mortality; to improve maternal health; and to combat HIV/AIDS, malaria, tuberculosis and other diseases.

The result of the global goal setting was an explosion of health activity as states oriented domestic policies towards the MDGs. Major bilateral donors and international organisations such as the World Bank and Regional Development Banks skewed their funding in the same direction. It stimulated the creation of new global health institutions such as the Global Vaccine Alliance (Gavi) in 2000 and the Global Fund to Fight AIDS,

Tuberculosis and Malaria (GFATM) in 2002. In contrast with UN agencies, they had different governance arrangements controlled by donors who channelled vast resources through them. Private philanthropy also joined in with the Bill and Melinda Gates Foundation (for example) deploying resources bigger than the health budgets of several developing states. Such monopolistic funding bought policy clout to determine preferred health strategies and technologies, and stifled dissent at a time when a narrow approach on specific, quantified targets was the fashion.

Tens of millions were pulled out of poverty and targeted diseases rolled back thanks to the MDGs. But it soon became clear that progress only came in those areas that were directly measured. What was not covered by a target was neglected. It was also clear that global aggregate progress was largely a by-product of rapid economic growth in just two states – China and India – rather than advancement among the scores of smaller states, especially in Africa. Everywhere, conditions such as maternal mortality proved more stubborn to improve because women's health required deeper changes in society and multi-pronged policies could not be captured by reductionist metrics. For example, the MDGs reduced women's progress to the limited ambition of school enrolment of girls.

As the MDGs hurtled towards their 2015 destination, impoverished governments became more and more dependent on foreign aid. Then the Global Financial Crisis led to donors slashing their aid budgets. Standard development policy was ripe for correction and the outcome of a worldwide debate was a very different 'Agenda 2030', adopted in 2015 by a UN summit of world leaders (United Nations 2015). Its transformative framework contrasted sharply with its predecessor. As outlined in the previous chapter, a more comprehensive programme of seventeen Sustainable Development Goals (SDGs) replaced the MDGs. They were underpinned by a staggering 169 targets. Health was assigned just one goal but SDG 3's call to 'ensure healthy lives and promote well-being for all at all ages' was more inclusive than the three disease-oriented health MDGs. Underpinned by thirteen new health targets, SDG 3 covered not just the unfinished agenda from the MDGs but other prominent challenges such as non-communicable diseases and mental health. Additionally, the SDGs' rhetoric recognised that the other sixteen goals also had health advancement responsibilities because of their impacts on the underlying social determinants of health.

The new health SDG liberated policy from earlier rigidity by recognising that in a diverse world, one size could not fit all. Good health could not be imposed from above down – least of all from a global level. The MDGs had been the construction of a small, self-selected group of UN bureaucrats and their counterparts in Europe, the United States and Japan. Futrthermore, real health progress had been hampered because crucial health determinants had been ignored for political reasons. For example, an alliance of the Vatican and conservative Islamic states caused reproductive health to disappear from the MDGs, and the target for affordable water was dropped at the insistence of neo-liberal Western states who wanted privatisation in the sector (Fehling, Nelson and Venkatapuram 2013). The SDGs brought a new vision of thinking globally but acting nationally through the notion of universal health coverage. Implicit here are the concepts of universalism and equity, the modern form of the basic values that have inspired the global health movement from its earliest beginnings.

Understanding the evolution of the universal health care concept is vital as this may be the battleground on which the future of global health will be decided. In 1978 the Alma Ata Declaration spawned an influential primary health care movement to serve as the foundation for achieving 'Health for All by the Year 2000' (World Health Organization 1978). It brought hope, raised expectations and energised international health collaboration. Learning the lessons from what subsequently happened is instructive for the future. For starters, there was no action plan agreed (unlike the more recent MDG/SDG initiatives). A major schism then appeared between the World Health Organization calling for 'horizontal' programmes (broad-based primary health care that covered all conditions) and the United Nations International Children's Emergency Fund (UNICEF) that argued for 'vertical' programming to focus on specific priorities such as immunisations and tackling diarrhoea in children. Scientific developments are overtaking this debate as today's citizens, in rich and poor states alike, expect both basic primary care for simple health conditions as well as sophisticated treatments using the latest technologies and treatments. Nevertheless, the competition between the World Health Organization and UNICEF continues to the present day, waxing and waning according to the politics of any given issue, and the institutional competition for limited resources. It illustrates the fundamentally political and competitive basis of the global health enterprise. Regardless of this tension, you can't keep good ideas down. Therefore, the vision of Alma Ata has clung on and slowly repackaged itself for a new age, embedded deeply within the SDGs.

18.3 – KEY PEOPLE: Jane Elizabeth Waterston

Photo 18.1 Dr Jane Elizabeth Waterston 1843–1932

Credit: Victuallers/Wikimedia Commons

Jane Elizabeth Waterston (1843–1932) was the first female physician in southern Africa. Born in Scotland, she was a pioneer of girls' education when she first arrived in 1867 in the Cape Province. She enrolled in 1873 at the newly created London School of Medicine for Women. After qualifying in 1880, she returned to Africa to practice in what is now Malawi. Battling misogynistic attitudes and appalled at the way that colonial institutions treated Africans, she set up free clinics for the poor in Cape Town, precursors of today's primary health care and universal health coverage. Her organisation also pioneered the training of midwives. She was an early, and vocal, proponent of health as a human right with her appointment to investigate conditions in concentration camps during the Boer War (1899–1902). Her European origins and African life spanned a tumultuous period of knowledge growth alongside value clashes, previewing contemporary debates in global health.

As universal health care covers the spectrum from personal care to public health provision, health systems become vital. Regardless of differences of national context, they have certain components in common such as: a financing mechanism, a workforce to provide services, diagnostic and other technologies, medical and other essential supplies, information for decision-making, laws and regulations, governance and management, and a machinery for the participation of stakeholders. However, in an interconnected world where key ideas, products and services can easily cross borders, global health policies have a strong influence on what states are able to do. For example, how to pay for health care has enormous economic, social and political implications. This is even more so in an era of rising expectations where ageing, chronic diseases and costly new therapeutics and technologies continue to push up costs.

Health care expends more than 10 per cent of global gross domestic product, an average of more than $1,000 per capita. Yet, this obscures huge disparities among states even at equivalent stages of development. According to a 2012 World Health Organization study, an average of $44 is needed for each person, each year, to get basic life-saving health-care services. But even this modest amount is not available to many of the health systems of poorer states. That means that people must find funds to pay for their own health care. Consequently, nearly a fifth of health-care spend worldwide is paid for out of people's own pockets. In many poor states, this makes up close to 80 per cent or more of health spending. As health-care costs increase, at least 150 million people are impoverished annually due to catastrophic medical bills. Ideological debates rage on whether health care should be funded directly from central government revenues (as in the United Kingdom's National Health Service) or by public and private sector insurance schemes.

Health systems are also constrained by shortages of workers. The World Health Organization projects a required density of 4–5 health workers per 1,000 population to reach a level where universal health coverage can be meaningfully realised. For that to happen, the global health workforce will need to nearly double from current levels. A major contributor to disparities in the distribution of the existing health workforce, and to realising such targets within states, is migration – as we first explored in Chapter sixteen. Convergence in global standards for education and training, and the aspirations of expertly trained workers who have highly marketable skills, are driving health workers to leave their homes and migrate to other states where they can be paid more for their skills. The richer states of the Global North are therefore often accused of poaching expensively trained professionals from poorer states, which endure severe shortages. In many cases the situation is acute. For example, the Philippines is well known for its large numbers of nurses and health-care workers who work overseas in a variety of states. Approximately 150,000 Filipino nurses work in the United States alone. Yet, when Covid-19 hit the Philippines' own health-care system, it had no fewer than 23,000 posts unfilled (Lopez and Jiao 2020).

Global health law

Good health initially meant tackling disease spread. When it was realised that pathogens recognised no boundaries, international legal controls emerged. For example, when the Silk Road brought plague to Venice in 1377, quarantine was invoked. A hotchpotch of national measures eventually consolidated in the International Sanitary Convention of 1892. This was the birth of global health law which is now part of the body of international law. Reflecting its messy beginnings, global health law is not a unitary framework but a patchwork of treaties and other quasi-legal instruments such as public health regulations at the local, state and regional levels. How this plays out and continues to develop over time is illustrated by the International Health Regulations (IHR) that came into force in 2007 as a legally binding treaty obligation of states (World Health Organization 2016). These cover any condition that could cause a 'public health emergency of international concern' (PHEIC). Importantly, the International Health Regulations contain strong injunctions to take scientifically justified and proportionate control measures, and avoid unnecessary interference with international traffic and trade.

18.4 – KEY TERMS: PHEIC

As set out in the International Health Regulations, the World Health Organization is empowered to make a Public Health Emergency of International Concern (PHEIC) declaration. The responsibility lies with the World Health Organization's Director-General who can declare a PHEIC after convening a panel of experts to discuss an emergency situation that is serious enough to affect the international community. It triggers a range of legal obligations on states – particularly those where the emergency originated – to detect, report and respond to the issue. Covid-19 was declared a PHEIC on 30 January 2020, and prior to that five others were declared between 2009 and 2018. These included H1N1 (Swine Flu), Ebola and Zika. The category also extends to emergencies that arise from chemical or radioactive accidents and exposures.

The International Health Regulations' flaws were shown by the 2014–16 West African Ebola outbreak when the World Health Organization prevaricated for a long time to declare a PHEIC because that would offend its West African constituency and panic other states to stop travelling and trading with the region. Yet the delayed response caused even greater uncertainty and damage. The inevitable enquiry that followed created an independent Emergency Committee that the World Health Organization Director-General is obliged to consult. The Ebola experience was also a wake-up call for states to invest much more into their own national disease surveillance and early response systems. It inspired regional organisations such as the African Union to set up their own centres for disease control to boost collective capacity in outbreak-prone regions.

The jury is still out on whether the International Health Regulations are working well. There are no sanctions against states that do not comply, and although the World Health Organization is the keeper of the regulations, it has no teeth to enforce them – once again due to the centrality of sovereignty in the global system. In health matters, just as in many of the others explored in this book, states do not look kindly on international organisations or foreign states that try to police their affairs. Yet, building up the health capacities of poorer states where future pandemics are likely to arise is an area that needs investment. Even in the wake of diseases like Ebola and Covid-19 this has been slow in coming. Additionally, there has been a steady criticism that richer states only feel compelled to act in health matters overseas when it is for their own self-protection – picking up a more realist line of thinking. Yet, this is clearly not viable as despite our best efforts, highly infectious diseases will spread.

One area of progress has been spearheaded by African states and came via the 2001 'Doha Declaration on the TRIPS Agreement and Public Health'. It outlined that if a government declares a domestic public health justification, generic drug makers can bypass patent laws and make their own cheaper copies of life-saving drugs – such as for cancer and HIV/AIDS. In doing so, they can significantly reduce the cost of those treatments. Enabling affordable access to medicines is a ground-breaking legal achievement giving primacy to the human right to health care above commercial and other rights and thereby advancing equity and fairness in global health. Examples like these show that the tentacles of global health law continue to spread, trying to keep pace with the good and bad drivers of health.

Health in waging war and peace

Worldwide disruptions caused by contagious diseases are now joined by other anxieties. These are the challenges of antimicrobial resistance, counterfeit drugs, access to pharmaceuticals, diminishing respect for health work in conflicts and growing health inequalities – alongside fears of bioterrorism and radiation and nuclear risks. Such an expanding menu has established direct links between health and security. Perceiving health as a matter of national security, termed as the 'securitisation of health' has created new problems. This became prominent post-9/11 when the War on Terror, and later the regional instability that broke out after the Arab Spring, spawned vicious conflicts. In consequence, attacks on hospitals and health workers became almost normal tactics of war. Civilians were directly or indirectly targeted via warring groups deliberately obstructing health workers in caring for the sick and wounded or stopping public health interventions such as immunisations or clean water for civilians caught up in conflicts. In this way, health care became 'weaponised' as a tactic of armed conflict (Thompson and Kapila 2018).

However, there is also a converse side: using health efforts to construct peace. A new field of 'health as a bridge for peace' has emerged as medical idealists and activists seek a deeper meaning from their endless labour of repairing wounded bodies at the frontline of unending conflicts. But humanitarian organisations such as Médecins Sans Frontières and the International Committee of the Red Cross are wary of deliberate efforts to construct a health-peace nexus because this can be construed as politicising the neutrality and impartiality of life-saving health work and thereby undermining the ability of humanitarians to access civilians on all sides of an armed conflict. We will come back to this idea in the second case study later in the chapter.

Psychological trauma arising from different forms of violence also adversely impacts human health and social development. Thus, in a society that has experienced high levels of trauma within itself, often spanning generations, this could be a major driver of continuing conflict and instability, thereby perpetuating violence. For example, many thousands of child soldiers were drugged and brainwashed into armed groups where they committed horrendous atrocities in Sierra Leone's 1991–2002 civil war. That trauma was likened to a contagious virus infecting family after family as even after the brutality ended, those who committed the acts (as children) often developed disorders that resulted in them continuing to exhibit violent behaviour, which in turn leaves an imprint on their own families and children. Similar interpersonal and intergenerational transmission of trauma has been blamed for the even longer second Sudanese civil war (1983–2005) during which the twenty-first century's first genocide occurred in Darfur. Global health and humanitarian practitioners have responded by creating 'psychological first aid' interventions, to try and heal traumatised minds, somewhat akin to traditional physical first aid to save wounded soldiers and civilians.

18.5 – KEY TERMS: Gavi

Created in 2000, Gavi, the Vaccine Alliance, is a public–private global health partnership that goes beyond traditional state-centred international collaborations with the goal of increasing global access to vaccines. It includes governments, the World Health Organization, UNICEF, the World Bank, the vaccine industry, research and technical agencies, civil society and philanthropies. Funded mostly by donors, it is the principal provider of vaccines for developing states. It also invests in strengthening their vaccine delivery systems. It uses the purchasing power of its multi-billion-dollar budget to secure vaccines in bulk at competitive prices. In return, vaccine manufacturers appreciate Gavi's mitigation of their commercial risks, which had previously stopped them from fully serving poorer populations. Gavi now vaccinates almost half the world's children. It has pioneered the development of innovative financial mechanisms such as the advance market purchase facility and the 'International Finance Facility for Immunisation' that issues Vaccine Bonds on the capital markets against long-term donor pledges. Gavi has also stimulated the research and development of new vaccines. Gavi co-leads the COVAX platform, which procures Covid-19 vaccines at negotiated prices to distribute to low and middle income states – as well as supporting procurement for many wealthier states.

Beyond war and violence, food systems that have come to rely on intensive production methods for both animal and plant-based food are depleting the nutritional value of what we eat and giving rise to anti-microbial resistance (due to the overuse of antibiotics in livestock), as well as malnutrition and obesity. In turn, this is fuelling the progressive rise of non-communicable or chronic conditions, even as novel types of communicable disease also arise. At the heart of the interconnected new health threats is the carrying capacity of the planet whose natural resources were once regarded as part of the global commons – a theme that will be explored in the next chapter. However, the respective ecological footprints of rich and poor are now in competition. A child born in a high-income state will consume several times more natural resources compared to a child born in a low-income state. For the health sector, that means a new thesis for safeguarding human health by also attending to the health of the planet on which we all depend. This new paradigm of 'planetary health' (Rockefeller Foundation–Lancet Commission 2015) or 'one health' (Zinsstaga et al. 2011) sets out aspirations for a rebalancing of the links between individual health, collective health, animal health and the health of the earth's natural systems that define the safe limits within which humanity can flourish.

CASE STUDY 18.1: Covid-19

The gaps and divisions created by the Covid-19 pandemic have profoundly affected international relations because everything about the origins and spread of the novel coronavirus has been contentious. China was accused of delay and cover-up as well as obstructing the conduct of independent enquiries into the origins of the virus. The World Health Organization was blamed for being slow and timid, and many states were accused of hiding behind their borders while competing with others for life-saving products such as personal protective equipment (PPE), therapeutics and vaccines.

The International Health Regulations, lynchpin of cooperation among states for their mutual safety, faltered as the pandemic became

Photo 18.2 Army Specialist Angel Laureano holds a vial of the COVID-19 vaccine, Walter Reed National Military Medical Center, 14 December 2020

Credit: Lisa Ferdinando/U.S Secretary of Defense/Flickr

politicised. Governments of all types – democratic and authoritarian – restricted human rights and liberties as populations were locked down, businesses collapsed, schools closed and unemployment soared. Science struggled to unlock the mysteries of the new virus, and misinformation, fear and panic filled the gaps. Latent prejudices surfaced in attempts to blame other cultures or states for spreading the virus – perhaps best signalled by the rise in anti-Asian racism in the United States. In addition, fake news, predominantly spreading on social media, directly endangered the health and well-being of all people, especially the poorer and least-educated groups. Even US President Donald Trump contributed to the torrent of confusion and misinformation, famously suggesting during a televised press conference that it may be worth injecting disinfectant into a person's body to treat Covid-19. While his advisors looked on in shock, cleaning product companies raced to issue guidance to remind the American public that their products should not be ingested under any circumstances.

During the peaks of the pandemic, health systems across the world became overwhelmed as they stopped attending to their normal business of caring for routine diseases. This created the unprecedented ethical dilemma that to save lives from Covid-19 meant accepting excess deaths and sickness from other causes

Photo 18.3 Man gets photographed after being vaccinated against Covid-19 at LNJP Hospital in New Delhi, 10 April 2021

Credit: Hindustan Times/Getty Images

(such as cancer) because of the pivoting away of health facilities to focus exclusively on the novel coronavirus. Amidst this, all types of inequality deepened as the virus drilled itself into the fault lines of societies.

Covid-19 showed that the interdependence of global health in a globalised world proved to be its Achilles' heel as states discovered how dependent they had become on others for health-care essentials, which were typically manufactured overseas and imported. Global medical supply chains collapsed with states bidding against each other for precious diagnostics, medicines and personal protective equipment. As governments turned inwards to safeguard their own populations, globalisation appeared to reverse. What was once proselytised as the engine for mutual prosperity was recast as a grave threat. National health security was seen as more vital than international solidarity.

The World Health Organization argued for states to get behind its COVAX facility (which it co-leads with Gavi and UNICEF among others) to make vaccines available equitably to all states according to need. Yet, a large number of richer states such as the United States and the United Kingdom scrambled instead to prioritise advance purchase agreements with vaccine manufacturers to guarantee privileged access for themselves. The implication was that states that could afford to buy vaccine stocks in advance would get first access, leaving poorer states to wait in line. Indeed, this is precisely what transpired. Underlining the situation in which some developing states were left, in February 2021 the Philippines offered to lift migration restrictions it had placed on its medical professionals leaving to work overseas if the United Kingdom and Germany donated vaccines in return – essentially trading nurses for vaccines.

Frictions also emerged as Global North states, which are home to the pharmaceutical companies that invented the bulk of the Covid-19 vaccines, wrangled with Global South states over protecting intellectual property rights as calls emerged to forgo patents to allow other states to independently manufacture the life-saving vaccines. In parallel, vaccines produced by China and Russia were offered to increase their soft power and simultaneously leverage the backing of weaker states over contentious issues on the global stage – such as human rights issues and territorial matters in Taiwan and Crimea. As the Covid-19 vaccine became a tool of both diplomacy and competition, those with access to the vaccines secured competitive advantage by resuming business and growth more quickly, and thereby deepened many of the underlying inequalities within the global system.

Covid-19 has demonstrated that the uncritical march of globalisation has hollowed out the capabilities of poorer, weaker states while expanding their exposure to external risks and leaving them ever more dependent on the mood and disposition of more powerful or capable states. Furthermore, when the chips were down – especially during the first eighteen months of the crisis – the global system was not seen to work fairly to protect the more disadvantaged when every state seemed to be engaged in the struggle to protect itself.

All was not bad, however. Crises often bring out the best in people. Communities across the world rediscovered an extraordinary spirit of solidarity as voluntarism flourished and people reached out to help the most vulnerable. As health workers became the new frontline heroes with many losing their lives to the virus, appreciation of the values of universal health-care provision was revitalised. The worldwide public mood infected governments, several of which, especially across Africa and Asia, vowed to revamp and recapitalise their publicly funded health systems.

CASE STUDY 18.2: Health as a bridge for peace

Photo 18.4 Former French Minister of Health, Bernard Kouchner, talks with soldiers in front of an ambulance outside the Hotel Dieu de France Hospital, 1 February 1990

Credit: Maher Attar/Sygma/Getty Images

Interest in the role of health in peace-making goes back a long way. In 1192, during the Crusades – as explored in Chapter three – the English King Richard fell sick. Saladin, Sultan of Egypt and Syria, sent his own physician to treat him. But the invaders repaid their hosts by launching further crusades of considerable barbarity. This, then, raises the issue of whether health can be a bridge for peace. To make 'peace' we must first understand 'war' and frame an analysis against which to assess the role of health. For example, during the Covid-19 pandemic, metaphors such as 'waging war on the virus' were widely used. The progressions of disease and conflict have many similarities, and a public health model can be used to analyse conflicts.

Conflicts, as with diseases, smoulder, flare up, die down and recur. Indeed, the best predictor of future conflict or disease is a past history of the same. Akin to the genetic basis of disease, the memory of conflict gets transmitted from generation to generation. Just as diseases come in waves and spikes, conflicts come in cycles and can be perpetually recycled. As with understanding an illness, dissecting the internal physiology of a conflict is useful to distinguish between underlying vulnerabilities, proximate triggers and perpetuating factors. For example, the Syrian regime's long-standing denial of democratic rights created the vulnerability of deep-rooted grievance. But the proximate trigger or 'match that ignited the fuel' for its civil war was the arrest and alleged torture of schoolchildren in 2011 for writing anti-government graffiti. The factor that perpetuates the Syrian conflict or the 'oxygen that keeps the fire burning' is, arguably, interference from other states, including through the provision of arms. Health work can be mapped onto such a conflict analysis model.

The first and default approach is that health institutions ignore a conflict and continue to work around it. An example was Sudanese hospitals at the height of the Darfur genocide in 2003–04 when rape by security forces was common. A police certificate was needed to confirm a rape before treatment was given because that was the administrative practice in 'normal' times. The second approach is 'palliative' – traditional humanitarian relief to reach the wounded and sick while a conflict continues around the workers. Health care is amongst the biggest components of humanitarian appeals with many agencies such as Médecins Sans Frontières and the International Medical Corps doing much-applauded work. The third approach seeks to use health's innate values that combine altruism with science in deliberate ways to 'transform' a conflict – such as using health as a bridge for peace.

Such a public health model of war and peace seeks optimal points for health interventions to break a conflict cycle. However, as with disease management, it is important to know where and when to intervene in a conflict, so as to positively influence its internal dynamics. Health peacemakers have to decide whether they are aiming only for violence containment, mitigation, or the more ambitious goal of conflict resolution. In public health language, this translates into primary prevention, secondary prevention and tertiary prevention. Studying conflict situations has resulted in the development of a framework of nine postulates (McMaster University 2005) to explain how health interventions could stimulate peacemaking:

1. Pursuing common issues or interests to bring protagonists together, such as when planning for recovery in Mozambique before its Peace and National Reconciliation Agreement was signed in 2019, thus pushing progress toward peace.

2. Evoking and extending altruism to generate positive feelings among parties, such as in polio vaccination days in Afghanistan and many other states.

3. Identifying and replacing rumours with facts to rebuild mutual confidence, such as that created between Crimean and Ukrainian authorities regarding a cholera threat in 2019.

4. Redefining prevalent norms to change the terms of the debate and open new space for discussion. For example, 'war' that is traditionally seen as a test of manhood and adventure may be redefined as a 'disaster'.

5. Confronting demonised stereotypes to bring about psychological healing, such as when Sri Lankan trauma counselling centres were established for all sides following its 1983–2009 civil war.

6. Regenerating a sense of shared identity to keep basic human connections going across the conflict divide. For example, with the establishment of a public health surveillance reporting system in Northern Alliance health districts in Afghanistan where workers were willing to report to the rival Taliban-controlled Ministry of Health in Kabul in the years before the US-led invasion in 2001.

7. Deploying negotiation skills to mediate across barriers to medical care distribution. For example, service delivery efforts by Philippines medical professionals to both sides of its civil conflict forged contacts that were subsequently maintained through formal diplomacy.

8. Personal solidarity actions by health-care professionals, especially respected doctors, to gain trust. For example, in the Maluku Islands, Indonesia, where 'personal witnesses' accompanied the war-injured following a 1999–2002 conflict, not just to provide care and protection but also to diffuse tensions.

9. Campaigning by health-care professionals against 'unjust' tactics in wars to assert moral authority to change public and official opinion. For example, when the documentation of the human impact of anti-personnel landmines by health organisations led to the 1997 landmark Ottawa Treaty and subsequently the 2008 treaty banning cluster bombs.

These mechanisms appear to achieve impact through at least four key routes. First, by addressing divisions, polarisation or discrimination, as grievance factors in conflict. Second, by providing common neutral technical space for confidence building. Third, appealing to shared or self-serving interests to solve a problem that cannot be easily tackled by one side alone. Fourth, by keeping connected amidst brutality through sustaining a sense of humanity among opposing sides and thereby rebuilding human relationships and ethical values.

However, historical experience from the examples cited suggests that although beneficial effects were experienced, these were too local or temporary to have any long-term significance on the course of the underlying conflict. And elsewhere, critics have argued that carelessly provided humanitarian aid, including for health care, might even have prolonged conflict (Thieren 2007). Thus, a balanced judgement on the impact of health as a bridge for peace would be that, at best, it might reduce or mitigate levels of violence only at the tactical level (Kapila 2007). If health aid is not the magic pill for conflict situations, the way to get the best value from any health-to-peace linkage may only be as part of wider political and security processes that better recognise health as a central issue.

Conclusion

Since time immemorial, health has symbolised the most noble of human values. Even as wars and pestilence challenged societies, the art and science of healing progressed steadily across many millennia, and within all cultures, providing a potential unifying basis for all humanity. Yet an understanding of global health depends on appreciating the continuous tensions inherent in the balance it must strike in its policies and practices. These have included the contentious role of human rights and the power of social determinants that shape the deeply unequal chances of people to receive health care or enjoy good health. As the chapter has shown, there are signs of unity of purpose for achieving universal health coverage, chiefly as part of the post-2015 agenda for sustainable development led by the United Nations. But there are also considerable challenges on how to get there. This is best underlined by the fact that, at its essence, the global system is one of sovereign states who sometimes (especially in emergencies as seen during Covid-19) instinctively look within rather than outwards – at least in the short term. Exploring these issues further and recognising how they overlap with the other global issues explored in this part of the book – such as security, migration and climate change – indicates that a better understanding of human health and well-being is not a tangential issue for International Relations. Rather, it is one of the key issues facing life in the global system and perhaps one of the issues that may, one day, serve to unite us.

 END OF CHAPTER QUESTIONS

1. Considering that universal health coverage is already difficult politically and economically to achieve within many states – in what ways do you think 'global' universal health coverage (to some extent) can be made more achievable?

2. How and when is it justified to restrict human rights and freedoms to protect and promote health?

3. Would stronger global health laws make the world safer? What do you think the various International Relations theories would make of such a development?

4. Considering how important vaccines are to health outcomes, is there more that can be done by states, international governmental organisations, civil society, individuals and transnational corporations to promote vaccine use, make vaccines more accessible and help to counter vaccine hesitancy?

5. What are the key lessons we can learn from pandemics such as Covid-19, considering their impact on international relations and state behaviour?

ENVIRONMENT AND CLIMATE

Raul Pacheco-Vega

Question: Does the global system have the tools to combat climate change?

Our planet carries approximately eight billion people. Yet its capacity to provide for each one of these individuals is threatened by population growth, climate change, deforestation, collapse of fisheries, desertification, air pollution and scarcity of fresh water. The full extent of our shared global environmental problems goes far beyond the well-publicised challenge of climate change. In fact, one of the elements often forgotten is the complicated relationship between human beings and their environment. In the early years of the conversation around environmental protection, some argued that the planet's resources were there for our collective consumption. However, there are limits to growth and this raises a range of important global issues. The human population quadrupled between 1900 and 2000. This growth, which continues, coupled with abrupt climate change events and further compounded by rapid industrialisation and urban expansion, have combined into a perfect storm of negative processes that put pressure on the capacity of Planet Earth to sustain life. Within the global system, the environment is one of the areas where much work remains to be done, particularly because cooperative approaches to environmental protection have had a mixed record despite the grave implications of failure.

Towards a global consensus

It is often hard to assess whether international cooperation efforts have had any real effect on society's well-being, the quality of our environment or even the construction of long-term relationships between states. One form of evaluation takes place through the study of environmentally focused 'megaconferences'. These large-scale events bring together representatives of national governments, intergovernmental secretariats, non-governmental organisations, academics and industry actors to engage in conversations about the state of the environment. They usually focus on a particular issue at hand. What makes these megaconferences interesting is that their goal is to engage in productive collaborative efforts to reach agreement and consensus on specific strategies to protect the environment and solve global challenges.

19.1 – KEY TERMS: Climate change, biodiversity and sustainable development

Perhaps no issue is more international than **climate change**. The earth's climate has never been constant. Yet, over the last century the effects of human activity – principally the burning of fossil fuels such as oil, coal and natural gas to fuel our economy and lifestyles – have driven global warming and a resulting large-scale shift in weather patterns. Climate change is a dynamic process that increases the severity of extreme weather events such as hurricanes, droughts and flooding as the earth continues to warm.

Biodiversity is a term that describes all the life forms on earth – in all their various forms, from the smallest bacteria, to plants, insects and the largest mammals. The different elements within earth's biosphere rely on the others to survive. Due to industrialisation and human activity, biodiversity loss is reaching critical levels.

Sustainable development concerns retooling how a state's development occurs so that it is cleaner, more aware of impacts on natural systems and produces fewer emissions and pollutants than in traditional industrial processes. This is all the more important as the large number of 'developing' states need to follow a development path in order to improve the lives and prosperity of their citizens and reduce poverty – much as the states of the Global North already have. If they do not do so sustainably then it will exacerbate climate change and biodiversity loss and endanger the health and security of future citizens.

Historically, the two environmental issues that have gained the most attention have been climate change and biodiversity. Both of these issues came up at the Earth Summit in Rio de Janeiro in 1992 – formally called the United Nations Conference on Environment and Development. Nevertheless, most scholars will recall the 1972 United Nations Stockholm Conference on the Human Environment as the first large-scale environmentally focused megaconference. The Stockholm Conference was also the starting point for the first global coordination mechanism for environmental protection, the United Nations Environment Programme (UNEP). This conference was also the first one where participants explicitly linked human health with environmental and ecosystem health in their discourses.

The second milestone in global environmental governance was the publication of the Brundtland Report in 1987. This report outlined the need for a new model for development that brought into play the notion that we cannot simply use (and misuse) the resources we have at our disposal. The new model, coined sustainable development, became an enduring part of the global conversation about environmental protection. The Brundtland Report defines sustainable development as having three main components: economic, environmental and social – an idea that was then put forward for implementation at the Earth Summit.

The third milestone was the aforementioned 1992 Earth Summit in Rio de Janeiro. A major outcome of this meeting was the recognition of two of the most important environmental issues – the loss of biodiversity and rapid climate change – and the need for intergovernmental secretariats and agreements to respond to these twin challenges. The bulk of the world's states, 161, signed a declaration on the need for a model of global development that enabled future generations to live within their means but also facilitated current generations' livelihoods. The fact that so many states reached an agreement on the concept of sustainable development, and the need to operationalise it, became the key contribution of the Earth Summit. Activist involvement became the norm in international conferences on environmental issues starting with the Earth Summit. Non-governmental organisations were considered part of the negotiations from the very beginning and over 2,000 non-governmental representatives attended.

The fourth milestone was the 2002 Johannesburg World Summit on Sustainable Development. The goal was to establish collaborative intergovernmental, cross-disciplinary and cross-sectoral partnerships. In theory, this would strengthen the way in which environmental activists interact and partner with national governments. Different types of partnership were elucidated and non-state actors were considered from the design stage up to implementation. However, following the summit there was a widespread perception that there had been very little progress on the implementation side, leading to a feeling of megaconference fatigue. To remedy this, the 2012 UN Conference on Sustainable Development (also known as Rio+20) created mechanisms for follow-up of commitments to sustainable development. It also highlighted the relevance of specific targets for development and the need for transition towards broader-reaching sustainable development goals. Moreover, the outcome document of this conference defines specific regional initiatives towards the implementation of sustainable development.

Finally, the 2015 Paris Agreement represented a moment of consensus among virtually all the world's states to put into place a long-term plan to address climate change. Among other things, it also established a global stocktaking process to be done every five years to monitor progress and make adjustments if needed. The fact that an agreement was reached was a landmark as prior negotiations were marked by disagreements on a strategy to compel states to reach internationally agreed targets on their carbon emissions. This is important as carbon dioxide, released primarily by burning fossil fuels for energy, is the main cause of global warming. Nevertheless, Paris showed that many states were able to agree on specific goals, targets and policies to combat climate change.

The Paris Agreement, whilst important, is not indicative of a single or comprehensive solution to climate change as much more needs to be done. Four important elements stand out, each of which indicates the challenges and opportunities ahead in dealing with climate change. Firstly, there is research (Broberg and Romera 2020) based on Article 8 of the Agreement that recognises that climate mitigation and adaptation strategies may not be sufficient. Consequently, mechanisms to help states deal with climate-induced losses and damage (such as flooding) are needed, together with funds and expertise to facilitate this. This reflects on the fact that although action is being taken to combat climate change, in the short and medium term the effects will still escalate and disproportionately affect the poorest and most exposed states.

19.2 – KEY PEOPLE: Christiana Figueres

Photo 19.1 Christiana Figueres (second from left) at the Paris Climate Change Conference, November 2015

Credit: hajue staudt/Unclimatechange/Flickr

The 2015 Paris Agreement was led by the Executive Secretary of the United Nations Framework Convention on Climate Change Secretariat, Christiana Figueres (Photo 19.1), a Costa Rican diplomat who came into the post following well-publicised failures of climate negotiations in 2010. It is an example of what can be achieved in global cooperation for environmental protection by just one intergovernmental secretariat. As an entity within the United Nations, with 450 staff, it played a pivotal role at a crucial time under Figueres' leadership in rebuilding momentum and securing agreement on the specific tactics and strategies that every state must undertake in order to reach the stated goal of holding increases in the earth's temperature below two degrees Celsius.

Secondly, the role of the United States in global climate politics has shifted due to the mainstreaming of climate change denial in the Republican Party, one of America's two major political parties (the other being the Democratic Party). When elected president, less than two years after the Paris Agreement, Donald Trump mainstreamed the already growing tide of climate denial. His rhetoric and his administration's policies, such as his emphasis on coal, dampened efforts to address climate mitigation and adaptation targets and undermined conversations around decarbonisation strategies. This mainstreaming was watermarked when, after several years of speculation, Trump announced the withdrawal of the United States from the Paris Agreement in November 2019. Although the successor Biden administration reversed this in 2021, having the world's most powerful state (and second biggest polluter behind China) mainstream climate denialism in its policymaking risks undermining global progress as the issue remains endemic in the Republican Party as we will explore later in the case study section.

The third element is the importance of ambition (Arroyo 2019; Röser et al. 2020). If states, cities, regions and communities approach climate policy in a way that remains close to the status quo instead of taking an ambitious and far-reaching approach, it is likely that we will not be able to reach our emissions and temperature targets within the timeframe that global agreements have proposed. This is closely related to a fourth development – an increased push for shifts in societal consumptive patterns (Alfredsson et al. 2018). Beyond the traditional conversations around the importance of reducing greenhouse gas emissions and developing adaptive strategies for cities and metropolitan regions, we have begun to witness a growing interest in changing how communities and societies consume, with a holistic goal of reducing emissions but also changing the ways in which commodity chains operate (Welch and Southerton 2019). Commodity chains are sequences of interconnected processes that firms use to develop goods (also called commodities). An example is the global coffee commodity chain. To have coffee on our tables we need to extract, transport, treat and process resources from all over the planet – even if the plantation is in, for example, Costa Rica.

There are different pathways for how to decide which goals in global climate governance should make it to domestic policies, but much of the work in International Relations (as outlined in previous chapters) has been focused on how globally popular, commonly held norms spread and diffuse across and within nations. Norm diffusion mechanisms suggest that internationally agreed goals and strategies to protect the environment can diffuse to nation-states and subnational governments through a broad range of informational strategies, human capital training, activist mobilisation, discourse building and consensus formation. In the climate governance field, the signing of the Paris Agreement appeared to signal global agreement on the importance of engaging in substantial collective action to reduce global greenhouse gas emissions (Held and Roger 2018). The bulk of scholars and policymakers agree that the importance of climate change as a global environmental issue is paramount, and therefore, we could argue that there is a global norm around a global strategy for emissions reductions that is slowly diffusing. If this logic holds in the way that other important norms have held internationally, the effects of shorter term setbacks, such as the United States' example during the Trump administration, will not be sufficient to change global momentum over the longer run.

Climate change is not the only ecological issue facing our planet. But its role in catalysing global action to protect the environment cannot be overstated. One of the most neglected issues is water. While the earth is two-thirds covered by water, the proportion that is freshwater (drinkable and usable for agriculture) is sometimes highly contested and in short supply for growing populations. One example of this is disputes over how (and where) water that runs across national boundaries is used and managed. For example, Pakistan and India have been in dispute over allocations of water from rivers that run across both states. Similar issues have arisen over the River Nile in north-eastern Africa, as explored in Chapter nine. When added to the effects of climate change, which can exacerbate drought conditions in one area and flooding in another, water is an issue of international concern. There has been some progress in developing global strategies for groundwater governance, for sustainable access and allocation, and for a nexus (water-energy-food) approach to managing water – but a unified global water governance framework is still to emerge. Two major obstacles that prevent this approach are the diversity of water usages and the multiplicity of stakeholders and actors across national boundaries that have an interest in how water is allocated, used and reused. Hence, addressing this issue will likely form one of the next major international challenges.

The environment as a global commons

The notion of public goods comes from the original definition of a good that is non-excludable and non-rivalrous. Think of it as something that anyone can access at any point in time without making it any less available for anyone else to consume. The best example of a public good is knowledge; in this case we can use the example of information that we find on the internet. All knowledge, once freed and put online for public consumption, is non-excludable and non-rivalrous in consumption. You cannot exclude anyone from consuming knowledge and learning, unless they do not have access to the means for knowledge transmission, which may be the case in some countries where specific websites are banned. You also experience non-rivalry in consumption. Air is another example of a public good. Under normal circumstances nobody can stop you from breathing air into your lungs, and the fact that you breathe air does not stop someone else from having the opportunity to enjoy it. This is the definition of a perfect public good: one that is always non-rivalrous in consumption and non-excludable in access.

19.3 – KEY TERMS: The resource curse

Being blessed with resources may be regarded as a wholly positive affair, giving a state vast riches under their land by virtue of the luck of their geography amplified by scientific and engineering developments. For example, when Saudi Arabia became a nation-state in 1932, they had no idea they were sitting on some of the world's largest pools of oil. Oil was not discovered there until 1938. Yet, such riches can also have negative consequences if not managed well. Addressing this, the concept of the 'resource curse' is defined as the negative effect that such natural resource wealth has on governance. States that are rich in minerals are often considered to be facing such a curse, because there is enormous interest on the part of outside entities to come into that territory, establish industrial mining operations and extract minerals from underground ores to process them into finished products or components. This can lead to corruption that diverts government attention away from the needs of its citizens and instead towards the centralisation of power and personal enrichment. Such scenarios have a negative impact on development – both economically and politically – that can affect a state for generations. In that sense, the 'curse' is not inevitable. But it does reflect the experiences of a significant number of newly formed nation-states in the twentieth century who found themselves blessed with valuable riches before they had developed robust political institutions, especially across the Global South.

Common pool resource theory derives from Hardin (1968), who said that if left to our own devices we would exhaust all the resources available for our consumption. Imagine if you were a shrimp fisher. You need to fish and sell your catch to sustain your family. Let's say that there are 10,000 shrimp available in the small catchment in which you fish. But there are 99 other fishers in the sea at the same time as you. If everyone cooperated and consumed only one-hundredth of the total available shrimp, each would have 100 shrimp to sell. If at any point any fisher catches more than a hundredth, there will be other fishers negatively affected. Hardin used a similar metaphor to make the point that if resource consumers behave selfishly, they would exhaust the resources they were supposed to preserve. Hardin called this the tragedy of the commons. Closed bodies of water, plots of land and large-scale areas of forests are all common pool resources. They are rivalrous in consumption, but non-excludable.

One can summarise the theory of common pool resources by placing goods in four specific categories: private goods, common goods, club goods and public goods. This categorisation framework has two dimensions. The first dimension is excludability. If you can prevent someone from accessing a good, that good is excludable. The second dimension is rivalry in consumption. Goods that are depleted are rivalrous in consumption. If I consume an apple, you cannot consume that same apple because I have already eaten it. Private goods, such as food, clothing and other material objects, can be purchased and acquired because they are tradable. As a result, these goods are both rivalrous in consumption (if I buy a car, nobody else can buy that exact same car) and excludable (you cannot buy a car unless you have the money to purchase it).

Goods that are non-rivalrous in consumption and non-excludable are called public goods. These are the things that everybody can enjoy. Consuming them does not reduce the possibility of someone else having the same opportunity of consumption. Air is a public good. Everybody can breathe air without worrying that at some point they will not be able to breathe simply because somebody else is also breathing. Finally, common goods, which are also called common pool resources, are those goods that are non-excludable but rivalrous in consumption.: fish in a fishery, trees in a forest, water in an aquifer or a lake. All these natural resources are common goods and, therefore, common pool resources.

What makes common pool resources so interesting is that the theory, developed by Elinor Ostrom (1990), argues that despite the fact that humans are supposed to be selfish, faced with conditions of scarcity we are able to self-organise and govern our

19.4 – KEY INSIGHTS: Forests

Map 19.1 The Amazon rainforest

Forests are one way to see how a resource can be viewed as a global commons. For example, the Amazon (Map 19.1) is a rainforest that spans nine states in Latin America – with the bulk (60 per cent) within Brazil. Preserving forests as vast as this, sometimes described as 'the lungs of the earth', are instrumental in any future climate mitigation as trees, and all plants for that matter, absorb cardon dioxide from the air as a food source. In that sense, the more trees there are, the more carbon we can remove and store naturally in trees. Conversely, when one state (such as Brazil) takes a path of clearing large areas of the Amazon (for agriculture and mining, predominantly) it is a local action that has global implications.

common pool resources (our 'commons') in a sustainable manner. One of the reasons why Ostrom's work had such an impact was because her theory of cooperative approaches to resources governance contradicted Hardin's tragedy of the commons model. Instead of being so selfish that they would want to fish all the shrimp (for example), Ostrom found that fishers would build a shared agreement to reduce their own consumption for the well-being of the collective. Obviously, this is an example on a relatively small scale. What remains to be seen is whether we can upscale this into global cooperation.Perhaps you would agree that a shared environment would be a resource community and individuals would work collaboratively to protect it. But there is another view, which is that responsibility for care of the environment rests with state governments. One way of thinking about this is to use the concept of the global environment as a global commons. After all, global environmental problems are by their very nature *global*. However, international cooperation is hard to achieve. As the example of the United States shows, there are powerful states that will (from time to time) avoid or withdraw cooperation for various reasons. It is hard to make states commit to specific conservation goals (in forest policy) or emission-reduction targets (in climate policy) or standards for pollution in rivers (in water policy) because each state has its own development objectives that may conflict with such goals, thus making it hard to find common ground for collaboration. Hence, a state's refusal to collaborate to solve an international issue is always concerning, but never surprising. Because of shifting state-level priorities, international collaboration on key environmental issues remains limited.

Global and domestic policy responses

The right to a healthy environment and the global commons are ideas that suggest that it is our shared duty to take care of our collective environment because everyone has a right to enjoy their environment and use some of its resources for their survival. It is possible to link human rights with global environmental regulation through the implementation of the international norm of a right to a healthy environment. Despite states having different abilities and varying degrees of technical expertise to implement the norm, the number of countries with constitutional environmental rights has expanded radically. No fewer than eighty states have now passed such legislation domestically, but we are still quite a long way away from having this norm as a fundamental human right. There is some evidence that a number of environmentally related norms have been emerging, such as a collective agreement on the pollution levels that microplastics bring along, but other norms have not yet achieved this degree of relevance across the board.

There has sometimes been a tendency to see environmental legislation as damaging to economic growth and prosperity. This can make it unpopular in domestic settings, making legislation difficult to pass – or even propose in some cases. Indeed, this was one of the key reasons for Trump's climate scepticism, particularly in regard to the Paris Agreement. Brazil's Jair Bolsonaro also took the same line by promoting (or overlooking) the large-scale clearing of land in the Amazon rainforest for agriculture during his presidency. There are, of course, many other concerns that divert government focus from environmental issues. Increasing regulation on certain heavy-polluting industries, such as steel and coal, can have a negative effect on jobs. Setting 'green' taxes – such as a tax on carbon emissions – either directly or through such measures as energy tariffs, can also cause a burden on taxpayers and businesses. Recent developments, such as the idea of the Green New Deal, have highlighted the importance of economic incentives to push forward greener, more environmentally friendly measures. Should such measures take hold, when added to the number of countries where the human right to a healthy environment is already enacted constitutionally, may help build better collaborative transnational networks to protect the global commons.

19.5 – KEY TERMS: The Green New Deal

Photo 19.2 Members of the US Democratic Party campaign for the Green New Deal, 7 February 2019

Credit: Senate Democrats/Flickr

The 'New Deal' was a package of policies pursued by the Roosevelt administration in the United States in the 1930s to create jobs and enable new regulations to help the nation recover from the Great Depression. In a similar vein, the Green New Deal refers to a series of climate-related policy measures that are intended to use government capital to invest in green jobs, establish zero emission targets – and in doing so both reduce environmental impacts and tackle inequalities. While this was originally a US-related policy package associated with members of the Democratic party in 2019 (Photo 19.2),

the idea has since taken hold in other states and therefore could set the stage for a *Global* Green New Deal. In this sense it may lead to the diffusion of a global environmental norm emerging from the United States.

Sharing a paradigm that pushes the human right to a healthy environment may also induce governments to actively seek participation in international environmental agreements. Nevertheless, it is important to find a way to coordinate these agreements, and this challenge raises the question of whether we need a global environmental organisation to make sure states comply. Given that collaboration between states is so difficult, international environmental agreements attempt to build a framework to help states talk to each other and agree on specific targets for environmental protection. Some of the most well-known international environmental agreements are specific to the area of climate change, but other less well-known examples – such as the Aarhus Convention on Access to Information, Public Participation in Decision-Making and Access to Justice in Environmental Matters – are equally relevant. States that are signatories to the Aarhus Convention make an agreement to share data that will enable their citizens to understand the potential risks that they face with regard to the processing and emissions of industrial chemicals. This information helps environmental activists bring industries to account and ensure that they reduce their polluting emissions.

You may recall from earlier in the chapter that there is now a consensus regarding one specific tool that may help achieve the goal of providing global public goods: international environmental agreements. These agreements, often produced at megaconferences, help protect our global commons by requiring nations to acknowledge and respect the human right to a healthy environment. However, the next big question is addressing who is in charge of implementing these international environmental accords. Some have argued that in order to compel states to cooperate in the protection of our shared environment, a global intergovernmental secretariat should be created whose sole purpose would be coordinating efforts to improve environmental quality. For many years there was a collective belief that the United Nations Environment Programme had been tasked with the challenge of protecting our global network of ecosystems and shared resources. This may have been true in the early stages of its creation following the 1972 Stockholm Conference, but protecting our global environment has proved to be an impossible task for a small agency with a limited budget and no power to compel states to act.

The reality is that even though there is increasing interest in strengthening global cooperation across states to protect the global environment, it is the number of institutions, agencies and programmes dealing with environmental issues at other levels that grows in size and complexity. And while there is still no agreement as to whether the United Nations Environment Programme is the agency that should be tasked with protecting the global environment or whether we should create a more substantial global environmental organisation, it is important to keep a focus on collective solutions at the international level rather than state, regional or local level. The example of the 2015 Paris Agreement, which built on the example of earlier megaconferences and movements, suggests that international collaboration to protect our environment may be on the rise, but there is still much more work to do.

CASE STUDY 19.1: Donald Trump and climate denial

Photo 19.3 Donald Trump holding 'Trump Digs Coal' sign while campaigning for president at the Mohegan Sun Arena in Wilkes-Barre, 10 October 2016

Credit: SOPA Images/LightRocket/Getty Images

One of the most challenging issues facing our global environmental governance model is the predominance of a specific state, the United States, in the international discourse and global policy arena. The United States, reflecting its disproportionately influential global position, has used that influence to drive international environmental politics in some arenas over recent decades. Yet it has also been inconsistent – or perhaps even negligent – in other arenas. This issue is compounded by the fact that the United States (second to China) is the world's second-largest emitter of the greenhouse gases that drive climate change. It is important to realise the risks in such a situation where one state is so influential – especially if the internal politics of that state should shift and its leadership become absent. Indeed, this allows us to also consider effects not just at the state level, but to consider the impact of one individual, Donald Trump, and his preferences on shaping global climate progress during his four-year term in office.

There is no question that a state leader with a strong personality can have an impact on global politics (see De Pryck and Gemenne 2017). Charisma, personality, wisdom, intelligence and being able to articulate a vision are all individual traits that can drive the way in which a message is passed on. For example, the joint announcement of then-US President Barack Obama and Chinese Premier Xi Jinping in September 2015 that they would both formally join the Paris Agreement was emblematic of the power of charisma and leadership gravitas to push the agreement over the line and secure the support of other more reluctant states. Nevertheless, individual personalities are not the only domestic sources of influence in international environmental politics. There are hundreds, perhaps even thousands of participants in global negotiations around every single environmental issue, from marine protected areas to the international carriage of hazardous waste, from climate change to biodiversity to bio-accumulable chemicals.

One of the reasons why Trump has had so much influence on global climate politics is because he unilaterally chose to leave the Paris Agreement and effectively terminate all substantive participation by the United States of America in global climate negotiations (see MacNeil and Paterson 2020). In doing so, Trump manifested an environmental sceptic's view, meaning that he did not seem to believe that climate change was worth his attention, or his state's actions. Environmental sceptics typically believe that any kind of collective concern about the impacts of industrial and human activities on ecosystems' health is overhyped or is a hoax by scientists and politicans. In line with this, Trump tweeted in 2012 that 'the concept of global warming was created by and for the Chinese in order to make US manufacturing non-competitive'. A range of other tweets and statements pointed to his lack of belief that climate change is driven by human activity, is widely exaggerated by scientists and that mitigating it is not worth the costs. Trump also actively worked to undermine the regulatory role of the Environmental Protection Agency (EPA) within the United States, arguing that such domestic agencies have a negative impact on business by producing too much regulation (commonly known as 'red tape').

Applying Trump's personal views more broadly within the phenomenon, climate sceptics (or deniers) do not believe the scientific consensus on climate change. Some do not believe it is occurring at all due to a misunderstanding between local weather and global climate (pointing to instances of cold winters for example) while others believe that it is occurring but is not driven by human activity. What most sceptics have in common is a rejection of attempts to change human and industrial behaviour. In addition to denial over the science, such global mandates also raise legitimacy issues at the political level for such thinkers as they tend to come from ideological positions that reject the authority of international agreements or organisations – seeing such attempts as tyrannical or illegitimate. Climate scepticism is therefore a cultural issue, more than just a political one (Dunlap, McCright and Yarosh 2016; Hoffman 2011).

Clearly, then, Trump is just one voice in an established discourse. This discourse is especially prevalent in the United States and the Republican Party where such thinking has become mainstream. Yet, because of the place of the United States in the global system, the unique ways that Trump wielded his executive power and his unique mastery of the media, Trump has had an undeniable effect on global discourse around climate change policy negotiations. When we are confronted with such marked political polarisation and strong domestic opposition to a global norm, as well as a powerful leader with a counterpoint view of the issue, a countervailing process emerges. This can be seen as follows: the counter-norm of climate scepticism works against the global consensus. In this case, that global consensus was the one agreed in 2015, at that time with the backing of the United States. Considering this from a normative framework, Trump's reversal was not just a domestic policy shift. Due to his unique impact, his actions have effectively mainstreamed climate denialism – something that was already well established before his election, but operating at a peripheral level.

Recalling the norm life cycle first explored in Chapter seven, Trump's example does not mean that climate denialism is so globally diffused that it has countered the already existing norm supporting international cooperation towards global climate change action and emissions reductions (Matthews 2015). For example, it took several decades and multiple acrimonious diplomatic encounters for the consensus of 2015 to be reached. We will have to wait for more time to pass to see the extent to which Trump's singular actions diffuse through the global system, but the International Relations' toolkit gives us the means to track this. If Trump's actions cause a cascade and become internalised, resulting in other states coming to follow his example, then any future global climate agreement is certainly going to be materially different, if it exists at all. This will be measurable beyond his presidency, as it has already been established that these views do not originate with Trump, but rather that he mainstreamed them. Yet it seems that few other global leaders have followed Trump's example. And, following Trump's defeat in the 2020 presidential election, the successor Biden administration swiftly rejoined the Paris Agreement.

 CASE STUDY 19.2: Governing extraction

Photo 19.4 Example of open pit mining

Credit: pixel2013/pixabay

Resource endowment is not spread evenly, it is mostly the luck of geography. Some states are rich, for example, in oil. Others have substantially large deposits of metal-rich minerals that are discovered under their soil and accessed through modern mining technology. There has been much interest in state resource endowments as pathways to prosperity in the economic development field. But it is only more recently that we have begun to pay more attention to how the dynamics of cross-state resource extraction has an impact not only on domestic governance conditions but also on the global system. Companies that engage in resource extraction in a state different to their own seek to benefit from the natural endowments of the target states. This does not always result in an equitable arrangement and has led to a concept known as the resource curse (see Box 19.3). This is exacerbated historically as during the colonial period, colonial powers often extracted vast amounts of wealth from the territory under their control. In the modern day, private companies are sometimes directly, or indirectly, connected to (or contracted by) a state, which raises some of the neocolonial critiques that we have explored earlier in the book.

Mining activities provide materials that enable the production of many of our most prized and important possessions – such as smartphones. However, they also have environmental impacts that are strongly differentiated. Extracting as an activity is as invasive as it sounds. Industrial plants with heavy machinery drill into the very surface of the Earth to extract minerals or other geological materials. Similar activities also take place over water by pulling large amounts of fish out of the depth of the oceans and other bodies of water. Bottling companies drill wells from which they can extract spring water to transform it into bottled water. This process is called 'commodification'.

Extractive activities can have impacts for much longer than their period of operation and this is particularly true of mining, which has the potential to start and sustain serious social disputes with affected communities. But even more concerning, mines can have extensive and long-term negative impacts on the environment. Polluted rivers, accumulating mountains of solid toxic waste, and effects on human health in workers and surrounding communities are just a few examples of these by-products of mineral extractive industries. Examples across the globe abound but in the modern era they are more prevalent in the developing countries of the Global South.

In Mexico, community groups have been battling against Newmont Goldcorp, a Canadian company, over the installation and operation of its Peñasquito Polymetallic Mine. Opening in 2010 in the state of Zacatecas, it is the world's fifth-largest silver mine and also holds significant deposits of gold and other minerals. This is an analytically rich case to consider because there are groups that oppose the installation of the mine, but there are numerous other stakeholders interested in making sure that the mine remains active due to the economic benefits it brings. This tension between economic well-being and environmental and public health damage is made even more visible when considering the global–local interconnections.

What is important for some groups at the local level is to have access to jobs, and the mine does provide a number of these, both direct and ancillary through other services that supply the mine and its workers. In contrast, other stakeholders are more interested in reducing the potential for negative ecosystem impacts, including species loss, deforestation, toxic chemicals and airborne particulate matter. In that sense, the idea of the environment (or climate) being global is only way to appreciate, or look at, issues such as these. The truth is, however, that (as indicated earlier in the chapter) such issues are operationally a state-level phenomenon that have their roots at the individual and group level.

There are many issues worth discussing in such a case as this, but there two main areas of interest. The first is the apparent disconnect between global corporate governance and local community struggles. Because mining companies are usually multinationals operating in foreign countries under various schemes, including subsidiaries, the domestic regulatory framework has limited effectiveness regarding what state regulators can do to force mining companies to comply with local environmental laws. Even at the domestic level, it is hard to make companies comply with legal requirements, emissions standards and cleaner production process guidelines. An example of this phenomenon is the case of the Buenavista del Cobre, a mine operated by Grupo México in Cananea, in the northern Mexican state of Sonora. In 2014, this facility had a toxic spill of about 40 million litres of copper sulphate into two Mexican rivers, the Bacanuchi and the Sonora. This accident reportedly affected more than 22,000 people. Five years later, these people and their families continue to face medical bills and health challenges that ought to be paid by either corporate insurance or directly by the company itself.

Such a case raises the charge that mining companies have a duty, if not legal, then certainly ethical, to protect their surrounding environment. Protective strategies that have emerged include ecosystems protection, water treatment, mechanisms for air quality protection, wildlife management strategies and waste governance. Yet, the bulk of these vary widely as they are within the purview of each state – and not all states evenly enforce the laws and regulations that exist. One potential pathway for addressing this is for mining companies to engage in corporate social responsibility strategies, which are developing across industries, including mining (see Hamann 2003). This is predicated as a response from such industries and corporations to a global call for environmental sustainability and a quest for reduced impact on communities, societies and regions. There is an implicit understanding that it has the potential to make companies more sustainable and humane. However, corporate social responsibility is not a panacea that will automatically achieve reductions in pollutant emissions, create spaces for best practice or develop responsible citizens, enterprises and corporations.

Going beyond leaving the setting of standards to corporations and states, an international framework would set a normative (and possibly legal) expectation for companies to act with more responsibility for the longer- and shorter-term impacts of their extractive activities.

Further, if a global environmental intergovernmental secretariat was established, we could infer that this agency would ensure that coordination across policy sectors and issue areas occurs and that there is a multidisciplinary group of people looking at the installation and operation of mines, such as those in Mexico mentioned above.

Conclusion

Developing new, and improving existing, ways to tackle environmental and climate challenges requires better integration between international initiatives and domestic policy strategies. This means creating the conditions for a model of governing the environment that is flexible and cuts across different levels, from the local to the global. It is also clear that frameworks based on ideas of global public goods and global commons are useful to aid our understandings of the shared opportunities and risks we face within the global system. However, at the same time it is important to recognise that these debates are daunting – and a rising tide of denial is perhaps an understandable, if unhelpful, reaction to this. Collective action on any scale, especially climate change, is an enormous challenge for humankind, the likes of which we have not faced in our history. Trying to find mechanisms, models and strategies to ensure cooperation across different levels of government, across a broad variety of issue areas and across a range of political and policy actors is a problematic and difficult process, as experience has shown. But the hope is that progress may continue, despite evident setbacks, and consolidate so we can all live healthily and happily on Planet Earth.

 END OF CHAPTER QUESTIONS

1. In what ways are biodiversity loss and climate change global issues that impact all of humanity?

2. How and when can more powerful states, such as the United States and China, disproportionally impact upon the development of global climate policy?

3. How do you assess the dangers of an ever-growing human population consuming more than our planet and its ecosystems can sustain?

4. What is the resource curse and is it only a problem of developing states or can it also happen in higher income states?

5. What kinds of issues do we need to balance out in order for mining and extractive industries to be more environmentally sustainable?

CONNECTIVITY AND EXPLOITATION IN THE DIGITAL AGE

Clare Stevens and Andreas Haggman

Question: In what ways are the devices and services that bring us together also the source of dangers and divisions?

As has become clear throughout this book, when we think of humanity we do not typically think of a single, homogenous, peaceful body. Instead, the global system comprises of a number of distinct factions competing, coercing and cooperating to achieve their own end goals. These may be groupings formed along ethnic, cultural or religious lines or they may be nation-states. Importantly, however, none of these groupings exist independently of the individual humans within them. Humanity consists not only of bodies, but also of the ideas contained within human minds. Central to the concept of connectivity is the ability to communicate with others, which we do more and more today via digital means – and at an intensity unmatched historically. The internet has put almost every individual within reach of each other in the sense that they can communicate instantly for leisure or even political purposes. Yet, it has also allowed criminals and state actors new avenues to operate. In this sense, our ever more connected world is simultaneously one of greater opportunity, but also one of greater risk.

The internet and digital commerce

Connectivity has taken many forms throughout history, most notably through trade and diplomacy, which typically moved slowly on horseback and over the sea until the invention of ever faster forms of transit that gradually shrunk the sense of distance between people through the twentieth century. However, this physical shrinking of space is nothing when compared to the advances in information technology that moves information at the speed of light. In contemporary industrialised societies, such information communication technologies are broadly and systematically affecting the forms human interactions take. Thus, age-old forms of human connectivity such as commerce, communications and political relations have now been intensified. Communications on the internet traverse any combination of these network links, and because this appears to challenge many conventional notions of state boundaries, they have become a hotly contested topic.

The World Wide Web is just one of many services operating on the internet. It is accessed through a web browser to display documents containing text, images and other media. Examples of other services on the internet include email, voice and video communications, online gaming and file transfers. Typically, these are accessed through separate programs or apps. Connectivity in the context of the internet refers to the availability and exchange of information, 'packets' of digital information flowing between physical nodes. However, the connectivity afforded by internet and communication technologies are not viewed or experienced in the same way everywhere around the world.

For example, internet access around the world closely reflects the geographies of uneven development, which was explored in Chapter seventeen. The proportion of people using the internet in advanced industrialised places is higher than those in lower income states (Map 20.1). In that sense, internet penetration simply reflects historical global distributions of per capita income, literacy rates and government openness to the internet in their respective states. Likewise, the effects of connectivity are uneven across geographic space too. For some states, it has democratised political debates, empowered marginalised groups or facilitated commerce. Conversely, in other ways and places, it has reinforced prevailing disparities of wealth and power, and intensified information asymmetries and intergenerational inequalities.

It is hard to get an accurate figure (and the figure is always rising) but somewhere between 50–60 per cent of the world's population has access to the internet. At the turn of the century, it was fewer than five per cent. Getting online has been made significantly more accessible in recent years due to the portability, ease of use, and the widespread distribution of smartphones that operate wirelessly and do not require a physical network connection point. Statistics like these allow us to put connectivity into a historical and social context in order to understand how our ever-growing connectivity simultaneously shapes and constrains political and social interactions across the global system. It also allows us to consider how both global and local political processes shape and constrain connectivity. To put it another way, digital connectivity is facilitated by technology, but it is also made up of laws and institutions that shape their use and regulate the individuals that design them or use them.

Map 20.1 The geography and penetration of the internet

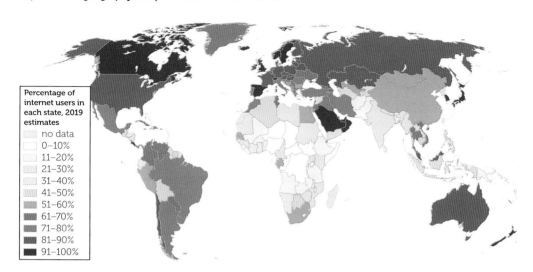

Source: International Telecommunication Union/World Bank/Our World in Data

The internet links tens of billions of devices across the globe. These include servers, personal computers, smartphones and video game consoles. Increasingly, other devices are also being connected to the internet, such as cars and domestic appliances in what is known as 'the internet of things'. Devices connected to the internet are connected to each other through network links. These links can be either physical cables or wireless connections. Physical cables come in an array of shapes and sizes, ranging from small cables used to directly link two computers together, to large undersea cables connecting continents. Wireless connections, though not visible, work on similar scales, from Wi-Fi networks and cellular networks to satellites in space.

As one of the oldest forms of human connectivity, commerce is a cornerstone of societal interactions. Throughout history, the trade of goods and services has provided opportunities for humans to physically connect and therefore necessitated cultural and linguistic methods of communication. Bartering, agreements and contracts have been made possible through verbal, written and visual means. The internet provided merchants and private traders with a whole new set of opportunities for their commercial purposes, whilst this adoption in turn fuelled the internet's growth. The shift of commerce from offline to online has repercussions for human interaction and communication. This also helps to bring to light the often-hidden complexity that occurs to get a product to market, and what occurs after you press 'purchase'. In the modern economy, commerce involves a long supply chain and multiple agents that affect the production and transportation of goods. To take a product from idea to conception to finally reaching purchasers requires first raw materials, then a manufacturer, a distributor, a seller and a customer (with possibly a marketer or two thrown in for good measure). Each step in this process requires individual human beings interacting with one another, especially at the point of sale.

Through digital commerce, however, customers can purchase goods without ever (directly) interacting with another human being. To buy a television, for example, would previously have required a person visiting a retail outlet such as an electronics store, speaking with a sales representative and making the purchase. The retail store would in turn have procured the television from a wholesaler, who would have bought it from an importer/distributor, who would have acquired it from the manufacturer. Thanks to the internet, however, a prospective buyer can now simply visit the manufacturer's web page, purchase the television and have it delivered to their door, effectively cutting out most of the traditional commerce chain and with very limited interpersonal communication. However, the growth of the internet did not take place out of the blue. The commercialisation of the internet in the 1990s and the speed with which it became a medium for such commerce depended on the extensive pre-existent logistical and technical infrastructures and capitalist institutions such as worldwide banking that could facilitate it. Some were therefore more ready to take advantage of its benefits that others.

20.1 – KEY TERMS: Cyber warfare, hybrid warfare and cyber security

Cyber warfare is a catch-all term that refers to the use of online technologies during conflict. This captures a broad range of activities: everything from the networked aspects of traditional conflict scenarios (such as a military intervention or military operations between states), to persistent low-level disruptions undertaken by state or non-state actors outside an official state of war. **Hybrid warfare** has also come into use describing a blend of traditional warfare (troops, tanks etc.) with information warfare. An example is Russia's use of weaponised fake news, bots and targeted disruption of elections in Ukraine whilst simultaneously using armed forces to annex Crimea in 2014. Finally, **cyber security** describes measures used by states, non-state groups and individuals to protect themselves from threats over the internet, such as antivirus software and other countermeasures. See Whyte and Mazanec (2018) for an overview of these issues, and Stevens (2018) for a more critical reading.

The anonymity and limited interpersonal communication that contributed to the new forms of commerce has also meant that other age-old human processes, namely criminal activities, have found new avenues online. While increased connectivity has intensified commerce in some ways, the anonymity that the internet affords also makes it a complex proposition to regulate. The internet's complexity means it also eludes simple or blanket international policy recommendations. Such complexity can be seen in various ways that often make the headlines. For example, first established in 2011, the Silk Road was a 'dark web' store. It allowed shoppers to make purchases without revealing any personal information as payments were made in bitcoin. People were able to buy and sell all kinds of materials, both legal and illegal. The Silk Road took advantage of the complexity of the internet's structure to hide the identities of its users, directing their traffic around multiple encrypted routers. It was eventually shut down by several US and European law enforcement agencies. The example highlights several things. First, bitcoin, one of many such virtual currencies, is not associated with, or made by, a sovereign state. This is a material change within the global system that the internet has facilitated – and in doing so poses deep questions about the power of states in the financial arena. Second, the Onion Routing (TOR) dark web system that is used to access websites such as the Silk Road is not as anonymous as many users once thought. As criminals and others who would wish to hide their activities (such as anti-government activists) have gained a new space to operate, the forces of the nation-state are also catching up and finding ways to penetrate this space. Indeed, TOR was actually built under the auspices of the US military – as the internet itself was in the 1960s when its prototype the ARPAnet went online.

Digital communications

At least as old as the idea of commerce is the idea of communicating across geographical space. A primary means for doing so is through the written word. Letters represented a key connection between humans for many centuries and were (in their various forms) a key element of diplomacy. In the digital age, email and instant messaging have usurped letters as the primary means of written communication, with countless digital messages sent each day. With email and instant messaging, the human middlemen are replaced by commercial entities such as internet service providers (ISPs) and technological processes and protocols that ensure the email or message arrives intact at the correct destination. A written letter (even in modern times) can take days or weeks to arrive at its destination. By comparison, a standard email or instant message usually arrives almost instantaneously. Even emails to the International Space Station take only a few seconds to transmit. Another important difference is that traditional letters were limited to one-to-one communication; electronic messages facilitate one-to-many interactions, turning an individual into a potential broadcaster. A third important difference is that traditional correspondence required considerable effort to duplicate in order to be able to pass on a message to even one other recipient, whereas electronic messages can be copied and widely propagated almost instantly. Given that digital communications travel almost instantaneously, messages can be effectively delivered to millions of people to spread ideas and organise movements.

There is also a wider economic and political structure that such digital communications operate within to consider. Writing practices and communications have been inextricably bound up with commerce. The earliest written texts, dated to about 2600 BCE in modern-day Iraq, were concerned with recording market transactions and relations, and such writings on clay tablets gave communications material form. Similarly, the widespread use of paper in later years, originating in China around 200 BCE–100 CE and later spreading through the Islamic world and into Europe, enabled the cartographic mapping of political and commercial empires to aid the flow of political power and trade. The internet is another materialisation of commerce's flows, ensuring that those private individuals and companies with access and capital are likely to benefit the most.

20.2 – KEY INSIGHTS: The 'Twitter Revolution'

Photo 20.1 Martin Luther posting the Ninety-five Theses in 1517

Credit: Karl Bauer/Wikimedia Commons

Photo 20.2 Hundreds of thousands of Egyptians gather in Tahrir Square to topple President Hosni Mubarak, 8 February 2011

Credit: Jonathan Rashad/Moment Open/Getty Images

The so-called 'Arab Spring' was also called the 'Twitter Revolution' due to the widespread use of social media to propagate ideas and mobilise protestors. In Egypt, the government even shut down internet services in acknowledgement of the role they were playing in the organisation of protests, such as the mass demonstrations in Tahrir Square, Cairo (Photo 20.2). It is worth putting this event in perspective with a historical comparison. When Martin Luther set in motion the Protestant Reformation in 1517, he did so by nailing a polemical document to a church door in Wittenberg (Photo 20.1). This act began a process of violent upheaval that culminated in 1648 with the end of the cataclysmic Thirty Years War. The full effects of Luther's public posting thus took some 130 years to come to fruition. Yet the revolution in Tunisia at the start of the Arab Spring took just a few weeks to spread throughout the Middle East and North Africa. This example suggests that digital communications can play an important role in enabling and speeding up political events, and the role of individual users can seem more immediate.

One of the unintended outcomes of the widespread convergence of mobile connectivity, social media and cloud computing has been a rapidly growing volume of personal information, (often) shared voluntarily with entities separate from the individual in order to access content. This 'exhaust cloud' of personal information and habits is a valuable commodity, hoovered up by large internet and social media companies – often for end-use that may be against the interest of the individuals whose data has been sold. This is explored further in the first case study of this chapter. The benefits of connectivity are not free of these wider economic and political structures, highlighting the (perhaps problematic) power asymmetries between individuals and the corporations providing these 'free' services such as Twitter and WeChat. There are both benefits and drawbacks to this phenomenon of digital connectivity. On the one hand, people living under repressive regimes may be limited in their ability to communicate both within and outside their state. With digital technologies this repression can be sidestepped, allowing the expression of grievances and a bringing to light of issues that might otherwise be shrouded from view.

With the greater reach of communications, the presentation of a novel idea is more likely to garner support, dissent or comments than an idea presented to a smaller audience. Consider, for example, crowdfunding platforms, where entrepreneurs can present their ideas to the public and appeal for funding to make them a reality. The idea does not have to be a physical product, it can also be the manifestation of a political or religious conviction. The internet makes it possible for ideas to gain traction that in the past might have fallen by the wayside. In this way, digital communications can increase shared knowledge and foster conversations that lead to the reformulation and improvement of ideas. It is these capacities for information's dissemination and reach that fuelled early narratives about the internet possessing some innate 'liberalising' essential nature. Yet, as has become evident over time with increasing polarisation in many of those states where the internet is widespread, polarisation is also a danger which can shake the foundations of liberal societies by dividing people into irreconcilable groupings.

In fact, as examples throughout this chapter seek to underscore, technologies can be used for a range of different ends. This is highlighted in the work of scholars such as McCarthy (2017). For example, these avenues of digital connectivity can also give a voice to unsavoury constituents of society. Just as the repressed can make themselves heard, extremists may find a foothold in the murky depths of the internet where bad ideas can be picked up and amplified. The Christchurch shootings in 2019 – which were livestreamed over Facebook – were perpetrated by a right-wing extremist who had disseminated videos and postings in online forums. This incident reflected a global growth in white supremacism and 'alt-right' extremism that has been facilitated by online connectivity. Another beneficiary of this has been Islamic State. Much has been made of their mastery of the internet to radicalise and recruit new members and spread propaganda – particularly through social media – as has been detailed in Chapter fifteen. There is no shortage of people, including Muslims, who renounce the group and actively seek to combat its message, but in the online world the majority view does not necessarily eliminate others being expressed. Previously, a bad idea might have faded into obscurity for lack of an audience, but with so many platforms and modes of expression even the most heinous ideas can find adherents.

20.3 – KEY INSIGHT: Everyone is a publisher

The expanding reach of ideas and information is a dynamic that has been intensifying since the invention of the printing press in the 1400s – which made it possible for text to be copied and distributed widely as pamphlets and printed books. Indeed, using such a pamphlet was how Karl Marx promoted his idea of a workers' revolution and inspired the rise of communism. Prior to this, painstaking and slow handwritten copies were the only means of reproducing a text. Printing presses were expensive, and some of those who owned them eventually became the publishing companies printing and distributing the books that we read today. Digital connectivity has changed this dynamic materially with messages not even requiring physical printing (or delivery) any more due to their readability on screens and the ability to share, forward and/or copy and paste information. In that sense, today (to an extent) everyone who has access to that connectivity is a publisher and there is little or no immediate cost involved.

Coming back to the idea of technology dividing people, this can be seen in the 'filter bubble' effect wherein people only access certain kinds of information. Digital algorithms also work to exacerbate this as the services or apps you use repeatedly serve you similar content in order to keep you engaged and/or to target you with advertising. This creates a digital echo chamber that serves to reconfirm the biases and political leanings of the user – pushing them further away from conciliatory or moderate positions. This is exacerbated further with the phenomenon of 'fake news', where false stories spread on the internet or other media because they are made to appear like stories from legitimate news outlets. Many of these are intended to stoke division, reduce trust in authority for profit-seeking or nefarious purposes and in some cases are even propagated by nation-states as part of an information warfare strategy. Russia, China and Iran have been heavily implicated in the latter, perhaps most notably Russia in its hybrid warfare campaign in Ukraine since 2014 and its attempts to influence voters in the 2016 US election.

Assuring the reliability of information has become increasingly difficult when tracing the origins of a story: both corroborating its complete factuality and countering the appeal of that false information can be very difficult with such a complex chain of human and computer (automated) interactions. All kinds of human activity have been afforded new avenues for proliferation, and fake news has parallels with age-old practices of propaganda, as the second case study in the chapter illustrates. With all these connectivity-enabled processes, some individuals are more vulnerable than others to its capacities for adverse uses. This highlights the important point that connectivity is often a reflection or intensification of pre-existent social structures and disparities, rather than containing any intrinsic emancipatory or authoritarian nature.

Reliance and vulnerability

Digital devices are inseparable from the new logistics and communications that are increasingly underpinning human activity. The most familiar devices are personal computers (desktops and laptops), smartphones and tablets. For many people it is impossible to imagine life without the instant connectivity and wealth of information provided by the internet and accessed through such devices. Devices have thus become an integral, perhaps indispensable, part of human life. Using the internet for many of our basic human functions, both individual and societal, effectively requires the internet to make up part of what it means to be human. These ideas have a long pedigree. In 1945 Vannevar Bush introduced his idea of a 'memex', which he described as:

> a device in which an individual stores all [their] books, records, and communications, and which is mechanized so that it may be consulted with exceeding speed and flexibility. It is an enlarged intimate supplement to [their] memory. (Bush 1945)

Eerily prescient, Bush's description accurately describes smartphones six decades before they emerged. The implication of this is that, thanks to such a device, the limited human mind can be freed up to perform greater capacities to imagine, associate and experiment. Of course, it is important to recognise that the spread of these technologies has by no means been total or equal. Even within relatively affluent societies such as the UK, 'the digital divide' still pares along those distributions of wealth, geography, gender and age that people were already experiencing. Connectivity and its undoubted benefits, like most things in human experience, do not afford the same opportunities to everyone equally.

20.4 – KEY INSIGHT: Contact tracing Covid-19

During the Covid-19 pandemic, governments around the world sought to utilise the near ubiquitous spread of smartphones in their societies to deploy contact-tracing surveillance technologies. If smartphones could be made to communicate with each other (for example through Bluetooth) they could help track the spread of the virus and alert people who had been in the proximity of someone who had contracted the virus. Apple and Google agreed to partner together to retool their software to provide these services through apps running on their respective smartphone platforms. This partnership specified that the apps governments develop cannot be mandatory for citizens, but must be opt-in (Google 2020). Much back and forth was done between Apple, Google and governments over how to ensure the personal data accumulated conformed to basic norms of privacy – for example concerning how and where it was stored and the degree to which is was encrypted. In this example, we have two corporations setting the terms available for a major aspect of sovereign states' technological management of a health crisis.

Of course, such reliance on technology can have negative consequences. If these technologies were to disappear or be denied to us, we could potentially lose some of our sense of identity and collective culture. Examples of Myanmar's internet services being shut down during the 2021 military coup demonstrate the large-scale vulnerability of the technology, as do the cyber-attacks on Estonia in 2007 that lost citizens access to essential services such as banking. Consider Facebook, a social networking platform with almost three billion users. Facebook, when taken together with Instagram (both owned by Meta), are used today (amongst other things) as photograph repositories, thereby becoming an archive of visual memories. If the internet malfunctioned, Facebook, Instagram and the memories they contain would be inaccessible, making abstract technological vulnerability relatable to us at an individual level. The example of memories shows how over-reliance on technology for important human functions may carry risks at new scales or scope.

State actors have also found ways to harness connectivity for their own ends. Revelations in documents leaked by the whistle-blower Edward Snowden in 2013 showed the extent of the United States' intelligence capabilities in cyberspace, many of which were predicated on the fact that most internet traffic originates from, terminates in or transits through servers based within the United States. This of course gives the United States a huge advantage, as it enjoys unprecedented access to the flow of information on the internet. The alarm expressed by American and British authorities in recent years to incursions of Chinese technology from firms like Huawei may well be born of this direct experience: there is no more vigorous a gamekeeper than an experienced poacher.

Recognising this disparity, and also reacting to alleged infringements of their own citizens' rights, several states have called for a move to a model in which states ensure data stays within their own borders. Where this is not possible, data would be handled in accordance with the law of its origin state, backed up by an international governance framework – see Kohl (2017) for more on these different state perspectives. Though this could redress the imbalance of power, it also has the potential to 'Balkanise' (carve up) the internet. Many of the benefits of the internet rely on the technology being uniformly functional and accessible across disparate geographical areas. A Balkanised internet would inevitably produce a range of operating standards that might well be difficult to integrate. China is an example of a state that operates a state internet policy, although for different reasons to those expressed above. Through the 'Great Firewall', the Chinese government blocks access to sources of uncensored information such as foreign news outlets and prominent websites like Facebook, Google and Wikipedia. The full benefits of global connectivity are clearly not available to the bulk of Chinese users, showing how control of the technology could be a powerful tool for controlling a population. Likewise, governments have been able to utilise connectivity for spying on dissidents and individuals using everyday items like WhatsApp and iPhones to target individuals they want to monitor.

Such reliance on networked technologies can bring societal-wide risks too. To understand why many industrialised state actors are so concerned about cybersecurity and cyberwarfare, it is necessary to understand how the technologies many of us use every day relate to these society-wide dynamics. Nearly every aspect of contemporary life has some aspect controlled by or connected to networked communications. Everything from the electricity and water supplies to our homes, to the roads and public transport systems, to the banking system, to the satellites that help us navigate. Each are reliant on the smooth functioning of a complex array of networked communication technologies. Bugs and vulnerabilities can thus emerge as undiscovered flaws in the software and hardware that make up cyberspace. Such flaws can be present in the systems from the day of their launch: discovering all the potential bugs in the millions of lines of code in a piece of equipment or software is time-consuming and not always economically viable for the vendors. They can also arise as different pieces of software, hardware and users interact and behave in ways that designers did not or could not anticipate given their enormous complexity and the way that new systems get added on to old systems. Vulnerabilities can also be intentionally exploited. This happens at all kinds of levels, from individual hackers accessing systems for personal or financial gain, to organised criminal groups exploiting vulnerabilities, to state-level intelligence and military agencies investing in the tools to spy and fight via cyberspace.

20.5 – KEY TERMS: WannaCry

Photo 20.3 Screenshot of a WannaCry ransomware attack on Windows 8

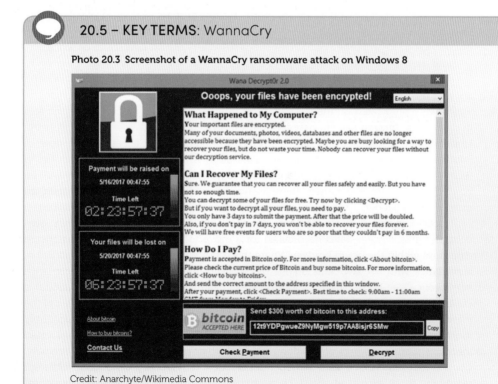

Credit: Anarchyte/Wikimedia Commons

In May 2017, a computer worm called WannaCry made headlines when it worked its way through unpatched Microsoft Windows systems across the world. A computer 'worm' is different from a computer 'virus' because a virus depends on a host program to spread itself, whereas a worm can self-replicate without human interaction. The worm was designed to encrypt the hard drives of affected systems, which could only be unlocked by users paying a ransom to the designers of the worm (Photo 20.3). This 'ransomware' locked the computers of schools, hospitals, factories and shops. The impact that the incident had on the UK's National Health Service (NHS) demonstrates how complex it can be to manage the risks of connectivity: the environmental challenges posed by the need for 'open' systems, combined with old infrastructure and the effects of fiscal constraint left them particularly vulnerable (Dwyer 2018). While it spread quickly and affected as many as 200,000 hard drives in 150 countries within 48 hours, the significance of the event lies in its story of its building blocks.

In August 2016, a hacker group calling itself the Shadow Brokers released data that originated from US National Security Agency servers. One of these hacking tools was 'EternalBlue', so called because of its tendency to inflict the blue-screen crash symptoms exhibited by malfunctioning Windows computers. The malicious code at the heart of the WannaCry ransomware was this same piece of coding, obtained from the internet and reconstructed by cybercriminals for the purposes of extortion. Here we see a worst-case scenario, whereby a government agency has invested significant resources into developing tools that can exploit the connectivity afforded by cyberspace, only for those tools to be repurposed by criminal groups. But this incident also underscores another issue: as Christensen and Liebtrau (2019) highlight, those nations that are most connected are also the most vulnerable.

At the international level, connectivity's effects and even the terminology and legal rules for how to deal with other states in cyberspace are still being worked out. On the one hand, states are concerned by the potential security issues that this reliance on connectivity may pose, both from accidental failures and malicious exploitation. But on the other hand, states are also spending a great deal of money in developing tools and techniques to exploit this connectivity for their own military and intelligence purposes. However, there are few 'cyber' terms for which there is universal agreement. Because cyberspace permeates so much of the global economy and infrastructure, governments have not been restrained in their use of the 'cyber' prefix, with activities as wide-ranging as warfare, terrorism and crime to e-government, commerce and social goods all being brought together under the concern of national security. For many advanced industrial states, 'cyberspace' and 'cyber security' are therefore prominent features of national security policy discourses.

CASE STUDY 20.1: Harnessing information for different ends

A smartphone is many times more powerful than the computer onboard Apollo 11 that guided NASA's astronauts to the moon in 1969. Smartphones are therefore not just powerful and compact, but the connectivity afforded by the internet amplifies their capacity and convenience. As a result, many people around the world have come to rely on these devices in their daily lives, storing the kinds of data, location history and personal preferences that historically would never have been concentrated in a single location. Such connectivity has afforded a huge range of benefits, offering individuals access to a vast array of information and social interactivity and new forms of expression.

The optimism in the early years of the new millennium suggested that the empowerment provided by individuals' unfettered access to information would have potentially revolutionary consequences, such as the overthrow of repressive regimes. However, the benefits of connectivity are not uniformly experienced as authoritarian regimes are

Photo 20.4 Mark Zuckerberg, co-founder and CEO of Meta, testifies at a joint Senate commerce/judiciary hearing in Washington, DC, 10 April 2018

Credit: Pool/Getty Images

harnessing a new arsenal of digital tools to maintain their positions, supplementing established repressive techniques but with increased intensity, scale or speed.

The 'Pegasus' software offers a useful insight into some of these dynamics. In October 2019, WhatsApp filed a lawsuit in US federal courts against a cyber surveillance firm, NSO group, claiming that technology designed by that company had piggybacked on WhatsApp to spy on more than 1,400 people in twenty states. This included journalists and human rights activists. NSO's technology, called 'Pegasus', silently deploys invisible software on an individual's smartphone or device. Controllers of Pegasus can then track users' calls, collect usernames and passwords, find the infected device's location and access the phone's camera and microphone. NSO claimed that it is 'lawful interception' technology designed to help governments prevent crime and terrorism. However, it is also easy for the governments and organisations that buy the technology to misuse it. Citizen Lab, a public interest organisation devoted to monitoring the freedom of the internet (see Maschmeyer, Deibert and Lindsay 2020), has tracked the use of Pegasus by operators of the spyware across forty-five countries, not all of them legitimate national law enforcement operations. NSO gained notoriety in 2016 after Citizen Lab produced evidence that the United Arab Emirates had used Pegasus to spy on human rights activist Ahmed Mansoor,

who has since been sentenced to ten years in prison for social media posts. In another case in Morocco, an activist targeted with Pegasus spyware described this surveillance as 'a type of punishment. You can't behave freely. It is part of their strategy to make you suspect you're being watched so you feel like you're under pressure all the time' (Amnesty 2019).

First, this illustrates that although connectivity has helped facilitate protests and political mobilisations, there are some digitally shrewd authoritarian regimes using those same innovations to reinforce older methods of control. Data from the *Varieties of Democracy*'s data set and the *Mass Mobilization Project* suggest that autocracies that use digital repression face a lower risk of protests than those autocratic regimes who do not. This same analysis also suggests that the authoritarian regimes that rely more heavily on digital repression are among the most durable (Kendall-Taylor, Frantz and Wright 2020). Regimes can use tools such as Pegasus to target their efforts more precisely, and this research suggests the dictatorships that use digital repression also tend to increase their use of violent 'real life' methods such as torture and killing. States can buy these capabilities on an international and unregulated market. Secondly, the Pegasus case study also illustrates the darker side of innovation afforded by connectivity: NSO's business is part of a multi-billion-dollar economy of digital surveillance tools. The benefits afforded by connectivity are therefore not uniformly experienced, with the vulnerability of individuals often a reflection of their wider social and political contexts.

This relates to a third point, namely that connectivity is not being harnessed by solely authoritarian regimes. In early 2018 it was revealed that a company called Cambridge Analytica had collected personal data from up to 87 million people's Facebook profiles without their consent and used it to develop 'micro-targeted' political adverts for Brexit in the UK and for presidential campaigns in the United States. This information allowed political campaigns to slice up the electorate into distinct niches and then appeal to them with precisely tailored communications. These highly partisan messages frequently get shared across social media platforms, amplifying the effect of the message. Due to the magnitude of the issue, Meta's CEO Mark Zuckerberg was summoned to the US Congress (Photo 20.4) to give testimony.

Despite the controversy around Cambridge Analytica, this utilisation of the 'data exhaust' generated by individuals is not unique to this company. Micro-targeted ads of one kind or another will be a feature of most party-political campaigns in the future, promising political campaigners a hitherto unparalleled precision in messaging to individual voters. Such examples make it harder to discern truthful and accurate information from disinformation and falsehoods intended to mislead or persuade. These dynamics are further complicated by the tendency for social media networks to produce 'echo chambers', where the preferences of individuals across the whole political spectrum reinforce the kinds of stories that fill their news feeds. Rather than empowering informed debate, this can have the effect of isolating different social groups from each other – which takes us back to the question posed at the start of this chapter.

CASE STUDY 20.2: 'Cyber warfare' or conflict?

Photo 20.5 President Putin chairs a meeting of Russia's Council for Strategic Development and National Projects, 13 July 2020

Credit: Alexei Druzhinin/TASS/Getty Images

In November 2018, the US military blocked the internet access of a Russian organisation that had been seeking to sow discord amongst American voters during the midterm elections. According to US government officials, this operation against a company called the Internet Research Agency in St Petersburg was part of the first offensive cyber-campaign intended to thwart attempts to interfere with a US election. The operation was undertaken by a joint task force at the National Security Agency (NSA) and US Cyber Command, both of whom operate as part of the United States Department of Defense. The United States is not alone in establishing a military branch dedicated to 'computer network operations' – those deliberate actions that employ devices, computer programmes and techniques to create effects through cyberspace. Dozens of states around the world now have dedicated military units with this focus, as seen on the Council on Foreign Relations' Cyber Operations Tracker (2020).

This case study seems to fit the bill for cyber warfare. However, when we look a bit more closely at the details and the political contexts of this operation, we can begin to see how the parameters of cyber warfare are still being worked out on the international stage. First, different states have different notions of what is 'cyber' about cyber warfare. This has important ramifications for the kinds of action they can take, and the kinds of organisations involved. In this example, the US military undertook this operation because the Internet Research Agency had been named as a key agent in a disinformation campaign that targeted American voters in the 2016 presidential election. Through falsified social media posts and targeted advertising, the campaign's goal was to 'provoke and amplify political and social discord' in the United States, according to court documents issued after an investigation in 2016. Russia-backed content reached as many as 126 million Americans on Facebook during and after the 2016 presidential election.

The Internet Research Agency was not a military organisation but was still able to undertake a form of cyber warfare. This is because Russia, led by Vladimir Putin (Photo 20.5), has a fundamentally different conception of the role of computer network operations. Russia does not generally use the term 'cyber' or 'cyber warfare,' except when referring to foreign approaches to the topic. Instead, like the Chinese, they conceptualise computer network operations within the broader rubric of information warfare (*informatsionnaya voyna*). The Internet Research Agency's activities were thus viewed as an extension of long-standing Russian ideas about employing all state means, short of war, to achieve its national objectives. These actions are just one element of a wider spectrum of political subversion techniques, disinformation and psychological operations. In Russia, distinctions between peace and war are not as ingrained as they are in American strategic thinking. This conceptualisation of information warfare means that it is not only military or intelligence organisations that take part in Russia but a whole-of-state effort. Unlike the US approach, the Russian approach to its offence is therefore not compartmentalised into military branches acting online.

Second, this case study highlights how cyber warfare is characterised by persistent low-level disruptions that are part of broader political actions, rather than a condition of a specified interstate conflict that takes place solely online. There may be many military units developing computer network operations capabilities globally, but this is not some devastating new form of warfare that a typical citizen can undertake. It takes a great deal of resources to undertake these kinds of operations. Furthermore, while state actors have reached broad consensus about what constitutes an 'act of force' in the context of cyberspace operations, in this example, both actors were careful to stay below this threshold under international law and the UN Charter. Instead, this new context is characterised by 'persistent engagement' – intense skirmishing that is part of a broader spectrum of actions rather than an isolated 'weapon-like' capability. As a case in point, the US government used criminal charges and indictments as well as sanctions in the case of the Internet Research Agency, demonstrating how computer network operations can also be used in conjunction with other tools of state power. Cyber-based retaliation is not the only way to respond to cyber incidents.

This affair underlines the extent to which the parameters for cyber warfare are still being worked out for many states domestically as much as internationally. While Russia had been using a private company to undertake information operations, long-held distinctions in US thinking between peacetime and wartime activities and military and non-military actors, together with the fact that the United States was not formally in a state of war with Russia, meant that US Cyber Command would have had to get special authorisations. For example, a presidential order in 2017 gave Cyber Command greater latitude to undertake offensive operations below the level of armed conflict, without which they would have been legally constrained from targeting civilian organisations like Internet Research Agency. Furthermore, the Cyber Command operations appear relatively contained, especially in comparison with the increasingly sophisticated efforts by Russia to use disinformation to sow widespread dissent in Western countries. The American campaign undertaken in response to Russia's information offensive is limited in large part to keep Moscow from escalating its response by conducting some reprisal that could trigger a larger disagreement between great powers.

Though the Internet Research Agency operations did not interfere with the election or voting processes themselves, which would have constituted an act of aggression under international laws of war, they did use connectivity to target individual voters' relationships with those election processes. The operations also undermined confidence in the election processes. This also suggests the new challenges that authorities will increasingly face in protecting the individual in the cyber sphere from malign actors' conduct. It also illustrates how cyber conflict is simultaneously a more prevalent and more mundane occurrence than the much more specialised practices of cyber warfare. Yet, regardless of categorisation, the cyber realm is already becoming one where states are racing to establish superiority. In much the same way as air superiority and nuclear superiority emerged at key strategic points in the twentieth century, cyber superiority will increasingly be a buzzword of the future in political and military disputes.

Conclusion

The devices and digital services that bring us together are also the source of dangers and divisions because the internet is an ambivalent technology that can be put to diverse uses. It can support, undermine or exacerbate any pre-existing social relations, depending on the context and actors involved. These uses can be empowering, but these effects can also be unforeseen, or even dangerous. In the era of digital connectivity, old human activities are finding new avenues. What is different is the intensity, scale and speed. These communication technologies have no inherent nature, no natural essence that make them either democratic or authoritarian. Like all human tools, networked communication technologies can be put to different uses at different times, whilst also shaping the social context in which they are used. While cyberspace is complex and decentralised, it is also important not to lose sight of the significance of individuals. Through participation in logistics and communications, digital or otherwise, each person has the potential to affect the process and progress of international relations. The rules governing this space are still in the making. Technology is not driving history: people are shaping technologies to their own ends, while those new technologies are simultaneously shaping society. This is what makes it such a fascinating topic and a central global issue.

 END OF CHAPTER QUESTIONS

1. On balance, do you think the internet has been a force for good? Put your thoughts in a 'for' and 'against' list. Compare and contrast your list with three other people. Where are the points of overlap and contrast?

2. Who, if anyone, is responsible for fighting disinformation that spreads over the internet? Do you think new tools are needed for addressing this – if so, where should these powers be located (with the state, transnational corporations or with international organisations etc.)?

3. In the internet-connected era, to what extent are private companies more powerful than nation-states? What implications does this have for the nature of the global system in the years ahead?

4. What role will communications and the internet play in the future development of conflict, such as with the idea of cyber warfare? Do you think such developments are as significant as when nuclear weapons emerged in 1945?

5. In what ways does it make you feel like an active global citizen knowing that you can 'publish' your thoughts and actions on the internet and potentially influence millions of people?

REFLECTING ON INTERNATIONAL RELATIONS

International Relations has grown from a discipline only interested in one major issue – warfare between states – to shine a light on virtually every element of the global system. As has been outlined throughout the book, this goes right down to the level of individuals and how we live our lives, and moves up to the most complex global structures that interweave through nation-states and international organisations. Attempting to draw a line under something as vast as this recalls an old lesson that endings are more difficult to write than beginnings. This is especially true of the idea that anyone can conclude something as vibrant, messy, incoherent, exciting and ever-changing as the discipline of International Relations. Instead of taking on such a futile endeavour, this final part of the book draws together some personal reflections that touch on many of the larger themes we have explored. More importantly, it also reaches beyond normal textbook debates to give you a sense of momentum to build a bridge towards the more expert literature and debates that will shape the rest of your studies. The hope is that it will leave a lasting impression, inspire you to stay engaged with the discipline, and to think more deeply and widely about how each issue within International Relations' gaze may affect all of us in one way or another.

CROSSINGS AND CANDLES

Peter Vale

Question: W. L. Watkinson once wrote: 'It is better to light a candle than curse the darkness'. Is this a helpful analogy to draw upon when reflecting on International Relations?

I have found it difficult to even begin writing about the world international relations makes without reflecting on a nearly fifty-year career in both the theory and practice of the discipline. This is because my engagement in it is indivisible from who I am. To make the same point in a slightly more elevated mode, although trained in the tradition that a scholar's gaze is objective, my academic journey has been one of continuous crossings between the personal, the political and the professional. My early career was conducted during a particularly nasty period of apartheid in 1970s South Africa. Not only was the minority-white-ruled government cracking down on all forms of political dissent, it was also wedded to a fierce anti-communism. In these circumstances it was difficult to exercise objectivity when it came to thinking about things political. Those years taught me a valuable lesson in life and learning: to believe that there is a totally objective or value-free view in International Relations is to call up the old Russian proverb that 'he lied like an eyewitness!' We all come to know the world through our own experiences. Because of this, even the most objective person has predetermined understandings about the world.

The four-minute mile

To appreciate why this all matters, I will begin with a story of a crossing between my colonial boyhood and my ageing self. Growing up in the post-Second World War South Africa, our home was littered with nostalgia for England – a country that my mother never visited until she was fifty. The cultural accoutrements in our home – books, music, food – signalled that our family's true place was in the Empire, not in Africa. In addition, the boarding school that I attended was loosely modelled on the English public school. Here, we were encouraged to participate in the forms of organised sport that were England's 'gift' to the world. Understandably, then, my earliest thinking about what made 'the international' was set by the cultural claims of England and the political sweep of the British Empire.

Given this, the story of Roger Bannister's sub-four-minute mile had a particular appeal for my young self. To explain: the measured mile became an important test in competitive athletics in the early 1950s. It was long believed that no person could run a mile in under four minutes. But, in the aftermath of the Second World War, when physical training and nutrition improved along with the instruments for timing, the four-minute mile came closer and closer to being 'conquered'. Indeed, breaking the barrier became a sort of milestone for both individual athletes and for the countries they represented.

 21.1 – KEY INSIGHTS: The British Empire

Map 21.1 The countries never invaded by the British

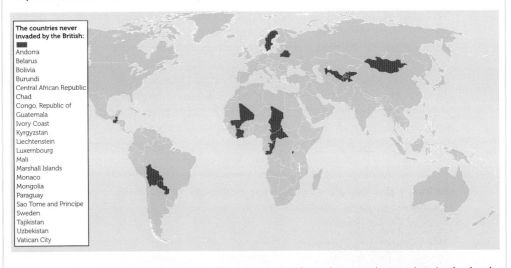

The countries never invaded by the British:

Andorra
Belarus
Bolivia
Burundi
Central African Republic
Chad
Congo, Republic of
Guatemala
Ivory Coast
Kyrgyzstan
Liechtenstein
Luxembourg
Mali
Marshall Islands
Monaco
Mongolia
Paraguay
Sao Tome and Principe
Sweden
Tajikistan
Uzbekistan
Vatican City

We have explored the idea, and historical experiences, of empire at various points in the book. However, none has had an impact as enduring as the British Empire. With its origins in the late 1400s, by the 1700s the British Empire had surpassed its rivals to become the world's most powerful empire. By 1913 approximately 23 per cent of the world's population and 24 per cent of the earth's landmass were encompassed within it. A more striking statistic that illustrates the sheer scale of the imperial competition between Britain and its rivals is that only twenty-two of today's 193 nation states were not invaded, colonised or somehow intruded upon by British forces at some point in history (see Map 21.1 and Laycock 2012). The legacy of the British Empire today endures in the Commonwealth of Nations – an association of over fifty of Britain's former colonies. But it can perhaps be seen more pervasively in the widespread use of the English language – which is the most spoken of the Earth's languages (when counting those who speak it as a second language). It is widely regarded as the primary global language of business, and for that matter the primary language in which International Relations communicates.

My initial fascination with the four-minute mile was ignited by an edition of the *Eagle Sports Album*, which had been sent to my school library from London. In its pages, much was made of the importance of Bannister's feat for Britain and Britons like my family, and others at the school, who were located in distant corners of the world. The drama of the event whetted a life-long interest in athletics. Finally, while on a trip to Oxford in October 2015, I visited the field on the Iffley Road where Bannister ran the famous measured mile. Two signs on Iffley Road declare Bannister's triumph. The first, which is mounted on a stone gatepost, announces, 'Here at the Iffley Road Track the first sub-four minute mile was run on 6th May 1954 by ROGER BANNISTER' (Photo 21.1). The second is positioned above a wooden fence facing the Iffley Road. Under the crest of Oxford University, proclaiming, 'Here, on 6 May 1954, Roger Bannister set a new world mile record of 3 minutes 59.4 seconds. The first mile ever run under 4 minutes'. If the first sign informs, the second proclaims Bannister's achievement as truth, and leaves no room for doubt – at this site history was made.

But more important was the slow realisation that what had happened on that famous day offered lessons in how I had first come to know and understand the world of International Relations. Until then, it never occurred to me that what had taken place on the day of the event was a quintessential moment of modernity – the conquering of space by time. The Iffley Road field was the site of the first 'timed', 'authenticated' or 'measured' mile run under four minutes. But – and this is why critical questioning is important in International Relations, as it is in all forms of knowledge – it seems unlikely that nobody else, anywhere else, across human history had ever run this distance in under four minutes.

In reality, Bannister had positioned the distance within a Western – and purportedly 'universal' – measure of time. This spectacle of the achievement was a moment of manufactured truth, a move that is integral to the idea of modernity wherein the West asserts its superiority. But time's averred authority has also been used to claim that the 'primitive', 'time-less', 'ungoverned' non-West is ready for 'timely' intervention (Nanni 2012). The analogue of measured time in International Relations is sovereignty: to become sovereign is to obliterate the past and arrive in the present. So, sovereignty delivers modernity's order to premodern, 'anarchic' spaces. Indeed, bringing ungoverned places into the modern idea of 'the international' is the first order of business in the discipline.

Photo 21.1 Blue plaque at Iffley Road Track, Oxford, UK

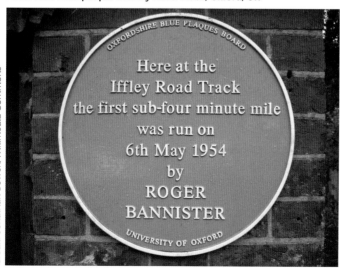

Credit: Jonathan Bowen/Wikimedia Commons

However, the divide drawn by the instruments of modernity is not the tightly patrolled frontier with its passports, visas, immigration documents and the like. It is a social space – contested, contingent and endlessly constructed – where inclusion and exclusion are continuously negotiated. So, there were (as there remain) forms of interaction between groups who have resisted incorporation into the command and control that sovereignty dictates are the 'gift' of statehood. This betwixt-and-between space has been a site of great tragedy, as endless migrant crises show. In many places, outside the authoritative gaze of state-centred reporting, these sites are killing fields. European colonisation, which drew the furthest corners on the planet into sovereign-centred order, was extremely violent. If killing was one dimension of this, another was the disruption to the ways of life of millions upon millions.

One example was a 1965 agreement in which late-imperial Britain 'gave' a number of islands in the Indian Ocean to the United States. The residents of this archipelago, known collectively as the Chagos Islands, were forcibly moved. Since then, the islanders themselves and their descendants have made numerous unsuccessful legal attempts to overturn this decision. Tragedies like these which occur at the margins of the world have often been ignored by the discipline.

Another thing that occurred to me at that field in Oxford is the power of who pronounces on these matters. This is the issue of 'voice': who gets to speak, how they get to speak and why this happens. At the policy end of International Relations, alas, the issue of voice is seldom considered a priority issue, notwithstanding the path-breaking insights that feminists have gifted the discipline. They have exposed the multiple ways in which women (and others at the margins) experience the international differently to men and how they are silenced in the telling of its story despite the significant roles they have played in its making.

21.2 – KEY PEOPLE: Graça Machel

Photo 21.2 Graça Machel, November 2014

Credit: Eric Roset/Africa Progress Panel/Flickr

Graça Machel was born in south-eastern Africa into a family that spoke the Shangaan language. Her father, a Methodist minister, died before she was born. A church scholarship enabled her to enrol at Lisbon University where she became politically active. In 1973 she joined the Mozambican Liberation Front (FRELIMO), which was waging a guerrilla war against Portuguese colonialism. Although trained to fight, Machel was devoted to education and helped to run a FRELIMO school while exiled in Tanzania. Following the liberation of Mozambique in 1975, she was appointed its Minister of Education and Culture. She was 30 years old. Within a decade, she had overseen large increases in school attendance and material rises in literacy. Today, her passion for these (and similar) issues extends far beyond Mozambique. Machel is a founding member and co-Deputy Chair of 'The Elders', a group of influential global figures working together for peace, justice and human rights. It was founded by her second husband, Nelson Mandela. Her first husband, Samora Machel, was Mozambique's first president.

For many, even today, International Relations remains mortgaged to the understandings of race, class and gender that were common in the decades of its founding. In many corners of the world, International Relations is called a 'mutant' discipline (Vale 2016). A field of knowledge that seems to have no conceptual capacity – no grammar or vocabulary, as theorists might say – to explain the everyday lives of people whom it has systematically excluded.

The fact of my early life was that the empire into which I was born was fading. The claims to its waning authority by the celebration of its history and achievements – like Bannister's run – must be seen in the context of Britain's changing place in the post-Second World War world. The dilemma it faced was best captured by the then US Secretary of State Dean Acheson, who famously pointed out that 'Great Britain … [has] … lost an empire and has not yet found a role' (1962).

Although no longer an imperial power, the United Kingdom's hold on the imagination of the world – and how it is organised and studied through International Relations – continues via its culture and language. It appears, however, in some perverse ways. In the late 1960s, Richard Turnbull, the governor of the colony of Aden (in today's Yemen), told a future British cabinet minister, Denis Healey, that 'when the British Empire finally sank beneath the waves of history it would leave behind only two monuments: one was the game of Football, the other was the expression, "Fuck Off"' (Healey 1989, 283). Though a vulgar phrase like this is seldom heard in polite circles, British cultural imperialism lingers in the discipline, which explains why English is its tongue. This suggests another relationship between International Relations and modernity. The third instrument of modernity, after time and sovereignty, is language. Like the other two, the English language has set the borderlines for inclusion and exclusion in the world and, in its study, through International Relations.

21.3 – KEY TERMS: Soft, hard and smart power

When Joseph Nye (1990) coined the phrase '**soft power**' to describe a state's power of attraction – its ability to persuade others to follow its policy preferences/directions – he helpfully contributed a term that could be used to account for the ways a state could influence other states to take certain courses of action short of any direct pressure. Soft power, then, has an opposite – **hard power** – which describes when a state uses coercive means to achieve its aims against a competitor. Typically, this would involve punitive economic sanctions or warfare of some sort. In the modern era, warfare does not have to be troops on the ground fighting (kinetic military action), but can be done via cyber, intelligence or other means.

Hard power and soft power are rarely used in isolation, especially as when both are taken to their extremes they become a liability to the success and survival of states (such as being too aggressive, or too passive in their international relations). It is more common for states to blend elements of the two into a **smart power** approach. This involves maintaining a significant deterrent through a powerful military – but also investing in multilateralism and international organisations to promote a good image internationally.

The place of language and culture in fostering international relationships is explained by the idea of soft power. This concept helpfully drew the issue of culture towards the centre of International Relations but, sadly, was silent on the controlling dimensions of language. This is because English has been proclaimed a 'global language' and purportedly is objective in its views of the ways of the world. But no language is neutral. Two observations suggest the limitations of having a monopoly of one language. The first draws upon the thinking of the Austrian philosopher Ludwig Wittgenstein, who pointed to the conceptual limitations of language, caught in his famous claim, 'the limits of my language mean the limits of my world'. So, however commanding language is as a tool to access the social world, its vocabulary sets limits on our understanding. Second, if English remains the language of International Relations, the discipline will not only be the domain of a global elite but will continue its long history of serving and servicing insiders only. Those who have no knowledge of English are excluded, or they can only access the discipline by developing a professional competence in the language. This is plainly limiting because the English language is sometimes unable to grasp concepts that lie outside its vocabulary. For instance, the Sanskrit word 'dharma' is sometimes translated as 'religion', but dharma in the Hindu cosmology includes a range of practices and conceptions of rights, duties, law and so on, which are not divinely ordained as in Christianity. Other important terms in the vocabulary of International Relations – such as the 'state', 'civilisation' and 'order' – are often lost in translation.

World-making

One disciplinary shibboleth is that International Relations is a neutral instrument of restoration – it does not so much 'make' the world as 'restore' it (Kissinger 2013). According to this logic, the discipline provides helpful tools and, sometimes, a hopeful heart that a world devastated by war can be restored by the discipline's science. But here too there is a need for a contrarian view. Largely absent from this optimism are the interlinked questions: who has the right to remake the world and whose interests will be served by any remaking? These questions would not have troubled those responsible for making (or remaking) the international community on three previous occasions: at the end of the South African War (1899–1902); at the end of the First World War (1914–18); and at the end of the Second World War (1939–45). Certainly, each of these is presented as a moment of despair interlaced with feelings of hope for what might come; each was marked by a particular configuration of politics, both local and global; and each was held captive by the vocabulary of the hour. Let's consider them in turn.

The South African War (also known as the Second Boer War and the Anglo-Boer War) was fought between the British Empire and the peoples of European descent on African soil known as Afrikaners who spoke a polyglot language. The war was fought over the riches that were found beneath the land which would come to be called South Africa. Although fought on the African continent, the war's form was decidedly European. This was because the Westphalian state, and the diplomatic routines developing around it, had migrated from its European heartland to Africa. It was the culmination of many contestations for the positioning of an alien social form, the modern nation-state, on a new continent. As recent work has shown, the making of the world after the South African War was concerned with reorganising the British Empire, which was then the dominant form of international organisation (Thakur, Davis and Vale 2017).

The idea of shifting understandings of what constituted sovereign identity away from an imperial setting towards a species of 'inter-nation' exchange, primarily between Britain and its four settler-ruled vassals – Australia, Canada, New Zealand and South Africa – gained salience in the years following the First World War. If the three other dominions showed that the local and the international could be seamlessly realigned, South Africa – with its diverse peoples – was a harbinger of the messy assumptions around this idea. Hence, for the theoreticians of the empire, the reorganisation of the colonies in southern Africa into the single state of South Africa foreshadowed a model for the reconfiguration of empire. Thus, the chosen path was the idea of an 'organic union', a system that gestured towards the importance of sovereignty within the semblance of an imperial brotherhood – in modern terms, it was a peculiar strain of multilateralism.

Out of this, in the 1930s, grew the idea of a white-dominated 'World Commonwealth', sometimes called a 'World State' (Curtis 1938). The thought crime (there is no other phrase for it) in this world-making was that all the imaginings of the international excluded other racial groups except in the quasi-religious category of 'trusteeship'. After the First World War, the latter status was awarded to states that could be 'trusted' to control foreign spaces in the interests of those who were deemed to be lower down the Darwinian ladder (Curtis 1918, 13).

In the lore of International Relations, the restoration of the world after the First World War has become sacred ground. The discipline's celebrated tale is how the international codified as science would build a better world. The discipline's institutionalisation was the founding of an academic chair, named after Woodrow Wilson, America's twenty-eighth president, at what is now Aberystwyth University in Wales. This gesture towards the United States suggests that the establishment of the discipline was in recognition of America's role in ending the so-called 'war to end all wars'. Not only did the United States help to deliver victory over Germany but its president proposed the League of Nations as an instrument for securing a future of world peace. But this was not to be. In the 1930s, the League failed to prevent another war – the idealism of early International Relations, around which the academic discipline was founded, was in tatters. The failure of this resolve, both institutionally and theoretically, is well documented in the histories of the discipline.

The folklore of international history holds that the post-Second World War order is indebted to the triumph of American interventionism. An end to supposed American isolationism in the 1940s beckoned it towards a reincarnation of its 'Manifest Destiny' – rooted in the nineteenth-century belief that settlers were foreordained to spread across North America. As the Maryland Democratic politician and judge, William F. Giles, succinctly summarised in 1847:

> We must march from ocean to ocean ... We must march from Texas straight to the Pacific Ocean, and be bounded only by its roaring wave ... It is the destiny of the white race, it is the destiny of the Anglo-Saxon race (quoted in Zinn 1980, 153).

With the Second World War at an end, Americans were seemingly called to embark on global responsibilities during the Cold War, a phrase first uttered by Bernard Baruch on 16 April 1947. The construction of a new world was to be sought through the idea of liberalism, which could marry free, strong government and multilateralism (Ruggie 1982). But the inconvenient truth remained: global apartheid was entrenched. Absent in the great councils of peace (and its making) were those excluded by International Relations' founding bargain – the non-white peoples of the world, although they were knocking at the very doors of the great chambers of deliberation. The fact was that sovereignty, and the passport it offered to participation, was still chiefly available to those privileged by birth and by skin colour.

Linked to the idea of 'self-determination', the new sense of freedom was infectious and spread to all spaces – especially colonised ones. Sadly, International Relations' engagement with this sense of optimism was quickly captured by the ideology of the Cold War with its zero-sum logic. Also lacking was an understanding of history, which would have taught us that the Haitian Revolution (1791–1804) was a powerful example of Black people making a state, conducting diplomacy and practising freedom. Instead the desirability of 'progress' rested on the conquest of nature by science. It is difficult today to underestimate 'the endless frontier' – as American scientist, Vannevar Bush (1945), called natural science – as the Second World War ended. Demonstrably, the atom bomb, the quintessential product of science, brought the fighting to a close – even though the effects on Japan foreshadowed different understandings of what science had delivered to the people of the world. After a second atom bomb was dropped on Nagasaki, Emperor Hirohito surrendered with these words: 'We have resolved to endure the unendurable and suffer what is insufferable.'

Conventional history has it that both politics and science – acting on their own and together – speeded the formal end of colonialism. This is certainly nominally so, but the reach of this freedom was, once again, to be framed within state sovereignty. These drew states, both newly independent and well established, towards the bureaucratic authority insisted upon by modernity with its technical know-how and mechanisms of social control. The international community was to be what anthropologists call an 'administered community' – both states and individuals would be controlled even as they celebrated their freedom.

So, the greatly praised multilateral structures of post-1945 – the United Nations, the International Monetary Fund, the World Bank and the General Agreement on Tariffs and Trade – were controlling institutions even if they gestured towards the protection of human rights. The archetype of this was the UN Security Council where the power of veto was vested in five states – China, France, Russia, the United Kingdom and the United States. Their 'override power', which aimed to control any threat to the interest (or interests) of an already advantaged group, remains a symbol of a global system that is grossly unequal.

In International Relations, one thread in the story is that the United States appropriated and adapted European 'understandings' of the international for the challenges it faced as 'leader of the free world'. The evidence supports this explanation: at least sixty-four first-generation émigré scholars (mostly from Germany) taught Political Science and International Relations in the United States. More than half of them came from the discipline of law, including figures such as Hans Kelsen, Hans Morgenthau, John Herz and Karl Deutsch. The ways of the world that they transmitted – culture, diplomacy, law – remained essentially white, Western and male. In disciplinary International Relations, the non-West was deliberately silenced by exorcising two of the most important issues – decolonisation and racism – from its theoretical concerns (Guilhot 2014). This legacy led Stanley Hoffman, who was born in Vienna, to declare that International Relations was 'an American Social Science' (1977).

21.4 – KEY TERMS: International Relations (again)

It may be near the end of the book, but it is worth revisiting what we mean by International Relations (upper case) and international relations (lower case) and how they are inexorably linked. A standard dictionary definition of international relations runs that the term 'is used to identify all interactions between state-based actors across state boundaries' (Evans, Newnham and Newnham 1998, 274). This is certainly suggestive of what the scholarly field of International Relations originally emerged to analyse over a hundred years ago. Yet, it is unhelpful in explaining the international relationships that fall between the cracks of the discipline's growing boundaries and the personal anxiety and fear around these issues. After all, at the height of the Cold War there was real fear that humanity would be destroyed by nuclear warfare. In these circumstances, it was difficult not to be anxious about the future or fearful for one's family. So, we ought to remember that a functional modern definition of both 'ir' and 'IR' does something more than simply demarcate (or analyse) boundaries and relations between states. A more reflective gaze points to a broader image that incorporates activities and actors across all of the levels of analysis – and especially the individual level that rises with importance as each year passes.

The ghastly technology of weapons certainly awakened ethical concerns within International Relations, the most important of which has already crossed our paths in this book: would humankind destroy the planet? Yet the counter-factual question on this issue, the question that should have mattered but which was seldom asked and never answered, is: would the United States have atom-bombed a white Western state? At the centre of International Relations was (and remains) the ideology of white supremacy. This is undergirded by the understanding that only whites of European extraction live 'within' history: all others, as Nandy (2003) has argued, 'live outside' it.

If these three moments of reconstruction – the South African War and the ending of the First and Second World Wars – represented the remaking of the world, what about the ending of the Cold War? It is difficult not to believe that the ending of the Cold War has been one of continuity rather than the much-anticipated rethink of the nature and idea of the international. The moment was certainly marked by a new vocabulary, of which the word 'globalisation' promised new horizons. However, it quickly became an encryption for neoliberal economics and a 'thin' form of democracy that was characterised by Francis Fukuyama (1989) as 'the end of history'. In essence, he argued that liberal democracy and capitalism had proved itself superior to other social systems. This theory was seized upon by International Relations scholars who had, embarrassingly, failed to predict the ending of the Cold War. For International Relations theorists, the bipolarity that had characterised the Cold War was a stable system for both superpowers. They therefore saw no reason for either power of the great ideological divide to end it. What they did not see was hidden in plain sight – the internal collapse of the Soviet economy matched with the rising opposition of subjugated peoples in Eastern Europe had corroded the Soviet system from within.

 21.5 – KEY INSIGHTS: Global 'insiders' and 'outsiders'

Just after the Berlin Wall came down in 1989 – the event that symbolised the beginning of the end of the Cold War – I was invited to participate in a high-level panel organised by what is said to be one of the so-called 'great' think tanks of the world, the New York-based Council on Foreign Relations. My co-panellists included former members of successive American cabinets, a former director of the US Central Intelligence Agency (CIA) and many academic luminaries from the International Relations community. During the course of several meetings, it became clear to me that Islam was being constructed as a threat to America's 'global interests' and that it would be targeted. This binary thinking created a kind of intellectual swamp that gave rise to successive wars in Iraq and Afghanistan and, dangerously, a tendency to focus disproportionately on such 'threats'. Given this background, it is no surprise that the War on Terror was a low-level race war. Even the circumstances that led to the horrific attack on the United States, known as 9/11, can only be fully understood through an optic which pitted global 'insiders' against 'outsiders' along racial lines.

In 1991, US President George H. W. Bush declared that the West had won the Cold War. What lay ahead was a new challenge, based on binary thinking of 'us' and 'them', that one disciple of realist thought called a 'clash of civilizations' (Huntington 1993). This same binary thinking has permeated international economic relations, which remain divisive. Rich industrial states in the Global North are tagged as 'developed' and are counterposed with poor 'developing' states of the Global South. With the exception of China, which has made enormous economic strides, and the promise that India might well follow this lead, global economic relations remain captive to the four features that the Caribbean economist, W. Arthur Lewis (1978), set out in a lecture over forty years ago:

1. The poor export primary products and the rich export manufactured ones
2. The costs of trading in the Global South are higher than those in the Global North
3. The Global South depends on the Global North for finance
4. The Global South can only grow economically if the Global North grows.

Underpinning this is a debate at the core of economics – the role of government intervention and planning against the so-called free market system. While this issue has hovered over International Relations, debates over security remain the staple diet of the policy end of International Relations, as is evident through the third part of this book.

Threading understandings and analysis of security and economics together is well within International Relations' conceptual range, however. One example was the Nixon administration's intervention in Chile in September 1973. This coup against Chile's democratically elected government was driven by Cold War anti-communist security concerns and involved the United States' determination to destroy the Marxist-oriented government of Salvador Allende. The coup was a precursor to a policy of social control, which gathered force from 1975 onwards, and was based on market principles. A negative example such as this can be reversed by considering a more positive example of how the bulk of the previously warring European states gradually surrendered bits of sovereignty due to economic necessity (food shortages and industrial decimation) following the Second World War and the need to find a security arrangement that would not lead to another war. This, of course, was the project of European integration which, as Brexit has shown, remains an interesting experiment in international relationships. This case confirms the wide range of analyses that International Relations can offer to just about any issue – from economic to security even as it struggles with the vocabulary of race.

 CASE STUDY 21.1: Think tanks

Photo 21.3 Headquarters of RAND Corporation, a US non-profit global policy think tank

Credit: Coolcaesar/Wikimedia Commons

No academic development has had a greater impact on International Relations' growth as a discipline than the rise of think tanks. This is a big claim, to be sure, so let me illustrate it with a story from South Africa. In the post-apartheid years, the emergence of a think tank founded by former members of apartheid's security apparatus shifted the hopes of the immediate post-apartheid years from the high idealism of the Nelson Mandela presidency towards a security-centred society. Generously supported by northern-based funders, this body securitised almost all features of public policy literally from A to Z – from AIDS to relations with neighbouring Zimbabwe. As others have shown (see Ahmad 2014), think tanks have played and continue to play a critical role in making the case for war against Islam in the United States, and in 2003 pushed the Blair government to enthusiastically support the invasion of Iraq (on this, see Abelson 2014). As Arendt (1970, 6), put it:

There are ... few things that are more frightening than the steadily increasing prestige of scientifically minded brain trusters in the councils of government during the last decades. The trouble is not that they are cold-blooded enough to 'think the unthinkable,' but that they do not think.

Rather than viewing think tanks as disinterested parties in the making of International Relations, we must search below their claims to neutrality. In economic-speak, they are 'norm-entrepreneurs': protagonists for policy outcomes who pursue particular agendas while claiming to provide objective analysis.

These days, think tankers are well schooled in the repertoire of International Relations; they have mastered its vocabulary and are familiar with its disciplinary traditions. Think tanks are encouraged to promote a policy fashion by drawing uncritically from a particular metanarrative. During the Cold War, for instance, think tanks in the West promoted the 'threat' posed by the Soviet Union (and its allies) in much of their work, which was also embedded within differing shades of realist thinking.

Early in my own career I worked for one such think tank: the South African Institute of International Affairs (SAIIA), which, nowadays, calls itself the country's 'premier research institute on international issues'. It was not branded as such when I first worked there – perhaps that was because I was one of only two academic professionals on the staff. The other was a liberal-Catholic, John Barratt, the director, who was a former South African diplomat. He had not studied International Relations, but had read modern history at Oxford after taking a first degree – also in history – in South Africa. The watchwords for our work were 'facts' and 'objectivity' – to seek 'truth' in the way that practitioners in the natural sciences do. In this view of scholarship, knowledge was neutral and the role of the SAIIA was to present as many opinions as possible on an issue so that the public could make up their own minds on the issues at hand. This was in the 'non-political' spirit of London's Chatham House on which the SAIIA was modelled.

Sustaining this position in the South Africa of the 1970s was bizarre. The apartheid government had cracked down on internal dissent with the result that censorship was pervasive, even in universities. It was, for example, almost impossible to access the vigorous debates on the liberation of South Africa that were taking place amongst exiled groups. More seriously, the Black community had absolutely no voice in the management and the affairs of the SAIIA: they did serve tea and sandwiches, however. In the 1970s I often thought that the good and the great who gathered in the Institute's classical-styled headquarters were of the view that those on the other side of apartheid's cruel divide had no imaginary, or, indeed, experience, of the international.

John Barratt was often as frustrated by this state of affairs as I was, and we made several efforts – mostly unsuccessful – to change its modus operandi. What the corporate sponsors of the SAIIA would have made of these efforts is unknown. What I do know is that on many occasions I faced the raised eyebrows of the white liberals – and the not so liberal – who gathered to deliberate on whether South Africa's outreach to independent Black states was compatible with the policy of apartheid, or on the unquestioning fealty of the white state towards the West in the face of sanctions that had been placed on South Africa due to its apartheid system.

We need to pause here and return to Hannah Arendt's concerns: who stands to benefit from the work of think tanks? In the main, the funding is linked to business. The assumption is that the work of think tanks – publications, public commentary, conferencing – reflects the interests of their sponsors and the status quo. Certainly, the conservative inclination of the SAIIA, when I worked there, reflected the interests of South African business in the 1970s, as successive waves of critical scholars, including myself, have been keen to point out. This personal experience confirms four things. First, access to the discipline – certainly in South Africa, but elsewhere too – was an elitist pursuit. Second, the conversations were limited by particular vocabularies. Certainly, they were not inclined towards Western Marxism, which was then reshaping the fields of history, sociology and literature. Third, the Cold War metanarrative framed all the analysis. But mostly, and fourth, think tanks are what theorists have called 'total institutions' – institutions with tight regimens, supervision and rules that 'routine' professional behaviour. These observations were confirmed when, a few years later, I spent some time as a research associate in a more cosmopolitan think tank community at the International Institute for Strategic Studies (IISS) in London.

Some wider points on think tanks seem to be essential as we look forward. As the discipline has become a popular academic subject, more and more graduates have entered the workplace, and think tanks are significant places of employment. Indeed, it is possible to talk about International Relations as an academic 'industry' grounded in think tanks. Then, the triangular relationship that runs between think tanks, sponsors and the press or social media must be appreciated for what it is – a closed epistemic group which threatens the credibility of the craft. Finally, the interaction of people trained in the same grammar and vocabulary often produces groupthink and insider terminology. It becomes impossible to see

beyond closed and often self-selecting groups – the so-called 'experts' – who repeat the same ideas to each other. Can any of these practices be conducive to sound policy outcomes? This is where the 'critical turn', which began in the early 1980s and spread in the course of the decade, has been important for understanding the future of how International Relations makes and remakes the world. The arrival of critical theorising opened up a space to question the inner sanctum of the discipline. It certainly enabled me to ask searching questions about the theory and practice of security in southern Africa (Vale 2003).

As in every discipline, and in every facet of life and knowledge, sources of certainty have to be questioned continuously and critical perspectives have freed the space for doing so in International Relations. The constant challenge in our professional lives, especially in International Relations, is to negotiate the space between understanding which questions are intellectually interesting and which ones will make the world a better place.

 ## CASE STUDY 21.2: Technology

Photo 21.4 'Sophia' at the AI for Good Global Summit, Geneva 2018

Credit: ITU Pictures/Flickr

Technology matters in the world that International Relations analyses. It always has, and it always will – as outlined in the previous chapter. Technology helps us understand and explain the global system and it also helps to shape it. Today, technology has irrevocably changed how scholars and students access

information and how it is processed and published in an acceptable and professional form. Certainly, technology is changing faster than our understandings of the world can keep up with. The internet and the smartphone, for example, allow individuals to carry the accumulated wisdom of all of humanity around in their pocket – just one tap away. Yet, such valuable information is fighting for the user's attention against a deluge of endless entertainment and distractions. Even if information is sought out, much of it distorts more than informs due to widespread misinformation and uninformed views.

Technology also constantly changes the very 'stuff' of International Relations. For example, the complex and still unresolved relationship between International Relations and economics may well be the result of the failure to understand the fact that new technologies have eroded the discipline's central tenets – those of sovereignty, order, power – indeed, the very idea of 'the international'. This is seen in the debate over globalisation – the idea of one world open for business with goods, services, people and information flowing freely between and among states and peoples. Technology has enhanced these movements, making them quicker and ever building in intensity. Hence, one useful way to think about the category of technology is to consider it as a game-changing element of the global system that has percolated into just about every area and issue, and, as such, something that we are yet to fully understand.

Even more striking than global trade, technology in the form of social media may well have finally shattered any hope of a detached, or objective, search for truth that the academic discipline of International Relations once hoped to tap from the practices of the natural sciences. Can scholars pretend to be objective on an issue when technology regularly reminds us that in some distant place, and sometimes much closer to home, bodies are piling up due to some type of conflict or an outbreak of disease? This ever-present connection to the world around us through technology draws us in, triggers our empathetic responses, and makes each observer feel involved in some way.

Notwithstanding International Relations' undertaking to provide understanding and rationality, technology seems to have widened conceptual cracks at the social, political and economic levels. There seems no end to the erosion of this order and the headaches that will certainly follow. Consider technology-generated security issues that immediately knock against International Relations' busy windows. The same kinds of technology that have helped to develop drones that are killing people in the Middle East and elsewhere have also enabled the delivery of more effective health care in remote parts of the world. So, how should we analyse this and is International Relations' theoretical toolkit suitable? Then, as viruses such as Zika, Ebola and HIV/AIDS arise and spread through the very mechanisms that the global system has built within itself, another question arises over whether technology can

halt this. We can see this clearly in the face of the Covid-19 pandemic where technology has shown a Janus face. On the one side technology can provide pinpointed capacity to trace the movements of those that have been infected by the virus. Yet, on the other, a worry persists that this same capacity will be used by governments to crack down on dissident voices and erode civil liberties and human rights.

For those who are interested in the story of International Relations, technology raises an uncomfortable prospect. Will it end one tradition of storytelling in International Relations – that of the place of the nation-state, the role of sovereignty and the making of the global system? This was a slow, ponderous process that took place over several hundred years as letters, directives and ideas travelled slowly between the metropole and periphery. Today, this is a near instantaneous process. The international is being made and remade by digital information travelling at near the speed of light.

The idea of the digital world also raises an idea known as the 'singularity', a time when technological growth becomes so exponential that it is irreversible and will forever change humanity. Ideas such as this are often connected to the rise of artificial intelligence (also known as 'AI'), which will come to exist (presumably) independently of human thought and control at some point in the future. This has been played out endlessly in Western science fiction, for example in dystopic movies such as *The Terminator* (1984), *The Matrix* (1999) and the television series *Black Mirror* (2011–). Yet, life has begun to imitate art. 'Sophia' (Photo 21.4) is a humanoid robot who became a 'citizen' of Saudi Arabia in 2017 (the first robot to achieve citizenship of any state) and has been recognised by the United Nations. Sophia is nowhere near as advanced as the robots depicted in fiction and is more of a fun stunt than a genuine artificial intelligence, but 'she' may embody what is ahead. More seriously, advanced militaries are already developing autonomous weapons systems that do not need a human hand to guide them. Simultaneously, international organisations –

principally the United Nations – are racing to make such weapons illegal. A good reading of history, drawing on past revolutions in technology, will suggest that this is likely to be in vain and the system will have to adapt to their inclusion. Technology in this sense is likely to revolutionise our global system and how International Relations interprets it in the years ahead, similar to how nuclear weapons recast the debate in the mid-1940s onwards.

Conclusion

I draw to a close by returning to the epigram at the head of this chapter from W. L. Watkinson, an English Methodist minister. It is also the motto of Amnesty International, a non-governmental organisation. The idea of 'crossings' in the title comes from my confession, made at the outset, that the personal, the professional and the political have been interwoven in my approach to the discipline over five decades. A parallel image drawn in the title encapsulates a belief that International Relations, especially in its critical mode, is a kind of candle that casts light in often very dark places. There is a paradox that stalks the discipline of International Relations: as it speaks of peace, the gift of sovereignty – which is its currency – looks out upon messy and often very violent social relationships. These pages have suggested that there are no uncontaminated places in the making and remaking of these social relationships. There is thus no space where International Relations can escape the hot breath of compromise, concession or conciliation. However, the task that lies beyond the pages of this book is to recognise that despite all that we are taught about the global system and what we experience as individuals, this is still a largely unexplored world. It remains a space of infinite possibilities and a site of great hope.

 END OF CHAPTER QUESTIONS

1. In an ever-changing world, does International Relations have enough tools to adapt and evolve to continue to analyse the global system effectively?

2. What place is there for International Relations in the academy – considering its position alongside other established fields such as Politics, History, Law and Sociology?

3. Do you see any emerging theories, insights or directions that might become 'the next big thing' in International Relations, helping it to evolve and develop further?

4. In what ways does language, and chiefly the English language, limit our imagination in International Relations?

5. Can International Relations be decolonised?

REFERENCES

Abelson, Donald E. (2014). 'Old World, New World: The Evolution and Influence of Foreign Affairs Think-tanks', *International Affairs* 90 (1): 125–42.

Abdelhaey, S. A. (2019). 'Bringing the Individual Back in', *Review of Economics and Political Science* 4 (4): 304–20.

Abu-Lughod, L. (2002). 'Do Muslim Women Really Need Saving? Anthropological Reflections on Cultural Relativism and Its Others', *American Anthropologist* 104 (3): 783–90.

Acharya, Amitav (2017). 'After Liberal Hegemony: The Advent of a Multiplex World Order', *Ethics & International Affairs* 31 (3): 271–85.

Acharya, Amitav (2018). *The End of American World Order*, 2nd edn, Cambridge: Polity.

Acharya, Amitav (2020). 'What "Introduction to International Relations" Misses Out: Civilizations, World Orders, and the Rise of the West', *Social Science Research Network (SSRN)*. Available online: https://papers.ssrn.com/sol3/papers.cfm?abstract_id=3750112 (accessed 10 April 2021).

Acharya, Amitav and Barry Buzan (2010). *Non-Western International Relations Theory: Perspectives on and beyond Asia*. Abingdon: Routledge.

Acheson, Dean (1962). 'Our Atlantic Alliance: The Political and Economic Strands', speech at the United States Military Academy, West Point, New York, USA, 5 December.

Acosta Arcarazo, Diego and Luisa Feline Freier (2015). 'Turning the Immigration Policy Paradox Upside Down? Populist Liberalism and Discursive Gaps in South America', *International Migration Review* 49 (3): 659–96.

Adebajo, Adekeye. (2002). *Building Peace in West Africa: Liberia, Sierra Leone, and Guinea-Bissau*. Boulder, CO: Lynne Rienner Publishers.

Ager, A., and J. Ager (2017). 'Challenging the Discourse on Religion, Secularism and Displacement', in Luca Mavelli and Erin K. Wilson (eds), *The Refugee Crisis and Religion: Secularism, Security and Hospitality in Question*. London: Rowman & Littlefield, 37–52.

Ahmad, Muhammad Idrees (2014). *The Road to Iraq: The Making of a Neoconservative War*. Edinburgh: Edinburgh University Press.

Ahmad, Zakaria bin (2012). 'ASEAN Beyond 40', *East Asia* 29 (2): 157–66.

Albright, Madeleine (2006). 'Extended Interview', *Religion and Ethics Newsweekly*. Available online: https://www.pbs.org/wnet/religionandethics/2006/05/19/may-19-2006-madeleine-albright-extended-intreview/2838/ (accessed 10 April 2021).

Alfredsson, E., M. Bengtsson, H. S. Brown, C. Isenhour, S. Lorek, D. Stevis and P. Vergragt (2018). 'Why Achieving the Paris Agreement Requires Reduced Overall Consumption and Production', *Sustainability: Science, Practice, and Policy* 14 (1): 1–5.

Allison, G. (1971). *Essence of Decision: Explaining the Cuban Missile Crisis*. Boston, MA: Little Brown.

Amin, Samir (1977). *Imperialism and Unequal Development*. New York: Monthly Review Press.

Amin, Samir (1982). *The Arab Economy Today*. Translated by Michael Pallis. London: Zed Books.

Amnesty (2019). 'Morocco: Human Rights Defenders Targeted with NSO Group's Spyware'. Available online: https://www.amnesty.org/en/latest/research/2019/10/morocco-human-rights-defenders-targeted-with-nso-groups-spyware/ (accessed 10 April 2021).

Amnesty International (2020). 'Death Penalty in 2019: Facts and Figures', 21 April. Available online: https://www.amnesty.org/en/latest/news/2020/04/death-penalty-in-2019-facts-and-figures/ (accessed 10 April 2021).

Anderson, K. S. (2000). 'The Ottawa Convention Banning Landmines, the Role of International Non-governmental Organizations and the Idea of International Civil Society', *European Journal of International Law* 11 (1): 91–120.

Andersson, Ruben (2014). *Illegality, inc: Clandestine Migration and the Business of Bordering Europe*. Oakland, CA: University of California Press.

Angenendt, S. and A. Koch (2019). 'How Germany Can Benefit from the Global Compact for Migration', *SWP Comment* 37, September. Berlin: German Institute for International and Security Affairs.

Anghie, Antony (2005). *Imperialism, Sovereignty and the Making of International Law*. Cambridge: Cambridge University Press.

Appleby, R. Scott (2000). *The Ambivalence of the Sacred*. Lanham, MD: Rowman & Littlefield.

Arendt, Hannah (1970). *On Violence*. London: Allen Lane.

Arroyo, V. (2019). 'Keynote Address: A Brief History of U.S. Climate Policy and a Call to Action', *Maryland Journal of International Law* 34 (1). Available online: https://digitalcommons.law.umaryland.edu/mjil/vol34/iss1/3 (accessed 10 April 2021).

Asal, V., B. Nussbaum and D. W. Harrington (2007). 'Terrorism as Transnational Advocacy: An

Organizational and Tactical Examination', *Studies in Conflict & Terrorism* 30 (1): 15–39.

ASEAN (2020). 'Cohesive and Responsive ASEAN'. Chairman's Statement, 26 June 2020. Available online: https://asean.org/storage/2020/06/Chairman-Statement-of-the-36th-ASEAN-Summit-FINAL.pdf (accessed 10 April 2021).

Ataguba, J., J. Akazili and D. McIntyre (2011). 'Socioeconomic-related Health Inequality in South Africa: Evidence from General Household Surveys', *International Journal for Equity in Health* 10 (48). Available online: https://equityhealthj.biomedcentral.com/articles/10.1186/1475-9276-10-48 (accessed 17 October 2021).

Attar, Samar (2007). *The Vital Roots of European Enlightenment: Ibn Tufayl's Influence on Modern Western Thought*. Lanham, MD: Lexington Books.

Baele, Stephane J., Lewys Brace and Travis G. Coan (2019). 'From "Incel" to "Saint": Analyzing the Violent Worldview Behind the 2018 Toronto Attack', *Terrorism and Political Violence*. DOI: 10.1080/09546553.2019.1638256

Barua, S. (2020). 'Understanding Coronanomics: The Economic Implications of the Coronavirus Pandemic', *Social Science Research Network*. Available online: https://papers.ssrn.com/sol3/papers.cfm?abstract_id=3566477 (accessed 17 October 2021).

Bellamy, A. (2017). 'Protecting People', in Stephen McGlinchey (ed.), *International Relations*. Bristol: E-International Relations, 123–34.

Berger, Peter L. (1999). 'The Desecularization of the World: A Global Overview', in Peter L. Berger, *The Desecularization of the World: Resurgent Religion and World Politics*. Grand Rapids, MI: Eerdmans, 1–18.

Besada, Hany, Franklyn Lisk and Philip Martin (2015). 'Regulating Extraction in Africa: Towards a Framework for Accountability in the Global South', *Governance in Africa* 2 (1): 1–12.

Betts, Alexander (2013). *Survival Migration: Failed Governance and the Crisis of Displacement*. Ithaca, NY: Cornell University Press.

Bilgiç, Ali (2018). 'Migrant Encounters with Neo-colonial Masculinity: Producing European Sovereignty through Emotions', *International Feminist Journal of Politics* 20 (4): 542–62.

Biscop, S. (2020). 'Weaker Together or Weaker Apart? Great Power Relations after the Coronavirus', *Asia Europe Journal* 18: 231–4.

Blackwood, Leda, Hopkins, Nick and Reicher, Steve (2013). I Know Who I Am, but Who Do They Think I Am? Muslim Perspectives on Encounters with Airport Authorities, *Ethnic and Racial Studies* 36 (6): 1090–1108. DOI: 10.1080/01419870.2011.645845

Blaney, D. and N. Inayatullah (2004). *International Relations and the Problem of Difference*. London: Routledge.

Bong, Youngshik (2019). 'Reconciliation and Context in the East Asian Region', ASEACCU 2019, Sogang University, 22 August.

Botha, Anneli and Mahdi Abdile (2014). 'Radicalisation and al-Shabaab Recruitment in Somalia', *Institute for Security Studies*, Paper 226: September. Available online: https://issafrica.s3.amazonaws.com/site/uploads/Paper266.pdf (accessed 10 April 2021).

Brady, D., A. Blome and H. Kleider (2016). 'How Politics and Institutions Shape Poverty and Inequality', *The Oxford Handbook of the Social Science of Poverty*. Oxford: Oxford University Press.

Breen, Suzanne. (2019). 'Ex-IRA Bomber Who Got 30 Life Sentences Has Words of Advice for Young Dissidents', *Belfast Telegraph*, 28 January. Available online: https://www.belfasttelegraph.co.uk/news/northern-ireland/ex-ira-bomber-who-got-30-life-sentences-has-words-of-advice-for-young-dissidents-37753754.html (accessed 17 October 2021).

Brigden, Noelle K. (2016). 'Improvised Transnationalism: Clandestine Migration at the Border of Anthropology and International Relations', *International Studies Quarterly* 60 (2): 343–54.

Broberg, M. and B. M. Romera (2020). 'Loss and Damage after Paris: More Bark than Bite?' *Climate Policy* 20 (6): 661–8.

Brooks, E. (2005). 'Transnational Campaigns Against Child Labour: The Garment Industry in Bangladesh', in J. Bandy and J. Smith (eds), *Coalitions Across Borders: Transnational Protest and the Neoliberal Order*. Lanham, MD: Rowan and Littlefield.

Brown, C. (2009). Democracy's Friend or Foe? The Effects of Recent IMF Conditional Lending in Latin America', *International Political Science Review* 30 (4): 431–57.

Brown, Katherine E. (2019). 'Once a Terrorist, Always a Terrorist? How to Respond to the Women of Daesh', *RUSI Newsbrief* 39: 1. Available online: https://www.rusi.org/sites/default/files/20190125_newsbrief_vol39_no1_brown_web.pdf (accessed 10 April 2021).

Bull, Hedley (1977). *The Anarchical Society*. New York: Columbia University Press.

Busby, J. W. (2007). 'Bono Made Jesse Helms Cry: Jubilee 2000, Debt Relief, and Moral Action in International Politics', *International Studies Quarterly* 51 (2): 247–75.

Bush, Vannevar (1945). *Science, the Endless Frontier. A Report to the President on a Program for Postwar Scientific Research*. Washington, DC: Office of Scientific Research and Development.

Bystrom, Dianne (2008). 'Confronting Stereotypes and Double Standards in Campaign Communication,' in Beth Reingold (ed.), *Legislative Women: Getting Elected, Getting Ahead*, Colorado and London: Lynne Rienner Publishers, 59–83.

Cakmak, C. (2008). 'Transnational Activism in World Politics and Effectiveness of a Loosely Organised Principled Global Network: The Case of the NGO Coalition for an International Criminal Court', *The International Journal of Human Rights* 12 (3): 373–93.

Cameron, Catherine M., Paul Kelton and Alan C. Swedlund, eds (2016). *Beyond Germs: Native Depopulation in North America*. Tucson, AZ: University of Arizona Press.

Carlin, Diana B. and Kelly L. Winfrey (2009). 'Have You Come a Long Way, Baby? Hillary Clinton, Sarah Palin and Sexism in 2008 Campaign Coverage', *Communication Studies* 60 (4): 326–43.

Carr, Edward Hallett (1939). *The Twenty Years' Crisis: An Introduction to the Study of International Relations*. New York: Perennial.

Carroll, Susan J. (2009). 'Reflections on Gender and Hillary Clinton's Presidential Campaign: The Good, the Bad and the Misogynic', *Politics and Gender* 5 (1): 1–20.

Casanova, Jose (2019). 'Global Religious and Secular Dynamics', *Religion and Politics*, Brill Research Perspectives 1 (1): 1–74.

Chang, Ha-Joon (2002). *Kicking Away the Ladder: Development Strategy in Historical Perspective*. London: Anthem.

Chankia, Emma, John L. Lwanda and Adamson S. Muula (2013). 'Gender, Gays and Gain: The Sexualised Politics of Donor Aid in Malawi', *Africa Spectrum* 48 (1): 89–105.

Charlesworth, Hilary (1994). 'What are "Women's International Human Rights?"', in Rebecca J. Cook (ed.), *Human Rights of Women: National and International Perspectives*. Philadelphia, PA: University of Pennsylvania Press, 58–84.

Charlesworth, Hilary (2002). 'International Law: A Discipline of Crisis', *The Modern Law Review* 65 (3): 377–92.

Chisholm, A. (2014). 'Marketing the Gurkha Security Package: Colonial histories and Neoliberal Economies of Private Security', *Security Dialogue* 45 (4): 349–72.

Christensen, C. (2011). 'Twitter Revolutions? Addressing Social Media and Dissent', *The Communication Review* 14 (3): 155–7.

Christensen, K. K. and T. Liebetrau (2019). 'A New Role for "the public"? Exploring Cyber Security Controversies in the Case of WannaCry', *Intelligence and National Security* 34 (3): 395–408.

Clayton, Lawrence. (2009). 'Bartolomé de Las Casas and the African Slave Trade', *History Compass* 7 (6): 1526–41.

Clifford, James (1986). 'Introduction: Partial Truths', in J. Clifford and G. E. Marcus (eds), *Writing Culture: The Poetics and Politics of Ethnography*. Berkeley, CA: University of California Press, 1–26.

Coggins, B. (2015). 'Does State Failure Cause Terrorism? An Empirical Analysis (1999–2008)', *Journal of Conflict Resolution* 59 (3): 455–83.

Cohen, B. J. (2008). *International Political Economy*. Princeton, NJ: Princeton University Press.

Cohen, Raymond and Raymond Westbrook (2002). *Amarna Diplomacy: The Beginnings of International Relations*. Baltimore, MD: Johns Hopkins University Press.

Cohn, Carol (1987). 'Sex and Death in the Rational World of Defense Intellectuals', *Signs: Journal of Women in Culture and Society* 12 (4): 687–718.

Collyer, Michael (2007). 'In-between Places: Undocumented Sub-Saharan Transit Migrants in Morocco', *Antipode* 39 (4): 668–90.

Cook, J. and Vale, G. (2018). *From Daesh to Diaspora: Tracing the Women and Minors of Islamic State*. London: ICSR. Available online: https://icsr.info/wp-content/uploads/2018/07/ICSR-Report-From-Daesh-to-_Diaspora_-Tracing-the-Women-and-Minors-of-Islamic-State.pdf (accessed 10 April 2021).

Council on Foreign Relations (2020). *Cyber Operations Tracker* website. Available onlne: https://www.cfr.org/interactive/cyber-operations (accessed 10 April 2021).

Courtois, Stéphanie (1997). *The Black Book of Communism: Crimes, Terror, Repression*. Cambridge, MA: Harvard University Press.

Cronin, Audrey Kurth (2020). *Power to the People: How Open Technological Innovation is Arming Tomorrow's Terrorists*. New York: Oxford University Press.

Cullet, P. (2007). *The Sardar Sarovar Dam Project*. Abingdon: Routledge.

Curtis, Lionel (1918). 'Windows of Freedom', *The Round Table* 8 (3): 1–47.

Curtis, Lionel (1938). *Civitas Dei: The Commonwealth of God*. London: Macmillan.

da Silva, Raquel and Rhys Crilley (2017). '"Talk about Terror in Our Back Gardens": An Analysis of Online Comments about British Foreign Fighters in Syria', *Critical Studies on Terrorism* 10 (1): 162–86.

Daghrir, W. (2013). 'Globalization as Americanization? Beyond the Conspiracy Theory', *IOSR Journal of Applied Physics* 5 (2): 19–24.

Danner, L. K. and F. E. Martin (2019). 'China's Hegemonic Intentions and Trajectory: Will it Opt for Benevolent, Coercive, or Dutch-style

Hegemony?', *Asia & the Pacific Policy Studies* 6 (2): 186–207.

Davis, Sara (2020). *The Uncounted: Politics of Data in Global Health*. Cambridge: Cambridge Studies in Law and Society.

De Haas, Hein, Katharina Natter and Simona Vezzoli (2018). 'Growing Restrictiveness or Changing Selection? The Nature and Evolution of Migration Policies', *International Migration Review* 52 (2): 324–67.

'Declaration of Quito, Ecuador, July 1990.' (1991). *The Latin American Anthropology Review* 3 (1): 46.

DeHahn, Patrick. (2019). 'More than 1 million Muslims Are Detained in China—but How Did We Get that Number?' *Quartz*. Available online: https://qz.com/1599393/how-researchers-estimate-1-million-uyghurs-are-detained-in-xinjiang/ (accessed 10 April 2021).

Dennis, J. (2018). Beyond Slacktivism: Political Participation on Social Media. New York: Springer.

De Pryck, K. and F. Gemenne (2017). 'The Denier-in-Chief: Climate Change, Science and the Election of Donald J. Trump', *Law and Critique* 28 (2): 119–26.

Dershowitz, Alan M. (2008). *Why Terrorism Works: Understanding the Threat, Responding to the Challenge*. New Haven, CT: Yale University Press.

Díaz, Pablo Castillo and Nahla Valji (2019). 'Symbiosis of Misogyny and Violent Extremism', *Journal of International Affairs* 72 (2): 37–56.

Doty, Roxanne L. (2006). 'Fronteras Compasivas and the Ethics of Unconditional Hospitality', *Millennium* 35 (1): 53–74.

Dunlap, R. E., A. M. McCright and J. H. Yarosh (2016). 'The Political Divide on Climate Change: Partisan Polarization Widens in the U.S.', *Environment* 58 (5): 4–23.

Dunne, Tim and Brian C. Schmidt (2020). 'Realism', in John Baylis, Steve Smith and Patricia Owens (eds), *The Globalization of World Politics*. Oxford: Oxford University Press.

Dupuy, K. E., J. Ron and A. Prakash (2016). 'Hands Off My Regime! Governments' Restrictions on Foreign Aid to Nongovernmental Organizations in Poor and Middle-Income Countries', *World Development* 84 (August): 299–311.

Dwyer, A.C. (2018). 'The NHS Cyber-attack: A Look at the Complex Environmental Conditions of WannaCry', *RAD Magazine* 44 (512): 25–6.

Easterly, William (2006). *The White Man's Burden: Why the West's Efforts to Aid the Rest Have Done So Much Ill and So Little Good*. New York: Penguin.

Ehrenreich, Barbara, and Arlie Russell Hochschild, eds (2003). *Global Woman: Nannies, Maids and Sex Workers in the New Economy*. London: Granta.

Elshtain, Jean Bethke (1999). 'Really Existing Communities', *Review of International Studies* 25 (1): 141–6.

Enloe, C. (1989). *Bananas, Beaches and Bases: Making Feminist Sense of International Politics*. Berkeley, CA: University of California Press.

Enloe, Cynthia (2001). *Bananas, Beaches and Bases: Making Feminist Sense of World Politics*. 2nd edn, Berkeley, CA: University of California Press.

Epstein, G. A., ed. (2005). *Financialization and the World Economy*. Cheltenham and Northampton, MA: Edward Elgar.

Erel, Umut (2007). 'Constructing Meaningful Lives: Biographical Methods in Research on Migrant Women', *Social Research Online* 12 (4).

Evans, Graham, Jeffrey Newnham and Richard Newnham (1998). *The Penguin Dictionary of International Relations*. London: Penguin Books.

Fairbank, John K., ed. (1968). *The Chinese World Order: Traditional China's Foreign Relations*. Cambridge, MA: Harvard University Press.

Fanon, Frantz (2004). *The Wretched of the Earth*. Trans. by Richard Philcox. New York: Grove Press.

Farrell, N., ed. (2019). *The Political Economy of Celebrity Activism*. Abingdon: Routledge.

Fassbender, Bardo. (2020). *Key Documents on the Reform of the UN Security Council 1991–2019*. Leiden: Brill Nijhoff.

Fehling, Maya, Brett D. Nelson and Sridhar Venkatapuram (2013). 'Limitations of the Millennium Development Goals: A Literature Review', *Global Public Health* 8 (10): 1109–22.

Fernández-Armesto, Felipe (1994). *Before Columbus: Exploration and Colonisation from the Mediterranean to the Atlantic, 1229–1492*. Philadelphia, PA: University of Pennsylvania Press.

Finnemore, Martha and Kathryn Sikkink (1998). 'International Norm Dynamics and Political Change' *International Organization* 52 (4): 887–917.

Fleischer, Ari (2003). Press Briefing, 24 March. Available online: https://georgewbush-whitehouse.archives.gov/news/releases/2003/03/print/20030324-4.html (accessed 10 April 2021).

Foreign Policy (2020). How the World Will Look After the Coronavirus Pandemic. 20 March. Available online: https://foreignpolicy.com/2020/03/20/world-order-after-coroanvirus-pandemic/ (accessed 10 April 2021).

Fox, Jonathan (2008). *A World Survey of Religion and the State*. New York: Cambridge University Press.

Freedman, Jane (2007). *Gendering the International Asylum and Refugee Debate*. Basingstoke: Palgrave Macmillan.

Freier, Luisa Feline and Nicolas Parent (2019). 'The Regional Response to the Venezuelan Exodus', *Current History* 118 (805): 56–61.

Frum, David (2003). *The Right Man: The Surprise Presidency of George W. Bush*. New York: Random House.

Fu, Zhengyuan (1996). *China's Legalists: The Earliest Totalitarians and Their Art of Ruling*. Armonk, NY: M. E. Sharpe.

Fukuyama, F. (1989). 'The End of History?' *The National Interest* 18 (Summer): 3–18.

Fukuyama, F. (1992). *The End of History and the Last Man*. New York: Free Press.

Gaddis, J. L. (1989). *The Long Peace: Inquiries into the History of the Cold War*. Oxford: Oxford University Press.

Giametta, Calogero (2017). *The Sexual Politics of Asylum: Sexual Orientation and Gender Identity in the UK Asylum System*. Abingdon and New York: Routledge.

Gilpin, R. (2001). *Global Political Economy*. Princeton, NJ: Princeton University Press.

Global Justice Now (2017). 'Honest Accounts'. Available online: https://www.globaljustice.org.uk/sites/default/files/files/resources/honest_accounts_2017_web_final_updated.pdf (accessed 19 October 2021).

Gómez, Nicolás Wey (2008). *The Tropics of Empire: Why Columbus Sailed South to the Indies*. Cambridge, MA: MIT Press.

Google (2020). 'Apple and Google Partner on COVID-19 Contact Tracing Technology', Company Announcements, published 10 April 2020. Available online: https://blog.google/inside-google/company-announcements/apple-and-google-partner-covid-19-contact-tracing-technology (accessed 10 April 2021).

Gross, Jaclyn (2018). 'Neither Here nor There: The Bisexual Struggle for American Asylum', *Hastings Law Journal* 69 (3): 985–1008.

Grotius, Hugo (1625/2019). *On the Law of War and Peace*. Trans. by Archibald Colin Campbell. Whithorn: Anodos Books.

Guilhot, Nicolas (2014). 'Imperial Realism: Post-War IR Theory and Decolonisation', *International History Review* 36 (4): 698–720.

Guterres, António (2020). 'Remarks at the New School: "Women and Power"'. Available online: https://www.un.org/sg/en/content/sg/speeches/2020-02-27/remarks-new-school-women-and-power (accessed 10 April 2021).

Haas, E. B. (1953). 'The Balance of Power: Prescription, Concept, or Propaganda', *World Politics: A Quarterly Journal of International Relations* 5 (4): 442–77.

Habib, B. and V. Faulkner (2017). ' The Belt and Road Initiative: China's Vision for Globalisation, Beijing-style', *The Conversation*. Available online: https://theconversation.com/the-belt-and-road-initiative-chinas-vision-for-globalisation-beijing-style–77705 (accessed 10 April 2021).

Hamann, R. (2003). 'Mining Companies' Role in Sustainable Development: The 'Why' and 'How' of Corporate Social Responsibility from a Business Perspective', *Development Southern Africa* 20 (2): 237–54.

Hansen, Lene (2016). 'Discourse Analysis, Post-Structuralism and Foreign Policy', in Steve Smith, Amelia Hadfield and Timothy Dunne (eds), *Foreign Policy: Theories, Actors, Cases*. 3rd edn, Oxford: Oxford University Press, 95–110.

Hardin, G. (1968). 'The Tragedy of the Commons', *Science* 162(3859): 1243–8.

Hartsock, Nancy C. M. (1984). 'Masculinity, Citizenship and the Making of War', *PS* 17 (2): 198–202.

Healey, Denis (1989). *The Time of My Life*. London: Penguin.

Heisenberg, W. (1963). *Physics and Philosophy: The Revolution in Modern Science*. Sydney: George Allen & Unwin.

Held, D. and C. Roger (2018). 'Three Models of Global Climate Governance: From Kyoto to Paris and Beyond', *Global Policy* 9(4): 527–37.

Henderson, E. (2015). *African Realism? International Relations Theory and Africa's Wars in the Postcolonial Era*. London: Rowman & Littlefield.

Henkin, Louis. (1979). *How Nations Behave: Law and Foreign Policy*. 2nd edn, New York: Columbia University Press.

Hennebry, J. (2014). 'Falling through the Cracks? Migrant Workers and the Global Social Protection Floor', *Global Social Policy* 14 (3): 369–88.

Hibbard, Scott (2010). *Religious Politics and Secular States*. Baltimore, MD: Johns Hopkins University Press.

Hickel, J. (2014). 'The "Girl Effect": Liberalism, Empowerment and the Contradictions of Development', *Third World Quarterly* 35 (8): 1355–73.

Hobson, John M. (2004). *The Eastern Origins of Western Civilisation*. Cambridge: Cambridge University Press.

Hodgkinson, P. and W. A. Schabas, eds (2004). *Capital Punishment: Strategies for Abolition*. Cambridge: Cambridge University Press.

Hoffman, A. J. (2011). 'The Culture and Discourse of Climate Skepticism', *Strategic Organization* 9 (1): 77–84.

Hoffman, B. (1945). Quoted in B. Cosgrove, 'Hiroshima and Nagasaki: Photos from the Ruins', *Time*. Available online: http://time.com/3494421/hiroshima-and-nagasaki-photos-from-the-ruins/ (accessed 10 April 2021).

Hoffman, Stanley (1977). 'An American Social Science', *Daedalus* 106 (3): 41–60.

Home Office (2019). 'Crime Outcomes in England and Wales: Year ending March 2019 '. Available online: https://assets.publishing.service.gov.uk/government/uploads/system/uploads/attachment_data/file/817769/crime-outcomes-hosb1219.pdf (accessed 10 April 2021).

Hopkins, S. and E. Louw (2019). 'Social Celebrity, Digital Activism, and New Femininity', in N. Farrell (ed.), The Political Economy of Celebrity Activism. Abingdon: Routledge, 66–84.

Hovey, Craig and Elizabeth Phillips (2015). 'Preface', in Christian Political Theology. Cambridge: Cambridge University Press.

Human Rights Watch (2021). World Report: Country Chapter, Egypt. https://www.hrw.org/world-report/2021/country-chapters/egypt (accessed 30 September 2021).

Huntington, Samuel P. (1993). 'The Clash of Civilisations?' Foreign Affairs 72 (3): 22–49.

Huntington, Samuel P. (1996). The Clash of Civilizations and the Remaking of World Order. New York: Simon & Schuster.

Hurd, Elizabeth Shakman (2017). 'Religion and Secularism', in R. Devetak, J. George and P. Percy (eds), An Introduction to International Relations. 3rd edn, Cambridge: Cambridge University Press, 356–70.

Hutchings, Kimberly (2018). Global Ethics: An Introduction. Cambridge: Polity Press.

Huysmans, Jef (2006). The Politics of Insecurity: Fear, Migration and Asylum in the EU. London: Routledge.

IMF (2018). Macroeconomic Developments & Prospects In Low-Income Developing Countries – 2018. Washington, DC: International Monetary Fund.

Independent Commission for Aid Impact (2020). 'The UK's Preventing Sexual Violence in Conflict Initiative: Joint Review'. Available online: https://icai.independent.gov.uk/wp-content/uploads/The-UKs-preventing-sexual-violence-in-conflict-initiative.pdf (accessed 10 April 2021).

Institute for Health Metrics and Evaluation (2016). Rethinking Development and Health: Findings from the Global Burden of Disease Study. Seattle, WA: IHME.

Jacobsen, J. K. (1996). 'Are All Politics Domestic? Perspectives on the Integration of Comparative Politics and International Relations Theories', Comparative Politics 29 (1): 93–115.

Jahn, B. (2000). The Cultural Construction of International Relations: The Invention of the State of Nature. Basingstoke: Macmillan.

Jervis, Robert (1978). 'Cooperation Under the Security Dilemma', World Politics 30 (2): 167–214.

Johnson, Paul (1986). 'The Seven Deadly Sins of Terrorism', in Benjamin Netanyahu (ed.), International Terrorism: Challenge and Response. New Brunswick: Transaction Press.

Johnson, Stanley (2012). UNEP: The First 40 Years: A Narrative. Nairobi: United Nations Environment Programme.

Johnson, Todd and Peter F. Crossing (2019). 'The World by Religion', Journal of Religion and Demography 6 (1): 1–86.

Johnston, Alastair Iain (1995). 'Thinking about Strategic Culture', International Security 19 (4): 32–64.

Jordana, J. and J. C. Triviño-Salazar (2020). 'Where Are the ECDC and the EU-wide Responses in the COVID-19 Pandemic?' The Lancet 395 (10237): 1611–12.

Joseph, J. (2010). 'The Limits of Governmentality: Social Theory and the International', European Journal of International Relations 16 (2): 223–46.

Juergensmeyer, Mark (2008). Global Rebellion: Religious Challenges to the Secular State, from Christian Militias to Al Qaeda. Berkeley, CA: University of California Press.

Justice News (2020). US Department of Justice, 9 November. Available online: https://www.justice.gov/opa/pr/former-elkhart-indiana-resident-sentenced-over-six-years-prison-financing-terrorism (accessed 10 April 2021).

Kaarbo, J. (2015). 'A Foreign Policy Analysis Perspective on the Domestic Politics Turn in IR Theory', International Studies Review 17 (2): 189–216.

Kahlina, Katja and Dušica Ristivojecić (2015). 'LGBT Rights, Standards of "Civilisation" and the Multipolar World Order', E-International Relations. Available online: https://www.e-ir.info/2015/09/10/lgbt-rights-standards-of-civilisation-and-the-multipolar-world-order/ (accessed 10 April 2021).

Kahn, Kim Fridkin (2003). 'Assessing the Media's Impact on the Political Fortunes of Women', in Susan J. Carroll (ed.), Women and American Politics: New Questions, New Directions. Oxford: Oxford University Press, 173–89.

Kaldor, M. (2013). 'In Defence of New Wars', Stability: International Journal of Security and Development 2 (1). Available online: https://www.stabilityjournal.org/articles/10.5334/sta.at/ (accessed 10 April 2021).

Kang, David C. (2010). East Asia Before the West: Five Centuries of Trade and Tribute. New York: Columbia University Press.

Kapila, Mukesh (2007). 'Healing Broken Societies: Can Aid Buy Love and Peace?' Global Governance 13: 17–24.

Kelman, H. C. (1970). 'The Role of the Individual in International Relations: Some Conceptual and Methodological Considerations', Journal of International Affairs 24 (1): 1–17.

Kendall-Taylor, A., E. Frantz and J. Wright (2020). 'The Digital Dictators. How Technology Strengthens Autocracy', Foreign Affairs. Available

online: https://www.foreignaffairs.com/articles/
china/2020-02-06/digital-dictators (accessed
10 April 2021).

Kennedy, Scott, ed. (2018). *Global Governance and
China: The Dragon's Learning Curve*. Abingdon:
Routledge.

Keohane, Robert (2002). 'The Globalisation of Informal
Violence: Theories of World Politics and the
"Liberalism of Fear"', *Dialogue-IO* 1: 29–43.

Keohane, R. O. (2016). 'Nominal Democracy?: A
Rejoinder to Gráinne de Búrca and Jonathan
Kuyper and John Dryzek', *International Journal of
Constitutional Law* 14 (4): 938–40.

Keohane, R. O. J. and J. S. Nye Jr (1973). 'Power and
Interdependence', *Survival* 15 (4): 158–65.

Keohane, Robert and Joseph Nye (1977). *Power and
Interdependence: World Politics in Transition*.
Boston, MA: Little, Brown.

Khagram, S. (2002). 'Restructuring the Global Politics of
Development: The Case of India's Narmada Valley
Dams', in S. Khagram, J. V. Riker and K. Sikkink
(eds), *Restructuring World Politics. Transnational
Social Movements, Networks, and Norms*.
Minneapolis, WI: Minnesota University Press,
206–30.

Khosravi, Shahram (2010). *'Illegal' Traveller. An
Auto-Ethnography of Borders*. Basingstoke:
Palgrave.

Khrushchev, N. (1962). Quoted in 'Nuclear Test Ban
Treaty', *John F. Kennedy Presidential Library
online*. Available online: www.jfklibrary.org/JFK/
JFK-in-History/Nuclear-Test-Ban-Treaty.aspx?p=2
(accessed 10 April 2021).

Kim, Andrew E. (2005). 'Nonofficial Religion in South
Korea: Prevalence of Fortunetelling and Other
Forms of Divination', *Review of Religious Research*
46 (3): 284–302.

Kirby, Paul (2015). 'Ending Sexual Violence in Conflict:
The Preventing Sexual Violence Initiative and its
Critics', *International Affairs* 91 (3): 457–72.

Kissinger, Henry (2013). *A World Restored: Metternich,
Castlereagh and the Problems of Peace, 1812–22*.
Vermont: Echo Point Books & Media.

Klabbers, Jan (2015). *An Introduction to International
Organizations Law*. 3rd edn, Cambridge:
Cambridge University Press.

Klausen, Jytte. (2015). 'Tweeting the Jihad: Social
Media Networks of Western Foreign Fighters in
Syria and Iraq', *Studies in Conflict and Terrorism* 38
(1): 1–22.

Koh, Harold Hongju. (2006). 'Why Transnational Law
Matters', *Penn State International Law Review* 24
(4): 745–53.

Kohl, U., ed. (2017). *The Net and the Nation State:
Multidisciplinary Perspectives on Internet

Governance*. Cambridge: Cambridge University
Press.

Konadu-Agyemang, Kwadwo, ed. (2018). *IMF and
World Bank Sponsored Structural Adjustment
Programs in Africa: Ghana's Experience, 1983–
1999*. Abingdon: Routledge.

Koplan, Jeffrey P., T. Christopher Bond, Michael H.
Merson, K. Srinath Reddy, Mario Henry Rodriguez
and Nelson K. Sewankambo (2009). 'Towards a
Common Definition of Global Health', *The Lancet*
373: 1993–5.

Kratochwil, Friedrich (2018). *Praxis*. Cambridge:
Cambridge University Press.

Krauthammer, Charles (1991). 'The Unipolar Moment',
Foreign Affairs. Available online: https://www.
foreignaffairs.com/articles/1990-01-01/unipolar-
moment (accessed 10 April 2021).

Kuhn, Thomas (1970). *The Structure of Scientific
Revolutions*. Chicago, IL: University of Chicago
Press.

Kynsilehto, Anitta (2019). 'Bearing Witness to
Violence at Borders: Intermingling Artistic and
Ethnographic Encounters', in K. Horsti (ed.), *The
Politics of Public Memories of Forced Migration
and Bordering in Europe*. Basingstoke: Palgrave,
71–86.

Lallerstedt, K. (2018). 'The Neglected Mega-Problem:
Illicit Trade in "Normally Licit" Goods', in H. Matfess
and M. Miklaucic (eds), *World without Order*.
Washington, DC: National Defense University,
251–73.

Laycock, Stuart (2012). *All the Countries We've Ever
Invaded: And the Few We Never Got Round To*.
Cheltenham: The History Press.

Lee, J. and G. Gereffi (2013). 'The Co-evolution of
Concentration in Mobile Phone Global Value
Chains and its Impact on Social Upgrading in
Developing Countries'. Capturing the Gains:
Working Paper 25. Available online: https://
globalvaluechains.org/sites/globalvaluechains.org/
files/publications/ctg-wp-2013-25.pdf (accessed
10 April 2021).

Lee, S. and S. Bartels (2019). '"They Put a Few Coins in
Your Hands to Drop a Baby in You" – 265 Stories
of Haitian Children Abandoned by UN Fathers',
The Conversation. Available online: https://
theconversation.com/they-put-a-few-coins-in-
your-hands-to-drop-a-baby-in-you-265-stories-
of-haitian-children-abandoned-by-un-
fathers-114854 (accessed 10 April 2021).

Leftwich, A. (2004). *What is Politics: The Activity and Its
Study*. Hoboken, NJ: John Wiley and Sons.

Lewis, R. (2020). 'This Is What the News Won't Show
You': YouTube Creators and the Reactionary
Politics of Micro-celebrity', *Television & New Media*
21 (2): 201–17.

Lewis, William Arthur (1978). *The Evolution of the International Economic Order*. Princeton, NJ: Princeton University Press.

Li, Xueqin (1985). *Eastern Zhou and Qin Civilizations*. Translated by K. C. Chang. New Haven, CT: Yale University Press.

Lister, C. (2015). 'Returning Foreign Fighters: Criminalization or Reintegration?' Brookings Institute Policy Briefing, August.

Liu, T. and W. T. Woo (2018). 'Understanding the U.S.-China Trade War', *China Economic Journal* 11 (3): 319–40.

Lopez, Ditas B. and Claire Jiao (2020). 'Supplier of World's Nurses Struggles to Fight Virus at Home', *Bloomberg*. Available online: https://www.bloomberg.com/news/articles/2020-04-23/philippines-sends-nurses-around-the-world-but-lacks-them-at-home (accessed 10 April 2021).

MacNeil, R. and M. Paterson (2020). 'Trump, US Climate Politics, and the Evolving Pattern of Global Climate Governance', *Global Change, Peace and Security* 32 (1): 1–18.

Mandaville, P. (2007). *Global Political Islam*. Abingdon, UK: Routledge.

Manley, John (2017). 'Leo Varadkar Doesn't Plan "First Gentleman" Role for Partner', *The Irish News*. Available online: https://www.irishnews.com/news/2017/05/29/news/leo-varadkar-doesn-t-plan-first-gentleman-role-for-partner-1037850/ (accessed 10 April 2021).

Marchetti, R. (2016). 'Advocacy Strategies for Human Rights: The Campaign for the Moratorium on Death Penalty', *Italian Political Science Review* 46 (3): 355–78.

Martin, G. (2019). *Essentials of Terrorism: Concepts and Controversies*. 5th edn, Los Angeles, CA: Sage.

Maschmeyer, L., R. J. Deibert and J. R. Lindsay (2020). 'A Tale of Two Cybers: How Threat Reporting by Cybersecurity Firms Systematically Underrepresents Threats to Civil Society', *Journal of Information Technology & Politics* 18 (1): 1–20.

Masters, M. and Salvatore Santino F. Regilme, Jr (2020). 'Human Rights and British Citizenship: The Case of Shamima Begum as Citizen to *Homo Sacer*', *Journal of Human Rights Practice* 12 (2): 341–63.

Matfess, H. (2017). *Women and the War on Boko Haram*. Chicago, IL: University of Chicago Press.

Matthews, P. (2015). 'Why Are People Skeptical about Climate Change? Some Insights from Blog Comments', *Environmental Communication* 9 (2): 153–68.

McCarthy, D. R., ed. (2017). *Technology and World Politics: An Introduction*. London: Routledge.

McGinley, Ann C. (2009). 'Hillary Clinton, Sarah Palin and Michelle Obama: Performing Gender, Race and Class on the Campaign Trail', *Denver University Law Review* 86: 709–25.

McGlinchey, Stephen, Rosie Walters and Christian Scheinpflug (2017). *International Relations Theory*. Bristol: E-International Relations.

McMaster University (2005). *Peace through Health*. Available online: https://www.humanities.mcmaster.ca/~peace_health/ (accessed 10 April 2021).

McNeill, William H. (1991). *The Rise of the West: A History of the Human Community*. Chicago, IL: University of Chicago Press.

Mearsheimer, John J. (1995). 'The False Promise of International Institutions', *International Security* 19 (3): 5–49.

Mearsheimer, John (2001). *The Tragedy of Great Power Politics*. New York: W.W. Norton.

Merger, Sara (2018). 'When is Terrorism not Terrorism? When the Political Motivations Are Misogyny', *The Gender and War Project*. Available online: www.genderandwar.com/2018/04/26/when-is-terrorism-not-terrorism (accessed 10 April 2021).

Ministry of Foreign Affairs of the People's Republic of China (2016). 'China's Territorial Sovereignty and Maritime Rights and Interests in the South China Sea'. Statement, 12 July 2016. Available online: https://www.fmprc.gov.cn/nanhai/eng/snhwtlcwj_1/t1379493.htm (accessed 10 April 2021).

Mlachila, M. and T. Moeletsi (2019). 'Struggling to Make the Grade: A Review of the Causes and Consequences of the Weak Outcomes of South Africa's Education System'. *IMF Working Papers* 19 (47).

Mohanty, Chandra Talpade (1988). 'Under Western Eyes: Feminist Scholarship and Colonial Discourses', *Feminist Review* 30 (1): 61–88.

Morgan, Chloe (2019). 'Give Us A Wave! World Leaders' Wives – and a Slightly Awkward-looking Philip May – Pose for Photos at G20 Summit in Japan (but Melania Trump Stays at Home)', *Daily Mail*, 28 June. Available online: https://www.dailymail.co.uk/femail/article-7191709/Wives-world-leaders-joined-Philip-pose-photos-G20-summit-Japan.html (accessed 10 April 2021).

Morgenthau, Hans Joachim (1948). *Politics Among Nations: The Struggle for Power and Peace*. New York: A. A. Knopf.

Morgenthau, Hans J. (1974). 'International Law and International Politics: An Uneasy Partnership', *American Society of International Law Proceedings* 68: 331–4.

Morokvašić, Mirjana (1984). 'Birds of Passage are also Women …' *International Migration Review* 18: 886–907.

Morozov, E. (2009). 'Drop Ipods, not Bombs!' *Foreign Policy*, June.

Morse, E. L. (1969). 'The Politics of Interdependence', *International Organization* 23 (2): 311–26.

Moyn, Samuel (2010). *The Last Utopia: Human Rights in History*. Cambridge, MA: Harvard University Press.

Mulligan, Stephen P. (2018). 'Withdrawal from International Agreements: Legal Framework, the Paris Agreement, and the Iran Nuclear Agreement'. *Congressional Research Service Report*, 4 May 2018. Available online: https://fas.org/sgp/crs/row/R44761.pdf (accessed 10 April 2021).

Murray, Robert (2015). *System, Society and the World: Exploring the English School of International Relations*. 2nd edn, Bristol: E-International Relations.

Mustafa, D. and K. E. Brown (2010). 'The Taliban, Public Space, and Terror in Pakistan' *Eurasian Geography and Economics* 51 (4): 496–512.

Mutua, Makau (2001). 'Savages, Victims, and Saviors: The Metaphor of Human Rights', *Harvard International Law Journal* 42: 201–45.

Nandy, Ashis (2003). *The Romance of the State and the Fate of Dissent in the Tropics*. New Delhi: Oxford India Paperbacks.

Nanni, Giordano (2012). *The Colonisation of Time: Ritual, Routine and Resistance in the British Empire*. Manchester: Manchester University Press.

Narayan, D. (2001). 'Voices of the Poor', in D. Belshaw, R. Calderisi, and C. Sugden (eds), *Faith in Development. Partnership Between the World Bank and the Churches of Africa*. Washington DC: Regnum Books, 39–48.

Narlikar, A. (2020). *Poverty Narratives and Power Paradoxes in International Trade Negotiations and Beyond*. Cambridge: Cambridge University Press.

National Treasury of South Africa (2020). *National Budget and Time Series in Excel Format*. Available online: http://www.treasury.gov.za/documents/national%20budget/2020/excelFormat.aspx (accessed 10 April 2021).

Neumann, P. (2013). 'The Trouble with Radicalisation', *International Affairs* 89 (4): 873–93.

Neuwirth, Jessica (2005). 'Inequality before the Law: Holding states accountable For Sex Discriminatory Laws under the Convention on the Elimination of All Forms of Discrimination against Women and through the Beijing Platform for Action', *Harvard Human Rights Journal* 18: 19–54.

Nkrumah, Kwame (1963). *Africa Must Unite*. New York: Frederick A. Praeger.

Nye, Joseph (1990). *Bound to Lead: The Changing Nature of American Power*. New York: Basic Books.

Nye, Joseph S., Jr. (2019). 'The Rise and Fall of American Hegemony from Wilson to Trump', *International Affairs* 95 (1): 63–80.

O'Brien, R. and M. Williams (2020). *Global Political Economy*. 6th edn, London: Red Globe Press.

OECD (2020). *Development Finance Data*. Available online: https://www.oecd.org/dac/financing-sustainable-development/development-finance-data/ (accessed 10 April 2021).

Oppenheim, Lassa Francis (1912). *International Law: A Treatise. Volume I: Peace*. 2nd edn, New York: Longmans, Green and Co.

Ostrom, E. (1990). *Governing the Commons: The Evolution of Institutions for Collective Action*. Cambridge: Cambridge University Press.

Otor, S. A. and M. Dornan (2017). 'How Does Foreign Aid Impact Australian Exports in the Long-run?' Development Policy Centre Discussion Paper 62, ANU, Canberra, Australia.

Oxfam (2019). *Public Good or Private Wealth*. Oxfam GB for Oxfam International.

Paris, R. (2004). 'Still an Inscrutable Concept', *Security Dialogue* 35 (3): 370–2.

Patomaki, H. (2002). *After International Relations: Critical Realism and the (Re)construction of World Politics*. Abingdon: Routledge.

Pedahzur, Ami (2009). *The Israeli Secret Services and the Struggle against Terrorism*. New York: Columbia University Press.

Penttinen, Elina (2008). *Globalization, Prostitution and Sex-Trafficking: Corporeal Politics*. London: Routledge.

Penttinen, Elina and Anitta Kynsilehto (2017). *Gender and Mobility: A Critical Introduction*. Lanham, MD and London: Rowman and Littlefield.

Peters, Anne. (2009). 'Humanity as the A and Ω of Sovereignty', *European Journal of International Law* 20 (3): 513–44.

Peterson, V. Spike, ed. (1992). *Gendered States: Feminist (Re)Visions of International Relations Theory*. Boulder, CO: Lynne Reinner Publishers.

Peterson, V. Spike (2003). *A Critical Rewriting of Global Political Economy: Integrating Reproductive, Productive and Virtual Economies*. London: Routledge.

Peterson, V. Spike and Anne Sisson Runyan (1999). *Global Gender Issues*. 2nd edn, Boulder, CO: Westview Press.

Pieterse, J. N. (1994). Globalisation as Hybridisation, *International Sociology* 9 (2): 161–84.

Piot, Peter (2014). 'Ebola's Perfect Storm', *Science* 345 (6202): 1221.

Piper, Nicola, ed. (2008). *New Perspectives on Gender and Migration. Livelihood, Rights and Entitlements*. London: Routledge.

Polanyi, K. (1957). *The Great Transformation*. Boston, MA: Beacon Press.

Qin, Yaqing (2018). *A Relational Theory of World Politics*. Cambridge: Cambridge University Press.

Qiu, L. D., C. Zhan and X. Wei (2019). 'An Analysis of the China-US Trade War through the Lens of the Trade

Literature', *Economic and Political Studies* 7 (2): 148–68.

Radicalization Awareness Network (2017). *Manual – Responses to Returnees: Foreign Fighters and Their Families*, July. Available online: https://ec.europa.eu/home-affairs/sites/homeaffairs/files/ran_br_a4_m10_en.pdf (accessed 10 April 2021).

Rapoport, David C. (2002). 'The Four Waves of Rebel Terror and September 11', *Anthropoetics* 8: 1. Available online: http://anthropoetics.ucla.edu/ap0801/terror/ (accessed 10 April 2021).

Rees, John A. and Stefania Varnero Rawson (2019). 'The Resources of Religious Humanitarianism: The Case of Migrants on Lampedusa', *Journal for the Academic Study of Religion* 32 (1): 172–91.

Reich, R. (2015). 'The Clash is no Longer between Left and Right …', *The Observer*, 8 November, 3–45.

Ridgwell, H. (2017). 'China Set to Spend Billions on "One Belt One Road", But Some Want Focus on Poverty', *VOA*. Available online: https://www.voanews.com/east-asia-pacific/china-set-spend-billions-one-belt-one-road-some-want-focus-poverty (accessed 10 April 2021).

Ringmar, Erik (2017). *'The Making of the Modern World'*, in Stephen McGlinchey (ed.), *International Relations*. Bristol: E-International Relations Publishing, 8–19.

Roberts, Christopher B. (2012). *ASEAN Regionalism: Cooperation, Values and Institutionalisation*. London: Routledge.

Robertson, H. (2018). 'Dutch Church Holds Non-Stop Service for Nearly 800 Hours to Prevent Refugee Deportation', *ABC*, 28 November. Available online: https://www.abc.net.au/news/2018-11-28/dutch-church-holding-non-stop-service-to-protect-refugees/10559676 (accessed 10 April 2021).

Robinson, Margaret (2017). 'Two-spirit and Bisexual People: Different Umbrella, Same Rain', *Journal of Bisexuality* 17 (1): 7–29.

The Rockefeller Foundation–Lancet Commission on Planetary Health (2015). 'Safeguarding Human Health in the Anthropocene Epoch', *The Lancet* 386: 1973–2028.

Rosenbaum, David (2004). 'A Closer Look at Cheney and Halliburton', *New York Times*, 28 September. Available online:https://www.nytimes.com/2004/09/28/us/a-closer-look-at-cheney-and-halliburton.html (accessed 10 April 2021).

Röser, F., O. Widerberg, N. Höhne and T. Day (2020). 'Ambition in the Making: Analysing the Preparation and Implementation Process of the Nationally Determined Contributions under the Paris Agreement', *Climate Policy* 20 (4): 415–29.

Ruggie, John Gerard (1982). 'International Regimes, Transactions, and Change: Embedded Liberalism in the Postwar Economic System', *International Organization* 36 (2): 379–415.

Sageman, Marc (2008). *Leaderless Jihad Terror Networks in the Twenty-First Century*. Philadelphia, PA: University of Pennsylvania Press.

Said, E. (1978). *Orientalism*. New York: Pantheon Books.

Sanderson, Marie. (1999). 'The Classification of Climates from Pythagoras to Koeppen', *Bulletin of the American Meteorological Society* 80 (4): 669–73.

Sargent, S. (2012). 'Transnational Networks and United Nations Human Rights Structural Change: The Future of Indigenous and Minority Rights', *The International Journal of Human Rights* 16 (1): 123–51.

Schmid, Alex, P. (1992). *The Definition of Terrorism, A Study in Compliance with CTL/9/91/2207 for the U.N. Crime Prevention and Criminal Justice Branch*. Leiden: United Nations.

Schmid, Alex and Albert Jongman (1988). *Political Terrorism*. New Brunswick: Transaction Books.

Schwartz, H. M. (2010). *States versus Markets*. 3rd edn, London: Red Globe Press.

Seib, P. (2012). *Real-time Diplomacy: Politics and Power in the Social Media Era*. Basingstoke: Palgrave Macmillan.

Sen, Tansen (2003). *Buddhism, Diplomacy, and Trade: The Realignment of Sino-Indian Relations, 600–1400*. Honolulu, HI: Association of Asian Studies and University of Hawai'i Press.

Shahi, Deepshikha (2019). *Kautilya and Non-Western IR Theory*. London: Palgrave Macmillan.

Shepherd, L. (2006). 'Veiled References: Constructions of Gender in the Bush Administration Discourse on the Attacks on Afghanistan post-9/11', *International Feminist Journal of Politics* 8 (1): 19–41.

Sherman, W. (2016). Interviewed on 'Our World: Iran's Nuclear Deal'. *BBC News*, 14 July.

Shirky, C. (2011). 'The Political Power of Social Media: Technology, the Public Sphere, and Political Change', *Foreign Affairs* 90 (1): 28–41.

Silber, M. and A. Bhatt (2007). 'Radicalisation in the West: The Home-grown Threat'. New York Police Department. Available online: http://sethgodin.typepad.com/seths_blog/files/NYPD_Report-Radicalization_in_the_West.pdf (accessed 10 April 2021).

Silke, A. (2008). 'Holy Warriors: Exploring the Psychological Processes of Jihadi Radicalization', *European Journal of Criminology* 5 (1): 99–123.

Sikkink, Kathryn (2011). *The Justice Cascade*. New York: W. W. Norton & Co.

Sikkink, Kathryn (2017). *Evidence for Hope: Making Human Rights Work in the 21st Century*. Princeton, NJ: Princeton University Press.

Simons, A. and D. Tucker (2007). 'The Misleading Problem of Failed States: A "Socio-geography" of Terrorism in the Post-9/11 Era', *Third World Quarterly* 28 (2): 387–401.

Singer, D. J. (1961). 'The Level-of-Analysis Problem in International Relations', *World Politics* 14: 77–92.

Singer, P. (1972). 'Famine, Affluence and Morality', *Philosophy and Public Affairs* 1 (3): 229–43.

Småberg, Thomas, Bruno Boute and Thomas Smaberg (2012). *Devising Order: Socio-Religious Models, Rituals, and the Performativity of Practice*. Leiden: Brill.

Spivak, G. (1985). 'Can the Subaltern Speak? Speculations on Widow Sacrifice', *Wedge* 7 (8): 120–30.

Steger, Manfred B. and Amentahru Wahlrab (2017). *What Is Global Studies? Theory and Practice*. New York: Routledge.

Steil, Benn (2013). *The Battle of Bretton Woods: John Maynard Keynes, Harry Dexter White, and the Making of a New World Order*. Princeton, NJ: Princeton University Press.

Stevens, T., ed. (2018). 'Special Edition: Global Cybersecurity: New Directions in Theory and Methods', *Politics and Governance* 6 (2). Available online: https://www.cogitatiopress.com/politicsandgovernance/issue/view/92 (acessed 10 April 2021).

Stewart, F. (1991). 'Are Adjustment Policies in Africa Consistent with Long-Run Development Needs?' *Development Policy Review* 4 (9): 314–36.

Stiglitz, J. (2002). *Globalization and its Discontents*. New York: W. W. Norton & Company.

Stiglitz, J. E. (2008). 'Is there a Post-Washington Consensus Consensus?', in N. Serra and J. E. Stiglitz (eds), *The Washington Consensus Reconsidered*. Oxford: Oxford University Press, 41–56.

Stiglitz, J. E. (2010). *Freefall*. London: Penguin.

Strange, S. (1996). *The Retreat of the State*. Cambridge: Cambridge University Press.

Temby, O. (2015). 'What Are Levels of Analysis and What Do They Contribute to International Relations Theory?' *Cambridge Review of International Affairs* 28 (4): 721–42.

Thakur Vineet, Alexander E. Davis and Peter Vale (2017). 'Imperial Mission, Scientific Method: An Alternative Account of the Origins of IR', *Millennium: Journal of International Studies* 46 (1): 3–23.

Thant, Myint-U. (2007). *The River of Lost Footsteps: A Personal History of Burma*. New York: Farrar, Strauss and Giroux.

Thieren, Michel (2007). 'Health and Foreign Policy in Question: The Case of Humanitarian Action', *Bulletin of the World Health Organization* 85: 218–24.

Thompson, Rachel and Mukesh Kapila (2018). 'Healthcare in Conflict Settings: Leaving No One Behind'. Report of the WISH Healthcare in Conflict Settings Forum. Doha: World Innovation Summit for Health. Available online: https://www.wish.org.qa/wp-content/uploads/2018/11/IMPJ6078-WISH-2018-Conflict-181026.pdf (accessed 10 April 2021).

Tickner, J. A. (2005). 'Gendering a Discipline: Some Feminist Methodological Contributions to International Relations', *Signs* 30 (4): 2173–88.

Todd, Zoe (2019). 'By the Numbers: Syrian Refugees Around the World'. *PBS Frontline*. Available online: https://www.pbs.org/wgbh/frontline/article/numbers-syrian-refugees-around-world/ (accessed 10 April 2021).

Toki, Valmaine (2010). 'The Treaty of Waitangi in New Zealand's Law and Constitution', *Commonwealth Law Bulletin* 36 (2): 398–400.

Tourish, D. (2020). 'Introduction to The Special Issue: Why the Coronavirus Crisis Is also a Crisis of Leadership', *Leadership* 16 (3): 261–72.

Tyndale, W. (2006). *Visions of Development: Faith-Based Initiatives*. Hampshire: Ashgate.

UN Women (no date). 'Facts and Figures: Economic Empowerment'. Available online: https://www.unwomen.org/en/what-we-do/economic-empowerment/facts-and-figures (accessed 10 April 2021).

UN Women (2018). 'Progress of the World's Women 2019–20'. Available online: https://www.unwomen.org/-/media/headquarters/attachments/sections/library/publications/2019/progress-of-the-worlds-women-2019-2020-en.pdf?la=en&vs=3512 (accessed 10 April 2021).

UN Women (2019). 'Facts and Figures: Leadership and Political Participation'. Available online:https://www.unwomen.org/en/what-we-do/leadership-and-political-participation/facts-and-figures (accessed 10 April 2021).

United Nations Human Development Programme (1994). *Human Development Report*. Oxford: Oxford University Press.

UNAIDS (2020). 'Seizing the Moment — Tackling Entrenched Inequalities To End Epidemics', 6 July. Available online: https://www.unaids.org/en/resources/documents/2020/global-aids-report (accessed 17 October 2021).

UNDP (2020). *Assessing the Impact of War on Development in Yemen*. Yemen: UNDP.

UNHCR (2021). 'Global Forced Trends in Displacement'. Available online: https://www.unhcr.org/

flagship-reports/globaltrends/ (accessed 17 October 2021).

United Nations (1948). 'Universal Declaration of Human Rights'. Available online: https://www.un.org/en/universal-declaration-human-rights/ (accessed 10 April 2021).

United Nations (2000). 'United Nations Millennium Declaration', UNGA Resolution 55.2, Document A/RES/55/2. Available online: https://www.un.org/en/development/desa/population/migration/generalassembly/docs/globalcompact/A_RES_55_2.pdf (accessed 10 April 2021).

United Nations (2001). 'The Responsibility to Protect: Report of the International Commission on Intervention and State Sovereignty'. Available online: https://www.un.org/en/genocideprevention/about-responsibility-to-protect.shtml (accessed 10 April 2021).

United Nations (2015). *Transforming our World. The 2030 Agenda for Sustainable Development*. Available online: https://sustainabledevelopment.un.org/content/documents/21252030%20Agenda%20for%20Sustainable%20Development%20web.pdf (accessed 10 April 2021).

United Nations (2018). Global Compact for Safe, Orderly and Regular Migration. General Assembly, 19 December. Available online: https://www.un.org/en/ga/search/view_doc.asp?symbol=A/RES/73/195 (accessed 10 April 2021).

United Nations General Assembly (2006). 'The United Nations Global Counter-Terrorism Strategy'. Available online: https://undocs.org/A/RES/60/288 (accessed 10 April 2021).

Üstübici, Ayşen (2016). 'Political Activism between Journey and Settlement: Irregular Migrant Mobilisation in Morocco', *Geopolitics* 21 (2): 303–24.

US Congressional Research Service (2014). 'Ebola: 2014 Outbreak in West Africa'. 24 November.

Vale, Peter (2003). *Security and Politics in South Africa: The Regional Dimension*. London: Lynne Rienner.

Vale, Peter (2016). 'Inclusion and Exclusion', *International Studies Review* 18 (1): 159–62.

Vaughan-Williams, Nick (2015). *Europe's Border Crisis: Biopolitical Security and Beyond*. Oxford: Oxford University Press.

Velasco, Kristopher (2019). 'A Growing Queer Divide: The Divergence between Transnational Advocacy Networks and Foreign Aid in Diffusing LGBT Policies', *International Studies Quarterly* 64 (1): 120–32.

Vitalis, R. (2015). *White World Order, Black Power Politics: The Birth of American International Relations*. New York: Cornell University Press.

Walker, Neil (2014). *Intimations of Global Law*. Cambridge: Cambridge University Press.

Waltz, K. N. (1959). *Man, the State, and War: A Theoretical Analysis*. New York: Columbia University Press.

Washburn, Wilcomb E. (1962). 'The Meaning of "Discovery" in the Fifteenth and Sixteenth Centuries', *The American Historical Review* 68 (1): 1–21.

Watts, Pauline Moffitt (1985). 'Prophecy and Discovery: On the Spiritual Origins of Christopher Columbus's "Enterprise of the Indies"', *The American Historical Review* 90 (1): 73–102.

Weber, M. (2004). *The Vocation Lectures: 'Science as a Vocation'; 'Politics as a Vocation'*. Indianapolis, IN: Hackett Publishing Company.

Welch, D. and D. Southerton (2019). 'After Paris: Transitions for Sustainable Consumption', *Sustainability: Science, Practice, and Policy* 15 (1): 31–44.

Weldes, J. (1996). 'Constructing National Interests', *European Journal of International Relations* 2: 275–318.

Wendt, Alexander (1992). 'Anarchy is what States Make of it: The Social Construction of Power Politics', *International Organization* 46 (2): 391–425.

Wendt, Alexander (1999). *Social Theory of International Politics*. Cambridge: Cambridge University Press.

West, R. (2017). 'For the Cost of the Tax Bill, the U.S. Could Eliminate Child Poverty. Twice', *Talk Poverty*. Available online: https://talkpoverty.org/2017/12/12/u-s-eliminate-child-poverty-cost-senate-tax-bill/ (accessed 10 April 2021).

Whyte, C. and B. Mazanec (2018). *Understanding Cyber Warfare: Politics, Policy and Strategy*. London: Routledge.

Wiktorowicz, Q. (2006). 'Anatomy of the Salafi Movement', *Studies in Conflict and Terrorism* 29 (3): 207–39.

Wilkinson, R. and K. Pickett (2009). *The Spirit Level*. London: Allen Lane.

Woodhead, Linda (2011). 'Five Concepts of Religion', *International Review of Sociology* 21 (1): 121–43.

Woolard, I. (2002). *An Overview of Poverty and Inequality in South Africa*. Working Paper prepared for DFID (SA).

World Bank (2018a). *Poverty and Shared Prosperity 2018: Piecing Together the Poverty Puzzle*. Washington, DC: World Bank Group.

World Bank (2018b) *Overcoming Poverty and Inequality in South Africa: An Assessment of Drivers, Constraints and Opportunities*. Washington, DC: World Bank Group.

World Bank (2019). *Belt and Road Economics: Opportunities and Risks of Transport Corridors*. Washington, DC: World Bank Group.

World Health Organization (1978). 'Declaration of Alma-Ata', International Conference on Primary Health Care, Alma-Ata, USSR, 6–12 September. Available online: https://www.who.int/publications/almaata_declaration_en.pdf?ua=1 (accessed 10 April 2021).

World Health Organization (2016). *International Health Regulations 2005*. 3rd edn, Geneva: WHO.

World Health Organization (2018). 'Adolescent Pregnancy'. Available online: https://www.who.int/news-room/fact-sheets/detail/adolescent-pregnancy (accessed 10 April 2021).

World Trade Organization (2019). 'Technological Innovation, Supply Chain Trade, and Workers in a Globalized World', *Global Value Chain Development Report*. Geneva. Available online: https://www.wto.org/english/res_e/booksp_e/gvc_dev_report_2019_e.pdf (accessed 10 April 2021).

Wynter, Sylvia (1984). 'New Seville and the Conversion Experience of Bartolome de Las Casas', *Jamaica Journal* 17 (2): 25–32.

Wynter, Sylvia (1991). 'Columbus and the Poetics of the Propter Nos', *Annals of Scholarship* 8 (2): 251–86.

Yan, Xuetong, ed. (2011). *Ancient Chinese Thought, Modern Chinese Power*. Princeton, NJ: Princeton University Press.

Zhang, F. (2015). *Chinese Hegemony: Grand Strategy and International Institutions in East Asian History*. Stanford, CA: Stanford University Press.

Zhang, Yongjin and Teng-chi Chang, eds. (2016). *Constructing a Chinese School of International Relations: Ongoing Debates and Sociological Realities*. Abingdon: Routledge.

Zhao, Tingyang. (2019). *Redefining a Philosophy for World Governance*. Translated by Liqing Tao. Beijing: Foreign Language Teaching and Research Press and Singapore: Palgrave Macmillan.

Zinn, Howard (1980). *A People's History of the United States*. London and New York: Longman.

Zinsstaga J., E. Schelling, D. Waltner-Toews and D. Tannera (2011). 'From "one medicine" to "One Health" and Systemic Approaches to Health and Well-Being', *Preventive Veterinary Medicine* 101: 148–56.

INDEX